THE TRUTH IS NO DEFENSE

THE TRUTH
IS
NO DEFENSE

Elisabeth Sabaditsch-Wolff

Published by New English Review Press
a subsidiary of World Encounter Institute
PO Box 158397
Nashville, Tennessee 37215
&
27 Old Gloucester Street
London, England, WC1N 3AX

Cover Art and Design by Kendra Mallock

ISBN: 978-1-943003-30-3

First Edition

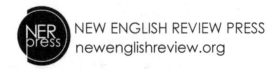

NEW ENGLISH REVIEW PRESS
newenglishreview.org

To Dymphna,

My late mother and

My daughter, on behalf of all the girls out there who deserve nothing but love and protection.

Contents

Acknowledgments

THANK YOUS INEVITABLY LEAD to leaving someone out. Even so, I will attempt to express my gratitude as comprehensively as I possibly can.

First and foremost, I thank my husband and my daughter. They are my fortress, my strength, my reason for being. They graciously gave their consent when I told them I would be away for two months to write my book, and they continue being gracious when I'm on the road—again. I love you more than I could ever convey.

Writing a book that includes autobiographical information entailed delving into my very young years. While my recollection of events in my early childhood was and is quite good, I am grateful to my father for our recent conversations, digging deep into our memories. More importantly, it was my father who sat behind me in court on every day I was there. For a father, this must have been a painful experience. Thank you.

My mother recently passed away, and those who knew her would agree that she was a formidable woman. She was certainly a powerful force in my life. She was never really able to deal with her daughter being persecuted by the Austrian authorities. I am certain she felt acute pain in seeing her daughter vilified by the media, the church, politicians and many others. Only much later did she come to the conclusion that the words leading to my conviction were not as evil as portrayed by others; many a friend apparently praised me and my actions, even calling me a "hero." This is what my mother always lived by: no matter the circumstances, smile, pick up the pieces and keep going. And this is what I try to embody and teach my daughter as well.

I know my mother-in-law worries constantly about my safety, yet she always supports me, knowing that I am doing the right thing. Thank you.

In the past decade, I have been through a steep learning curve with regard to Islam, Socialism, Marxism and other totalitarianisms; oftentimes, I felt like I was working hard toward a PhD. My teachers were the best of the best. In no particular order: I am grateful to Christian Zeitz, Stephen Coughlin, Clare Lopez, Diana West, Robert Spencer, Andrew Bostom, Rabbi Jonathan Hausman, John Guandolo, Frank Gaffney, Allen West, Karen Siegemund, Trevor Loudon, James Simpson, Bat Ye'or, Katie Hopkins, Christopher Hull.

Where would I be without my fearless group of warriors who are joining me every year in the lion's den at the OSCE conferences in Warsaw and Vienna. Thank you for standing up for Western civilization, for freedom, for our children's future.

Whenever a milestone of a verdict passed I thanked the army of supporters.

I wrote the following words shortly after the first verdict in 2011:

Yesterday was a crucial day in our fight against the Islamization of Europe and for the future of our civilization. As most of you know, I was acquitted of the charge of hate speech, but found guilty of denigrating religious teachings of a legally recognized religion. I am sure that you also know that this religion is Islam.

I can tell you that I am shaken to the core; not so much about the guilty verdict—that was a given from the start—but about the judge's explanation for the verdict. [...] It was indeed a dark day for young girls in Austria. What shocks me most, however, is that the judge is a woman who should know better. The reasoning used in her judgment is despicable, and a slap in the face for every woman and girl, from every race, religion, or nationality. Marrying and molesting a child is not to be tolerated, not in the 6th century, not in the 16th century, and definitely not in the 21st century. One would expect a woman, let along a judge, to know this. But the future and the appeals court will hopefully show that this judgment is morally and factually wrong.

Since the curtain has now fallen on the first act of this tragedy, I now want to do a round of thanks. I am indebted to so many people from all over the world, and I will try to do my best to mention most of them here.

First and foremost, I want to honor the Counterjihad Collective, especially Baron Bodissey of *Gates of Vienna*. Without the tireless and selfless effort of these fine people, all of whom I am privileged to call friends, my case would have remained what it currently is in the mainstream media: ignored, at best vilified. It is amazing for me to see the results of this fine-tuned effort on a daily basis.

Imagine the following: My lawyer sends me a document regarding my case; I in turn send it to the German-English translators JLH and Rembrandt Clancy, who in no time return the translation to me. Baron Bodissey edits and posts on *Gates of Vienna*. Once the document is published, other translators grab the post and disseminate it in their blogs; other English language bloggers publish on their blogs.

If I am interviewed on camera, Vlad Tepes and KitmanTV are on hand to YouTube these reports, and Baron Bodissey is on hand to post. Transcribers are called to action, with translators, to subtitle if needed.

The result is without a doubt the most comprehensive reporting about Counterjihad activities currently available. The MSM are not doing their jobs, we are. And we should be proud of this achievement. A big Thank You to all involved in this.

Second, I want to thank my family and friends for their support in these hard times. On many an evening was I cranky after having spent more than ten hours poring over the Qur'an, the *hadith*, and *The Reliance of the Traveller*. You all know just how horrible the contents of these books are, and I can now tell you that studying Islamic texts can affect your psyche. I want to honor my daughter, who was more than patient when Mommy had an important Skype call to discuss some point raised by my lawyer.

Which brings me to my brilliant legal team. Dr. Rami and Mr. Strobl have been thrown into the cold water of Islamic doctrine. In little more than a year, they both became more knowledgeable in Islamic teachings than the majority of the population. They are now aware of the teachings of the Qur'an, they now know all about the *shariah* and its implications on our free society. And they did a marvelous job defending me and Western civilization. Thank you.

Heartfelt thanks and appreciation are also more than due to my supporters, be they politicians, bloggers, donors, and those who comment in those blogs and newspaper forums, whether you are from Europe, the United States, Canada or Australia.

Thank you to many political leaders for repeatedly bringing up my case. Those political parties who so far have not understood the ramifications of this case will be judged by history.

Thank you also to the Wiener Akademikerbund, ACT! for America, Citizens' Movement Pax Europa, Riposte Laïque, and all other organizations that support me and continue to support me so generously. Without you I could not have gone through with this.

Thank you to the numerous well-wishers and supporters who have written to me in the past hours and days, or have written thoughtful comments about yesterday's outcome.

I want to present one representative example here:

A man from Koblenz:

> As an ex-Muslim from Iran I want to wish you all the best and would like to support you if possible.
>
> I also want to wish lots of strength and endurance in your fight against mafia called politics and law, which is controlled by the political left.
>
> It is people like you who were in the resistance during the Nazi era, instead of swimming like dead fish in a stream of conformism and shutting up.
>
> I hope that your appeal will be transferred to a judge who is still sane and who doesn't retroactively legalize child abuse like the previous actor-judge.

After the appeal in 2012, I had the following to say to my supporters:

Dear Friends,

As many of you know, Sunday December 20 was a dark day for freedom of speech.

The Austrian justice system decided that the truth may not be spoken if it is deemed "excessive" (*nota bene*: and thus "denigrating" from the point of view of pious Muslims). Although the verdict was shocking, it did not come as a surprise.

Before I continue with my thoughts about the impact and implications of the ruling, I want to thank a few people:

First of all, my deepest gratitude to my unwaveringly supportive husband. He has stood behind me and continues to do so, despite the fact that his wife is now a convict. Without him, I could not have survived this ordeal.

Next comes my beautiful, caring daughter, the light of my life, for whom I have decided to fight. She and all girls are the future, our future: she will have to live in the world we shape now. She will one day judge our accomplishments because she will have to live with the consequences. And it is for my daughter and all of your daughters that I will continue.

The rest of my family has also been extremely supportive, especially my father—who, when I started this journey, believed that Islam is a religion we must respect. He has come a long way since then. Kudos to him for having the courage to learn. I wish more would follow in his footsteps.

Once again, I thank my lawyer, Dr. Rami, for his incredible work. When I first entered his office back in November 2009, he probably knew as much about Islam as the rest of the population—which is not much. Two years and many books later, he has become an expert. And he has done magnificent work in organizing my defense—which, by extension, is a defense of our right to freedom of speech.

What would I do without the unflinching help and support of Baron Bodissey and the *Gates of Vienna* community? What a difficult year lies behind *Gates of Vienna*, and Baron and Dymphna have not given up, and are not giving in. We have lost a few friends during the storm, but so many new friendships have been made. There is reason for optimism. Please continue your support of *Gates of Vienna*, the beacon of free speech in an angry ocean of lies and misinformation.

It goes without saying that my deepest gratitude also extends to the associated networks. These include, but are not limited to, EuropeNews, PI-News, ACT! For America, and Vlad Tepes. The larger network also includes the countless translators who give up their free time to make this and so many other stories available to the English-speaking world—not to mention those parts of the world that speak Danish, Dutch, Swedish, Finnish, French, Italian, and all the other languages in which the information has spread.

Daniel Pipes and his immensely important Legal Project were among my greatest allies, offering assistance from the day I began this legal quest through the manifold courts. I cannot overemphasize their important work with respect to many other victims of Islamic lawfare. My legal options would have been reduced greatly had the Legal Project not stepped up to support me.

A final thank you goes to Alliance Defending Freedom and the European Centre for Law and Justice, both of which supported my lawyer and me in various stages once my case was accepted for review by the European Court of Human Rights.

A heartfelt "God bless you" to all of you who organized prayer groups, lit a candle for me in church, or prayed for me in a synagogue. Although I do not fathom God's will right now, I don't have to. There is a reason for all of this, and by going on, by not giving up, I will one day be able to understand His plans.

To all of you who drove and flew to Vienna, to you who took a day off from work to stand with me on this day: THANK YOU. Your presence meant more to me than you will ever know.

Finally, I am used to the process of editing thanks to Ned May's meticulous "nediting," as my colleagues and I like to call it. Very little of what I produce in written form is printed or posted without Ned's careful inspection. With this book, I added another layer of editing, and I'd like to express my sincere gratitude to William P. Eigles, who in turn made the life of my editor and publisher, Rebecca Bynum, a whole lot easier. What I love about Rebecca is that her editing was respectful of how I chose to say what I said. This is what made the work of Ned, Bill, and Rebecca so outstanding. Thank you!

FOREWORD

BY DR. KAREN SIEGEMUND

THERE'S NOTHING QUITE AS CHILLING as reading hate-filled lies about oneself. One minute, you're going about your daily business —making breakfast for the kids, getting ready for work, feeding the dog, engaged in your mundane routine—and the next, your stomach lurches, your skin tingles, you feel the blood drain from your face and your breathing gets a bit tougher as you look at the words that change your life, change the way you look at yourself, and change your relationship to those around you. Your friends, your family, will never see you the same way again. Perfect strangers will now have strong opinions about you, and they won't be good ones.

In an instant, your life has changed.

The book you hold in your hands tells a story of exactly this. One day, Elisabeth Sabaditsch-Wolff was "just" a mom, a housewife, leading her life in Vienna, and the next, her entire world has been transformed. She was labeled with all the usual hate-filled insults, brought before the Austrian court, her family life turned topsy turvy and her private life pretty much obliterated.

Elisabeth Sabaditsch-Wolff's journey is as wildly implausible as any fairy tale. Except "once upon a time" is now, and the happy ending is, esteemed reader, up to you.

This is a story of freedom versus totalitarianism; of a perspective that sees rights as granted by God and protected by government, as in the United States Constitution, versus a view that sees rights as bestowed by government and therefore which can also be denied by government, as in the European constitutions.

It's the story of tolerance versus intolerance, of the Right's support of the individual versus the Left's supremacy of the state, of liberty versus suppression, of facts versus feelings, of law versus whimsy. It's the story of love versus power, of values versus surrender, of truth versus agenda and finally, of fight versus submission.

The actual basis of the story is of political Islam versus cultural sovereignty, but each of these fault lines is played out in the most chilling fashion and one that we must pay close attention to because each of these, regardless of our opinion of Islam, has a direct consequence on our own lives. And while it might be tempting to slough off this dire tale as irrelevant because, well, who really cares what happens in tiny bucolic Austria, let me point out that there are countless reasons why it's relevant far beyond Austria's borders. Some of these reasons are historical, but others pertain to the present-day context in which freedoms are being suppressed all over the Western world including the United States, and stories like Elisabeth's are being played out in one arena after another.

And it could happen to you.

Imagine, for a moment, that out of love of your country and concern for your children's lives and future, you undertake to give your time and experience to teaching a course that you hope will provide enough information to people so that they can make good choices in their lives. Knowledge is power, and you offer your knowledge to others with the goal of empowering them. It's something that's part of our civic life here in the US, as it is in Austria.

Now, imagine this: after one of your seminars—which are open only to event registrants, by the way; these aren't held on street corners or aren't part of a school curriculum—you find that you are being sued for hate speech over a factual statement you'd made, accompanied by a question. Truth, and a query. Seems harmless, right? Wrong.

All of a sudden, you've gone from being a concerned citizen doing your part to protect those you love, to being branded as a hater, a bigot, a racist, and worse. In the blink of an eye, you've lost your privacy; you're vilified by the media and shunned by people who once were your friends, hated by those who don't even know you.

Free speech? If the government grants it, the government can take it away, and that is exactly what happened to Elisabeth Sabaditsch-Wolff in Austria.

Here in the US, the First Amendment to the Constitution protects our right to free speech, but even so, those whose speech isn't in accordance with the Left's narrative are finding themselves shut out of the public sphere in a myriad of ways. They are losing their voices on so-cial media, which also means a loss of livelihood for many; Google and YouTube use a variety of tactics to restrict access to conservative sites and videos; a number of conservative individuals and groups have been de-banked by institutions kowtowing to Leftist bigotry; it's shockingly common for fundraising platforms like GoFundMe and Amazon Smile to deny their services to those on the Right; many are being shut out of Uber and other similar crowd-provided services as a result of their con-servative stance; and increasingly, those on the Right are losing jobs as I and countless others have.

All of these are now the consequences of speaking "freely" in the United States. No, we're not sued, and voicing one's opinion is, at this point, not a criminal activity, but we are being increasingly silenced throughout the civic space, and it's terrifying. This is a loss of freedom to totalitarian forces, a pervasive intolerance of "diverse" voices. It's evi-dence of the Left's turning the Right into the "other" and thereby justify-ing any action that diminishes them—that diminishes us.

Regardless of which side of the aisle you're on, this kind of vilify-ing and "othering" should scare every single one of us. One of history's painful lessons is that once this othering starts, and once the population at large stands by while groups are shunned, punished or worse, then the tentacles of bigotry and persecution only grow broader, deeper and more pervasive, putting everybody at risk. In addition, group persecu-tion destroys the health and prosperity of a culture with a rot that is impossible to wash away without a catastrophic upheaval.

But let's be clear: a culture stands on the strength and virtue of its values, and of the extent to which those values are woven through and upheld by those who comprise that culture. No society can exist without a set of shared values; no society can exist with a literal rejection of the notion of shared values at all. And that kind of values-rejection is one of the cancers infiltrating the United States and much of Europe, and is destructive in ways we can't even imagine.

And this is what Elisabeth Sabaditsch-Wolff was trying to contend with—the preservation of her culture in the face of destructive forces so that her daughter could grow up with the freedoms, prosperity and cultural foundation that are the cornerstones of the Austrian life she herself grew up with.

Elisabeth had a highly unusual upbringing, as you'll find out, one that set the stage for what was to follow. The daughter of an Austrian career diplomat, then later part of the Austrian diplomatic corps in her own right, she led a life that was Forrest Gumpian in how she found herself in one global conflict zone after another—Iran at the onset of the Revolution, followed by Iraq, then, Kuwait of all places. She was living in Libya when the Muslim terrorists attacked the United States on September 11, 2001.

Throughout it all, she experienced life under theocratic dictatorships and learned how they affect a culture and its citizens. She learned about Islam and Ramadan, the month-long Islamic holiday where even non-Muslims were essentially forced to comply with the various religious restrictions. She learned, among other aspects of Islam, about Mohammed's marriage to 6 year old Aisha, a marriage consummated when the little girl was 9. Perhaps more importantly, she learned that while Muslims were aware of this, a good Muslim never spoke of it, and during the time she lived in Islamic countries, she, too, remained silent.

Two other aspects of her unique upbringing come into play. Aside from living in these various Middle Eastern hot spots, she spent her younger formative years in the United States, attending middle and high school in Chicago where, at least at that time, the school curriculum included learning about the Constitution. Elisabeth, then, was steeped in the American view of rights, including Freedom of Speech, being endowed by our Creator and protected by the Constitution. In addition, the idea of rights as construed by the founders is that they are "restrictive" rights, limiting government's power in order to protect the individual. There seems little doubt that her years in the US instilled in her both the perspective regarding the provenance of rights and their nature, but also the independent spirit of the American heartland. It was the combination of these two traits that contributed to the unfolding of the rest of the story.

One final element of her time abroad also played a role in the saga: her frequent returns home to Austria from the various outposts made obvious the subtle but unmistakable change in the Viennese culture. It was no longer homogeneous; an increasing number of refugees had settled there without any attempt at assimilating into their new country. The effect of an always-growing number of people who rejected Austrian values, and Western values generally, was blindingly apparent to Elisabeth, more so than to a resident, as, for example, a visiting grandmother is more likely to notice a child's growth than his mother does.

So these three factors: time in Islamic theocratic dictatorships, learning about the US Constitution and independent spirit during formative years, and the repeated shock of watching Vienna become less and less Viennese, all played a role in this story.

So what is it that happened?

In a very tiny nutshell, Elisabeth had been conducting private seminars on the topic of Islam. During one session, she described the relationship between Mohammed and Aisha, specifically, as noted above, that they married when Aisha was a six year old, and consummated the marriage when she was nine and he was 53.

One can't help but recoil at the idea of a nine year old in such a situation—it's a hard thing to write, an impossible one to contemplate. Think of the nine-year-girls you know. Now think of the 53-year-old men you know. Enough said, surely.

After stating the facts about Mohammed and Aisha, Elisabeth then asked: "What would one call this, if not pedophilia?"

This is the question that brought the wrath of the Austrian judicial system down on Elisabeth Sabaditsch-Wolff.

In the chapters that follow, you'll read about the original trial, the second trial, the acquittal of the original charge and then the subsequent Kafkaesque out-of-thin-air new charges leveled against her.

And you'll read about the final verdict brought down by the Austrian court: that the issue was to balance "free speech" with the "right" to not have your feelings hurt, and guess which side won?

The right to not have your feelings hurt. A magnificent and chilling example of the Utopian Left crafting "rights" that are impossible, and yet that make the courts the arbiters of what does and doesn't hurt people's feelings, and that are enforceable by these same courts eager to suppress anything with which they disagree.

This also highlights the different perspective of rights between the American Constitution and the European ones. The rights protected by the American Constitution are described as "restrictive" or "negative" rights, intended only to preserve freedoms and limit the interference government can have on our lives. European "rights," on the other hand, are "positive" ones, intending to guarantee various things like housing, or the right to not have one's feelings hurt, which can only be provided by others.

These fundamental differences in attitude toward rights plays a central role in this story; it took a person raised in the philosophy of Creator-endowed rights that should be protected from government incursion to stand up to the outrageousness of a "right," codified in a government document, for an individual not to have his or her "feelings hurt."

And that person, thankfully, is Elisabeth.

Elisabeth exercised her right to free expression in speaking about Mohammed and Aisha, but this right was trumped first by a law against "religious denigration," a law crafted to protect Islam from criticism, a vague and bizarre restriction on free speech, especially if such "denigration" happens to be the truth. Then it was trumped by the law against hurting others' feelings.

And the legal battles went on for ten years. Ten years of being mired in legal proceedings, with the cost, the stress, the publicity, the weight of it all hanging over her life, while hoping, hoping that free speech and the facts of the case might actually prevail—hoping, that because one only spoke the TRUTH, that her right to free speech might be protected.

That the freedoms so proudly proclaimed in EU and Austrian documents might actually be upheld.

But in the end, that wasn't the outcome, as you'll discover.

From the minute I'd first heard of Elisabeth's case I was appalled. As the President of the American Freedom Alliance, a non-profit organization in Los Angeles that protects and defends Western civilization including the US Constitution, free speech, freedom of religion and other hallmarks of our culture, the idea that free speech can be so trampled upon dismayed me. That the words she'd said were in a private seminar rather than rabble-rousing on a soap box in a park somewhere only made it that much more shocking. In addition, I am highly sensitized to the incursions made by the Left into our free speech. My father was raised in Berlin during the 1930s and 40s, and that tyranny's first steps are always to limit free speech and freedom of expression generally; so when I see this kind of reaction to free speech, it chills me.

Elisabeth and I have a shared indignation and anger at rights trampled on, at freedoms stolen, and at the implications of a loss of free speech; we immediately felt ourselves to be kindred spirits in our determination to speak up and speak the truth, not only for ourselves but for others as well—she in her fighting her lawsuit and I as president of AFA. We are both mothers—I have two daughters and she has one, and as Elisabeth is engaged in the fight to ensure that her daughter can grow up with the freedoms we take for granted, so, too, do I fight for a future of freedom for my own daughters, rather than the totalitarianism that is seeping into our social and political fabric.

We also are kindred in our love of Austria and its culture—I was exceptionally fortunate to have spent summers in the Austrian Alps as a child, visiting my grandmother who had fled West Berlin after the wall went up. Austria has a very special place in my heart.

But we also have a new kinship. My own free speech cost me my teaching job. Here's what happened. On May 5th, the American Freedom Alliance held a conference on the "Long March through the Institutions," with the subtitle, "the Left's Revolution by Other Means." While it's apparent that our political and civic institutions have been infiltrated and are being destroyed, the aim of the conference was to reveal how this has been a deliberate, concerted, orchestrated undertaking over the past several decades, and what we're seeing now is the consequences of this "long march." We had speakers on the topics of the media, the schools, religious institutions, national security and many more, and the entire day provided an unparalleled education.

The very next day, May 6th, I was informed that my teaching contract at the local private school where I'd taught math for four years would not be renewed due to my "widely publicized views." A further explanation included this quotation from a speech I'd made as president of AFA: "Each of us here, believes in the unparalleled force for good that is Western Civilization, that is OUR heritage, whether we were born here or not." The complaint was this, and this is a direct quotation from the email: "one can deduce from these comments that… she rejects anyone whose roots are not grounded in Western Civilization."

The frank absurdity, complete illogic and downright mean-spiritedness of the fake inference is outrageous, and the accusation is, obviously, utterly unfounded. In short, though, I was let go from my teaching job on the sole basis of my political beliefs, and on the speech which reflects those beliefs. This had nothing to do with my actions, with my teaching ability, or with my interactions with my students. The only issue cited was speech. Elisabeth and I, then, both had our voices suppressed because they reflect an ideology that is deemed unacceptable. Both of us had our worlds change in an instant; that sick feeling I described in the beginning of this chapter is the feeling I had the moment I lost my job, and it's a feeling I relive daily. It's a sick, sickening, sinking feeling, and Elisabeth and I are only two of countless people who have also suffered tremendous consequences from being ideologically on the "wrong" side. We both know, day in and day out, how it feels to be vilified, silenced, persecuted, when quite literally all we do, both of us, is seek to preserve that which is valuable about our world, and protect it for our children. We both know how precious free speech is, that there are forces doing all they can to suppress it, and that this is a fight we must engage in, even though neither of us sought to be on the frontlines of this fight. We're both sort of accidental culture warriors, moms who care about our families and their future, and who, just through speaking truth, have been made the targets of the Left's juggernaut of suppression, serving also to reveal how real the attacks on our freedoms actually are.

This is a similarity between the Left and Islam: neither can support the truth being told, and both succeed only where the truth is concealed. The Left has done this through the Long March and its relentless imposition of policies that are cloaked in compassion and caring, but that at their core are totalitarian power-grabs. The spread of Islam does this through silencing, as in the case of Elisabeth and countless others. The startling thing is how they've been working hand in hand, as we've been seeing in Europe and now in America, with alliances that are damaging to the very fabric of society.

"The truth shall set you free," is another phrase attributed to Jesus but one that many of us believe and live by, especially in self-governing nations. We set a high premium on the truth as it is what we require to make the best possible decisions about our lives and our governance. But take note: If the truth about what you believe is something you're ashamed of—as in the case of Elisabeth's Jordanian friend who made clear that the truth about Mohammed and Aisha isn't to be spoken—or that you strive to conceal, even to the level of legislatively prohibiting speech, then there's something perverted about the fundamental situation. When the truth, in other words, doesn't set you free, but is a threat, then perhaps one is aligned with a belief system that is harmful rather than beneficial. Then perhaps a better course of action would be to re-examine one's own beliefs rather than persecute those who speak the truth about them.

The attacks on the truth, and on free speech, are pervasive and increasing. Dennis Prager, one of the world's premier radio show hosts and creator of Prager University, recently testified before the US Senate on the topic of social media's treatment of conservative voices. This was the beginning of his statement: "[Social media's] suppression of internet content on ideological grounds threatens the future of America more than any external enemy. In fact, never in American history has there been as strong a threat to freedom of speech as there is today." And of course, it's not only social media's suppression of internet content that is the threat, but also the punitive consequences of all speech that is ideological unaligned with the Left. It's real, it's daily, it happened to Elisabeth and to me, and it's extremely important to note that it can happen to any one of us, on either side of the big puddle. And the erosion of free speech, as noted before, is one of the first major steps in the erosion of all freedoms generally and that is why people like Elisabeth feels she has no choice but to refuse to capitulate.

Brent Bozell, founder and president of the Media Research Center, said in his talk to AFA at the Long March conference: "The attacks on freedom are real. The attacks on what you believe are real. It is not that they're fighting you on what it is you believe, it is that they do not want to allow what you believe to be in the public conversation." And once you limit what can be part of the conversation, what would you call it other than totalitarianism? Most specifically, the truth must be allowed to be spoken—if the truth is banned, then we are truly doomed.

I'd said this is a story of freedom versus totalitarianism, of a perspective that sees rights as granted by God and protected by government, as in the United States Constitution, versus a view that sees rights as bestowed by government and therefore which can also be denied by government, as in the European constitutions. And indeed, it is so.

I'd said it's the story of tolerance versus intolerance, of the Right's support of the individual versus the Left's supremacy of the state, of liberty versus suppression, of facts versus feelings, of law versus whimsy. It's the story of love versus power, of values versus surrender, of truth versus agenda and finally, of fight versus submission.

I'd said it's a fairy tale, but so far, the ending hasn't been happy. It's up to us, all of us who believe in truth and freedom, to stand shoulder to shoulder with Elisabeth to bring a happier ending to the story.

Elisabeth didn't choose this fight, but she has values which she won't surrender; she's a truth teller because that is the right thing to do, and it is simply not her nature to submit. We all owe her a debt of gratitude for her refusal to be suppressed and her determination to fight for freedom and bring a happy ending for all of us.

—Dr. Karen Siegemund
President of American Freedom Alliance
Los Angeles, California
August 2019.

Meet Emma and Aisha

EMMA IS NINE YEARS OLD. She gets up every morning, dresses in her pristine uniform, has breakfast with her Mommy and then heads to school. In fourth grade, she is taught reading and writing, math, science and some history. Her classmates are boys and girls who do everything kids at that age do: they laugh together, they study together, they get along, sometimes they don't. Their future is set: finish primary school, go on to grade school, high school, graduation and perhaps college or university.

Sometimes doing her homework, doing household chores and even her friends annoy her. But Mom and Dad have given their permission for her to go on a week-long school trip to England. It will be just her teachers and her classmates. And lots of sightseeing in London. What a thrill!

Emma's life is simple. All she has to do is love her parents, study, do some sports, read good books, and enjoy her friends. She is free to choose how she wants to spend her time—she loves going to the library to pick up the latest books or meet her girlfriends for an ice-cream. She knows she will be free to choose what to do with her life, because Mom and Dad have told her so, even though she hasn't really made a decision about what to study at university because she thinks she has plenty of time until she graduates high school. Emma is excited about her future.

⬥

Aisha is nine years old. She also gets up in the morning, dresses in her school uniform, which includes a hijab, or headscarf, which she struggles with every day. She doesn't want to cover up her beautiful hair. It took so long for her hair to grow this long! And anyway, the hijab itches her scalp in the summer months, and it is generally a nuisance when she and her girlfriends play catch in the school yard. Sometimes she even cries when she looks in the mirror with only her face showing. However, she obliges her parents and, most of all, Allah, because she wants to please Him.

Aisha enjoys going to school even though she doesn't know how much longer her mother and her father will permit her to study. Sometimes her teacher tells the girls that it's more important to cook well rather than knowing how to do math. Her best friend Amina agrees. She is not interested in anything taught is school because she will leave school after the end of the school year. She already knows her future husband, her second cousin whom she met a few days ago, and who she thinks will treat her well. They will be married as soon as the school year is over. Amina is looking forward to her wedding day, when she will be dressed like a princess. Her father picked a good boy, she tells Aisha. She believes she's lucky with her future husband, because she observes her sisters' unhappiness with their husbands. One of her brothers-in-law even married a second wife!

Aisha shudders at the thought. Her older sister only made it to seventh grade when Father introduced her to a cousin, an older boy she hardly knew and didn't particularly like, and to whom she was married right after her school year ended. Aisha remembers the sadness in her sister's eyes; she had wanted to become an engineer, but her husband did not approve of her continuing school. In any case, her sister is now expecting her third child in as many years.

Aisha is really good at math and hopes her father will allow her to attend university. Perhaps she can study engineering for her sister. Perhaps she can even work as an engineer. Perhaps she doesn't have to get married to another cousin, or maybe not at all. Perhaps she can choose where and how she wants to live.

But perhaps all of this will remain a dream. Aisha is sad.

Introduction

When words lose their meaning, people lose their freedom.
—Confucius

A DECADE AGO, Europe as well as the United States was still bliss-fully unaware of the impact of an Islamized society. Granted, (almost) everyone had been shocked—rightly so—and strongly condemned the numerous Islamic attacks against targets representing Judeo-Christian values in Europe. The memory of the September 11, 2001 slaughter in the U.S. was still vivid and the country held annual commemoration events in New York, Washington, and Shanksville, Pennsylvania, to keep that memory strong.

A decade ago, Europe had yet to experience the brutal slaughter in Paris, both the cold-blooded murder of journalists of the Islam-critical *Charlie Hebdo* magazine and the concerted attacks in November 2015, the deadliest since World War Two.

A decade ago, discussion of the undeniable Islamization of non-Muslim societies was nearly non-existent, despite the very obvious presence of "no-go" zones in countries such as Sweden and Belgium, and despite the fact that the fallout of the Great Migration of 2015 had yet to take root in European societies. Those of us who dared to examine the encroachment of Islam into European societies were few in number and already ostracized. Today, there are countless Islam critics, while social shunning has progressed to successful "old-fashioned techniques such as peer pressure and shaming."[1] The number of court cases in Europe aimed at suppressing this discussion has reached into the thousands, and sentences have even included prison terms.

And finally, a decade ago, I embarked on an inadvertent journey

---

1 https://www.nationalreview.com/corner/doj-followed-obama-clinton-un-resolution-against-negative-speech-about-islam/ accessed June 23, 2019.

through the Austrian and supra-national legal systems to defend my right to free expression.

While a new survey in Germany suggests that barely 20 percent of respondents agree that free speech is possible in public, most Austrians believe they absolutely have the right to free speech. Unfortunately, this sentiment is more than naïve. A random poll taken in the streets of Vienna would reveal that nearly 99 percent of respondents would answer in the affirmative, that, "yes, we can say whatever we want."[2] The reasons are twofold: First, Austrians likely feel no real need for freedom of speech as whatever they want to say they can, be it a discussion of the latest cellphone, the advantages of a LED television set, or the latest episode of *Designated Survivor*. What they do not realize is that the right to free expression protects—or rather, should protect—speech that shocks or offends, or it is worthless.

Second, Austrians have never really lost free speech because they never truly had it to begin with. Most of today's population has no recollection or, thanks to lacking history lessons, even the most basic knowledge of the 20th century's National Socialist terror regime with its brutal repression of free thought. The right to freedom of expression is an abstract right granted by the European Union to Austrians. The sentiment is, "We have it, so why discuss it further or even test it?"

What you are about to read is definite proof that there is no freedom of speech and thought in Austria today. While Austrians have grown up accepting that Austria's law concerning any form of (neo) National Socialism or anti-Semitism is prohibitively strict and encompasses the public denial, approval, or justification of National Socialist crimes (including the Holocaust), there are legal precepts that now apply to ban any discussion of Islam—that is, any discussion emanating from a non-leftist or non-Islamic point of view. Yet, this is precisely what I was asked to do in 2008: The Austrian Freedom Party, the country's right-of-center political party, commissioned me to hold seminars on Islam; however, in 2010, I had to stand before a judge in a court of law and defend myself for explaining the basics of Islam via fully sourced Power Point presentations. And, as I learned ten years later, the truth is no defense.

This book is not an autobiography of Elisabeth Sabaditsch-Wolff. I am not a lawyer, nor have I any training in legal matters; as such, I will leave discussion of legal fine points to the experts, some of whom will

---

2   The remaining one percent will be the astute "losers of globalization," demonized by the mainstream media as the haters and xenophobes.

weigh in on the same in this book.

What this book is about is my story, why I say what I say and do what I do. As I like to quip, "I could be catching up with Danielle Steele's most recent novels, all of which I have missed because of my 'job.'" I will tell about how I, as a diplomat's daughter, grew up and lived in the United States, Iran, Iraq, Kuwait, Libya, and Austria, and how all of these distinctive places have shaped and influenced me. What I saw and experienced in Iran, Kuwait, and Libya molded my way of thinking, complemented by reading and studying Islamic texts, and left me no other course but to become a critic of Islam and an advocate for freedom and human rights as enshrined in the Universal Declaration of Human Rights and the United States' Bill of Rights.

Through this book, you will be introduced to the strange Law on Islam in Austria and why Islam is a protected religion there, along with Christianity and Judaism. In addition, you will learn about the warped verdicts handed down by judges both in Austria and at the European Court of Human Rights in Strasbourg, France, and about the terrible repercussions for the free world, both in Europe and the United States, of those verdicts. My case is unique in that I called upon the European Court on Human Rights to decide whether the right to have religion shielded from fact-based criticism trumps the right to freedom of expression, or vice versa.

Due to the legal case filed against me, I have been invited to speak in numerous countries and venues. As a result, in this book, you will read excerpts from my speeches that duly reflect my observations of and points of view on various aspects of Islam, free speech and thought, and free societies and democracy. Finally, I present the most important and material court documents and verdicts (translated into English) in the appendix.

—Vienna, Austria
  June 2019

A Note on Names

In the interest of protecting my family and friends against any future harassment or harm as a result of the publication of my account in this book, nearly all names of the people involved have been changed.

Prologue

The future must not belong to those who slander the Prophet of Islam.
—Barack Hussein Obama

The reason why people are silenced is not because they lie, but because they speak the truth. When people lie, their own words can be used against them. But if they tell the truth, there is no other means than violence.
—Theodor Fontane

February 15, 2011

I AM WALKING along the sidewalk toward the main entrance of Landesgericht Wien, the Vienna District Court. It's an imposing building on the corner of Landesgerichtsstrasse and Frankhplatz in downtown Vienna, not far from the Rathaus (the Town Hall). With me is my attorney, Dr. Michael Rami, with Gheneff-Rami-Sommer Rechtsanwälte, an established Viennese legal firm.

It's early morning, chilly, and dim on this bleak February day. Our breath makes cloud-puffs in front of us as we walk up the steps and through the arches to the front door. As we enter the close warmth of the building, we have to pass through a security screening. Just like the airport, I think to myself. Nobody says anything about it, but without the threat of Islamic terror attacks, we wouldn't have to go through all this rigmarole. If I asked, I'm sure they'd tell me it "has nothing to do with Islam."

Dr. Rami and I don't say much to each other as we pick up our bags from the security inspection table and continue down the hallway. Everything that needed to be said prior to today's court appearance has already been said. We had spent countless hours in preparation for the first two days of the trial, and then in the courtroom itself during my two prior appearances. He is calm. I am calm, too. But inside me there is a different reality; my mind is swirling with contradictory emotions. On the one hand, I am furious at the injustice that has forced me to appear in front of a judge for speaking the truth. On the other, I am apprehensive about the outcome of the trial. I also feel a sense of relief that the whole ugly mess will finally be over. I've been carrying this weight on my shoulders for well over a year, and now I long to be rid of it!

I wait outside the courtroom before going in, while Dr. Rami talks to some of his colleagues. I look around—there aren't many people here, though I am grateful for the friends who did show up. One of them flew in from Denmark; the other arrived by train from Germany. "Thank you," I mouth to them.

It's not the trial of the century. Still, I know the media will be present, as they were on the other two days. The media started this whole charade—in particular the magazine *NEWS*—and they wouldn't want to miss the dénouement.

I enter the courtroom and take my seat, waiting for Judge Bettina Neubauer to appear. There is muted conversation around me, the shuffling of papers, muffled footsteps, the shifting of chairs. I stare straight ahead, just waiting—waiting—waiting for all of it to be over!

Back in December, on the opening day of the trial, Dr. Rami said to the judge, "Your Honor, today it is not Mrs. Sabaditsch-Wolff, but freedom of expression that is on trial." Then, Judge Neubauer seemed unconcerned. Today, when she walks into the room, she still seems unimpressed. She wears the same slight smile—some observers call it a "smirk"—that she has worn throughout the trial. Everyone rises and looks toward the judge as she takes her seat.

When Judge Neubauer addresses me, I feel all the eyes in the room turn toward me and my attorney. Dr. Rami turns to Judge Neubauer and once again declares, "Your Honor, today it is not Mrs. Sabaditsch-Wolff, but freedom of expression that is on trial."

Once again, the judge seems unimpressed. What did I mean when I said what I said about rape, she wants to know.

"When a Muslim marries a nine-year old," says the defendant, that is, I, "he can invoke Islam, which allows him to do that."

"How do you conclude something like that?" asks the judge.

"Muslims are supposed to emulate the Prophet in all things," is my answer. "That is what it says in the Qur'an." I hold up a copy of the Muslim holy book. "And because Mohammed married a six-year old, Muslims, in Yemen among other places, still assume the right to marry and abuse children." I give the judge a penetrating look. "I have a six-year-old daughter. I do not want something like that to happen to her."

Judge Neubauer asks matter-of-factly, "Why should that happen?"

"Because Europe is under threat of Islamization," I say. "I give my seminar to inform and warn people."

"What do you think you call forth with such statements, if not hate?" asks the judge, who seems somewhat unnerved.

"I do not create hate," I reply calmly. "Reading the Qur'an causes far more hate than my seminars."

I stare blankly at the judge. Even now, more than a year later, I am amazed to find myself here, charged—and soon to be convicted—of "hate speech" for giving a factual description of the sexual relationship between Mohammed, the prophet of Islam, and his nine-year-old "wife." It's not as if I made the whole thing up. The story is right there in the Sira or biography of Mohammed. It's part of the canonical scripture of all major branches of the Islamic faith.

The words that caused me so much grief were spoken in September 2009 at one of my seminars about Islam. A reporter for the magazine *NEWS*, having heard about the dangerous "Islamophobe" Elisabeth Sabaditsch-Wolff, had been there secretly taping the session. She delivered the tape to the authorities, prompting them to lay a charge against me.

The original charge was "incitement to hatred," but that isn't the charge for which I would ultimately be convicted. By the time we reached the second day of the trial on January 18, 2011, it had become obvious that there was no way I would ever be convicted of "incitement to hatred." So the judge, at her own discretion, added a second charge, "denigration of religious beliefs of a legally recognized religion," and it was on that charge that I would be convicted this day.

In other words: presenting the "religious beliefs of a legally recognized religion" in a factually accurate manner may constitute "denigration," if that religion happens to be Islam.

It was clear from the moment the second charge was added that the Austrian state needed to convict me of something, *anything*, to set an example so that other "Islamophobes" would be warned. The judge obliged and concocted this absurdity. Is there any other country in the world where the charges against a defendant can be revised at the whim of a judge? But this is Austria, where anything goes, apparently.

The case against me hung on my intention. The prosecution claimed my intention was to stir up hatred, but how do they know what or whom

I hate? As it happens, hatred was not my motivation, but in any case, isn't it my own personal prerogative to decide what I like, what I dislike, or even, what I hate? And how is the judge able to gauge my level of hatred? Can she look inside my mind? Can she see into my heart?

All I ever wanted to do with my seminars was to wake people up to the dangers of Islamization, to help them to realize that we are swimming in treacherous waters, that we are on our way to very dangerous times. My only goal is to warn people, so that we never have to say, "Now it's too late."

CHAPTER ONE

A Rebel at Heart

The right to agree with others is not a problem in any society; it is the right to disagree that is crucial.
—Ayn Rand, *Capitalism: The Unknown Ideal*

I T IS A MYSTERY TO ME why I became the rebel in the family. What I *can* say is that, as far as I can tell, no one else in my family has a defiant streak. My father is often painfully obedient, especially to the authorities; my mother mostly followed suit. I suppose that the reason may be found in the years of their births: the early 1940s, after World War II had begun. Both Mom and Dad experienced the war firsthand, my father in Vienna, and my mother in a town in southern Austria.

I remember my grandparents' apartment in Vienna. They proudly showed me their refurbished bathroom and explained that the old one had been blown away by a bomb during the war, leaving a big hole in the outside wall. As a child, my Dad could look through the hole into a courtyard filled with rubble and debris.

My mother, on the other hand, was evacuated to the countryside in southern Austria to escape the relentless Allied bombardments. She once told me the story of how she, as a very young girl, found a metal milk jug on the roadside, which she promptly picked up and shook, because it made a delightful clanking sound. The sound emanated from a small bomb inside...

Growing up in postwar Austria under the nearby influence of the Iron Curtain and the rise of hard communism only a few kilometers away in Hungary and Czechoslovakia, my parents were part of a generation which knew that, in order to be successful, one needed to be obedient to authority. This obedience to the government—the belief that paternalistic government was generally good to its people, its voters—was rampant then, as it is today.

As for my sister, I suppose that she was too young to comprehend what had happened in Tehran—the transformation of a relatively free society into a totalitarian theocratic one. I can think of no other reason why we are so very different. So it seems that I am the black sheep in my family. And guess what? I can live with that!

My rebelliousness appeared early in my life, although it took me a while to realize it. There is one story I always tell when I am asked about my rebellious streak: I attended a strict gender-segregated Roman Catholic school in Chicago which forced its students to wear uniforms and taught us to be good in the Catholic sense. That is all very well; I do believe that the world would be a better place if the Ten Commandments led the way. However, what I strongly dislike is hypocrisy.

I was in high school when my best friend Liz was in tears once again because of her family. She had always had a tough family life, and I was always by her side to dry her tears or just hold her. I also had to take a Latin vocabulary test that day, one that I was prepared for and for which I had studied. So, when Liz asked me to stay with her and listen to her problems, I made a conscious choice to skip Latin class (which I was acing anyway) and risk detention rather than leave her in her misery. Of course, I skipped the Latin test; and, of course, I got a detention. But I had made the right decision, one I believed should have made the Catholics in that school rethink their position. I deserved the F, but a detention? No. It is no surprise that cutting class to be with a distressed friend made absolutely no difference to my (academic) career.

In all of the schools I attended (and there were quite a few), I was an outsider trying to fit in. In Vienna's schools, I was different because I had returned from Tehran, having experienced a revolution as well as having traveled to places that my classmates had only studied about in history class. Furthermore, my handwriting was different. I had learned the German style, which I then proceeded to change to Austrian handwriting. So, what does a seven-year-old discuss with her fellow classmates during break? The latest news about her Dad, who is still in Tehran and about whose fate she knows very little? Or, perhaps how cool it was in Babylon? Or, how much she misses Iranian bread? Or, how she's counting the days until she can place a phone call to her Dad? Kathryna, a Polish refugee girl,[1] was the only one who could relate to my situation.

---

1 Austria accepted many refugees from Poland in the early 1980s as a result of the Polish uprisings against communist rule, especially following the rise of the Solidarity

We became good friends as a result.

In school in Chicago, I was once again different. Again, I had to adapt my handwriting. I was an Austrian who learned to speak flawless English within a very short time; I even regularly beat my classmates in spelling bees and homonym contests. I devoured books by Judy Blume and Danielle Steele. And, because I lived in Chicago; spoke perfect, accent-free English and had integrated well (I love cheese popcorn and light beer), everyone naturally assumed that I would eventually become an American citizen. I was asked more than once, "When are you becoming an American citizen?" When I explained that I would never become an American citizen, my classmates were taken aback.

Today, I understand why. For an American, it is natural that everyone's goal be to gain citizenship; after all, most legal aliens long for the day when they can become American citizens. Back then, during puberty, my feelings were hurt. Why could no one understand that I was Austrian? That it was never my intention to be anything else? That I wanted to return to Austria, today rather than tomorrow? Impossible for an American to understand; I get it now. And I respect that to be an American is to be a citizen of an exceptional country.

I am sure that I was insensitive to all of that back then. I was searching for my own identity while trying to be someone else, someone I would never be. Today, I am a proud Austrian with deep love and respect for all things American. I am a traveler between both worlds, America and Europe, which misunderstand each other more often than not.

๛

Another story that epitomizes my rebelliousness: When I was stationed in Kuwait, I always wanted to drive from Kuwait to Bahrain. Yes, I could have flown to the capital, Manama, but I wanted to experience the excitement of driving through a "forbidden" country, one that does not allow women to show their hair and that does not issue visas to single women. All of those "not alloweds" were sufficient for me to challenge them. And that is what I did.

I was in possession of a diplomatic passport, which made my quest easier. In addition, my boss, the ambassador, was amenable to my plan. So I entered his office, visa application in hand, and asked him to sign

---

(*Solidarnosc*) movement and its leader, Lech Walesa.

a so-called *note verbale*,[2] which was required for a visa application by a member of the diplomatic corps. The ambassador asked me why I wanted to drive to Bahrain. I answered, "Because it is a challenge, especially since I am unmarried." The ambassador, with a smile, said, "Then get married." I replied, "I already have someone in mind, just for the duration of the trip." His smile turned into a grin and, with that, he signed our applications as well as the required *note verbale*.

Only a few days later, I embarked with a close friend of mine (to whom I was married, according to the visa application) on the long drive from Kuwait to Saudi Arabia. It goes without saying that I did not wear a headscarf; my only concession to the conservative Saudi Arabian laws was to tie my back-length blond hair in a ponytail. I also did not don an *abaya*, but wore a t-shirt and long pants. No one ever questioned me or my companion during the entire trip, even when I took a "potty break" along the route to Bahrain.

I will admit that my rebellion against the Saudi modesty laws was eased by my diplomatic status. However, I went through with my plan despite the fact that I was single. I wanted to know what it was like in Saudi Arabia—unpleasant for a Westerner who values freedom above all, especially on our return leg when we stopped for lunch in Khafji (the last town before the Kuwaiti border) and experienced gender segregation at a fast-food restaurant; we, however, were considered a "family" and therefore allowed to sit together.

Ramadan (the 30-day period when devout Muslims fast from sunrise to sunset) was also a time for me to challenge the status quo. In Kuwait, I was lucky to live on the third floor of the embassy building, where I was assigned a decent-sized, two-bedroom apartment with a huge (although, due to the heat, useless) terrace. The workflow during Ramadan was even more sluggish than at other times, so I often snuck upstairs and began cooking my lunch. I was secretly pleased when the aroma began wafting throughout the building—I imagined the Muslim embassy staff's collective bellies growling with hunger pangs. In addition, when I manned the visa section or simply supervised the discussions between staff and visa petitioners, I would enter the visa section with my breakfast roll in hand, filled with delicious (pork) salami that had come straight out of my freezer that morning. Mind you, I was not trying to antagonize or make fun of anyone; I was simply protesting!

Moreover, under international law, the premises of the Austrian em-

---

2 A diplomatic communication prepared in the third person and left unsigned, it is less formal than a note but more formal than an *aide-mémoire*.

bassy were not considered Kuwait proper and so, strictly speaking, I was not breaking any rules. In the late 1990s, Ramadan took place in the late fall and winter months, and so the sun set around 5:30 pm. I always enjoyed doing my grocery shopping shortly before the breaking of the fast, because the stores would be empty due to everyone else's waiting at home for the sun to finally set. By the time that people were done with their first meal of the day, I was back in the embassy enjoying my evening.

Thus, there was no need to be a rebel (and perhaps a nuisance) in the streets. The situation would definitely be much different, and a greater challenge for me, if Ramadan had taken place during the summer months, as now.

I was friends with a Kuwaiti man who hailed from a very prominent Kuwaiti family. He hated all things Muslim, and Ramadan in particular, with a passion. He visited me often during Ramadan for some sanity and a beer, telling me that, in the office, he would hide behind his newspaper while devouring a sandwich. The poor guy was stuck with this life; he could never escape, as I did, and always had to pretend to be a good Muslim, while at the same time professing to me how much he hated his religion. There was never any question that he would ever leave Islam, because leaving Islam meant leaving his family. Apostasy always entails loss: Loss of family, respect, livelihood, and, in countries such as Pakistan, Iran, or Saudi Arabia, even one's life. I wish our politicians and Non-Governmental Organizations (NGOs) could understand all of that. Apostates from Islam are treated abysmally, even in Europe.

Yet back in the late 1990's in Kuwait, I always suspected that a sizeable number of Muslims would love to leave their religion, to leave bondage, and free themselves from oppression. I witnessed so much "snitching" going on both in Kuwait and Libya. If you did not live a perfect life according to Islam's rules, you would be at your family's mercy and would experience their wrath. You would be ostracized, and who wants to be left out? This is the terrifying cleverness of the system called Islam, along with all other totalitarian ideologies: As a Muslim, you were part of a group, a collective—the Ummah—and any non-conformity, any attempt to break away from the collective, was seen as turning your back on the group, becoming a traitor..

I witnessed this frequently. For instance, my landlord in Tripoli, Libya, and his immediate family were not devout; his wife did not cover her hair. However, the family followed Ramadan's rules, and so when they visited family during Ramadan, the wife did cover her hair. The same went for our Jordanian interpreter in Kuwait: He wistfully showed me photos of his wife from the 1980s and early 1990s, when her hair was still uncovered. He was very unhappy about her decision to wear a hijab, but he was unable or unwilling to do anything about it. I even suspect that he was secretly proud of her decision. There was no doubt her family back in Jordan reacted to her decision very positively.

My greatest and most consequential rebellion was to go against mainstream opinion as early as 2007, when I finally realized that Austria and Europe were faced with accelerating Islamization and I felt compelled to educate my fellow Austrians about it. Perhaps (and in hindsight) I was naive back then, thinking that what I had to say would be welcomed and even lead to political action. Despite the fact that human rights, and in particular women's rights, are nonpartisan, only the Austrian Freedom Party was willing to listen to me, by offering me the opportunity to hold seminars under the auspices of the party's education institute. I am still grateful for that; it took a leap of faith for the Freedom Party to give me a chance because they had no idea who I was or what I was going to say. I did not have to present my presentations for their prior approval.

My seminars took place biannually, once per semester, on three Saturday mornings, each one lasting for at least four hours. At first, only about six or seven people attended, although I was honored to have a few politicians present. What they now know about Islam, its doctrines, and its tenets is what I taught them. My PowerPoint presentations were always fully sourced, and they explained Islam and its consequences for democracy, freedom, and human rights. I loved the vigorous discussions that ensued, especially since many of the attendees found my explanations challenging to their worldview. However, as Islamization progressed over the years and its implications became increasingly obvious in the public sphere, attendance increased, and so it was inevitable that one day, those unhappy with what I had to say—those who view me as an "Islamophobe" or "racist"—would intervene to destroy the work of all those who, like me, criticize the tenets of Islamic doctrine.

CHAPTER TWO

Early Years in Iran

There are no jokes in Islam. There is no humor in Islam. There is no fun in Islam. There can be no fun and joy in whatever is serious.
—Ayatollah Khomeini

I am a "diplomat's brat." My father was a career diplomat for the Austrian Ministry of Foreign Affairs, and I was born in Geneva, Switzerland, during his first posting. He followed a regular career path, working his way up the diplomatic ladder. Following a short stop in Vienna and the birth of my sister, Dad was offered the post of deputy consul general in New York City. That two-and-a-half-year stay there presented me with the priceless opportunity to learn English for the first time, including the Pledge of Allegiance, in preschool and kindergarten. My mother, the perfect diplomat's wife, decorated our apartment in Riverdale in her trademark manner, creating sweet comfort for our family. Memories of my years in New York are sketchy other than the celebration of the Bicentennial of the founding of the United States in 1976 with its stunning display of old ships on the Hudson River and my dancing the "can-can" on the occasion of my graduation from kindergarten.

How differently my life would have turned out had the Austrian Ministry of Foreign Affairs not decided against transferring Dad to Moscow! I don't remember any of this, but from what Dad told me, he was already taking Russian language lessons in preparation for a move to the Soviet Union. And I suppose I would have become expert in all things Soviet at the height of the Cold War, with flawless Russian language skills as well—a fascinating thought. Alas, it was not to be.

Instead, my mother packed up our belongings, and we traveled halfway around the globe to Tehran, Iran, where life could not have been more different than in Moscow or New York City.

My early memories of Tehran during the time of the Shah, Mohammad Reza Pahlavi, are spotty at best. Before our family was able to move into our own place, we were housed on the premises of the Austrian Cultural Institute for a couple of months. Due to the high number of foreigners—there were about 44,000 Americans alone!—the real-estate market was extremely tight and rent comparatively high. While my father was offered a respectable house, the Austrian Ministry of Finance refused to release funds to pay our rent,[1] thus forcing us to camp in the Cultural Institute until the matter was finally resolved. Living there must have been tough on everyone, especially my mother. Not only were the living quarters cramped, but Dad went off to work every morning and Mom was stuck in a foreign city, without Farsi language skills, without friends, and with two small children. How to feed the family must have put an incredible strain on her.

This is a photo of the house and garden that I loved roaming as a child.

---

1 Moreover, a Westerner could not just live anywhere in the city, but had to take into account the security situation. The same situation presented itself to me later on in Libya. Fortunately, the Ministry of Finance had, by that time, understood that local situations in countries like Iran and Libya could not be compared to the one in Austria.

After what seemed like a long wait, we finally moved into our own home, a big house with a big garden and an even bigger pool, located on a street named Kuche Dariush in the northern part of Tehran. Dad picked the location in northern Tehran, near a barracks, for safety and security reasons. You couldn't drive straight onto our street from the main avenue (back then called Saltanatabad, but renamed after Khomeini's revolution), because of what is called a "tchoub" in Farsi, an open canal with water carrying sewage which flowed from north to south. I vividly remember the yucky, greenish, slimy color of the water inside the tchoubs. You always had to know where these tchoubs flowed in order to bypass them, whether on foot or by car. Once Dad reversed our green Volvo into a tchoub and got one of the tires stuck; friendly Iranians helped haul the car back onto the street again.

It was only a few minutes' walk to the Saltanatabad main-street thoroughfare, where Mom would take my sister and me for grocery shopping. There wasn't a grocery store like those we knew in the Western world; instead, Mom had to learn all the parts of a cow very quickly, as there was no meat processing. I remember standing in a butcher's shop with a whole cow hanging upside down on a meat hook, and Mom pointing to a part of the cow, which the butcher then proceeded to process. After that, we moved on to a greengrocer's for our vegetables, then on to a small convenience store for staples, followed by a bakery that offered exquisite, tasty cookies. To this day, I long for Iranian flatbread called "barbari," which tasted best straight from the oven. There was a special bakery near our house, located on a street called Dowlat. I loved driving or walking there with Dad to pick up stacks of barbari bread, which I then devoured. In those pre-Islamic Revolution days, Dad also treated us to delicious French bread and ham.

Dad loved to hike, so Tehran was perfect for him because its northern part is delimited by the Alburz mountain range, which included Mount Tochal with its ski area, and the Damavand, Iran's highest mountain (5,600 meters/18,400 feet high). Dad climbed Damavand during Ramadan 1978; during his rest breaks, his Iranian mountain guide sat at a separate table because he was fasting, while the rest of the group ate. An Austrian cable-car supplier had been engaged to build a chairlift to the peak of Tochal, and though the chair and cables had already been delivered, the chairlift was never built.

In addition, an Austrian mountain guide was hired to train Iranian mountaineers for an ascent of Mount Everest. Apparently the devotion of the Iranian mountaineers was limited because the guide had plenty of time on his hands to instruct Dad, culminating in his own successful ascent of Damavand. Even more appreciated (not least by me) was the hiring of an Austrian ski instructor who, due to the Iranian skiers' lack of training enthusiasm, skied with us every Sunday afternoon.

On one of our family trips to Iraq, we visited the ancient city of Samarra, 78 miles north of Baghdad, with its famous mosque and spiral minaret. I even climbed the minaret as a young girl. In 1990, on our way to the Turkish border, we passed Samarra.

Reaching school age, I was duly enrolled in first grade at the Tehran German School where I learned to read and write, along with some basic math skills, in addition to some Farsi, which was mandatory. I remember my parents waiting in our car for school to end on Sundays so that we could all go skiing in the nearby Dizin ski area. I loved skiing in Dizin but not the serpentine drive up the mountain (invariably, my sister or I, or both of us, would throw up). Nevertheless, we were rewarded with an amazing ski area (one that was in a league with medium-sized Austrian ski areas, according to Dad). Due to Dizin's elevation, the season would last as late as May, which we would take advantage of as often as the weather permitted. There is nothing like spending the morning skiing and then jumping into a pool in the afternoon—life was not bad for us in Tehran!

My parents also wisely decided that we should do as much sightseeing as possible. We drove north to go swimming in the Caspian Sea or south to spend a weekend camping with friends in the desert. To this day, I am not a fan of camping, but I do remember the excitement of those road trips. For instance, once after a heavy rainfall, the tires of our car got stuck in the deep mud and the stifling heat enabled us to fry an egg on the hood of the car. We also went on a road trip from Tehran to Baghdad, Iraq, then south to Basra, and returned north to Tehran. I spent time in places such as Babylon and Ur, the ancient Sumerian city in what was Mesopotamia. I was always aware that these were places that one studies in history class, but that I was able to actually be in these historic places amazed me.

I always like to tell the story of how and when I starting drinking beer. I was no older than six or seven, and we were spending another weekend in one of the many desert areas that surround Tehran. As camp was being set up by the adults, I became increasingly thirsty. Pointing to one of the many canisters of water, I asked for a drink; Dad said, "No, no, we use water for washing. Have a drink of beer." The presence of an Austrian entrepreneur importing and selling Austrian and German goods, including beer, made life easier for Western expats, especially when camping in the desert.

One of my other hobbies as a six-year-old consisted of jumping up and down on mountains of carpets. My parents had decided to invest in Persian rugs, and periodically we would pay a visit to our favorite carpet seller, an Iranian Jew, whose shop was conveniently located in the vicinity of our house. Carpets were sold in (what seemed to me at my young age) huge warehouses with thousands of carpets stacked on top of each other. Our carpet seller would then present his best carpets by fishing out one of them from the stacks, which drew lengthy approving "oohs" and "ahhs," and oftentimes "nooos," followed by drawn-out negotiations of the final price. My sister and I didn't care much about the carpets, only about the fun we had racing through the shop while my parents picked out the most beautiful and valuable carpets. My parents spent many afternoons with the carpet seller in the summer of 1980, after the revolution. He asked my mother to carry his wedding jewelry with her to Austria, which she did. Her diplomatic status did not impress the airport guards and they proceeded to body-search her. How she managed to save the jewelry from being confiscated will remain her secret forever. Unfortunately, she passed away before I found out about this incident. We also took some of his own carpets with us when we finally left Iran, and he was only reunited (tearfully) with his possessions in Vienna. Sadly, we never heard from him again.

Pre-revolutionary Iran was a fine place to live, even if you were not Muslim. At no point did I, as a young child, *feel* Islam (as we do now in Europe and the United States). We Westerners were free to live as we liked; there was nothing I missed or wanted. Islam in pre-revolutionary Iran was unobtrusive; it is widely acknowledged that the Shah was responsible for this freedom. Seldom did I see a covered woman; as a matter of fact, the only covered women I saw were outside Tehran, and they certainly made no impression on me at all.

One of my parents' most cherished memories was attending one of the final cocktail parties attended by the Shah and his wife. In August 1953, the Shah had been forced to flee Iran due to an attempted coup d'etat staged by the pro-Soviet Prime Minister Mohammad Mosaddegh, who had suspended the Iranian constitution of 1906, was ruling by edict, and had expropriated British and U.S. oil properties without due process or recompense. After British and American intervention, Iran was restored to its constitution and the Shah was able to return to the country, whereupon he fired Mosaddegh in accord with the Iranian constitution. Thereafter, every August, the Shah's mother commemorated his return to Iran by hosting a lavish cocktail party in her palace in northern Tehran. Iran's entire high nobility and dignitaries were invited, with the diplomatic corps also present but only for decoration purposes. As this was the middle of summer, most ambassadors were out of the country, so the *chargés d'affaires* took part in this extravaganza. Many Iranian women flew to Paris to have their hair coiffed especially for the event, while the buffet included mountains of oysters (despite the heat!) and lobster with free-flowing alcohol. The bloody demonstrations that took place simultaneously in the southern part of Tehran left a hollow aftertaste.

Following the Shah's lavish state visit to Washington, D.C., in November 1977, President Jimmy Carter and the First Lady flew to Tehran and spent New Year's Eve toasting the Shah, which enraged the Iranian clergy, leading to protests and deaths. Opposition groups formed throughout 1978, with the revolution beginning in earnest with the Black Friday protests, culminating in the use of excessive violence by the Shah's security forces on September 8, 1978. I personally do not remember when the turmoil inside Iran started or when Ayatollah Khomeini began causing trouble; most of what I know is what I read in my young adult years, accounts of how the revolution began and how Khomeini stirred the masses from exile in Paris with the help of tapes of his sermons that were smuggled into Iran. However, the trouble started when the Shah, due in part to his failing health, was incapable of responding properly and decisively to the uprisings. There were myriad reasons for his failure to stop the revolution that resulted in the establishment of a theocracy, which to this day destabilizes the entire region and terrorizes its people. As for me, the Islamic revolution laid the groundwork for who I am today.

My parents must have kept their concerns about the revolution from my sister and me because I only realized there was something wrong when, early one morning in December 1978, my Dad, my mother, my sister, and I were driven to the airport. I remember saying good-bye to our cat, closing the heavy white gate behind me, and getting into the embassy car. Something was up; the situation felt ominous.

My mother's ID card issued by the Iranian Ministry of Foreign Affairs

There must have been thousands and thousands of Iranians, and other nationals, flocking to the airport because the terminal was packed. At one point, I lost my parents. I was lifted above people's heads so that I could be reunited with my parents, who were sick with worry. My father had thrown up all over his turquoise-colored turtleneck. The massive crowds at the airport and in the streets have had a lasting effect on me: to this day I avoid large crowds.

My parents, my sister, and I arrived in Vienna to celebrate Christmas. Dad then returned to Tehran, leaving us behind. He was not allowed to leave his post as only dependents had been expelled from Iran. The Islamic Revolution had begun. As a result, we were separated from my Dad for most of the next two years, with the exception of school holidays, which we spent with him in Tehran.

My mother's Herculean efforts and the graciousness of friends enabled us to stay at a furnished apartment and attend school in Vienna. (My parents' condominium had been rented—a lesson they took to heart and never rented it out again.) My mother suffered immensely from the stress of worrying about my Dad's safety, her daughters' happiness, and dealing with her own helplessness, despite weekly phone calls from Tehran. Most of our possessions were still in our house there, not in Vienna. It must have been an awful time for her.

Returning to Tehran during school holidays became normal for me. It was great to be reunited with Dad. Although his life seemed so much easier than my mom's, I am certain it was not. The supply situation had deteriorated dramatically, with many food staples unavailable. Many embassy officials had become bachelors because there families had been expelled (like my father) and spent their free time playing cards. There were frequent curfews, which made evening entertainment a challenge (how to return home in time for curfew?), and the daily demonstrations in the streets added to security concerns.

The mass demonstrations in the city changed me. I remember riding in my Dad's car and witnessing the chaos, but what frightened me most was the countless number of women in the streets, fully veiled in black chadors, raising their fists in the air, chanting "*Allahu akbar*" and "*Marg bar Amrika*" (Death to America). Seemingly overnight, the country that had once seemed so free, had given me so many precious and enduring memories, and had been a pleasure to live in, had morphed into a country of mass protests and angry-looking black-clad women demonstrating for the Islamic revolution. Ayatollah Khomeini billboard portraits were everywhere. The image of his face, so full of hatred and rage, is one

I will never forget. As a seven-year-old, I was baffled at this hatred. Why would anyone want to look or feel this way? What made people look or feel that way? I came to understand this only decades later.

Demonstrations in front of the US Embassy, 1978.

Nighttime was especially eerie for me. When the revolution began in the fall of 1978, I would stand outside the house, separated from the street by the fence, and listen to desperate-sounding chants of "*Allahu akbar*" from our neighbors' roofs. At one point, our street was almost deserted—most of the Iranians living there had fled Iran or been arrested. The Iranians next door stayed; they would later save our lives.

Did we ever feel unsafe during the revolutionary turmoil? According to my father, the answer is yes, no, and maybe. At the time, no one knew for sure whether we as Austrians were a target, so one had to choose safety over sorrow and assume we were a target. However, Americans,

British, and French most definitely were unsafe in Tehran and the rest of the country. In general, it was unsafe to be anything but Iranian, simply because there was no way for Iranians to distinguish between an Austrian, a French person, or an American.

From our point of view, the transition from Shah-ruled Iran to a revolutionary Iran was very gradual. In the summer of 1978, for example, we spent a few days in the city of Isfahan, about 250 miles south of Tehran and known for its famous Islamic architecture and beautifully tiled mosques. In Isfahan, we encountered demonstrations for the first time. Because we were sitting in our car, we were able to quickly turn into a side alley to escape getting caught; at no point were we afraid.

While there was always plenty of barbari bread and sabzi (vegetable greens), ham, baguettes, and alcohol vanished from the shelves. Shipments of alcohol covered by diplomatic immunity took forever to clear customs. Suddenly there was no Coca-Cola or Sprite to be had, the former because it reminded people of whiskey, the latter because it reminded people of vodka. Such was the logic of the Islamic Revolution. The Austrian import/exporter had to shut down his business, while friends went into hiding, went to jail, or emigrated

We got used to the many Pasdaran, or Revolutionary Guards,[2] roaming the streets. They posed a threat simply because they did not know how to handle a weapon. Interestingly enough, skiing was not banned by the revolutionaries. The reason was a very unrevolutionary, non-Islamic, almost capitalistic one: there were simply too many jobs associated with the running of the ski area.

Even with a full-blown Islamic takeover of Iran, we were still able to attend church services every Sunday at 6 pm in a large Catholic chapel in northern Tehran. Despite the presence of at least two aloof-looking Pasdarans, there were no incidents. The locally based Catholic priest in charge of German-speaking Catholics in Iran was a good-humored Bavarian and a close friend of my parents. He once asked Dad if he could drive the bishop to the airport with his diplomatic license plates. While the drive was safe, one just could not guarantee safe passage and many of the young men carrying arms in the streets were illiterate.

Despite all of this, my parents tried to make life as easy as possible for my sister and me. I enjoyed the summer months. I loved swimming in our enormous pool and wandering about the beautiful garden with its more than one hundred rose bushes, as well as our free-roaming

2 The Islamic Revolutionary Guard Corps (IRGC) is designated as a terrorist group in Bahrain, Saudi Arabia, and the United States.

chickens. I do not remember going hungry at any time; however, there are photos of my sister looking worryingly skinny, with her collarbone protruding.

This photo depicts the segregation of the sexes enforced at the beaches of the Caspian Sea following the Islamic Revolution. My father tells me enjoyed his time, even relaxed, while my mother had two small children at her hands.

The summer of 1980 was particularly memorable in many ways. A gas station near our house exploded, but that did not warrant any further concern; we shrugged and moved on, as did everyone else. The Islamic revolution was in full swing and going well from Khomeini's point of view. So-called students had attacked and taken over the U.S. embassy with a sizeable number of American hostages, causing outrage outside of Iran but increasing support within the country. From his office window, Dad was able to follow some of the goings-on in the American embassy, especially the frequent demonstrations with the battle cries of *"Marg bar Amrika"* and *"Allahu akbar."* None of this really impressed me because I was enjoying my time, although I remember Mom discussing the preparation of food for the two hostages held in the Iranian foreign ministry. My sister and I were tasked to paint some pictures using our watercolors and write some uplifting words, which were then delivered along with the food. Bruce Laingen, one of the hostages and, as *chargé d'affaires*, the highest-ranking U.S. diplomat in Iran, returned the favor by writing letters to us and painting beautiful landscapes of what he imagined Austria looked like.

July 31, 1980, is a day I will never forget, and neither will my parents. After a morning of fun in the pool and a hearty lunch, Mom, my sister, and I retired to my parents' bedroom on the first floor for our afternoon nap in order to escape the worst of the summer heat. My sister and I snuggled against my mother and tried to fall asleep. Suddenly, I was roused from my half-sleep—there was unusual noise and ruckus in the street. I got up and peeked out the window. There were indeed people standing in the street, gesticulating, looking nervous. Following their gaze to my left, I saw angry black clouds of smoke rising from what was our storage area, a kind of annex to our house. Mom and my sister had woken up in the meantime and were also looking out the window, while I went to open the bedroom door. What I saw frightened me to death—the entire house was engulfed in smoke, and there was no way we could escape using the stairs. We were forced to find another exit. "Let's jump in the pool!" I screamed, opening the door leading to our sizeable terrace overlooking the pool and the garden. Mom was unhappy about my idea because she had holes in her eardrums and generally avoided getting water on her head. By the time we were on the balcony and examining our options, we noticed two men carrying ladders and making their way to save us. The men, our next-door neighbors, leaned the ladder against the balcony wall while motioning to us to climb over the rail and wiggle down until we reached the top of the ladder. A scary thought!

Only a few minutes later, we were safely on the ground and rushed out into the street. What a sorry sight we were! Mom in her nightgown, my sister and I in our underwear. Even at my young age, I was self-conscious in my near-nakedness, especially considering the religious fervor in place at the time.

No sooner had we made our way out of the smoky house than Dad arrived, followed by a red fire engine—an American one! I was fascinated by the fire engine's mighty appearance. The fire in the little annex was extinguished very quickly, and soon we were allowed back into the house. What a sight! What a smell! I will always remember the pungent odor of burning plastic, and to this day I am frightened of fire, even to the point that I am overly careful when lighting a candle for fear that my house will once again burn down. The entire ground floor was flooded with water, the parquet destroyed. We soon found out the fire was set in the annex storage room, where incidentally two propane gas canisters had been stored. We were very lucky to be alive.

We never found out officially who had set the fire, although my parents had strong grounds to point the finger of suspicion at Mariam, our Iranian maid, of whom I had always been very fond. When my mother returned to Tehran at the beginning of July, she noticed that a lot of her clothing and wedding mementos, including silver candle-holders, as well as other trinkets, were missing. So Mom accused Mariam of stealing, which must have enraged her, leading her to set the fire. However, to prevent Mariam's family's wrath and retribution, Dad never pressed charges with the police. There was no point in the exercise, especially since we were due to leave the country in a few weeks.

So how does a diplomat and his family end a day this exciting? Well, they keep their chins up and attend a party at the Austrian ambassador's residence, what else? The show must go on.

Our Iranian adventure officially ended in September 1980. Mom, my sister and I returned to Vienna to start school again, while Dad left Tehran on September 20, mere hours before the Iran-Iraq war broke out, vowing never to return to Iran during his lifetime.

My mother cleaning up and looking over what was left after the fire.

In hindsight, my time in Iran, and what I witnessed and experienced there, set the stage for who I am today. It is only natural that I became a critic of Islam, after witnessing the dramatic change in Iran, from a relatively free and rather secular country to a staunchly theocratic society based on the Shari'a (Islamic law). I am fairly certain that one reason for my outspoken criticism of Islam is my having observed women in Iran from a young girl's point of view. In the early 20th century, the Shah's father decreed the removal of the veil and opened schools for girls. Women's freedom later included the choice for or against the veil and the ability to work in formerly male domains such as legal professions, science, and technology. The revolution—actively supported by most Iranian women while adopting the chador and/or hijab as a sign of protest and the symbol of the revolution—quashed many of the advances for women that were realized in the preceding decades. One of Khomeini's first decrees following his return to Iran and assuming political power included lowering the legal age for girls to marry from eighteen to nine lunar years, and, while the age of consent was later raised, the laws of the Islamic Republic refer to Shari'a law for the settlement of disputes. The shift that I witnessed, from free Iranian women to women in bondage, including the age of consent, made a lasting impression on me. It would lead the way to the courtroom I would find myself in many decades later, where I would fight for the rights of girls, including my own daughter, to live as free human beings.

CHAPTER THREE

Living in Iraq and America

Congress shall make no law respecting an establishment of religion, or prohibiting the free exercise thereof; or abridging the freedom of speech, or of the press; or the right of the people peaceably to assemble, and to petition the Government for a redress of grievances.
—US Constitution, First Amendment

AFTER OUR ADVENTURES in Iran, my family settled in Vienna. Primary school was uneventful—despite the fact that I attended three different schools in four years—followed by two unremarkable years in what is called "gymnasium" in Austria. When I say "uneventful" I refer only to school, because...

In the fall of 1982, the Austrian Ministry of Foreign Affairs found itself in a challenging situation. The Austrian ambassador to Iraq was due to depart for an extended home leave, and it was decided that the *chargé d'affaires* was too young and inexperienced to be in charge of the embassy for a prolonged period of time. No one in the ministry was willing to spend two months in Baghdad without their family, because the ministry, inflexible as ever, was apparently unwilling to fund the presence of diplomatic staff's family in Baghdad. This is when my father stepped in: He was prepared to take the ambassador's place, and he had my mother, sister, and me flown in to join him. To him, having his family present for the Christmas holidays was worth whatever he had to pay in return. So, once again, my mother packed and prepared herself for life in a country at war (the Iran-Iraq war), which included the purchase of a Christmas tree, frozen game meat and vinegar essence, among other supplies. We traveled to the airport with a lot of luggage. An Austrian

Airlines airplane was to fly us to Baghdad via Larnaca, Cyprus, a flight I would remember quite well because our flight from there to Baghdad was delayed due to fog at Baghdad airport, which caused my mother to become increasingly concerned. This was entirely understandable as she feared the frozen meat would thaw and the rest of the food in our luggage would spoil, yet there was nothing she could do but show patience. Thankfully, our arrival at Baghdad International Airport took place after midnight and therefore the airport was deserted. My father was waiting for us at the baggage carousel. After our piles of suitcases arrived and we hoisted them onto carts, we noticed on our way out that we were leaving a trail of blood behind us. The meat must have thawed. Oops! (We were wondering about the light security presence, especially for a country at war.)

We made it to the ambassador's residence without a hitch. The night was calm despite Iraq being at war with Iran. During my two weeks in Baghdad, I hardly noticed that there was a war going on. I say hardly because there were some indicators: I saw artillery positions and light anti-aircraft guns located throughout the city, and I heard artillery fire. In addition, we knew from the condition of the stores that the country was in a war economy. While we never went hungry, we had to adapt to whatever was available at the moment, which is why my mother shopped so extensively prior to our trip. The nature of a war economy was such that one day the stores offered a wide range of fish, including lobster, while at the same time there was no chicken. On another day, we would find chicken but no red meat. The following week, we bought fantastic steak, but there was no fish. The supermarket aisles were always filled to capacity but only with two or three more-or-less useless products—a stark reminder of what people in the Soviet Union were experiencing at that time (according to what we had seen on television). Most of our daily nutritional needs were provided by private markets, not official stores. In my father's view, the reason for the supply shortages was a combination of the fact of there being a war on (70 percent) and local incompetence (30 percent).

On my father's days off, we visited historical sites near Baghdad. Leaving Baghdad required special written permission from the Iraqi Ministry of Foreign Affairs, which Dad once forgot about prior to his official visit to Basra, a city in southern Baghdad. While his visit took place without incident, he was officially reprimanded upon his return, happily without any consequences, by the Iraqi Ministry of Foreign Affairs.

When we drove around the city, I remember not only the countless posters and gigantic depictions of Iraqi president Saddam Hussein in every imaginable pose—although not nearly as frightening as Ayatollah Khomeini in Tehran—but also how my parents and I marveled at the many pedestrian bridges over the highways with escalators on both sides of the road. What made us laugh, though, was the very idea of building escalators in a desert area—the dust that seeped into the intricately built escalators destroyed the mechanism in mere weeks. They were never maintained and thus rotted away in the desert heat. The presumably German manufacturer must have made a fortune. The Iraqis also loved the reflectors on the roads because they were made with Swarovski crystals—so much so that these reflectors were installed all over Baghdad, not just in the streets, which turned out to be counterproductive to driving at night. We found this quite amusing.

Dad likes to tell what, in his memory, is a very spooky story about how one day in late November, Palestinian Day,[1] a representative of the Palestinian Fatah terror organization (more commonly known as the Abu Nidal Organization) entered the scandalously unsecured embassy premises unannounced, through the kitchen door, to thank my father, the ambassador, for Austria's Palestinian-supporting—and Jewish!—chancellor Bruno Kreisky. Then, the very friendly Abu Nidal representative handed over a modest gift, a small wooden box with inlays, and left as quietly as he had come.

Another event also stayed in my father's memory: the longest whiskey bar he had ever seen. In early December 1982, he was invited to attend the National Holiday observance of what was then the Republic of South Yemen, to be celebrated in one of Baghdad's largest hotels. Dad marveled at the whiskey bar, containing about 100 bottles of fine whiskey, which was also served to the guests while they were entertained by a ladies' orchestra from East Germany. All of this took place at a reception hosted by an Islamic country in an Islamic country, both of which consider women and whiskey haram (forbidden). Very surreal but illustrative of life in wartime Baghdad.

On December 25, 1982, my family attended Christmas mass at a Catholic church in Baghdad; this was a very special mass for both religious and political reasons. Dad had held preliminary discussions with the Catholic leader in Baghdad at the embassy. The religious leader then

---

1 "International Day of Solidarity with the Palestinian People," a UN-organized observance commemorating UN Resolution 181 (the UN Partition Plan for Palestine), is held each year on November 29th.

asked Dad to preach the Gospel in German, a very exciting moment for him—this was the religious reason. The political reason was that the three masses held (the final one specifically for Filipino Catholics) were celebrated in filled-to-capacity churches and without any interference.

My two weeks in wartime Baghdad taught me two lessons that are still valid today: First, while democracy is always to be preferred, in some cases secular dictatorships, such as the ones I witnessed in Iraq and later in Libya, were good for Christian minorities. Christian life thrived under Saddam Hussein in Baghdad and Mosul, where Christians were numerous and still spoke Aramaic, the language of Jesus Christ. Since Saddam Hussein's death and the subsequent political and military turmoil, we have seen Christians systematically driven out of these lands in large numbers, brutally persecuted, and often killed. Certainly, nowadays, following the ousting of Saddam Hussein, Christians in Iraq can no longer move around as freely as they did in 1982.

Second, the secular dictatorship under Saddam Hussein kept Islamist forces at bay. Iraq in 1982-83 reminded me of pre-revolutionary Iran—a nominally Muslim country where Islam was kept in the background and so did not usurp everything non-Muslim. Saddam Hussein was a devout Muslim only when it suited his purposes and goals; similarly, the Shah of Iran appeared to be almost completely secular. In contrast, both countries are now back to being fully Islamic, to the detriment of the Christians still living there.

Normal life resumed after we returned to Austria in January 1983, though not for long, because my father was once again to be transferred. This time we packed up and moved to Chicago. I admit that as excited as I was in the beginning—and who wouldn't be with a room on the 67th floor facing the seemingly endless Lake Michigan?—I struggled very hard during the coming four years: with myself and my identity, growing from a girl into a young lady, with the all-girls school and its strict uniform code, with the frigid winter weather, with the flat geography (I desperately missed the mountains and skiing), with my loneliness and homesickness. And yet, growing up in Chicago has affected me more than I care to admit. By the time I reached my 40s, I was able to recognize the profound influence Chicago had over me.

As consul general of Austria, my father (and, by extension, my mother, my sister and I) represented Austria in the American Midwest, which we traveled and visited extensively. I danced at an Austrian ball in Eau Claire, Wisconsin; I gave my very first speech at a Christmas celebration in Indianhead, an Austrian-run ski area in the upper Michigan peninsula; I skied in Michigan's Devil's Head and Boyne, but also in the Rockies; and I cried alongside homesick Austrian emigres wearing their 60-year-old traditional Austrian costumes. The latter experience especially made a profound and lasting impact on me:

I vowed then and there to never leave my country because I did not ever want to cry as hard as these emigrated Austrians did. They missed their home country as much as I did. Unlike me, though, they could not return to Austria, because when they had made their way to America, which warmly welcomed them, they had left a war-torn homeland, a fledgling post-World War I Austria that offered them nothing but starvation and inflation. The memory of these Burgenland-Austrians in Milwaukee, who were now Americans and grateful to America and the American Dream, but still mourned the country they had left behind when they heard the Austrian national anthem, has stayed with me all these years.

Much as I disliked the rigidity of uniform requirements at my school, Academy of the Sacred Heart on Sheridan Road, I did profit immensely from my teachers, in particular, my social studies teacher, Mrs. Felix. Her sister had been my sister's and my English language tutor in the summer of 1983, teaching us how to read, write and converse in English so that we would be able to follow the classes, and she prepared us well, because I was an honors student by the second trimester of seventh grade.

Mrs. Felix's social studies class was especially thought-provoking. On the first day of class, she described the historical significance of the Bering Strait and how some of the early settlers may have crossed it to come to what would become the United States. In the process of describing the trek across the continent, she told us that if ever we were caught in an emergency situation and we ran out of food, she insisted that she would want us to eat her flesh. Gross... perhaps, but her offer made a huge impression on us.

I always enjoyed Mrs. Felix's English language classes, though perhaps my classmates did not. We often had spelling bees and homonym exercises; because I always was an avid reader I won most of these contests—me, an Austrian, whose first language wasn't even English. Naturally, I did not make many friends.

However, Mrs. Felix' most important contribution to my future turned out to be her eighth grade social studies class, which required us to pass a test on the United States Constitution. We had heard rumors from previous students that this test was among the most difficult they had ever taken and that we should study exceptionally hard in order to pass it. If we did not pass it, we would not be able to graduate grade school. We were warned! And so it was: we were prepared well for many months and I admit I found the Constitution a challenge to study, but at the time, I marveled that an eighth-grader was able to comprehend a legal document drawn up two centuries ago. Nevertheless, the rebel in me asked why I, as an Austrian, was forced to study the US Constitution; shouldn't I study my own constitution first? The adult in me today says: Yes, perhaps that would have been good, but look at how you profited from the US Constitution, how you learned to appreciate the concept of freedom, how you understand the beauty of the Bill of Rights, and how amazing the simplicity of what is arguably the greatest and most defining document ever drawn up and which has guaranteed the freedom and the pursuit of happiness for countless millions of people.

I have the greatest respect for the US Constitution, and I wish we Europeans were fortunate to have a document like it. Alas, we don't. Instead, the Europeans have been more or less subtly forced to accept a monstrous multi-thousand-page "Treaty of Lisbon," a document that even the drafters admitted they do not comprehend. It took several referendums to literally shove the treaty down the Europeans' throats. No wonder the Brits have chosen Brexit.

The test itself went fine for me; I passed with a C, and I still have the original test in my possession. But the test meant so much more: to this day, I see, and define, freedom the way the Bill of Rights does. Only later in life did I recognize that my greatest mistake, one that ultimately led to my court conviction, was caused by my naive belief that Austria prided itself in "granting" its citizens the right to free speech. As I would find out twenty years later, Austrians have a right to "free speech, but..."

Compare, for instance, how the freedom of speech is enshrined in Europe and the United States.

Constitution of the United States:

"Congress shall make no law (...) abridging the freedom of speech, or of the press..."

European Union Charter of Fundamental Rights:

Article 11 1. Everyone has the right to freedom of expression. This right shall include freedom to hold opinions and to receive and impart information and ideas without interference by public authority and regardless of frontiers.

2. The freedom and pluralism of the media shall be respected.

Analogous to the charter, Article 10 of the European Convention on Human Rights is also relevant:

> 1. Everyone has the right to freedom of expression. This right shall include freedom to hold opinions and to receive and impart information and ideas without interference by public authority and regardless of frontiers. This article shall not prevent States from requiring the licensing of broadcasting, television or cinema enterprises.

> 2. The exercise of these freedoms, since it carries with it duties and responsibilities, may be subject to such formalities, conditions, restrictions or penalties as are prescribed by law and are necessary in a democratic society, in the interests of national security, territorial integrity or public safety, for the prevention of disorder or crime, for the protection of health or morals, for the protection of the reputation or rights of others, for preventing the disclosure of information received in confidence, or for maintaining the authority and impartiality of the judiciary.

Aside from the content, notice the sheer number of words required to "grant" Europeans their right to speak freely. While the First Amendment protects speech with very few exceptions, the European Convention on Human Rights ascribes more duties and restrictions to freedom of speech. Call me a "free speech fundamentalist," if you will, but I prefer the simple "make no law to abridge free speech" over the wordy "you can say whatever you want, but only under the following circumstances." As my attorney so aptly argued during the court proceedings: "We do not need freedom of speech for the president's Sunday talk show appearances."

In 1987, after four long years, we moved back to Vienna where I finished high school at the Vienna International School because I attended school in the United States and the curriculum at my school in Chicago had nothing in common with the Austrian curriculum requirements. In addition, I believed that my German language skills were not good enough to return to a regular Austrian school. Even in an international setting, with kids from all over the world in my class of more than 100, I stood out like a sore thumb. This time the reason was that my old school in Chicago and my new one in Vienna were literally and figuratively speaking worlds apart: in Chicago, I attended a Catholic all-girls school with a strict uniform dress code. There was little to no interaction with boys my age. Classes were small, with a maximum of ten girls. In Vienna, at the age of sixteen, I suddenly found myself sharing a classroom with boys my age. I had to decide what to wear every day, and class sizes were much larger. I was bewildered and uncomfortable. Plus, just like in Chicago, when I entered seventh grade, I joined an already established group as an outsider two years before graduation. This is never good, and it is never easy. Thus, it is no surprise that I never felt a part of the class of 1989, and was more than glad to graduate and get on with my life. I have no fond memories of school.

Instead of going to college after graduation and doing what was expected of me, I followed my passion and became a certified ski instructor. I was on skis in every kind of weather—winter storms with gale force winds as well as pouring rain or sunshine—from November until late April. I loved teaching people what I love most: becoming one with nature, the snow, the mountains, on two skis. I loved hanging out with the other ski instructors, both male and female. We were all close friends as well as co-workers. In the early 1990s, it did not matter what your sex was; you simply did your job, whether it was lugging heavy poles up and down the slope for the weekly ski races or escorting the young kids to the bathroom.

Despite the possibility of continuing skiing into summer due to the availability of glacier ski areas, I decided to take up my father's offer for a summer job: one of his close friends was Austrian ambassador to Kuwait and needed some help in the visa section, so I removed my ski boots, said good-bye to the mountains and hello to the desert heat of Kuwait.

CHAPTER FOUR

I Was Saddam Hussein's Hostage—A Diary

Wednesday, July 24, 1990

WE HAVE BEEN stuck in the Austrian embassy in Kuwait City for almost a week now, held prisoner by the Iraqi regime.

I was with Nancy H. (a Saudi national) and several other friends because Nancy had to leave for Austria the next day. She mentioned that Iraq had stationed troops on its border with Kuwait; it was looking like an impending conflict. My first thought was, I hope that Saddam Hussein does not follow through on his threat and march into this peaceful paradise.

At any rate, I had no chance to follow the situation because the local media were reporting almost no details. I was also too preoccupied with my life there[1] and with my Kuwaiti friends, Jassim and Khalil. And, the preparations for the arrival of my friend from Vienna, Alexandra. I was really looking forward to her visit.

Wednesday, August 1

In the afternoon, I drove to Mowasat Hospital with Uli, the Austrian embassy secretary, because she was feeling sick. On the way home, driving on Gulf Road, with a gorgeous view of the sea, I couldn't help thinking how beautiful this country was, how peaceful.

At 9:30 PM, as usual, I listened to the news on the radio and then

---

1   In the course of my summer job at the Austrian embassy in Kuwait, I issued up to 250 visa applications a day.

went to sleep.

View from the Austrian Embassy balcony toward Kuwait City with smoke rising in the direction of the US Embassy.

Thursday, August 2

At 5:35 in the morning, the telephone rang. It was Mr. L, the interim Trade Commissioner, and he asked me if everything was okay and whether I had heard anything. I was completely confused and asked him to call the ambassador in the residence. I thought he was drunk. I looked out the window for a second, and then I went back to bed.

Ten minutes later, the phone rang again. It was Uli[2] on the phone, and she told me that war had broken out. I ran upstairs to her apartment and heard on the news that Iraq had crossed the border, and tanks were rolling toward Kuwait City. I was vacillating between complete calm and being upset. Then I called my parents in Vienna to let them know that there were problems here, but they shouldn't worry.

Soon after that, the ambassador called and told us that we could leave on an Austrian Airlines plane, but Uli and I didn't want to do that yet.[3] Shortly after this, the flight was canceled. The airport was being shelled and was under small arms fire. We repeatedly heard shooting in

---

2 Embassy secretary, Uli H., and I are housed in the embassy.

3 The Austrian Airlines plane was already on its way from Damascus to Kuwait but had to return. For this reason, an Austrian Airlines crew is stranded in Kuwait, because they would have flown back to Vienna on this plane.

the streets and helicopters circling our district.

At 8:00 AM, the Austrian Ambassador, Mrs. H. (another embassy secretary), and Muhammad S., the embassy translator, came and told us what was new. Mrs. H. was on the phone, frantically trying to reach all the Austrians in Kuwait and determine the exact number of them (there were currently 70). I heard intermittent shots outside, and received countless calls from various newspapers and from ORF out of Vienna. Alexandra made a final call from Austria at 9:45 AM local time and explained that she couldn't come because of the situation. I couldn't keep from laughing at the obviousness of her conclusion.

The ambassador described the situation as follows: At 2:00 AM, Iraqi troops crossed the border. Beginning at 4:00 AM, they bombarded the inner city, especially the Bayan and Dasman palaces,[4] where they met with resistance.

One casualty was the emir's brother who was, among other things, the President of the Olympic Council of Asia, to whom I had made a presentation for Austria a few days before. He wanted to organize a friendship game with his soccer team in Austria, against Stockerau, I believe. He died fighting alongside the Kuwait Emiri Guard commanders in the Battle of Dasman Palace.

Kuwait Towers, the city landmark, was also hit. The area from the First Ring Road inward became a no-go zone, with military headquarters in the Sheraton Hotel, which was one of the first buildings taken over. With the many Americans, English, and Germans, there was also a 45 year-old Austrian businessman, Peter A., about whose whereabouts we could learn nothing. We only knew that at 4:00 AM, he was taken from his room by Iraqi soldiers and made to lie down in the street with the other guests.[5]

The tank cannons were thundering constantly; soldiers were shouting in the street.

Kuwait's resistance continued.

More bad news and wild rumors reached us. Meanwhile, the tanks rolled tirelessly southward on the once beautiful Gulf Road, through Salmiya, Ahmadi, Fahaheel, and toward the neutral zone near Saudi Arabia. The Gulf Road was completely destroyed by the lines of heavy tanks.

During pauses in the firing, each of which lasted longer than the

---

4 These are two of the city palaces of the ruling family.

5 Mr. A. was taken by the soldiers to a camp in the area of Baghdad and held there. We did not see him again until much later when we were at the airport in Baghdad.

last, Wedad (Uli's domestic help) and I drove hurriedly to the co-op,[6] which was still open, and bought the most necessary things—water, packaged food, and the last newspaper available. Amazingly, the co-op was not crowded yet. People were also relatively calm but, at any rate, were buying water, oil, and rice. We were really lucky because it was quiet in the streets. In the course of the day, we went up onto the roof several times and, from there, watched the awesome spectacle. Helicopters were circling over the inner city. Smoke was rising everywhere. One of the helicopters landed by the co-op and let soldiers off. And, smoke could be seen over the industrial district, Shuwaikh. Apparently it had been heavily bombarded.

Friday, August 3

I spent the nights with Uli, punctuated by many phone calls with as much rumor as substance. I got through to Vienna one last time (8:30 PM local time), but unfortunately nobody was home to answer the phone. From this point in time on, international connections were broken, and so making contact outside the country was impossible. In the morning, we still had contact with our embassy in Riyadh by teleprinter; we were also able to take a couple of calls from there. This connection with Riyadh was very important because Riyadh was then able to inform Vienna about our situation. Telephone messages came repeatedly from Andrea (a secretary in the Austrian trade commission) in the Messilah Beach Hotel, where all the women and children from the Kuwait International Hotel had been sent. The word was that the Americans had already landed and were going to bomb the hotel. Reports like that were coming into the embassy constantly. It was unnerving. Nobody knew what to believe.

At 11:00 PM, the phone rang. A member of the emir's family, who had turned in his passport to me several days before for a visa to Austria, asked me if I could bring his passport to him. I had to tell him that we were not allowed to leave the house. Then he said that he would send his brother, although it would be dangerous for him. As we agreed, I waited downstairs by the main entrance. After a short time, the man came, took the passport, thanked me, and disappeared.

I was barely back on the fourth floor when the telephone rang. The man who had called before thanked us profusely for our help. He wished

---

6 The co-ops (cooperatives) are state-subsidized grocery stores. There is a co-op in every district in Kuwait besides the expensive supermarkets like the Sultan Center (with largely imported and high-quality merchandise).

God's protection for us. He gave us his lifelong gratitude and hoped to see us again sometime.

Saturday, August 4

In the morning, we were still in contact with the embassy in Riyadh. After that, only radio contact through the German embassy was possible, which could send reports for us to Vienna via Bonn.[7] The fact that there was no radio in our embassy building for this kind of crisis situation seemed unbelievably foolish to us.

Sunday, August 5

The first Austrians from the surrounding hotels came to us in the embassy. Psychologically, that was incredibly important for Uli and me. They were Andrea, Nadja, Reinhard, Werner, Petra, and Christoph. Of course, we got along wonderfully. Fortunately, the embassy's first-floor apartment was empty but still very comfortable because there was some furniture left behind. The previous occupant had been transferred to another post only a few weeks before.

We got lucky with Christoph. He was a trained cook and a confectioner, and he conjured up tasty dishes for us from our emergency rations. Since there was still no cooking gas in the apartment, our first dinner together was in Uli's place upstairs.

Monday, August 6

We sent the men out shopping. Werner walked to the co-op and the greengrocer. Reinhard and Christoph were driven to the Sultan Center grocery store, where they also got fresh bread from the Austrian baker. The supply situation looked super—we wouldn't go hungry. *Inshallah!*

Then, in the afternoon, the Austrian Airlines crew turned up, as well as Mr. and Mrs. B. (Austrian Airlines representatives in Kuwait) who had been driven out of the SAS hotel by the Iraqis.[8] Apparently, an Iraqi colonel had arranged for porn films and girls. This made staying there less than pleasant, especially for the female crew members, so the ambassador evacuated them. The rooms in the first floor apartment were

---

7 There was much criticism about the lack of emergency contact possibilities for the personnel at the Austrian embassy in Kuwait. It was ridiculous that messages had to be sent from the German embassy in Kuwait to the German ministry of foreign affairs in Bonn, Germany, and then on to the Austrian ministry of foreign affairs.

8 Mr. and Mrs. B. had previously lost almost everything. They had to give up their residence; it was subsequently plundered and vandalized.

divided up.

My room is converted into a food storage area.

Bit by bit, we got more provisions and also, finally, gas, so that Christoph was able to cook a set meal again. The current "menu" was always hung near the main entrance. What had been my room next door to the apartment was transformed into the storage room, and the provisions were stored there.

We adjusted so that each person in this peculiar commune was given a job. The Austrian Airlines captain listened to the news on his shortwave radio every hour. Christoph cooked. I helped in the kitchen. The Austrian Airlines crew cleaned the dishes. Others washed, ironed, etc. Now and then I issued visas but very seldom. Most people just picked up their passports, so they could leave the country as quickly as possible.

The emir and his government fled to Saudi Arabia and tried to save what could be saved—without much success at any rate, because as of yesterday Kuwait had become a part of the Republic of Iraq. It was annexed—a tragedy.

In a speech by Saddam Hussein, we heard that everyone wanted to make war on Iraq; that the U.S. Air Force was only disguised Israeli airplanes, and that all the U.S. allies were insane. I (all of us) see this differently. It is so macabre. Everything seems so calm, too calm. Yesterday we were told about precautions against Iraqi poison gas, and we sealed several windows.

Tuesday, August 7

In the street in front of our embassy, women and children with banners and pictures of the emir are demonstrating and loudly calling on us for help.

Wednesday, August 8

At midnight, several desperate Kuwaitis run down Shawki Street, our street, waving banners. They are demanding the return of the emir. *All we want is to get out*, go home, and back to peace.

We hear repeatedly that several people have managed to cross the border to Saudi Arabia. That bolsters us, although unfortunately we do not have this option. We have neither the necessary equipment nor the necessary know-how to survive in the desert. Besides, we heard that several people had died in the desert.

In spite of that, one of our activities is sitting in front of the map and looking for an escape route. After some days, though, we give up because of the limited chances of success.

Also, I feel relatively safe here—though, what is safe?

I remember thinking, "When will the spell be broken? I am still okay."

In a way, I am living in a make-believe world—soaking up the reports like a sponge, registering them, and yet I cannot *not* comprehend what is going on. We are all in a trance. We act as if nothing had happened, and then are shocked out of our dream world by new reports of savage violence.

2:20 PM: We receive two reports. Allegedly, the Iraqi foreign minister has been shot and killed. And 40 Iraqi tanks with their occupants have supposedly fled to Saudi Arabia. But, that is not confirmed.

The Austrian ambassador went to see the Iraqi ambassador this morning, to talk about the whereabouts of Mr. A. The Iraqi ambassador promised to look into it. We don't hold out much hope. I think the Iraqi has other things on his mind than looking for an Austrian.

Well, I have something else on my mind as well. Fortunately, I am still in contact with Jassim by telephone; he sounds very depressed, obviously. The poor guy is separated from his mother and worried because she needs dialysis. He is sitting at home and waiting—like all of us. I would like to see him, but unfortunately that won't happen.

Supposedly, the gas station in Hawalli (the district next to the embassy's) was blown up, by accident.

I would like to know how my Saudi friends, the H. family, are. I am worried about them.

Friday, August 10

We learned that we are now hostages.

Last evening, there was bad news again. Iraqi television announced that all diplomats had to go to Baghdad within 14 days, and all embassies here would be closed. A second report said that all embassies and personnel were just consulates, starting immediately; all ambassadors were demoted to consuls, but diplomatic immunity would remain in effect. We want to believe the second version because it seems more plausible, but the first version was reported on the BBC news.

Moving us to Baghdad would be a disaster—we would be used as leverage against the Western powers to prevent them from making any moves to liberate Kuwait. The Austrian Airlines captain does not believe it will come to that; he thinks that the Western powers are getting stronger every hour and will soon attack. I hope that we won't be wiped out in the process. I am worried about my parents. What is going on with them?

It is strange how values change in such a situation. Two weeks ago, it still mattered whether I could fit everything in my luggage to take back home to Austria; and now, I don't even know if I am going to go home again, and we are expecting the worst.

Family B. has to start all over again, because their residence was ransacked three days ago.

But I believe—the way things look now—that anything except for your passport and your life is worthless anyway. Everyone is fantasizing about the airplane, the airplane that will save our lives.

Saturday, August 11

After several attempts, two Austrians have finally managed to leave the country by way of the desert. I envy them.

Yesterday it was announced that the border between Iraq and Jordan was closed. Furthermore, West Europeans, U.S. citizens, Canadians, as well as Australians would not be allowed to leave the country.

Several Palestinian leaders have spoken up for Saddam Hussein. They are the first foreign leaders to support him.

I just want to go home. Peace and quiet again. I miss everyone so much.

Adi definitely wants to be mentioned, so I am mentioning him. He is a great mental support for me. Without him, I would probably go crazy. Our many conversations are good for me.

This afternoon, I dreamed about my parents for the first time. It shocked me a little, because I dreamed that they are here too, in deep doo-doo.

Mr. Klestil, general secretary of the Austrian foreign ministry,[9] informed us via Austrian shortwave radio that everything is being done to get us out. It was also reported that all Austrians are fine. It makes us feel good, somehow—this report—because it shows that we are not forgotten. That is incredibly important. I don't want to be forgotten.

Jassim got in touch; he didn't sound well. He told me his businesses in Salmiya[10] were plundered. I just cannot believe it; he does not deserve that. The Kuwaitis are such a sincerely good people, a peaceful people, and now everything is ruined. A wonderful city. And I keep asking myself, why all of this?

Monday, August 13

Yesterday there was some hope of finally being able to leave, but it was just a rumor. For a short time, there was a glimmer of hope.

Several Austrians have tried—and some have managed—to flee Kuwait. Anyway, yesterday a Brit was (accidentally?) shot and killed at the border, and that only strengthens us in our belief that we should not venture a step outside the embassy without complete security. We can hope that it will all be over soon. It is unnerving, not being able to leave the house. Thank goodness, we are not all on top of each other and wrangling. That can (still) be avoided.

One can more or less imagine how the American hostages in Iran felt in 1979. Of course, it is not possible to empathize with everyone exactly, but it is similar in a way. When the Iranian revolution broke out, I

---

9 He will later be elected Austria's president.

10 This is a city district of Kuwait.

was 8 years old and living in Tehran. My mother cooked at home several times for the American hostages and then found ways to get the food to their embassy while it was still comparatively warm. We still have the china that she had to buy for that.

Well, the most important thing is that we still have enough to eat[11] and are not being badly treated. We are living in decent conditions. But, for how much longer?

Tuesday, August 14

I cut my hair this morning. There were several reasons for that. I once said that I would never again let it be cut short, but I also thought that Kuwait was a peaceful country where war and unrest would not prevail. I was wrong on both counts.

Besides, this haircut has a practical side—but it is also a kind of protest. Who knows how long my hair will grow before we go home? The general secretary of the Austrian foreign ministry announced by radio that he would close the embassy, but only if the Austrians are allowed to leave the country. It sounds good, but I do not believe that Saddam Hussein will take this deal. He does not care about us at all.

I notice that I am getting grouchy, and I am sorry about that, but what am I supposed to do? I am trying to pull myself together, as well as I can, but it is hard. I feel so closed in. And yet, I should be happy that I have it so good and that we are all relatively secure. It could be worse.

Thursday, August 16

Today is the day I should have gone home. No doubt, nothing will come of that. Oh well. The day before yesterday, I heard from my parents by radio. I was surprised that they asked about the whereabouts of my diplomatic passport. Where should it be? In my possession, of course.

Friday, August 17

The message brought me back to reality. I don't want messages like that. That sounds hard, but it hurts more to hear something than to hear nothing. (We don't want any personal messages, because it makes us uncomfortable for those who hear nothing from home. So, we decided: No personal messages).

Between the day before yesterday and yesterday, there were what we

---

11 We are very well fed by the SAS hotel. The Swiss director general is emptying all of the larders and freezers in the place, so that the Iraqis get nothing. No wonder we are having mostly shrimp and veal on our menu!

call Iraqi "fireworks"—shots and flares, and also soldiers shouting. It is still eerie and frightening, even after so many days of experiencing these fireworks.

Yesterday, we also heard officially that we will lose our diplomatic immunity at noon on August 24th. Our "umbrella"—as Adi appropriately likes to call immunity—will be gone for good then, and we will be even more vulnerable to the Iraqis than we already are. I try not to think about that. I am trying not to think about anything at all. There are constantly rumors and announcements, but I've learned the likelihood of something actually happening is nil.

Sunday, August 19

There is news yet again. Last night, the Americans and British were taken prisoner. They will be held in camps at strategic points to prevent an attack by hostile (allied) troops. Later, the word went out to all Western European and Australian citizens that they had to gather in hotels. But we are not following this command and staying as quiet as possible, so as not to attract unwelcome attention (BBC urged its listeners to "keep a low profile"). In principle, that makes no difference because the Iraqis know that the Austrians are holed up in the embassy, and they can get them anytime. But at least we have our protection until the 24th.

Yesterday I had my first meltdown. We had heard that there was a European Community convoy to Baghdad and that we could attach ourselves to it. Everyone was free to decide whether they wanted to ride along. Naturally, the groups got together to talk and consult —the Austrian Airlines people, the "International" people (co-workers from the Hotel International), and the embassy group. That is when I truly understood how alone I really was. I no longer actually belong to the embassy staff, since I served my last day on the 14th. I am not with the Austrian Airlines or the "International" group. I am completely alone. I alone may decide for myself, but that is made more difficult by the fact that I have no one to consult with. So, the roof kind of fell in on me. After 17 days, I just couldn't control myself. I felt so terribly alone and deserted. Adding to that, I had a little fight with Christoph.[12]

Yesterday, we got two more housemates—Mr. and Mrs. H. (he was a baker in the Sultan Center). Their house in Salwa,[13] or at least the streets leading to it, was closed off by soldiers, so they came to us. They are nice

---

12 Each of our fellow residents had a crisis at some point, but no one is alone. The feeling of community is fantastic.

13 This is a district of Kuwait City.

people, and we have things to talk about again.

This evening there was news again. Our "friend," Saddam Hussein, gave a speech to all foreigners and laid down completely unrealistic conditions, and attached the fulfillment of them to permission for us to leave. At the end, something was said that we at first didn't hear, or understand—that is, that Austrian, Swiss, Swedish, Finnish, and Portuguese citizens are allowed to leave because these countries have sent neither troops nor weapons to Saudi Arabia. This step, according to Hussein, is a "gesture of goodwill."

At first, we laughed at the top of our lungs, but when we watched this announcement again, we just smiled and then shouted loudly.

Tomorrow, the ambassadors of these countries will go to the Iraqi ambassador to learn details. Until they come back, we will just have to be patient.

Monday, August 20

In the morning, our ambassador (after consulting with the other ambassadors) drove to the Iraqi embassy and learned that we actually could leave, but only by way of the Iraq-Turkey border. Then there was a vote inside our embassy community, and everyone thought that we had to take the chance. It might be our only chance to get home.

That was at 3:00 PM. From that point on, our departure was planned feverishly. The Swedes are organizing buses, we are organizing private and company cars. Then the route was set: Kuwait City – Jahra – Basra – Amara – Baghdad bypass – Samara – Mosul – Zakho – Turkish border. If possible, all would go together.

Christoph and Ingrid are currently preparing travel provisions, which are piling up in the former entry hall. Uli, Andrea, and Korina are using the telephones to inform all remaining Austrians in Kuwait of the exact plans. Adi, Bernd, and Wolfgang are discussing the technicalities of the implementation.[14] All of the rest is packing and talking about what was going to happen.

In the evening, my friend Munir brought me my clothes, which were still at the dry cleaner's. To do that, he had to drive through the whole city. He took an enormous risk just to do me that service. Saying goodbye was hard for me. I will never forget him, but what hurt the most was

---

14 This refers to the organization of the number and order-in-sequence of each car, as well as the number of persons in each car. Every car needs an exact route plan—this according to the permits issued by the Iraqi embassy. Furthermore, each car is identified by an Austrian Airlines sticker.

that I couldn't phone either Jassim or Khalil to say goodbye.[15]

Unfortunately, Uli can't come with us; her position requires her to stay with the ambassador.

Tuesday, August 21

We all slept very little and very badly; most of us are nervous. 5:45 AM was wake-up call for all of us. A final shower, a little food and the rest of our things packed or, alternatively, luggage carried to the store-room, which is stuffed with our remaining things. I think to myself: the Iraqis will be happy about the things we leave behind.

At 7:00 AM, all of the Austrians who are prepared to leave are starting to dribble in and wait for the Letters of Protection provided by the embassy.

At one point, I almost faint when I suddenly see Hisham standing in front of me. He graduated from high school with me last year and is the last person I expect to see in a situation like this in Kuwait. I chat briefly with him and his parents, greet a few other Austrians, and say goodbye to Uli. I am really annoyed that my (rental) car is not being taken along and I am being shipped by bus. I, at least, want to be in a car with Adi, but I can't even have that. The convoy starts out toward the Swedish embassy at precisely 7:30 AM. We cross the Third Ring Road, and what we see there is awful. Houses shot to pieces and houses burned down, bullet holes everywhere, dozens of burned-out wrecks on the side of the road, pictures of the emir stuck over the directional signs and torn, traffic lights out of order—but no military in sight yet. The city is quiet this Tuesday, almost spooky. Except, on this day, there are almost a hundred cars and several buses from Switzerland, Sweden, Finland, and Austria parked in front of the Swedish embassy.

At 9:00 AM, our journey into the unknown begins. My stomach is turning over from pain, anger, sadness, and fear. To take my mind off of it, I chat with Hisham and his mother, wave at the people in the other cars and turn around once more in the direction of Kuwait City. A last look at Kuwait Towers. I vow to return one day.

---

15 Not until October did I speak with Jassim again. He made it to Baghdad and managed to reach me by phone. His mother had died in the meantime because the Iraqis had taken the dialysis machine away.

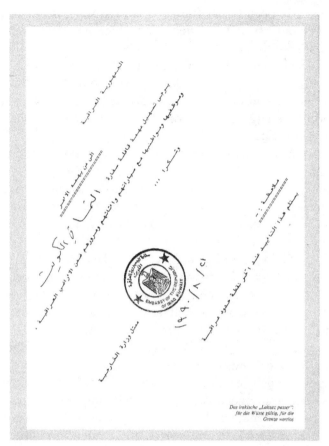

Das irakische „Laissez passer":
für die Wüste gültig, für die
Grenze wertlos

A so-called *Laissez Passer* (Letter of Protection), issued by the Austrian Embassy Kuwait, a formally useless paper indicating that I am an Austrian citizen. Arab authorities love papers with stamps, so we hoped this one would impress an official if needed.

We soon come upon the first Iraqi soldiers, who are standing at a traffic circle to Jahra (a small town outside Kuwait City) and eating watermelons.

After leaving Kuwait City, on the Jahra road northward in the desert, we see an even greater military push—an unbelievable number of soldiers jammed into large vehicles, and an immense number of tanks and artillery dug into the desert sand, right and left.

Many Kuwaiti cars are traveling on our side of the road, packed full—also fleeing, apparently to Jordan. The rich refugees are riding in their usual cars—BMWs, Mercedes-Benzes, and the like. Poor refugees are traveling in open trucks (formerly used as watermelon transports, now as Filipino transport) stuffed full of luggage next to the most unlikely things (tricycles and swimming tubes). The mass of children on the trucks make a pathetic impression, because they are stuck between the bars and the baggage in the glowing desert sun and can't move. The heat, the flies, the filth—it is awful. The adults' faces express everything from sadness to aggression. A concert of horns beeping, when everything comes to a standstill.

During the trip to the Iraq-Kuwait border, I feel terrible. The bus is filthy and uncomfortable. The driver is not just a worry, he is a nightmare. First, he drives at 40 km/h, then at 100—always so that we are losing the convoy, and that makes me the most nervous. We are at the mercy of this monster, and I am furious. I feel so helpless. Cars pile up massively at the border.

Suddenly, I don't see any Austrian cars and panic. We lost the rest of the convoy with Swedes, Finns and Swiss a while ago. Somehow, though, we get through the traffic jam. To my great relief, the other vehicles of our convoy are sitting on the right side of the road and waiting. Only two cars are missing, and one of them is Mike's.[16] But, apparently, he went over the border ahead of us. I use the opportunity of the stop to talk with the others and empty my bladder, which is not so simple with such a crowd of people and soldiers. Then we all have to go back to our vehicles because an Iraqi officer wants to take down our names.

He is quite friendly and speaks good English. He even points out that my name on my Letter of Protection is written wrongly in Arabic. After this procedure, we are finally able to travel at 1:30 PM. Shortly after crossing the border, we encounter the other cars from the convoy again.

Here is where we begin to have serious problems with our driver, who wants to change buses but not bother with the luggage. We do not agree—we will never see our bags again. Then he suddenly demands another $2,000.00—which we do not have—to continue. He can only be persuaded to go on after tedious talks and discussions. I do not know why he ultimately decides to do so. I am growing more and more afraid.

The convoy stops shortly before Basra because the bus is too slow again. People said they waited a full two hours for us. That is too much for me. I grab my things and ask Karl and Jasmin to let me ride in their car. I can't stand the bus any longer. Thank goodness that this is not a

---

16 Trade delegate, Mike L., took over the leadership of the convoy, with Kuwait's Austrian Airlines representative by his side.

problem, and I settle down in the car, very relieved. Hamid, Jasmin's son, is very nice. So, besides cold water, I also have friendly people to talk with.

On our way from Kuwait to the Turkish border we refueled at a gas station, which we had been told we scarce. It was so hot I wrapped a wet towel around my head. I always carried my water canister with me.

From this point on, I feel good again. The landscape near Basra is beautiful, and everything is green because of the nearby Tigris river.

Again and again, we see large military units, all going toward Kuwait. We stop often because cars are frequently missing. This is taking a lot of time. It is clear that our convoy is not well organized. We also stop at the astonishing number of gas stations. We heard that the gasoline supply in Iraq is very bad, but this does not prove to be true. During these short stops, we are able to stretch our legs, eat a little something, and talk briefly with the others.

The local people are all very friendly. Only the huge posters with the picture of Saddam Hussein are a little frightening, even intimidating. Anywhere and everywhere, Saddam is laughing, grinning, or staring at us. He is ubiquitous, omnipresent. You could never forget that you were in Iraq. The road takes us further toward the city of Amara, away from the greenery next to the Tigris, back into the desert, where there are now and then villages of mud huts and children playing barefoot in the dirt or hawking watermelons at the roadside, which no one buys. There is neither electricity nor water in these villages. It is like being transported back to the Middle Ages. The poverty is indescribable.

At a brief stop in one of the larger towns, we watch 12 year-old boys go by, a plastic bag with the uniform in one hand, the weapon for shooting people in the other. There are no words to describe that. You have to see it to believe it.

After that stop, we travel until dark. We learn by shortwave radio that our convoy is on the way to the Turkish border, nothing more. At least the war has not begun yet. That is what we fear most.[17]

Nighttime is pleasant because the air is finally cooler, so that it is possible to drive without the air conditioning. But, of course, it is also more dangerous because the streets are not lighted. There are no roadblocks, though; it is very calm. At midnight, we make a longer stop at a roadside café, a place where many travelers, including soldiers, are stopping. The drivers can have a rest and sleep; the others eat, talk and stand around. Adi is listening to Austrian shortwave and again there is nothing new except that the American troop deployment is continuing and Saddam Hussein is making threats. Everyone's mood is very gloomy. People are just standing around and talking softly. Somehow Karl finds a block of ice, which brings the luxury of cold water.[18] Jasmin and Hamed are already sleeping, and so are most of the others. I cannot.

Wednesday, August 22

We start out again at 2:00 AM, and I am finally able to empty my bladder on the side of the road in peace. I have never been as afraid as I am at this moment. I hear odd sounds behind me and have the feeling that a soldier could jump out of the debris at any second and take me with him. I am relieved in every sense of the word when I am sitting in the car again. Shortly after that, I fall asleep and do not wake up again until the convoy is making a stop in the morning dusk, just outside of Baghdad.

We received information that the Turkish border is closed and we are taken to the Austrian embassy in Baghdad. I am surprised because we heard in Kuwait that, whatever happens, we should bypass Baghdad and get to the border as quickly as possible. But, I fall asleep again and only wake when we stop in front of the Austrian embassy building in Baghdad. It is 6:30 AM.

---

17 We were not given military escort, and it is hard to defend against attacks in a desert, so that is why we were afraid.

18 Nobody gave thought to the diverse illnesses you could contract from drinking thawed water.

ISHTAR SHERATON
QUARTIER VOM 22.-23.8.90

This is the hotel where we spent the night in Baghdad.

We have a friendly reception from Mr. Tschürz's wife and Mr. Krauss, the embassy's second-in-command. They lead us into a small room and pamper us with coffee and more. I dash to the bathroom right away, where I brush my teeth and wash my hands. After a short and somewhat depressing discussion of the situation, I try to telephone home. Unfortunately, it is impossible to get through. Adi has just managed to inform Austrian Airlines in Vienna about our situation. In my case, the line is dead, so I try by radio, but the message is not received in Vienna. I also learn then that the Austrian Airlines representative (in Baghdad) held up the convoy on his own responsibility, so that we won't go on to the border to no purpose. We are very grateful to him. It is decided that we will all be accommodated in the Baghdad Sheraton Hotel so that we can catch up on our sleep. We are really looking forward to that.

Some are so exhausted that they fall asleep on the embassy floor.

Many of us are surprised that the ambassador is not there to help us, but it will only get worse. Everybody is very impatient. Checking into the Sheraton hotel, everyone wants a room as soon as possible. I share one with Jasmin and Hamed. It is glorious to shower again. We stink; our hair and bodies are full of sand and dust and sweat. We breakfast, go to bed at 11:00 AM, and sleep like the dead. A meeting is announced in the evening to discuss our next steps. Now, rested and washed, everyone is feeling so much better. Mike, his family, and Andrea, who slept at the residence of the Austrian trade delegate as well as the Austrian Airlines crew, gradually arrive at the hotel.

Shortly after that, the Austrian ambassador arrives and greets us with the ominous words, "I have bad news for you." He tells us that he was in the Iraqi foreign ministry with the Swedish ambassador, to arrange for our departure, which, however, was not approved. After four hours sitting with "bread and water" (his words), he was granted permission for the departure of 23 percent of the Austrians in the convoy, that is, 17 people.[19] We are now supposed to choose them, and they should set out immediately.

There is a great uproar, and many people complain justifiably. The ambassador sticks with the seventeen; he has no choice. In any case, only the diplomats are allowed to depart—but we are supposed to leave immediately. That was all he can tell us, and that makes us pretty angry.

The ambassador leaves us, and Mr. Tschürz and Mr. Krauss remain to help with any likely problems. Mike holds a vote on whether we should try it; a bare majority is for it. So, Mike and Andrea begin to select the people for the possible trip to the border. And that just barely works out with the head count.

The "Sobolak" drivers[20] come by too and tell us about the trip to the border and the dangers they encountered. I am afraid all over again; the others too. The reports of the Swiss and the Swedes are also not exactly encouraging. In the Sheraton at 3:00 in the morning, it is finally agreed to discuss this further, according to what news is available by radio. Everyone is understandably very uncertain and nervous. At 7:00 PM, shortly before the meeting, I reach my parents by telephone for the first time in three weeks and receive a brief preview of what was waiting for me in Vienna: The media is going wild; a whole television series is being planned on us, and the telephone is ringing constantly. All of Austria is

---

19 We never find out the reason for this seemingly arbitrary percentage.

20 Employees of a hauling firm, who are stuck in Baghdad with Mr. Krauss's furniture transport and try repeatedly to escape Iraq by way of Zakho.

waiting for our return. It is very flattering but also daunting. At any rate, it feels good to have a telephone call with home.

After the meeting, depressed, I sit with Jasmin, Karl, and two Austrians residing in Baghdad who are having a vigorous discussion. They tell me that my diplomatic passport makes it possible for me to go to Amman, Jordan, by plane. It will just take several days for a seat on a plane to be free for me, and it will cost $125.00. I wonder why no one has told me this before. Anyway, I ask Mr. Freissmuth if that is true, and he confirms it. But, he advises me to travel with the convoy nonetheless. If things do not work out at the border, I can still get out, but "diplomats have certain problems leaving." I am completely confused and don't know what I should do. I want to try to reach my parents again and log a call. At 11:00 PM, I get through and impress on them that they should say nothing to the media, as it can threaten my departure.

Thursday, August 23

At 2:00 AM, I shower again, pack, fill the thermos with water and escape into the lobby, because Jasmin and Hamed are throwing up, and I am almost to that point. Everyone is already gathering in the lobby. Mr. Tschürz's wife takes me aside and shows me a telex that says we should start out immediately; it is an opportunity to leave. Ten minutes later, she tells me she heard from the Swiss that several of them have been allowed to cross the border. Nonetheless, it is decided after several arguments to stay in Baghdad and not leave until the next day.

I am quartered with Mrs. Tschürz because I do not want to stay in the hotel any longer; I can't say why. So, Mr. Krauss drives me to her house. It would have been much more comfortable in the hotel because there is no bed for me at Mrs. Tschürz's house. I sleep on a mattress on the floor. It is already 5:30 in the morning; the discussion in the hotel lobby lasted that long.

In the morning, the two "Sobolak" drivers wake me and tell me over breakfast about their trip to the Turkish border. It does not sound very encouraging. The doorbell suddenly rings at 10:00 AM. A staff employee at the embassy was told to get me and bring me to the hotel. I cannot learn anything more from him. I am worried but pack my things without a word and go back to the hotel. During the ride, the man tells me that there are big problems in the embassy, which, in these sad circumstances, is not very encouraging. Everybody from the convoy is assembling in the lobby again. The ambassador once again is not there, only Krauss, Tschürz, Freissmuth, and Mr. I., the Austrian Airlines representative in

Baghdad, who stopped the convoy outside the city.

It is announced that it is best for us to go to the border, in spite of everything, and leave immediately so that we can be there as soon as possible. The departure is set for noon. I say goodbye to Krauss, Freissmuth, and Tschürz and then go to the second floor of the hotel to get something to drink and meet up with the others.

To keep the convoy together, the cars are given numbers before we leave (stickers from Austrian Airlines' baggage check). This causes a small delay, but we start off at 12:30 PM, past the intersections manned by the military. The soldiers wave at us. The convoy comes to a standstill after less than five minutes; several cars are missing, lost in traffic.

The heat in the cars was brutal in spite of the air conditioning. At the first stop, we wait a quarter of an hour, then we cross a bridge to a highway where we wait on the roadside in the blazing heat for half an hour—nothing. It is terrible. Finally, we drive to the edge of the city and find the ones who were lost; they took another route. After that, keeping the convoy together goes smoothly. All of the cars stay in place in line, and we proceed expeditiously. The road seems familiar to me. It leads to Samara, a town known for its prominent minaret, where I was back in 1982. Hamed and I, however, fall asleep and sleep with few interruptions until sunset.

The scenery is monotonous—desert, mud huts, very poor, and depressing. Shortly before Mosul, at 8:00 PM, we come upon a military blockade, which gives us no trouble. I expected a lot more military, especially after what we heard in Baghdad. Thank goodness, little of that is turning out to be true. Mosul is still very lively at this time of day. Cars are driving like crazy, but the convoy is staying together in the trip through the city. After Mosul, we come to another barricade, but no problem there either. At the next one, which monitors vehicles entering the border area, longer and more vigorous discussion is necessary because the soldiers did not want to recognize our special permit.[21] But, after a long back and forth, we are sent on with a smile.

I can't interpret this smile. It's giving me a strange feeling.

The road to Zakho border crossing was very busy. Many cars are passing our convoy. A short breakdown—a car needs a change of tires— gives us the chance to take a breather and stretch our legs. It is slowly getting cooler, and the landscape appears hillier, and when the road leads upward in serpentine curves, we know the border with Turkey is

---

21 While the Iraqi embassy in Kuwait gave us no military escort, it did give us a travel permit intended to secure "unhindered travel to the Iraq-Turkey border."

close. Suddenly, the convoy stops. In front of us, stretching to the next curve, are up to 50 cars, with their lights out. No one can tell what is waiting for us behind the curve. It is 10:30 PM, and the mood is good because a soldier who is hurrying by let it drop that maybe all Austrians will be allowed to depart. We hug each other, and we all have happy expressions on our faces. Adi listens to the 11:00 o'clock news on his shortwave radio as usual and smiles.

But first, we have to get by the line of cars, and so an Iraqi dressed in civilian clothes is bribed with a camera and leads us to the next post. The scene on the right and left is awful—hundreds of Asians lying on the ground or on the roofs of cars, a picture of abject misery.[22]

The next military position returns us to reality—there is an insistence on the 17 heads mentioned in Baghdad, minus two, because two Austrians exited on their own without a diplomatic passport[23] and that is being counted against the quota. So, Mike is going from car to car to ask people, who urgently needs to leave?—just the question itself sounds ridiculous. Jasmin and Hamed check in, and I do too, but later I tell Mike I will not go so that his wife can leave with their son, David.

At midnight, we make it to the Iraqi border post, 400 meters from the Turkish border, on the verge of freedom. Here, too, thousands of Asians lay sleeping on the ground on both sides of the street. We ask the border guard whether everyone will be allowed to leave. He says no, only 15 people are allowed to leave. So, the infamous list is pulled out, and a new one with 15 people is drawn up. What an eerie scene—Mike, standing on the hood of his car, lit up by the other cars' headlights and surrounded by his fellow travelers, asking, "Who really needs to leave?" The question draws an uneasy laugh.

Then a guard comes over and says that 15 passports can leave, which is in our favor because the children listed in the passports can go along too. We quickly manually add children to the passports of adults who are not even related, just to get the children out of Iraq. Suddenly, diplomats count in the quota, so I remain. The back and forth about the passports lasts a relatively long time, until it is decided that this is a passport count, not a head count.

Mike tries, as well as he can, to keep families together. Mike's wife and his son, David, are also supposed to go. Understandably, she does

---

22 The border is generally closed to refugees of Asian countries. For refugees from Western nations, an exit—as allowed by Saddam—is possible only during daylight hours.

23 I think it was the two Sobolak drivers I met in Bagdad.

not want to go, but changes her mind because David is sick. Jasmin and Hamed come along too; Ingrid, the purser from our Austrian Airlines crew, gets the last place, so she can give a competent account in Turkey of what happened with us. Their luggage is stuffed into two cars, which are allowed to cross the border. The rest are left behind.

The pathetic blockade—a barbed barrier against cars—is opened. The cars drive through, and the people follow on foot, holding hands with their children. The passports are examined carefully beforehand. There are several foreigners in the group, Godfrey[24] and his wife, as well as the driver of the convoy's supply vehicle and his wife. Austrians with dual citizenship go along too. Nobody is turning around; they might start crying, as we are. We traveled so far (1,250 km) to see just 31 people crossing the border, and we are still in Iraq! So close to freedom and yet so far.

I will never forget the feeling from this morning, the helplessness, the dependency on the whims of the Iraqi authorities. We wait another 30 minutes to see that everyone got across, then divide the remaining cars anew, and at 5:00 AM drive back to a hotel in Mosul. I apologize to Karl because I immediately fell asleep. I know how important it is for Karl for me to keep him awake with conversation, given that he is just as exhausted as I was. But, I just cannot hold out. I do not wake up until the convoy stops, because Mr. Krauss is coming to meet us.

Friday, August 24

We get out at Hotel Mosul, located directly on the Tigris River and, dead tired, we argue over the rooms. Everyone wants to be first. I take a room with Andrea and fall asleep immediately. We get up at noon and go to eat. There is a great buffet, better than the food in the hotel in Baghdad—chicken, rice, steak, and other really good things.

At 1:00 PM, there is a short meeting, where we learn nothing new. During the night, Mr. Krauss received permission to leave Baghdad[25] and followed us to Mosul so that he can assist us with any likely difficulties at the border. There is nothing to report from Baghdad, but he is in constant contact with the Austrian embassy. We decide to stay a few days in Mosul for safety's sake, in case the situation changes.

In the afternoon, Karl, Peter, Andrea, and I drive into town to run errands for other people, as there is nothing to do in the hotel but go

---

24 Godfrey is the chauffeur of the foreign trade commission in Kuwait.

25 Members of the diplomatic corps in general are required to get special permission to leave the capital city of Baghdad.

swimming. (And besides, my swimsuit was not one of those "absolutely necessary things" that we were allowed to bring from Kuwait.)

The excursion is depressing. When we walk through the souk,[26] we see only men, the young ones all in uniform. The old and the very young are working as vendors in the shops, which admittedly offer everything but at ridiculous prices (if you exchanged your money officially). Bargaining is impossible, no more than half-a-dinar reduction. We buy underwear, shirts, and ghastly shampoo. You can even see the first plunder from Kuwait—canned goods, Coca-Cola (with price tags from the plundered Sultan Center grocery store in Kuwait), electronic equipment, and much more. The heat is killing and, even so, the shopping street are crowded with people.

Our first impression is that the food situation in the market is not so bad. With a closer look, however, you can see that there really is nothing. What there is is cleverly built up and covered, in an attempt to mislead. So, we return to the hotel and deliver the goods that were requested. Dinner is scheduled for 7:00 PM. After that, we all sit down at the bar again.

At 10:00 PM, we hear on the news about a planned Waldheim[27] trip, but we can't make much of it.

A party is set for Christoph's and Werner's room. The vodka is flowing freely; we are celebrating Mike's birthday, with tears and a lot of gallows humor. An unforgettable night.

At 1:00 AM, we separate, and we do not know what the next day will bring.

Saturday, August 25

At breakfast the next day, I learn that I am to leave for the border immediately.[28] I don't really understand, but Mr. Krauss says he will drive me to the border and anyone who wants to can ride along. I am bewildered, but I pack my things and say my goodbyes. Adi and Mike ask me what I think of the idea of not leaving until 3:00 PM because (Austrian) President Waldheim is in Baghdad and possibly something will develop for all of us out of that. If not, then I can still go. I already had the idea myself but did not want to say anything. So, we sit at the bar and

---

26 The Arabic word for "market."

27 Kurt Waldheim, the former UN secretary general and current Austrian president, is on his way to Amman, Jordan, in an attempt to meet with Saddam Hussein in Baghdad.

28 We never learned from where this announcement originated.

wait. Mr. Krauss is staying in his room the whole time and appears in the lobby at 3:15 PM. He announces that we are being allowed to leave, but how, when, and to where are still unclear. We all hug. This report somehow sounds credible, but we want to wait for further information because the embassy does not yet know all of the details negotiated by Mr. Waldheim.

After another telephone conversation, we know that Mr. Waldheim was successful with Saddam Hussein. We should be patient. The military will fetch us from the hotel and take us back to Baghdad. That is annoying; we do not want to go back to Baghdad. From here, it would be much simpler to be allowed to reach freedom at the Turkish border. But there is no choice but to accept it. Adi projects that we will have to wait at least five hours for the available military to arrive in Mosul, and then we will have another five hours' travel to Baghdad. Not very appealing. So, we sit down at the bar again, but this time to celebrate our upcoming freedom.

Suddenly, someone cones and tells us that the military is already in the lobby and talking with Mr. Krauss. We hear that we are going to be brought to Baghdad by plane. We should take all of our luggage and get into the buses that are waiting for us outside the hotel.[29]

Several people are angry because they do not want to leave their cars behind, knowing that they will be gone forever. In the end, though, there is no choice except to get on. The buses are modern, clean, and had air conditioning. Our route cuts diagonally through the city to the airport, where we take notice of the anti-aircraft batteries and bombers. What shocks me is a Kuwait Airways plane sitting beside the runway with its cockpit shot to pieces—the evidence of war.

Then we see an Iraqi Airways plane that seems to be waiting for us on the tarmac, with its engines running. We load what is left of our luggage ourselves from the buses to the cargo area of the plane, and, after a thorough inspection of passports, we are allowed to board. A gloriously appointed machine—Saddam Hussein's private plane, as we learn later.

I sit down near Adi and can't grasp it all. A few hours before, we said goodbye to the others at the Turkish border and envied them their freedom. And now, we are on our way back to Baghdad. It is just incomprehensible. On board, security officials are running around, checking our passports for the umpteenth time. When I open the overhead compartment, I find weapons of all sorts.

---

29 My first thought is, so now that they are letting us go, all the gentlemen of the military are suddenly organized!

During the flight, those with diplomatic passports are invited into business class; several pilots are sitting there and talking. The flight itself is nothing spectacular, but, landing in Baghdad, I feel a little queasy. I think we all are having odd thoughts.

Only when we are on the ground do I realize that we did not land at the Baghdad International Airport but at Saddam Hussein's private landing strip in central Baghdad. The plane parks right next to the reception building, and we are treated like kings. Drinks of all kinds, friendly smiling soldiers, television sets, leather-covered furniture. Meanwhile, the plane is surrounded by the military and closely guarded. We are invited to make ourselves comfortable, although most of us are too nervous to sit.

We learn that other Austrians are being flown in from Basra, to fly to Amman with us and President Waldheim. First, a small plane from Basra arrives, then the Baghdad Austrians in buses.

At 8:30 PM, it is time: President Waldheim, Austrian foreign minister Alois Mock, and crowds of reporters arrive and get standing ovations. Mr. Waldheim greets each Austrian personally, in the popping of flashbulbs and in front of filming cameras. Many Austrian reporters who traveled with Mr. Waldheim are eager to interview us, but none of our group agrees to it. We are still too much in shock to say anything, and we don't want to either. After a short speech by Mr. Waldheim, we are allowed to board Saddam's private plane again.

Mr. Waldheim holds a press conference before our departure and then, at 10:00 PM, we are finally off to Amman. The mood on the way is already wonderful. Uli I. opens a bottle of champagne and it is passed around, and, aside from that, it is pandemonium. Now and then, reporters try to squeeze us for information but do not succeed. Out of consideration for the hostages from other countries, we agreed in Baghdad to say nothing. I am embarrassed when Austrian newspapers are being passed out. I am quoted several times in the *Kurier* newspaper, in spite of my parents' promises to pass nothing on. I am angry and annoyed. Still, it is a party on the plane; there are only laughing and relaxed people. Just wild.

After an hour's flight, we land at the military airport in Amman where an Austrian Airlines plane is sitting right in front of us. An unforgettable moment! An Austrian Airlines plane never looked so good—the plane we've been dreaming of for so long had become a reality. We pay no attention to our luggage. We do not know until we arrived in Vienna whether it was reloaded, but that does not really bother anyone.

If the mood on board during our landing approach to Amman was wild, what followed surpasses everything. The waltz music, the smiling faces of the crew, and the free-flowing alcohol makes for a glorious continuation of the party that started on Saddam's plane.[30]

At any rate, we sit in Amman for another one-and-a-half hours because Mr. Waldheim has to give an interview to CNN. At about midnight, he comes back on board with a smaller number of reporters, and we finally take off. With a euphoric, if off-key, singing of the national anthem, we are off to Austria!

---

30 No food is served because there is none. The Austrian Airlines crew rightly assumed that we will want to celebrate with alcohol.

CHAPTER FIVE

My Time in Kuwait

Against a stupidity that is in fashion, no wisdom compensates.
—Theodor Fontane

FEBRUARY 27, 1997. In my mind I was humming Sarah Brightman's "Time to say good-bye," an apt tune while waiting in line at security at Athens airport, with four huge suitcases and a Greek cat in an animal carry-on box. I would be lying if I said I was as cool as the ice floating in my drinking bottle, and neither was Poldi, my cat. I had spent ten days with my parents in Athens, Greece,[1] for some last-minute pampering and shopping before I was due to start work at the visa section of the Austrian Embassy in Kuwait. And now, armed with my red diplomatic passport indicating that I was an embassy employee, I was prepared to open a new chapter in my life.

⸺

In August 1990, as the bus I was traveling on was racing towards the Iraqi border on what would six months later be dubbed the "Highway of Death,"[2] I turned around one last time. I observed the famous Kuwait Towers gleaming and glistening in the already scorching early morning sun. I made a vow then and there, in the middle of nowhere, and with all

---

1 My father was Austrian ambassador to Greece and Cyprus at the time.
2 The Highway of Death is actually called Highway 80, a six-lane road running from Kuwait City to the city of Basra in Iraq. It was used by the Iraqi army to stage the invasion of Kuwait. The coalition forces liberating Kuwait attacked the retreating Iraqi army from the air, resulting in destruction and deaths in the piled-up military vehicles.

the uncertainty ahead of me, that I would one day return to Kuwait and leave it on my own terms. Saddam Hussein may have forced me to leave that day, but next time, I would be the one to make that decision. I was the master of my life, and no one else.

In the days, weeks and months following my harrowing journey through Iraq and my integration into what could be called "normal life," I fought a gargantuan battle with a common condition that today is treated as post-traumatic stress disorder. From the moment I stepped off that Austrian Airline plane at Vienna airport on that August morning, I was left to fend for myself. Unlike the Austrian Airlines crew, who were immediately separated from the rest of us and put into medical care, I was never medically evaluated or militarily debriefed by anyone. I was basically returned to my parents' care and that was that. As far as I know, the situation was similar for everyone else who got off that airplane and was shoved into the media limelight.

This is unthinkable nowadays. Upon their return to Austria, hostages today are immediately taken to the army hospital, subjected to extensive medical tests, given psychological support if needed, are debriefed and segregated until they are ready to be discharged. The way the Austrian foreign ministry treats its employees was and still is a disgrace. For instance, I never heard from the ministry again, other than an official letter informing me that my contract and therefore the payment of my salary would be extended from August 16, the day I was supposed to leave Kuwait, until August 26, the day I arrived in Vienna.

There was pandemonium at the airport; that much I remember. I gave interview after interview, both for television and print media, even though I was mentally completely and utterly exhausted. Only a few hours earlier I had been in Mosul fearing that I would be shipped off to a camp as one of Saddam Hussein's "foreign guests," and now I found myself answering the sometimes silly questions of journalists. I had the nagging feeling that this media attention was not a coincidence, because it seemed that my mother knew exactly where and to whom to push me. With 20/20 hindsight, I should have told her and the journalists to leave me alone, but I was too emotionally drained, and grateful that I no longer had to fend for myself. To this day, I am strongly critical of my mother and her need for media attention, both for herself and me. Now that I am a mother, I don't want to spend even one day worrying about my daughter the way my own mother suffered when I was missing in Iraq. She told a journalist in one of her interviews that her problem wasn't so much falling asleep or sleeping through the night; the worst for her was waking up in the morning not knowing where I was and whether I was still alive. I don't think she was offered professional help in her situation, so I assume the limelight was her way of coping with a psychologically exceptional situation.

Having made my way through the throng of journalists and having said good-bye to my fellow hostages, I was relieved to arrive home at 7 am. I had not slept in almost 30 hours, but first I wanted to sit down and give an account to my parents of what had happened to me during the past three weeks. Imagine my surprise when they told me they did not want to hear anything, and sent me to my room to get some sleep. "You should get some rest. You are scheduled for an 11 am Sunday talk show and you need to be awake for that."

Again, I was too emotionally drained to reply, so I just went to bed, but to this day I don't understand why my parents never wanted to know what happened. Were they afraid to hear something they were not prepared for? They need not have been afraid, because nothing untoward had taken place. And so they were left with not knowing, which in my view is worse than knowing. However, there were also few people in my circle of friends who asked me about those three weeks in August. Why? I suppose most people must have thought: "She's back safely; thank God for that. Now let's move on." For someone suffering from PTSD the way I was, this was a disaster. Glued to CNN all day, I agonized over my Kuwaiti friends. In the days before the Internet, there was no other way to find out what was happening on the ground in Kuwait. I may have been physically home in Vienna, but emotionally I found myself in Kuwait. I suffered from nightmares, insomnia, and sudden crying fits.

One of the worst manifestations of my PTSD took place in November, a full three months after my arrival in Austria. I spent a week on a glacier in the province of Salzburg, the ski area where I worked all winter, and was due to take another ski instructor's exam. While I was waiting for my turn to ski down my favorite, incredibly steep slope, one that I normally would ski down at high speed with three turns, something happened inside my brain: I began shaking uncontrollably, and all of a sudden I was deathly afraid of the slope in front of me. In my mind, there was no way I could get down the way I was supposed to in a gracious manner. Instead, one of the instructors was tasked with gently coaching me to snowplow down the mountain like a beginner! I was deeply embarrassed about my behavior, which I did not recognize, but was still able to continue working at the ski school. I successfully retook the exam the following spring.

In order to cope with what the distant liberation war did to my psyche, I skied, talked a lot with my students and picked up the latest copy of *USA Today* ordered especially for me. I then went back to my private accommodation, changed from my ski instructor's uniform into something more comfortable and caught up on the latest news from Iraq and Kuwait. No matter the weather, every morning when I strapped on my skis I was grateful to be safely back in my beloved Austria.

In August 1991, against the explicit wishes of my parents—which I totally understood, but ignored—I found myself on a Lufthansa airplane full of businessmen returning to Kuwait. My plan was to search for whatever I had left behind in the embassy on the day we traveled to Iraq the previous year. I wanted to find friends I had not heard from. I wanted to see the so-called Highway of Death for myself in order to deal with my PTSD. I was searching for some semblance of closure.

As the plane was approaching Kuwait Airport, everyone was peering out the windows; some passengers even appeared to be frightened. The scene was indeed very eerie: we descended alongside hundreds of oil wells ablaze with huge plumes of smoke extending into the atmosphere. I thought I was prepared for this sight, but the reality of this wanton destruction only set in on approach to the airport. After passport control, I saw throngs of Kuwaitis in their glaringly white dishdashas (traditional male Kuwaiti dress) in tears, hugging returning family members. As usual, guest workers picked up their Kuwaiti bosses.

The hotel shuttle took me to my hotel, and there were a few military security check-points on the way to Kuwait City. Upon check-in, I had to surrender my passport, which I only grudgingly did because I was reminded of how many Austrians were stuck in the midst of the invasion without passports. I decided to find private accommodations and thankfully, I was once again able to reside in the same room in the embassy I had stayed in in 1990 and which had been turned into a storage room after the invasion. I also found a rental car, which was not easy to accomplish so soon after liberation and very expensive. Cruising down my beloved Gulf Road, I saw countless graffiti thanking the United States: "Thank you, Bush!" "Thank you, America!" Cars sported Saudi Arabian and Qatari license plates rather than Kuwaiti ones. Strangely enough, Iraqi occupation graffiti was not yet removed, whereas the renaming of Kuwaiti street names and, bridges and buildings was immediately reversed.

And I located some of my friends, who not only had survived the occupation and the war, but were also kind enough to take me on a tour of Kuwait. And so I cruised up and down the Highway of Death and wandered among the countless burned out vehicles, carcasses really, saying a silent prayer for those who had perished: the Iraqi soldiers in that carnage in front of me, the Kuwaitis who had been tortured at the hands of the Iraqi occupants, as well as soldiers from the coalition forces.

During the liberation war, the Iraqi army leadership had been duped into expecting a coalition attack from the sea, so I was also shown a beach fortification with trenches near the city of Fahaheel, which I proceeded to explore. I was very conscious of landmines left behind by the retreating Iraqi army; however, because I followed already present footsteps, I assumed I was somewhat safe. On our drive back north to Kuwait City, I was shown the destruction of bridges riddled with bullet holes, the remnants of checkpoints at roundabouts, and ravaged neighborhoods with wrecked mosques; it seemed as though every neighborhood in Kuwait was affected in some way, though inexplicably the area around the Austrian embassy was left unscathed. Even the embassy building itself appeared to have been spared, although I did not find much of what I had left behind, which I thought was curious.

My friends also introduced me to their family by inviting me to join them for a simple lunch. Their home was located in Keifan, a Shiite neighborhood, which had been overrun with Iraqi soldiers during the occupation, but was also a center for the Kuwaiti resistance movement. The family recounted how the resistance hoarded and cached weapons in the mosque—the reason for which I would understand only many years later when I studied Islamic texts—and how the mosque exploded and was completely destroyed for unknown reasons toward the end of the occupation. When I asked the women about how they spent their time during the occupation, they told me how they read the Qur'an, taught their children in private lessons, baked bread and washed the many dead. My two friends proudly show me the spot where they lobbed grand grenades against Iraqi tanks, showing no remorse at the resulting deaths.

I was served a very simple but delicious meal of chicken and rice in Kuwaiti spices, set traditionally on a plastic spread on the ground. Even though the family was obviously devout Shia Muslim as evidenced by the Islamic garb worn by the women, the lunch was not segregated, likely in my honor. During the meal, I asked one of the girls, who was about my age, a simple question, and the answer has stayed with me ever since, guiding my criticism of Islam.

"What would happen if you were stuck in a burning house and the only way out would mean shedding your *abaya* (Islamic garb)? Would you do it?"

"No, I would rather die than take off my *abaya*." She said those words very matter-of-factly, without any hesitation.

These are the two girls who told me they'd rather die than take off their
***hijab* and *abaya*.**

All I could do was stare at her in shock. I mean, what can one say in reply? How I wish our politicians would listen to Muslim women speak these words, and then perhaps they would understand what exactly the *hijab* means to those women wearing it. The *hijab* is not just a piece of cloth; it is a way of life. Take away the *hijab* and/or the *abaya*, and these women feel violated. So there is really only one way to deal with the issue of *hijab*: either remove it when outside an Islamic country, or stay away from a non-Islamic country. There is no accommodation of the *hijab* in a Western, non-Muslim country. I learned this from the smiling girl squatting next to me at that lunch in Kuwait, answering a question that to her seemed very silly. I often wonder what her life is like today, although I would not be surprised if she married only months after my departure and is now already a grandmother many times over. Perhaps her husband even took other wives. She is probably leading a very "normal" life.

During the lunch I was also able to question one of the men sitting next me, a Kuwaiti army captain, who was captured on the second day of the invasion and taken to Basra, a town in southern Iraq. While his wife knew nothing of his whereabouts until November 1990, he leaned about Austrian President Kurt Waldheim's successful mission on the radio in his cell. He was released in March 1991, one month after the liberation of Kuwait.

The oil fires caused by the retreating Iraqi army impacted Kuwaitis and non-Kuwaitis alike until the fires were extinguished. Around 700 oil wells were set on fire as soon as the coalition forces initiated air strikes in January 1991, causing an unprecedented environmental disaster, though thanks to the ingenuity of Western engineers, the smoke plumes did not start the feared nuclear winter. The desert, usually a drab light brown, was now pitch black from the free-flowing oil. I feared the worst for the environment.[3] The fumes affected me; in the afternoon, when the winds changed, I would notice dark clouds appearing in the sky from a westerly direction. There are no clouds in Kuwait in August, so I knew smoke from the burning oil wells was on its way, darkening the otherwise blue sky, sometimes so dark that the street lights were turned on. There was also a weird smell that came with the smoke clouds, leaving my throat scratchy and my eyes tearing up.

Given that whatever was in the atmosphere could not be healthy, I was not all that sad to board the Lufthansa plane taking me back to Austria and my family.

After another long winter season in the mountains, my father let me know it was time to get a real job, which I grudgingly did in mid-1994. I joined the real world by accepting a job as secretary to an American investment banker, a huge mistake, since I am not cut out for the world of banking. Bored stiff by the nascent investment opportunities in the Bulgarian dairy business, I hoped to be able to leave sooner rather than later. The opportunity presented itself in early 1995, when my father informed me of a job opening in the office of the vice chancellor, whose adviser for European Union affairs was looking for an assistant. In many respects, my decision to leave the banking world which had offered me nothing but terminal boredom, while accepting a loss in income, would dramatically change the course of my life. This is not to say my life would have remained dull, but working in the political center of the Austrian

---

3 Later, when I returned to Kuwait, I would visit farms utilizing the advantages of what the oil left behind: fertile soil.

government held so much more appeal. I knew the current chancellor—of whom I was not particularly fond—was due to be replaced by Mr. Wolfgang Schüssel, the minister for economic affairs, which was all the more thrilling. Not only was Mr. Schüssel an acquaintance of my father's, but more crucially, I was fascinated by his formidable and keen intellect as well as his political savvy. During the party congress of the Austrian Conservative party at which I volunteered, Mr. Schüssel finally won me over during his rousing, uplifting acceptance speech. However, I was not sure if he would want me to remain a part of his cabinet, so when he went to cast his ballot, I bumped into him when I was cordoning off the stairs. He recognized me.

"How are you doing?" he asked.

"Oh, I'm fine, but I'm probably even better if I knew you'd keep me in your office."

Cheeky, yes, but his smile told me he liked my response, because a few days later I was ordered to move to Mr. Schüssel's secretariat, where I became his and his chief of staff's personal assistant. Now that was a job to my liking!

Working in the government's inner sanctum was a dream come true for me. I felt like a fish in water. I had been a political person all my life, whether in the United States glued to the televised Oliver North hearings as a 16-year-old, or in Iran experiencing the political influence and impact of a religion taking over a heretofore mostly secular society. Austrian politics became a factor in my life when my father's job as representative of Austria in the American Midwest included defending the election of Austrian President Kurt Waldheim. The way the Austrian social democrats colluded with other (non-political) parties, both nationally and internationally, to smear Waldheim preoccupied and disgusted me.

As a member of the cabinet of the Austrian vice chancellor and foreign minister, I received a comprehensive political education no university could ever have provided me. Soon after Mr. Schüssel's inauguration, he called for snap elections, so I had a front-row seat to a thrilling election campaign as well as the ensuing coalition talks with the social democrats. I also held the fort during night sessions of budget talks, connecting Mr. Schüssel by telephone conference call with his closest advisers, followed by midnight celebratory drinks after a successful conclusion of the negotiations. I learned the steps of how a law came into existence; I wrote up the minutes of consultatory meetings between Mr. Schüssel's chief of staff with the chancellor's chief of staff; and, I explained political decisions to concerned citizens on the phone. Finally, I answered his fan mail, sometimes even sending out small caricatures Mr. Schüssel did, as he was a talented painter, spending many a trans-atlantic flight sketching his latest cartoons, which we then proceeded to collect for him.

Always the pragmatist, Mr. Schüssel was not excited about his new position as foreign minister, which forced him to deal with the world of diplomacy. He made no secret of his feelings, much to the chagrin of the ambassadors in the foreign ministry, who often left meetings miffed and disappointed about the lack of passion and concern for world affairs they witnessed during the proceedings. I did not share Mr. Schüssel's aversion to international diplomacy; I personally was very excited about the opportunity to shake hands with the myriad foreign dignitaries who ambled past my desk. The visit of Alija Izetbegovic, known for his pres-idency of the newly created country of Bosnia-Herzegovina, is one that stands out in my memories. I am fairly sure he visited Mr. Schüssel to discuss the Dayton Agreement. Little-known, however, is that in 1970 Mr. Izetbegovic authored the *Islamic Manifest*, which clearly stated that "There is no peace or coexistence between the Islamic faith and non-Is-lamic social and political institutions." (p. 26) Thanks to Mr. Izetbegovic we (ought to) know what Islam really is:

> The briefest definition of the Islamic order defines it as a unity of re-ligion and law, upbringing and power, ideal and interest, the spiritual community and the state, willingness and force... An Islamic society without an Islamic authority is incomplete and without power; Islamic government without Islamic society is either utopia or violence. Gen-erally speaking, a Muslim does not exist as a sole individual. If he wish-es to live and survive as a Muslim, he must create an environment, a community, a system. (p. 8)[4]

Of course, at the time no one, including Mr. Schüssel and myself, had any knowledge of this manifest. Only recently did I learn of the existence, and I wish our politicians would take the time read it in order to understand Islam. Much of what I would say more than a decade later is similar to the above quote, but unlike Mr. Izetbegovic I would be required to defend my words in a court of law.

In late 1996, my life was about to be transformed once again when

---

4 http://www.angelfire.com/dc/mbooks/Alija-Izetbegovic-Islamic-Declara-tion-1990-Azam-dot-com.pdf.

a job notice made its way across my desk one day. While this was very common, what made my heart flutter was the destination: "Job opening at the Austrian Embassy Kuwait." I was single at the time, free to go wherever my heart desired, and so I immediately set out to stake my claim to this job, which turned out to be easier said than done. In a harbinger of what was to happen to me many years later, I became a political pawn between the foreign affairs representatives of the two coalition government parties. If this sounds ridiculous, believe me, it was. Here I was, a low-ranking member of the vice-chancellor's cabinet vying for an equally low-ranking job at an embassy in a completely irrelevant country, but the commission in charge of these overseas appointments decided to punish the vice-chancellor by blocking my application. What the members of this commission were trying to accomplish is beyond my most fanciful surmise. As it happened, Mr. Schüssel was extremely supportive of my intention to move to Kuwait: "I am sad to let you go, but you are young and need to live and work internationally. Go and get experience!"

Finally, in late 1996 I received my marching orders and made preparations to move from Vienna to Kuwait. Having watched my mother do this all my life, I had the necessary organizational skills to plan everything I would need in Kuwait while still working full-time: new furniture, food staples unavailable in Kuwait, and my library of books.

∝

The airplane was on approach to Kuwait airport. Petting my cat in his cage at my feet, I admit I felt queasy. Had I made the right decision in returning? Would I be happy with my choice of post? On the other hand, I had the advantage of knowing where I would sleep that night, where I would work and what the country was like. I would not be stuck in culture shock as everything would feel familiar. And so it was: My cat and I settled into our new life problem-free, with the support of the embassy personnel. My first task included renewing my Kuwaiti driver's license and purchasing a car—my first one ever! Was I ever proud of my little midnight blue Suzuki Swift, which would be my loyal companion, especially when hauling heavy loads of alcohol across the city. More on that later.

I settled into my new life and enjoyed myself. The temperatures rose markedly in early April, prompting the arrival of the annual visit of the exterminator (cockroaches!) and the servicing of the air-conditioning in my apartment, which was then turned on full-blast until the end of October. I never had an issue with air-conditioning like many others did; it was an absolute necessity and a part of life, with temperatures hovering continuously above 105°F from May until early October. As with everyone else in Kuwait, my life revolved around the heat. Working hours were adjusted accordingly; shopping was done either very early in the morning or late evening with ice boxes in the trunk to prevent the spoiling of perishable food, and there were always bottles of water rolling around the back seat, so that in an emergency I would not dehydrate while waiting for help, a habit which much to my husband's annoyance I have not been able to break ever since.

The Austrian Embassy in Kuwait

At the embassy I was in charge of consular affairs, which included the issuing of passports to Austrians residing in Kuwait, Bahrain or Qatar, and other administrative paperwork, particularly for general elections. I also oversaw the visa section staffed with a Jordanian translator and interpreter, Hussein, as well as the embassy houseboy, an Indian man named Dioge, whose job included accepting visa applications, but also caring for the embassy building and running small errands. In the summer months, when the number of visa applications rose to a sometimes staggering two hundred a day, Dioge was assisted by Hussein. Oftentimes there were cases requiring more questions or paperwork, which was when I was called into the visa section to enter the discussion and make a final decision.

My beloved first car

I enjoyed working on these challenging cases, since more often than not the visa applicants were trying to cheat. The visa rules for Kuwaitis and passport holders from the so-called GCC countries (Gulf Cooperation Council, consisting of Kuwait, Bahrain, Qatar, the United Arab Emirates, Saudi Arabia and Oman) were quite relaxed: only a valid passport and a filled-out application form with two passport-size photos were required. Matters became more challenging with respect to other passports: What was the legal status of the—Indian, Pakistani, Filipino, Sri Lankan, Bangladeshi—applicant? Was he or she traveling with their sponsor, i.e., the Kuwaiti family, as a maid or driver? Was the applicant's passport completely new or were there several entry and exit stamps indicating a likely return to Kuwait? How long was the residence permit valid? If the applicant did not travel with a Kuwaiti family, what was the purpose of the trip? What was the income? If the income certificate showed a monthly salary of the equivalent of $200, how did the applicant intend to pay for an extended holiday in Austria? Or was the trip planned to illegally migrate to Austria, or Europe? I always demanded a bank statement showing steady income for the previous six months; more than once I debunked bogus bank statements. Sometimes the hotel reservations the applicants produced were fake, too, as a quick phone call to the hotel in Vienna or elsewhere in Austria revealed. And in one case, I even proved that a passport from Kazakhstan was counterfeit. I often felt like the Sherlock Holmes of the Austrian Embassy visa section.

The issue of second and third wives was one I found most challenging to deal with. Even if this was not a frequent issue, it forced me and my superiors to reconcile the existence of polygamy with Austrian law which bans polygamy. How do we, as representatives of the Austrian government, view the visa application of a large Kuwaiti family with father, wives and mothers, numerous children and the corresponding number of maids? Are we the enforcers of Austrian laws banning polygamy, or do we look away, issue the visas and hope the family spends a suitable amount of money in "*Zal am Si*" (*Zell am See*, a favorite holiday location for Kuwaitis in the Austrian province of Salzburg) for the economic good of Austria? Much as I felt an acute need to deny the visas to ease my conscience, in the end I followed the internal embassy rules by issuing the visas. I firmly believe polygamy is morally wrong, even if it is legal in Kuwait. By issuing the visas, I was forced to tacitly approve of polygamy.

I ran a strict regimen in the visa section. I had to, because the annual heat during the summer months meant that the number of visa applications rose steadily from mid-May onward, culminating in up to 200 visa stickers, as I described previously. This situation was reflected not only in the need to start my work day before everyone else, but also in a certain work sequence: first came the application, which included filling out the above-mentioned form, adding the two photos and the required additional paperwork, depending on the applicant's nationality. After the payment of the fee and the checking of the information on the application, the paperwork made its way to my office, where I double-checked everything, entered the information into a special computer program connected with the Schengen Information System (which does a quick background check), and upon receiving the go-ahead from the system, I printed the visa sticker and affixed it to the passport. Because my system worked so efficiently, we were able to return the passports the following day.

The only times I ran into trouble with my carefully-laid plan was when I was called into the visa section to intervene in difficult cases. Most of the time I was able to resolve the queries; if not, I presented the case to my immediate superior, either the consul or the ambassador.

In one case I made an executive decision. According to the Vienna Convention on Diplomatic Relations, the visa section is legally considered Austrian premises, so when one day a Kuwait army officer entered the visa section wearing in his uniform I politely asked him to leave and return in civilian clothes. Hussein, who witnessed this exchange, was astounded that the army officer did as he was told, and by a woman no less!

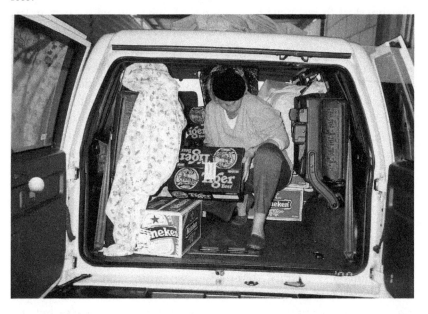

Believe it or not, ordering alcoholic beverages from a catalog and picking up the shipment was also part of my job description, albeit an unofficial one. The Kuwaiti ministry of foreign affairs permitted foreign embassies in Kuwait to import alcohol twice a year. Every embassy had a catalog offering the sale of tax-free alcoholic beverages, which included everything a non-Muslim heart desired. So along with my colleagues I would peruse the catalog and draw up a list of beer, red and white wine, whiskey for my friend Agnes, and a few bottles of vodka to bring as a gift for dinner party invitations. The ambassador would then hand over our orders to whichever embassy was in charge of the full order of all embassies, always one with a large warehouse-like storage facility on its premises. A few weeks later, we were notified about the pick-up date. I would grab some duvets to cover the boxes and make my way to the embassy building across the city. The large heavy doors were unbolted, allowing me to back the car into the driveway and then—usually with the help of strong Austrian army personnel which I enlisted with a smile and the promise of a homemade dinner—the copious cases of illegal-legal booze were carefully stacked in my car. I drove back to my own embassy ever so gingerly, even more careful than usual, imagining the disaster in every way possible if I were to be hit by another car. Once again, I cautiously maneuvered the car into the driveway, making sure no one in the street was stopping to watch while my friends and I hauled the cartons from the car into my second-floor apartment.

I really did lead a weird life!

If the summer months were the toughest and heaviest in terms of workload, the rest of the year was the exact opposite. It was hard not to get bored; that's how quiet my office became. Apart from taking my annual vacation in the early spring to go skiing or visit my parents in Athens, I immersed myself in a long-distance university degree in "Diplomatic Studies." I was very much aware that this degree would never be accepted by Austrian authorities, yet it forced me to read books I otherwise would never have read (such as *The Prince* by Niccolo Machiavelli) or study in depth topics I otherwise would not have bothered with. For instance, in late 1998 and early 1999, with the support of the Austrian ambassador, I wrote a final paper on women's suffrage in Kuwait, a captivating and timely subject at a time when Kuwaiti women were finally due to be granted the right to vote.[5]

I was not in the least surprised that

> in May 2009, four female candidates won parliamentary seats in a general election out of fifty available seats. Although this was 8% of parliament, by the 2013 election, no women had been elected to the current parliament, and the last woman elected resigned in May 2014,

because a decade earlier, when I questioned Kuwaiti women from all strata of society—from Bedouin women to businesswomen—in the course of gathering primary sources for my research paper, one answer predominated: "Why do I need the right to vote? Everything is currently all right. My husband votes for me." This view was joined by a conservative/Islamist Kuwaiti member of parliament and Islamic scholar, Waleed Al-Tabatabaie, who did not shake my hand when I interviewed him.

---

5 According to *Wikipedia*, In May 1999 a decree that allowed women the right to vote and run for office was issued by the emir, which was overruled again by the parliament 6 months later. https://en.wikipedia.org/wiki/Women%27s_suffrage_in_Kuwait.

Although my interview with him was off the record, he is on the record saying the following in 2005, which is basically the same thing he said to me:

> We have no problem with women voting, but we do have a problem with women standing for elections. Islam dictates that the head of the nation must be a man, and we are technically the head of the nation here.[6]

Visiting the State Mosque of Kuwait in 1998

---

6 https://www.nytimes.com/2005/05/04/world/middleeast/lawmakers-block-women-from-voting-in-kuwait.html. accessed July 3, 2019.

When I researched the paper and listened to the various views on Kuwaiti women's right to vote, I understood for the first time that we in the West have no right and no reason to force the Western notion of freedom and democracy onto the rest of the world. To me, the honest reply "Why do I need to vote?" epitomizes the vast gulf between the West and the non-Western, Muslim world with respect to democracy and human rights. If one questions the necessity for the right to vote, then the logical next step is to question the right to free speech and all other rights.

Not surprisingly, Ramadan, the Islamic month of fasting from sunrise to sunset, influenced me greatly. Whereas the first Ramadan felt weird and different with a sprinkle of fascination, I found myself increasingly annoyed in the years that followed. When I was in Kuwait, the end of Ramadan coincided with Christmas, which was convenient for both non-Muslim and Muslim embassy employees—we all had the same days off.

Two stories exemplify the way Ramadan concerns both Muslims and non-Muslims alike. The husband of a friend and embassy colleague, a Coptic Christian from Egypt, carried his family's Christmas mail to a Kuwaiti post office. As he was licking the stamps to affix them to the letters, he was accosted by men in the post office expressing their anger that my friend's fast was broken. Another friend, a blond lady working for the German embassy, stopped at a red light and was reprimanded for chewing gum.

Ramadan itself was not an issue on the embassy premises and, unlike Kuwaiti government and municipality offices, our working hours remained the same. However, because our Muslim embassy workers didn't eat or drink, there was a noticeable slowdown in dealing with the workload, which thankfully was mostly inconsequential. In any case, I was always of the opinion that whether or not my co-workers were fasting, the work had to be done. What annoyed me was the ambassador's secretary, a Yemeni woman, who kept reading her Qur'an, which I thought was inappropriate. No one said anything, so I wisely kept my mouth shut as well. The secretary's behavior was in sharp contrast to my own: Ramadan was the time I most enjoyed eating my breakfast sandwich and drinking my water. The more my Muslim co-workers fasted, the more I bent unwritten rules, which thankfully I did not have to follow inside the embassy. Only when I was in public did I refrain from breaking Kuwaiti law. Well, at least most of the time…

My field of work also included the monitoring of the two English-language newspapers, *Arab Times* and *Kuwait Times*. I enjoyed reading the two dailies, even though the quality of their reporting was mediocre at best. The Amir did this, the Amir did that, ministers were grilled by members of parliament, the summer heat is on, sandstorms batter the State of Kuwait, Filipino maid committed suicide, Filipino ambassador opens safe house, Indian maid raped by her sponsor. On and on the news went.

In Ramadan, however, both newspapers devoted ample space to questions and answers about the various rules during the month of ab-stention. For instance, I learned how the fasting Muslim decides when he must stop eating and drinking:

> It has been made permissible for you the night preceding fasting to go to your wives [for sexual relations]. They are clothing for you and you are clothing for them. Allah knows that you used to deceive your-selves, so He accepted your repentance and forgave you. So now, have relations with them and seek that which Allah has decreed for you. And eat and drink until the white thread of dawn becomes distinct to you from the black thread [of night]. Then complete the fast until the sunset. And do not have relations with them as long as you are staying for worship in the mosques. These are the limits [set by] Allah, so do not approach them. Thus does Allah make clear His ordinances to the people that they may become righteous. (Qur'an 2:187, Sahih Interna-tional)

Another amusing question concerned the accidental swallowing of a fly. The answer included the following:

THINGS THAT DO NOT BREAK THE FAST
To eat and drink something unintentionally.
A mosquito, fly or any other object going down the throat uninten-tionally.

These questions were characteristic of the challenges of Ramadan etiquette for devout Muslims. Back then I had not yet studied Islamic law or read the Qur'an, so I merely snickered at these no doubt serious questions.

To this day I am thankful for my ignorance of the Qur'an, the *hadith* and the *sira* during my time in Kuwait. Imagine the trouble I would have found myself in had I turned into the critic I am today then and there in Kuwait. I don't think my diplomatic status would have saved me from being recalled to Austria, that is, I would have faced deportation.

And the greatest shock was yet to come.

One morning I was perusing the newspapers when I read an article discussing the relationship of Mohammed with a young girl named Aisha, and how he married her when she was six years old, and consummated the marriage when she was nine. I was so shocked about what I had just read that I raced to Hussein in the visa section and asked, "Oh my God, I just read about Mohammed and Aisha! Did you know about that, I mean, is this something that people know about?" He became verbally aggressive towards me and hissed, his face contorted in what appeared to be pain: "You must never talk about this ever again." When I retorted, desperate to hear something positive, that I thought religions were inherently good (yes, I was once that naïve!), he impatiently shook his head as if he felt sorry for my stupidity and ignorance and said: "Religions are good, people are bad." He never said whether what I had just read about Mohammed and Aisha was true or not. And I never raised the subject again.

Hussein would later make me an immoral offer: his wife and his children were away in Jordan for the summer months, so how about if he and I entered a summer relationship? Needless to say, I turned down this proposal. In any case, I was friends with his wife, too, so this was definitely a no-go. What a ridiculous and disgusting thought!

My life in Kuwait did not consist solely of work. As a matter of fact, I had copious free time at my disposal, which I devoted to exploring Kuwait. Some evenings I scouted the *souks* (markets), especially the ones specializing in selling beautifully embroidered fabrics in silk and cotton. Many a time I splurged on a fabric, which I then took to the Pakistani tailor across the street from the embassy, but first I picked out my favorite pants or shirts for the tailor to copy.

I also hung out with my Kuwaiti friends, who on many Fridays invited me to ride on their boat to an uninhabited island off the Kuwaiti coast, which incidentally was the first Kuwaiti land to be liberated from Iraqi occupation. I thoroughly enjoyed these trips, with barbecuing and drinking, chatting, swimming, or simply relaxing. The calm sea water surrounding the island was a deep Caribbean blue-green, and had I been an avid snorkeler, I would have been doing just that all day long.

My friends were typical of Kuwaiti society. Ghazi hailed from a prominent family and was required to meet certain expectations: as a (seemingly devout) Muslim, he was forced to marry an equally devout Kuwaiti girl and father as many children as possible. Ghazi had a problem on his hands, because he fell in love with a Polish woman, Agnes, who had moved to Kuwait with her Palestinian husband and their daughter. Divorced from the husband, she met Ghazi and became his…, well, I am not sure what to call their relationship, but I guess concubine or second wife would describe it. Theirs was true love, which I witnessed firsthand, but the circumstances of their relationship were dreadful, with horrific consequences. Ghazi took great care of Agnes and her daughter, providing them with a house and a maid and plenty of money, but Agnes had become an alcoholic in a country that strictly speaking had no alcoholics. When Ghazi was finally forced to marry his chosen wife, I visited Agnes in the hospital where she detoxed for a few days. Of course, official hospital records indicated a different illness, yet in essence she was treated for her alcoholism. Agnes' life revolved around Ghazi, about when he would finally be able to spend time with her rather than his wife, all the while nursing multiple bottles of whiskey and smoking *shisha* pipes nonstop. Even when she came over to my place or on our weekend trips to the island she would carry her *shisha* with her. Ghazi had to tap into his sometimes shady contacts to provide her with plenty of booze. Imagine the pain she endured when she knew Ghazi and his wife spent their vacation in Thailand. Agnes then had to fight for her own vacation with Ghazi. Such were the rules for a second wife, which Agnes was, according to Islamic law.[7] My heart ached for her, but I also knew there was no way out for her. Her home was now Kuwait, not Poland; she had no job, and her daughter would later marry a Kuwaiti man. She was stuck in Kuwait, fully dependent on a man who loved her, but for traditional reasons could not and would never make their relationship official. I am sorry to say I am no longer in touch with her.

I was also friends with an Egyptian expat, Mohammed, who worked for a German company and spoke perfect German. He and I had dinner once in a while, and, as a pious Muslim, he tried to do *dawah* (inviting me to Islam), only I didn't know the *modus operandi* at the time. Now and then he would drop a comment about Islam or offer to tell me more about Islam. As a naturally curious person, I started reading a book about Islam; I think it was a German book called *The True Imam*. A few weeks later, in his car on the way back to the embassy after another dinner, he asked me what I thought about Islam now that I had read the book. His face was beaming with excitement. "How can anyone believe

---

7 Agnes had converted to Islam upon marrying her Palestinian husband, but never lived an Islamic life. As a matter of fact, she hated everything Islamic.

this crap?" I answered honestly, which turned out to be a mistake, because no sooner had those words left my mouth, I received a hard slap to my cheek. I turned to Mohammed and hissed, "You better take me back to the embassy RIGHT NOW, and I never want to see you again." Without another word, he did as he was told, and while he tried to call me in the days following, I never spoke to him again. I learned *dawah* the hard way.

If you think that by living in Kuwait I stayed away from military activities, or they from me, think again. In 1998, Kuwait's northern neighbor once again played cat and mouse with the United States, and with the United Nations weapons inspectors who were required to inspect various sites suspected of containing the production or stockpiles of weapons of mass destruction. As Iraq continuously challenged Security Council resolutions, US president Bill Clinton launched Operation Desert Fox in December 1998. What sounds like just another limited military confrontation to the rest of the world greatly impacted Kuwait's inhabitants. For weeks leading up to Desert Fox, we received notices and warnings from both Kuwaiti media and UN personnel stationed in the UN-monitored and enforced demilitarized zone (DMZ) between Iraq and Kuwait about the threat of Iraq using chemical weapons against Kuwait in retaliation. Every time I drove to the grocery store during that time of crisis, I listened to the news on the radio, when suddenly the program would be interrupted with a warning and instructions on the construction of a safe room in case of a poison gas attack. Our Austrian UN contingent was kind enough to provide the embassy personnel with an army-issued NBC (nuclear, biological and chemical) protection kit containing decontamination powder, an atropine injector, a light NBC protection suit and potassium iodide tablets. I remember thinking upon receiving my kit: "I hope I never have to use this. I wouldn't have a clue what to do with any of this." We were never given instructions.

During the actual bombing campaign I remember talking on the phone one night with a German friend stationed at the border, when we both abruptly halted our conversation because we could hear the explosions of targets near the DMZ. While I was acutely aware of a military confrontation going on in the vicinity, I was never actively afraid. Perhaps I simply resigned myself to a low chance of survival after a chemical attack following a close look at my apartment's poor-quality windows. They could hardly keep out the desert heat and the dust, so how would they withstand a chemical attack?

Warm oasis in the desert of Oman

With the military confrontation resolved after only a few days, my life returned to normal, whatever normal means in Kuwait. I did some traveling, occasionally visiting an already bustling Dubai or driving around the capital city of Oman, Muscat, a country I enjoyed very much because it is not oppressively Islamic and also because of its gorgeous scenery. The view of the blue sky and the barren mountains coupled with a small river and a lush oasis here and there was breathtaking.

The trip that left me with a lasting impression was one that took me to the Demilitarized Zone (DMZ) between North and South Korea. In early 1998, I had the priceless opportunity to visit South Korea when I was invited to attend World Cup ski races held in Yong Pyong, a ski resort near Seoul, after the end of the winter Olympic Games in Japan. Not only did I ski in Yong Pyong,[8] but I also toured the DMZ and stepped into North Korea. Once again, the stark contrast between communism and capitalism was so vividly displayed and reaffirmed my commitment to a capitalist and free society and rejecting all forms of socialism.

Inside the corrugated steel hut where North and South Korea negotiated the armistice following the Korean War.

With the millennium ending in 1999, I met my future husband, an Austrian United Nations military observer, in Kuwait, of all places! I wanted to get married in Kuwait, simply because I like doing things differently, but *shariah* law precluded that plan. My best friend was to be my maid of honor, but because according to *shariah* a woman's testimony is worth only half of that of a man, my future husband and I decided that getting married in Vienna, after all, was the way to go. It was also time for me to leave Kuwait.

---

8 I specifically had my ski boots delivered by courier from my parents in Athens to me in Kuwait, and which I then carried from Kuwait via Singapore to Korea.

CHAPTER SIX

My Time in Libya

Just stay quiet and you'll be okay.
—Mohammed Atta, 9/11 attacker

AFTER NEARLY FOUR YEARS of living and working in Kuwait, I decided it was time to move on. I had gotten married in October 2000 and my husband was still studying at medical school in Vienna. As an Austrian embassy attaché, I could choose my assignment: Albania or Libya.

Why these countries? Well, because accepting a post in, say, Paris, London, or New York costs you money, while in countries known as "shitholes" you are able to save money; this has to do with a number of factors, not least being the living conditions. And, as compared to France, Albania and Libya were certainly considered to be hardship posts. I also picked these countries due to their relative proximity to Vienna, our home, where my husband was studying and shuttling back and forth to be with me.

Before I made my final choice, I asked colleagues at both embassies for their assessments. In the end, I opted for Tripoli, Libya. The reasons were quite simple: I had always wanted to visit Libya, especially because of its ancient historical significance, but also due to its proximity to the sea. While living in Kuwait, I had really loved driving along the Persian Gulf every day. And then, of course, there was "the money." I never made a secret about this. And, I would venture a guess that nearly all other expats were in Libya because of "the money." Only I was open about it.

So, Tripoli it was. Before moving there, I spent a few days in the city looking for an apartment and getting a feel for the living conditions. I knew they would be harsh, but I was willing to "bite the bullet" in order to save money for my married life.

What about Tripoli was harsh? First, there was absolutely nothing to keep me busy. In Kuwait, one could at least go shopping, acquire a membership at one of the finer hotels in order to swim and sunbathe, or eat out as there were some fine restaurants with very high standards. In Libya, in contrast, there was nothing of the sort—no cinema, no symphony, no opera, no shopping malls, not even a decent grocery store. This meant having to buy greens at the vegetable market, milk and cream (not pasteurized and therefore undrinkable after two days in the fridge) at a special dairy outlet. Milk, for example, was packaged in plastic bags. And there was only one type of white bread to be had. I never did find out what it cost. I was never told because the staff in bakeries spoke no English. I just handed over whatever coins I had and never knew the actual cost.

A photo of my house in the Gargaresh area of Tripoli. As is becoming more and more common in Europe, Libyans close off streets to erect tents for wedding celebrations. If you are caught in between, tough luck.

My apartment was located in the Gargaresh neighborhood of Tripoli. The apartment was on the first floor of a two-story building; the top floor was occupied by my landlord, his wife and children. He was a high-ranking official in the Libyan Ministry of Fisheries. Although he was always friendly to me, he also tried to rip me off many times. There were many repair jobs in the apartment that needed to be done, but for which he charged too much or failed to do at all. This meant that I had to wait until my husband returned from Austria, so that the two men could "get down to business." I was a woman, and the landlord made me feel like one, in the Islamic sense: respected, but a bit dense, and not fully human.

My apartment was huge, too big for me, but there was nothing smaller available; apparently, there are no single apartments. A typical couple in Libya does not live alone like my husband and I did, but usually has at least three kids. So, I stacked my 500 imported water bottles in the huge living room. The furniture in the apartment can only be described as "tacky." I used the dining room table as a massage table when my Bulgarian masseur came once a week. The kitchen was of decent size, although I had to bring my own dishwasher, fridge, and freezers. (I needed two huge ones because I imported a lot of food from Austria.) Using the dishwasher was no fun because the electrical plug was not grounded. I got a shock from the unit every time I used it.

Drinking water depot in otherwise useless living room.

The apartment had two bedrooms. Both were filled with low quality, ugly furniture left for me by the landlord. The wardrobe was cheap, too. I used the other bedroom for ironing and for guests, though there were admittedly very few. Who would want to spend a week in Libya doing nothing?

There was a narrow balcony that I used for sunbathing when I didn't head to the beaches with my friends. Leading to the balcony was a sitting room, which I used for watching satellite TV, and which doubled as my working area. I had a telephone landline because cellphones were too expensive (more than $1,000 for a contract). It was common knowledge that all phone calls were monitored. The clicking sounds on the line were the tell-tale signs. Surprisingly, I had decent bandwidth for my internet connection.

In Libya I had to learn patience. There is little point in getting annoyed when the air-conditioning stops working in the middle of a sizzling summer day because of a blackout—what's the point? You just sit around, wait, and hope that the blackout will not last so long that all of your precious food hoarded in the freezer will spoil. Or, you read a book. Or, you re-count the 400 or so water bottles in your storage room.

I worked at the Austrian embassy as a visa officer, with working hours from 8:00 am to 2:30 pm. When I arrived at work each day, I opened the big window in my office to let in the fresh air. My office was adjacent to a school, so every morning I would listen to military chants and some sort of pledge of allegiance to Libya's leader, Muammar Gaddafi, sung by the students. Austria and Libya then had generally good relations which resulted in my work on the visa desk being quite dull. The more interesting work was done on trade relations, but this was taken care of by the trade delegation that was located in a different area of Tripoli. Boring work at the embassy resulted in tense relationships between staff members.

My free time was spent attempting to remain sane, done primarily by walking my friend's dog after lunch and watching Austrian TV via satellite. My husband and I also visited the world-famous excavations in Leptis Magna, a prominent city in the ancient empire of Carthage, and Sabrata, an ancient Phoenician port city with a magnificent amphitheater.

Now and then, there were private invitations to a dinner or a party, but otherwise it was just surviving and dealing with the boredom. Or, dealing with basic needs—for example, where to find a hairdresser to freshen up my blond streaks? Well, someone knew of a Filipino man, who then came to my apartment to touch up my hair. (He was gay, which, I'd imagine, wasn't conducive to working in the public sphere in an Islamic country.) And, where to find a vet to take care of my cat? What about a doctor in case of severe diarrhea, which happened frequently? My husband decided to take a water specimen taken from the tap water in my apartment with him for analysis in an Austrian lab. The result was devastating: I was poisoning myself every time I took a shower, but I had no choice but to continue to shower with the bad water.

I spent many weekends at the beach in my effort to stay sane. I would typically wake up my friends by telephone (some were hung over from the night before), and, in the late morning (too late for me), a group of expats (Austrian, Spanish, German, and other Westerners, most of whom were employed in the oil business) would set off in a convoy to find one of the many fantastic beaches. However, these beaches offered us no comfort at all—no sanitary places, running water, sunbeds, or showers—absolutely nothing but the raw beauty of a fairly untouched beach. We would set up camp—that is, start a barbecue and open our (illegally imported) beer—and enjoy ourselves. There were many such beaches, both to the east and the west of Tripoli; one was aptly named Paradise Beach.

Leptis Magna, a famous archaeological site to the west of Tripoli.

Sometimes, we even managed to forget that we were in Gaddafi's Land. Although, in passing the excavations and the huge pipes for the Great Man-Made River project on the way back to Tripoli, we were catapulted back to reality.

What is noticeable in general in Arab-Muslim lands is the amount of litter in the streets. There were plastic bags everywhere—in the bushes, in the trees, stuck to fences, in the ditches and no one cleaned them up.

There were also many unfinished projects. You could see half-finished apartment buildings left to rot. There were train tracks leading from Tripoli to the west toward Tunisia. (This was an Austrian-led project.) The tracks ended suddenly and no train ever rode on those tracks to nowhere. The tracks ran parallel with the main street-cum-highway leading to Tunisia. My husband and I frequently traveled this highway to go shopping in Djerba, an island off the coast of Tunisia; it was a four-hour drive, with the desert to the left and the sea to the right of the highway, and then a lengthy wait at the Tunisian/Libyan border crossing. The Libyan border officers always seemed very surprised when checking our passports. While we both had diplomatic passports, my husband got his due to my job. His passport read "husband of Mrs. Elisabeth Sabaditsch-Wolff, attaché at the Austrian Embassy in Libya." That was "a huff" to the men at the border crossing—a man dependent on his wife? Impossible, to their way of thinking. There was lots of chatter among the border agents while we waited in the searing heat, until finally, they waved us through. When we returned to Libya, the same scene was replayed.

I recall breathing a sigh of relief when we stepped onto Tunisian soil. We felt free again; in Libya, we were unfree. Tunisia was much more open than Libya—we felt it as soon as we crossed the border. Freedom is not only tangible but it is also a feeling; there are degrees of freedom. Tunisia is less free than Austria, for example, and I always breathed a sigh of relief when my plane touched down in Vienna. But, when you are stuck in a totalitarian country such as Libya, Tunisia meant a certain degree of freedom, even if that only meant the freedom to buy beer and wine. Every summer, thousands of Europeans flock to Tunisian beaches like the ones on the island of Djerba, which is something I cannot relate to, particularly nowadays with the ever-present threat of terrorist attacks on beach resorts.

How else do you know you are in an unfree country? One clue is the exit procedure at the airport. All expatriate workers need an exit visa to be able to leave Libya; my diplomatic passport exempted me, but I found the procedure very humiliating when police checked passports for exit visas at the door of the aircraft. Western companies made sure that their staff always had their exit visas stamped, even if they weren't immediately needed. As soon as they expired, the next ones were applied for. Better safe than sorry.

On Tuesday, September 11, 2001, I drove to work just as I did every day. And, as on every day, I had stomach cramps due to the situation at the embassy; I felt so uncomfortable working there. The kids at the school chanted next door; the visa section was crowded as Filipino workers applied for visas they were unlikely to be granted. Because I was due to fly home to Vienna that night, I meticulously handed over my workload to my colleague before I drove home. As I did every day,

I marveled at the ugliness of socialism combined with Islamic architecture while I drove out of the city on Gargaresh Road. All of the storefronts were painted in Islamic green, the buildings themselves were usually painted white. Gaddafi's portrait was to be seen everywhere, in very different poses: Gaddafi as the benevolent father with smiling children, Gaddafi in uniform with tanks in the background, Gaddafi the pious leader with both the Qur'an and his revolutionary treatise, *The Green Book*, and Gaddafi with his female bodyguards. I felt catapulted back to Iraq—Saddam Hussein had created the same type of personality cult.

When I first traveled to Libya prior to moving there, visiting the remains of the city of Sabrata was on top of my to-do list.

On September 11, 2001, I entered my apartment, fed the cat, prepared my lunch, and settled down to watch TV. It was 2:45 pm local time when German television RTL interrupted its normal programming to report a plane had crashed into the World Trade Center in New York City. Even before the second plane crashed (which I saw live on TV), I knew this wasn't an accident and prayed that Libya hadn't been behind it. I really did not want to experience another war. After the second plane crashed into the other tower, the satellite connection crashed as well, which angered me, but I knew there was nothing I could do. I grabbed the phone, called my friend Doris, who worked at an Austrian oil company, and told her what I had seen. She told me later that I sounded confused and agitated; she thought I was drunk. Far from it, I was very sober. I then lay down on the sofa in front of the TV and fell asleep because the restart of the satellite receiver was to take about 45 minutes; I knew I would not miss much. This was a serious crisis, and it wouldn't make a difference whether I watched TV now or in an hour.

Indeed, the crisis had worsened when I switched on my lifeline to the world. It was all there—the shock, the horror, the towers aflame, the damaged Pentagon and the crater in Shanksville. I was still fairly calm, although I didn't know whether Austrian Airlines would be flying into Tripoli that night. I was also worried about leaving my cat behind, something I'd never done before. This time I couldn't take him with me; I knew that if Libya was behind the attack, I not only wouldn't return to Tripoli but would also lose my beloved cat. It was a risk I had to take, but I was unhappy about leaving him behind, though a friend would take care of him.

The day ended with the TV running full blast while I packed my suitcase. During late evening, the Austrian Airlines departing flight was confirmed. But, before I left for the airport, my landlord stormed into my apartment without even bothering to knock on my door. He ran up and down in the hallway, screaming, "The Jews did it, the Jews are behind this. I know it!" I looked at him, crazy man that he was, and calmly told him that I was fairly certain that the Jews had not been involved in this carnage. I wanted to add that I hoped that his beloved leader wasn't behind this, but I bit my tongue. I merely showed him the way out.

It was very late at night. The feeling at the airport was generally subdued. Everyone asked whether there was anything new to report; it was word of mouth, as there was no wireless internet at the airport, and not even a TV set. In the days before smartphones, once you left your home, you were disconnected from information, something that was not helpful in times of crisis such as this one. Security checks took even more time than they usually did; the guards and security personnel were even more meticulous in checking identities.

Maybe I was wrong in thinking that Libya hadn't been behind this. But, what would they gain? Libya had just returned to the community of responsible nations by giving up its nuclear weapons, but, then again, Gaddafi wasn't exactly a beacon of sanity. I was emotionally drained when I passed through the last security check at the door of the airliner. I was surprised to see a larger aircraft – usually Libya only permitted Austrian Airlines to fly into Libya using the small 100-seat Fokker aircraft. But tonight, there was an Airbus 321, seating more than 200 passengers. Was Austrian Airlines expecting an exodus of expatriates? Was there another reason? I never did find out.

As I looked out of the window as the plane flew out of Libya, leaving behind the African coast, I was relieved. Whatever had happened in New York City, Washington D.C., and Shanksville, whoever was behind those terrible attacks, I knew in my heart that the world we knew would never be the same. When the sun arose, I was again back on Austrian soil. Back home. Safe.

9/11 was not the epiphany for me that many others had with regard to Islam. I had known a long time before September 2001 that there was something seriously wrong with Islam and the effect it had on people, both old and young. I had witnessed it firsthand in Tehran, then in Baghdad, in Kuwait, and now in Libya. What I was still lacking was knowledge in Islamic doctrine and that was to come soon.

I do not regret making the choice to work in Kuwait and Libya. They were and remain an important part of my life, of who I am and the values I live by and believe in. Actually living in Islamic countries, rather than just vacationing there, has given me the insight to say: This is not the way I want to live. I want to live a free life, making my own choices with regard to what I eat, drink, whom I associate with, what I read, what movies I watch. I am an adult, and I am responsible for myself and my daughter. I make the choices myself. My decisions are not made by a religion-cum-ideology that I do not subscribe to. Only when you lose your freedom do you value freedom; I have lost it many times, which is why I am fighting this fight—for my daughter, for her children, for the future. I will never give in to ideologies—Islam, socialism, Marxism, environmentalism, etc.—whose goal is the bondage of men and women. Never!

CHAPTER SEVEN

Back in Vienna

The essence of stupidity is not not knowing, but rather not wanting to know.
—Roland Baader

I N OCTOBER 2001, my husband and I left Libya (and with it the Islamic world) and settled in Vienna. I returned to the Ministry of Foreign Affairs, knowing full well that I was going to leave as soon as humanly possible. After the disaster of Tripoli I was ready for a change of pace and environment. I also knew that I would easily get a job in the private sector—and I did. One of Austria's richest entrepreneurs hired me as his personal assistant. However, in hindsight, I should not have accepted the job offer.

First of all, I had not yet come to terms with what had happened to me in Tripoli and the ensuing serious medical problems; I needed time to heal. But I ignored the nagging in my stomach, that feeling telling me not to do something stupid. This is what happens when you are raised in a way that we would today call "old-fashioned," meaning: you *must* have a job, no matter how much you like it or whether you are ready for it, and in the workforce you must not be an embarrassment to yourself and the rest of your family.

Secondly, my job as personal assistant consisted of sitting around all day doing nothing while waiting for my boss to show up from his numerous meetings either in Prague or in Vienna. I felt I was wasting my time, and the older I got, the more I felt that way. I had done plenty of sitting around in Kuwait and Libya, and I was ready for a change. Even the decent paycheck did not make up for this feeling. I learned that money isn't everything, and it certainly doesn't make up for a lousy job.

While I was transitioning from what would be my last "normal" job, I decided to return to school and finish my master's degree in "Diplomatic and Strategic Studies." Plagued by mind-blowing migraine headaches as a result of the stress I had been subjected to during my year in Libya, and even now in Vienna, I was let go from my job after a short check-up in the hospital. I was relieved in so many ways and in every sense of the word. For the first and only time in my life I drew unemployment benefits until I was officially a student, i.e., in exactly six months.[1]

At university, I was a teacher-student: I had no money for tuition,[2] so the university offered me a position as instructor for undergraduate English composition and preparation for the TOEFL—Test of English as a Foreign Language, a challenging prerequisite for students aiming to study at English-language universities worldwide.

In my teaching classes, I was confronted with students from Saudi Arabia, Kuwait, Libya and other Arab-Islamic countries. Not only was anti-Semitism[3] rampant among these students (and openly exhibited), but the quality of their written assignments left much to be desired. I could not believe that these students honestly thought they were going to be successful, considering they could not pen a simple essay with an introduction, a body, and a salient conclusion. I was oftentimes presented with was the semblance of an essay telling me they did not need to know English because they would inherit their father's company with a secretary who knew plenty of English. I was astounded. No matter how hard I tried to explain that this attitude was not going to lead to a degree, the quality of their work—or lack thereof—remained exactly the same. Even failing grades did not make the slightest impression on these students.

There were, however, students from other countries as well. I was fascinated to observe that the most hard-working students came from Western countries; the attitude they exhibited was completely different from that of the Arab students. The difference was even more pronounced during Ramadan, which back then took place in Novem-

---

1   Interestingly, the unemployment agency was quite happy that it did not have to process me for a job placement. I was told they could not place me anywhere because I was overqualified. This was even before I had my university degree!

2   My best-laid plan to save money for married life went wrong when I was repatriated after only a year in Libya.

3   And with it, conspiracy theories as to how the Jews were responsible for the 9/11 attacks. When I informed the university president, it was I who was reprimanded.

ber; thankfully, I must add. November was a useless month in terms of teaching my Muslim students anything at all. The minute the sun set—usually during class—they stormed out of my classroom to break their fast. Homework was generally ignored as there was simply no time to get it done during their nights of binge-eating and praying. In short, just like nowadays, Ramadan is a month of disruption for schools and universities. I admire all those brave teachers who today try their hardest for some semblance of normalcy during Ramadan without any support from school authorities.

I must add that despite these challenges, I truly loved teaching. I learned so much from my students when they opened their souls in essays they turned in. I remember in particular a Slovakian girl who was very gifted and whose essays I always looked forward to reading. I made sure to encourage her to write more; I hope she is still writing today.

My own classes were satisfactory in terms of academics, although I did butt heads with one specific professor, ironically from the US. The class itself was very stimulating and rewarding; however, when the professor included the viewing of the movie *Black Hawk Down*, I refused to watch it. I had seen parts of the movie before, and when I informed the professor that I could not watch the movie because of the brutality it depicted, and would sit outside the classroom for the duration, he was very upset with me. I told him I was afraid my post-traumatic stress disorder—which, following my Kuwait adventure, was present but never treated—would be triggered. I had my way, however, and sat right outside the classroom, reading papers or grading homework. The most striking aspect of this class was that many of my classmates hailed from the Balkans, where they had experienced that war first-hand. When I questioned them whether they minded the violence, they told me they were excited about the movie and did not mind the violent parts at all. They laughed at me, and I'm sure they, along with the professor, thought I was a craven coward. I didn't care.

In late July 2003, only days before the university lost its accreditation, I graduated *magna cum laude* with my degree in Diplomatic and Strategic Studies; I was now certified as smart. I loved walking down the aisle in my cap and gown, something that I had always dreamed of. I had no intention of returning to diplomacy, though. Instead, I began teaching English to students and adults at an English-language institute in Vienna.

During that time, I also became pregnant. My daughter was born a week after I taught my last class in late 2004. With the help of my mother, who took great care of her beloved granddaughter, I juggled being a full-time mother and a teacher. This situation worked out very well, also for my health, as the frequency of my migraine headaches decreased.

My husband and I frequently drove to the sea to introduce our daughter to salt water. On one of those trips to the island of Majorca, I brought with me a heavy book that would change my life. It was called *Gabriels Einflüsterungen* (*Gabriel's Whisperings*),[4] written by Jaya Gopal, an Indian atheist. The book explained Islam—its history and teachings—using only Islamic sources rather than Western sources, which at the time were still popular. (The apologist Karen Armstrong was widely read after the 9/11 attacks.) Reading the book widened my already open eyes. I was horrified and deeply frightened by what I read. All of a sudden, everything I had experienced and questioned in Tehran, Kuwait and Libya made perfect sense: the child marriages (which are frequent also in Kuwait,[5] not just in "backward" countries like Yemen), the strict requirement for headscarves, the definition of *jihad* and why it must continue for all time, the prophet as warlord and sexual predator, the terrible consequences for non-Muslim societies.

There were so many questions going through my head at the time: Why didn't anyone seem to know this? If people did know about this, why didn't anyone do anything about it? Where were the feminists with regard to child marriages and mandatory headscarves? How could anyone ignore this dangerous situation, especially in light of how Austrian society had obviously already changed in the past decade?

I had noticed the first signs of the transition of our majority Christian society into a minority Muslim one[6] as early as 1998, and it was 2006 or 2007 when I read the book! How naïve I was back then!

I had swallowed the Red Pill;[7] there was no way back. I began ed-

---

4 The official English translation of book was published much later. Its title is *The Misery of Islam*.

5 When I checked passports in the visa section at the embassy in Kuwait, I would always do the math. There were many marriages with brides as young as thirteen and grooms as old as forty or fifty years.

6 As of this writing, at least 10% of the Austrian population is Muslim, with Muslim students making up more than 60% of primary school classes in Vienna. It's all about demographics.

7 According to *Wikipedia*: "The red pill and its opposite, the blue pill, are a popular cultural meme, a metaphor representing the choice between: the Red Pill leading to a life of harsh knowledge, desperate freedom, and the brutal truths of reality; and the Blue Pill leading to a life of luxurious security, tranquil happiness, and the blissful ignorance of the harsh realities of life, basking in an (essentially dishonest) illusion."

ucating myself about Islam, devouring every book, even the apologetic ones, available at the time, including the *Qur'an*, and read websites devoted to explaining Islamic doctrine from every angle. The more I read, the more knowledge I had, and the more I was frightened. However, I believe fear is never the right emotion; I was resolved to fight. My weapons are words and education. My goal was to prevent my daughter, and, by extension, all girls, from experiencing any of the atrocities I had read about. She had the right to grow up as a free person, to make her own decisions, to be educated, to be able to speak her mind without repercussions. An Islamic society, as I had observed firsthand in post-revolutionary Iran, in Kuwait, in Libya, offers none of these freedoms. Thus, I decided, Austria must not become Islamized.

Along with reading everything in sight about Islam, I also became active online, reaching out to American blog talk radio.[8] This drew some interest in my reports from Austria, which were made easier because of my perfect English. On one of these shows, I was noticed by the organizers of an upcoming conference to be held in Brussels. In addition, fortuitously, I joined an Austrian activist group and later became a member of the *Wiener Akademikerbund* (Vienna Association of Academics), which had already been actively warning about the dangers of multiculturalism and Islamization for at least three years.

In October 2007, I was invited to and attended the Counterjihad Brussels conference and delivered the country report on the state of Islamization in Austria. I was honored to finally meet and exchange views with the authors of those books and online articles I had been devouring for the past months. I also got to know activists from all over Europe and the United States. I no longer felt isolated and alone.

In early 2008, I was asked by the Austrian Freedom Party to hold a series of fully sourced seminars in Vienna on Islam, explaining to interested parties what the *Qur'an* and the *hadith* [official collections of the sayings and doings of Mohammed] actually teach, along with the basic tenets of Islamic law. At the time, the Freedom Party was considered a right-wing extremist party. Truth be told, though, the Freedom Party was the only political party exhibiting interest in listening and learning about this challenging topic. I would gladly have held my seminars for all other political parties in Austria, including the Social Democrats and the Greens. Alas, no one was willing to listen. As I like to say: "You may choose to ignore Islam, but Islam does not ignore you." To this day, as far

---

8 *The Gathering Storm Show* (no longer active).

as I am aware, no other party has offered seminars on Islam. The other parties merely have devout Muslims advising them, to their and their voters' detriment.

For the next year and a half, the interest in my seminars grew and attendance increased. It should not have come as a surprise that the success of my lectures drew the interest of Austrian leftists, who are as determined as leftists in other Western countries to discredit and destroy the work of those they view as "racists," "fascists," and "Islamophobes." Unbeknownst to me, the left-wing weekly magazine *NEWS* sent a reporter to one of my seminars in October 2009 to make a surreptitious recording of it.

CHAPTER EIGHT

The Crucial Year

The smart way to keep people passive and obedient is to strictly limit the spectrum of acceptable opinion, but allow a very lively debate within that spectrum.
—Noam Chomsky

WEDNESDAY AFTERNOON, November 25, 2009, 3.15 PM, was a dreary day. I was busy doing household chores when my cell phone rang. It was Martin, a close friend of my husband's, and a media spokesperson for the Freedom Party. He asked whether I had seen the latest edition of *NEWS* magazine. "No, I haven't," I replied. "But it's Wednesday, so I assume you have the preview edition in your hands. What's the matter?"

Within minutes he faxed me the relevant pages of the cover story. My life would once again be changed dramatically.

"Strache's School of Hate—Undercover in the Freedom Party". The cover story presented my seminars in such a perverted way that I didn't recognize myself or what I had said. The reporter, a young lady by the name of Veronika Dolna (whom I remembered from a private conversation she had with me during one of the breaks for her over-enthusiasm), did what the mainstream media nowadays do best: she accused me of presenting Islam in a distorted and hateful way, while simultaneously doing the exact same thing concerning me. In her report, she accused me of "Islam-hatred," "Islam-bashing," "quoting selectively from the Qur'an," "interpreting at my own discretion," To her, I was a cold woman who spreads vitriolic rhetoric against Islam. Furthermore, she scolded me in print for "binge-eating donuts and bacon sandwiches during the break." This is what the mainstream media considers balanced reporting.

In a further story published by *NEWS*, bishops, rabbis, politicians, none of whom had ever attended any of my seminars and who knew nothing of the content, were asked to weigh in and condemn me. What pained me most was the comment of a Catholic bishop who said: "One must never speak about any religion the way Ms. Sabaditsch-Wolff did about Islam."

Dolna's report also showed a facsimile of the criminal complaint filed by *NEWS* and sent to the public prosecutor's office. The complaint showed that my "crime" was "hate speech" under Article 283 in the Austrian criminal code. This is when I decided I needed legal representation. Thankfully, my old friend Sylvia, also a journalist, but an honest one, was kind enough to get in touch with me right away and recommended Dr. Michael Rami. She also assisted me with my increasing media presence, coached me on what to say and what not say. I am very grateful to her. She also interviewed me for another weekly magazine, something unheard of nowadays.

My interview with Sylvia M. Steinitz in *Profil* magazine:

"I Am Against Dialogue"

A criminal complaint is being filed against Elisabeth Sabaditsch-Wolff for "hate speech" under Austrian law, essentially the same thing that Susanne Winter was convicted of early this year.

Elisabeth gave a presentation about Islam at an FPÖ-organized seminar, and said some of the usual things that anti-*jihad* advocates say when they talk about Islam. A left-wing magazine, which had planted someone in the audience, caused charges to be brought against her at the same time it was publicized in their magazine.

Elisabeth held the controversial Islam Seminar at the FPÖ-political academy. Charges of defamation of a religious group have been filed against the daughter of a diplomat. This is her only interview in which she explains her views.

Mrs. Sabaditsch-Wolff, are you afraid of Muslims?

No, I am afraid of political Islam, which is massively gaining influence in Europe. That is what I am against.

What is your goal?

I want to preserve Europe and its democratic and secular values.

What bothers you about the Islamic way of life?

Islamic doctrine discriminates against women and non-Muslims. Islamic law, or *shariah*, cannot be reconciled with democratic principles and universal human rights.

Do you see the need for that?

There are powerful groups who are working towards the Islamization of Europe. That is a fact. What can we gain from closing our eyes and ignoring this? Even Libyan leader Muammar Ghadafi says: "There are signs that Allah will grant victory to Islam in Europe without swords, without guns, without conquest. We don't need terrorists, we don't need homicide bombers. The 50+ million Muslims [in Europe] will turn it into a Muslim continent within a few decades." A head of state confirms what our politicians deny. What else has to happen until we finally get it?

There are people who see the growth of Islam in Europe as an opportunity for a completely re-engineered pluralistic society.

The vision of a pluralistic society does not withstand a reality check. Show me one example where this has been a success. Wherever Muslims have been given the opportunity for self-organization they have established parallel societies. See Berlin-Kreuzberg, see Lyon. See also Great Britain, where parts of shariah have been implemented.

Do you really think that Austrian culture is endangered?

I see signs of an erosion of our way of life. In large cities massive changes are evident in the streets. There are discussions about a ban on teaching the Turkish sieges of Vienna; St. Nicholas is banned from visiting children in [public] kindergartens.

And you want to change that.

Yes, very much. But why is that so bad? In Bhutan, the king is applauded because he allows only a certain number of foreigners into the country. He prescribes a certain dress code and mandatory cultural events. Bhutan is a small country that wants to retain its cultural identity in a globalized world. Austria is also a small country with similar challenges. Why is the one country commended and the other berated?

According to NEWS, you defamed Islam. That is why NEWS has filed charges citing defamation of religion. Your reply?

One can report anyone to the authorities. I am not guilty of defamation. And even if some consider my words harsh, I definitely did not make them in a public forum, since the seminars were held before a group of people who registered beforehand.

You are accused of making the following statements, among others: "Muslims rape children because of their religion," or "Mohammed enjoyed contact with children." Why the polemics?

This is a clever strategy. You and all the others who are now crying wolf are locked in a choice of words. As a result you are able to maneuver yourselves away from the main point. It is a fact that Mohammed married a six-year-old at the age of 56. To this day, men in Islamic countries view this as legitimizing marriage to a minor, thereby causing rape and life-long trauma. This is the problem we need to address, and not how to circumscribe this bitter reality.

Are you afraid that these customs will become part of Europe?

There are groups who have this goal. In every Islamic system you find that the human rights of young girls are in grave danger. Look at Saudi Arabia. Look at the former socialist South Yemen. When Khomeini came to power he lowered the minimum age for girls to get married to nine years.

You are being accused of Islamophobia. Does this bother you?

A phobia is an irrational fear. My worries are not irrational, but justified. One of these days our politicians will have to recognize this fact. People like me are not right-wing xenophobes.

But what are you?

We are people defending the principles of freedom and equality in a secular society. I criticize political Islam and its political manifestations. No democratic country can take this right away from anyone.

Why do critics of Islam nearly always use polemics?

And what [if not polemics] did the article in *NEWS* use? There are comments about my body, there is ridicule about how I eat. Sexist attacks below the belt against women making unpopular statements are a manifestation of a male-dominated system. There are many critics of Islam. However, it's always women like Brigitte Bardot or Oriana Fallaci who are attacked below the belt.

Leading politicians have sharply criticized your seminars. Are they all members of a male-dominated system?

These politicians do not know the contents of my seminars. All they know are out-of-context quotes from an article in a glossy magazine. I also find the reaction of these politicians strange. They get away with much worse.

For instance?

SPÖ secretary general Laura Rudas, who calls for a public ban of the headscarf. I would not do something like that.

On the other hand, you are being compared to Susanne Winter (FPÖ). She was convicted of defamation because she accused the prophet Mohammed of pedophilia.

I do not want to be compared to Susanne Winter. There are no similarities between us. She is an active politician; she acts in a public forum. I do not.

You hold your seminars for the FPÖ-Political Academy.

But I am not politically active. I am also not a member of FPÖ. What I do is offer seminars on the topic of Islam, and I can be booked. The FPÖ academy did just that. I do not want to comment on Susanne Winter's statements. But in my opinion she does not know much about Islam.

In what way are you qualified to hold these seminars?

I have an M.A. in Diplomatic and Strategic Studies. I spent part of my childhood in Islamic countries, worked and lived there. I have personally experienced life in Islamic societies and I see evidence of a trend towards the Islamization of Europe.

How do you view yourself?

I am a mother and a feminist. I want my daughter and my niece to grow up in freedom and dignity. I want the same for all Austrian citizens, and that includes Austrian Muslims.

In your seminar you do not distinguish between Muslims and Islamists.

Oh yes, I do. I do that because I know how much Muslims worldwide are suffering under the Islamic yoke. I say that in all my seminars, only *NEWS* did not bother to quote that. Why do think so many Muslims try to escape from Islamic countries like Iran and Afghanistan? Because life there is unbearable.

So you want to liberate Muslims from Islam?

Muslims have to liberate themselves from this static and tenacious Islam that is hell-bent on following norms from the seventh century. The result is that wherever there are Islamic societies there is no progress, but steps backwards, especially in the realm of human rights and democracy.

But isn't the referendum on the minaret ban in Switzerland also a step backwards?

The result of the referendum is the best proof that politicians should finally take the Islamization of Europe seriously.

What do you think about the reaction from the Islamic world regarding the referendum?

The Islamic world leads in discrimination against religious minorities. Christians are persecuted and discriminated against in all Islamic countries. You have to remember that the Christian culture is not one that immigrated or is foreign; it is indigenous. There is a complete ban on building churches in Turkey. And now Erdogan speaks of discrimination against Muslims in Switzerland? Where are Muslims being discriminated against in Switzerland? The European elite allows Islamic countries to walk all over them, all the while bowing down to them.

Are you in favor of a ban on minarets in Austria?

I will not answer that. Instead, I will quote the now so agitated Turkish prime minister who once said, "The mosques are our barracks, the domes our helmets, the minarets our bayonets and the faithful our soldiers."

Do you feel misunderstood?

Above all, I believe that my rights are being curtailed. Currently, I do not believe that I have freedom of speech or opinion.

Haven't you yourself strained this right?

No, I don't believe I did. Above all, I did not speak publicly. What is all the commotion about?

But now it has become public.

I only say out loud what others are thinking. But these concerns are not taken seriously.

Are you against a dialogue with the Islamic world?

I am against a dialogue with political Islam. I am, however, in favor of a broad discussion about human rights and personal freedoms.

You criticize Islam as discriminating. What do mean by that?

Just one example: In Islam non-Muslims are called kuffar, non-believers. These infidels are all defamed and not considered equal. This is offensive. Where are the protests?

What are your negative experiences in Islamic countries?

People in these countries are continuously restricted. This leads to aggressions and reporting people to the authorities and other absurd situations. For example, a (Coptic) member of the

Austrian embassy in Kuwait was verbally abused at the post office because he was mailing Christmas letters. It was Ramadan and he must not eat or drink publicly. He said, surprised, "But I am not eating!" "Oh yes, you are. You are licking off the adhesive part of the stamp." This is daily routine in an Islamic society.

Can you really use a single occurrence as an example?

I can tell you hundreds of similar single occurrences. This story is not a single case, but a social program.

Will you continue with your seminars?

Yes. There are requests coming in from all over Austria. I will continue to defend my right to freedom of speech. I will not be gagged.

My initial reaction to the *NEWS* report was one of utter shock, of disbelief, and of disgust. I was disgusted by the actions of a left-wing magazine, whose only goal was to destroy the Freedom Party and its popularity with voters. The Freedom Party was and still is reviled as a "xenophobic party" by leftist media and politicians. To this day I believe I was collateral damage; had it not been for my presentations, it would have been someone or something else.

I cannot deny that the days following the *NEWS* report were anything but easy. Understandably, my memories are blurry, but I did have meetings with Dr. Rami and the Freedom Party Education Institute about the strategy we would pursue. The biggest and most disappointing surprise was the reaction among some of my family. "You shouldn't have said that." Or "If you hadn't said anything, nothing would have happened." Now that is the worst one can say to me, the utter submission to speech codes. I was left speechless, and not just figuratively speaking. What a lack of understanding of the concept of free speech! In an interview with Diana West, I recounted the way my family reacted to the story:

> Elisabeth's husband, a military surgeon, is very supportive of her. "My mother had to come to terms with her daughter being maligned in the media," she says. "My sister has cocooned herself and believes the NEWS story rather than confronting reality. My father, who has attended all of my seminars, knows the truth and supports me 100 percent."
>
> Of course, when she enters that Vienna courtroom, she will face the state alone. "The thought that the state—a state that I

love very much and that I represented proudly all my life—is prosecuting me for thoughts is a painful one. It is hard to understand that I should have to stand trial for thoughts that are not only based on experience but are the product of careful study of the texts that make up Islam."

But Elisabeth Sabaditsch-Wolff is also standing trial for her courage, which threatens all states of denial. "It is interesting to note that once the topic is raised, most friends out themselves as feeling the exact same way I do, however, there is fear. They do not want to become active out of fear for losing their jobs (which is a very real possibility) or getting hurt by some Muslim wacko. My response is always, 'Fear is the wrong feeling here. We need to stand up and say, No to *Shariah*, gender apartheid, theocracy, parallel legal systems.'

"By the way," she adds. "I am being charged for saying all of this!"[1]

With the threat of a courtroom appearance hanging over my head I was immediately contacted by Pamela Geller and Robert Spencer, both of whom invited me to speak at the launch of their organization "American Freedom Defense Initiative" at CPAC in 2010. Not only would this be my first visit to the United States in nearly fifteen years, but it was there that my speaking career began. Because I was still teaching at an English language institute at the time, a job I would later lose as a direct result of the investigations for hate speech, I could only get away for two nights, but I was incredibly excited to travel to Washington D.C., of which I had fond memories from a week-long field trip during eighth grade. I spent the flight writing and rehearsing my first public speech, discussing my background, why there was a hate speech charge pending, and how I would henceforth focus on the right to free speech, which was increasingly coming under threat in Europe thanks to the ominous "European Union Framework Resolution for Combating Racism and Xenophobia." I also quoted Monika Maron, a former East German dissident and writer:

The debate [should not be] about Islam and its critics. It is about us, about our trust in democracy and our rights to insist on maintaining laws and a way of life which was achieved in centuries-long battles

---

1 http://dianawest.net/BlogArchive/tabid/56/EntryId/1579/Elisabeth-Sabaditsch-Wolff-Versus-the-State-of-Denial.aspx

against tyrants of both church and state.

The room Pamela Geller had rented at CPAC was jam-packed, leaving many of those who came late with standing room only. The event marked the beginning of my great and long lasting friendships with heroes such as Col. Allen West and Maj. Stephen Coughlin.

My first speech roused a crowd of 250-plus to standing ovations. I was flabbergasted that an Austrian housewife who only spoke the truth and who was accused of hate speech was suddenly considered a hero. I certainly don't see myself as a hero. A role model, perhaps, but I am essentially doing what everyone else should be doing every single day, that is, exercising my God-given right to free speech. That doesn't make me a hero, but normal and human.

The next day I had a meeting with the Austrian ambassador to the United States (an old friend of my dad's), and when I told him the story of my hate speech charges, he couldn't believe what he was hearing. While officially he could not agree, he did so privately. I asked myself: What good does that do?

The embassy driver took me and a young journalist to Capitol Hill, where I was due to speak to congressmen and staffers on the case at the invitation of the Center for Security Policy. The journalist was a young lady from a newspaper called *The Jewish State* (a newspaper for New Jersey's Jewish communities), and I enjoyed the interview with her because she was well-prepared and listened intently. To her I was a "high-profile personality in the growing movement against radical Islam's steadying foothold in Europe." She certainly got that right. She also wrote:

> Sabaditsch-Wolff insists that all she is doing is telling the truth, and she fully expects to stand trial on charges of hate speech.
> "We're going to reply to the charges and we will do that in full detail," Sabaditsch-Wolff told *The Jewish State* in an interview Feb. 19. "It remains to be seen whether the truth is a defense. I don't think it will be."
> If her case makes it to trial, it will be the first challenge to Austrian laws that ban hate speech against officially recognized religions, of which Islam is one. According to Austrian law, if a religion is recognized by the country, it is protected against hate speech unless the tenets of the religion go against the Austrian constitution. Christianity and Judaism have both been challenged and cleared in Austria, but Islam has not been challenged since it was incorporated under this law in 1912. While she did not intend to bring any case to court, now that

the opportunity has fallen in her lap, she plans to run with it.

Upon my return from my whirlwind trip to the US, a formal interview with the police brought me back to reality. I gave a deposition in the presence of my attorney, and neither of us could shake the feeling that the entire scene was surreal. In my seminars I defended democracy and freedom of speech, rejecting theocracy and calling for the rule of law, and here I was sitting before the Office for the Protection of the Constitution and the Prevention of Terrorism! This was ludicrous. At the time, my lawyer and I were still somewhat confident that the authorities would show some insight and come to the realization that my words were the truth and certainly not prosecutable. Boy, were we wrong!

After that, there was nothing from the prosecutor's office. Finally, on September 15, I found out that a formal charge would be filed against me. The travesty of the matter is that I did not learn of the charge filed against me through a court document.

I received no official summons.

It was not communicated through my lawyer.

No, that's not the way we do things in modern multicultural Austria. As is typical of the corrupt soft-totalitarian state known as the "European Union," I learned of the official charge via the Austrian media—in *NEWS*, the very same magazine that had published the undercover report and filed the complaint against me.

As I wrote at the time:

> I just had a long talk with my legal representation. This is a huge judicial scandal. My lawyer has tried to get the documents detailing my case and the charges. In vain. The public prosecutor cited "computer problems", the clerks said there is a note in my case that nothing is to be made public (wonder why the media knew about it then), and he was shoved from clerk to clerk, getting nothing. So, a far we know, I will be tried, but nothing else.
>
> I have nothing whatsoever in my hands. I cannot defend myself at the moment because neither my lawyer nor I know the precise charges.
>
> It makes me wonder about our judicial system. It is outrageous that the media in both Germany and Austria knew about this before the accused did.

A few days later, I received official notice from the court: my trial date would be November 23, 2010.

CHAPTER NINE

The Trial

What we will speak now?—The truth, even if it is a crime.
—W.A. Mozart - *Die Zauberflöte* (The Magic Flute)

EXACTLY A YEAR before my trial, in November 2009, *NEWS* magazine broke the story about the "hate school" against Islam and Muslims, with me stirring up hatred of innocent people, people from all walks of life—including a so-called journalist. After thoroughly researching Islamic doctrine, reading about it both online and offline, I had been so deeply disturbed by what I had read that I felt it was my duty to share what I had learned and experienced.

So it was with a heavy heart that I drove my daughter to school on November 23, 2010, all the while trying to explain to her that Mommy had a very hard day ahead of her. I asked her to be lenient with me in case I was cranky when she got home from school. When she inquired about what was going on, I answered: "Sweetheart, you are too young to understand, and I don't want to burden you with all of this. But I promise you I will explain everything as soon as you are old enough to understand." Satisfied with my words and a final "I love you," she jumped out of the car and made her way to school. I sighed, turned the car around and drove home to prepare for a day I would wish on no one.

The weeks before the trial were spent with hours of preparation. I searched for and found sources for every single accusation made by the prosecutor. I filled two files just answering these accusations.

The book that enjoys the central place of honor in the photo is *'Umdat al-salik wa 'uddat al-nasik*, or *The Reliance of the Traveller and Tools of the Worshipper*. It is commonly referred to as *Reliance of the Traveller* when cited in English.

A sample of books I consulted when preparing for the first round of my trial. Most important were copies of the Qur'an, the *Hadith* and *Reliance of the Traveller.*

This particular version is the Revised Edition (published 1991, revised 1994) and is *The Classic Manual of Islamic Sacred Law 'Umdat al-Salik by Ahmad ibn Naqib al-Misri (d. 769/1368) in Arabic with Facing English Text, Commentary, and Appendices*, edited and translated by Nuh Ha Mim Keller. The publisher is listed as Amana Publications in Beltsville, Maryland.

It is considered an authoritative source on Sunni Islamic law, because it is certified as such by Al-Azhar University in Cairo. There is no higher authority on Sunni Islamic doctrine than Al-Azhar; it is the closest equivalent to the Vatican that can be found in Islam.

So whatever you find in *Reliance of the Traveller* is definitive Islamic law. No Sunni Muslim jurist would argue against anything cited there.

And, as we would soon discover, everything that "denigrates religious teachings" in my seminar could be supported by one or more passages in al-Misri's treatise. From beating your wife to excising your daughter's genitalia: it's all in there.

However, this book still was unlikely to be an adequate defense for quoting and referring to it. It has been well-establis hed in a number of jurisdictions—including several in the West—that a non-Muslim who quotes the Qur'an accurately can still be convicted of "hate speech." This aligned with the definition of Islamic slander (also to be found in *Reliance*), which considers anything that insults Islam, whether true or false, to be defamation. I could still be convicted. Under the Shariah rules used in the brave new world of the Islamic Caliphate of Eurabia, I actually was guilty.

Nervous before the trial with Dr. Rami

Below is the original live blogging from that first day of my trial, as posted on the website *Gates of Vienna*:

10:34 (3:34 am): Opening remarks
The room has seats for 15, but 25 spectators are there. ATV[1] and other press asks for comments, but on advice of the lawyer I say "No comments now—after the hearings."

The judge informs me about my rights, that all I say can be used against me.

The public prosecutor makes a short summary of various conclusions from me, taken out of the context from eight hours of lectures. Without the context, they sound ominous, like speaking of a "Burqa ghost," comparing my statements to those of Susanne Winter, mention-

---

1   Private Austrian television station.

ing that Muhammad married a child of six, as well as the risk that we will eventually have a civil war.

I can't believe that the prosecutor apparently did not consider it necessary to prepare for the trial. No, he says, he has no questions for the defendant. The tape recording of my comments, the basis for the charge against me, he only heard "in excerpts."

The defense lawyer speaks of the principles of gender equality, freedom of religion, and the lack of reciprocity that exists in Islam, for example that other religions cannot be freely exercised in several Islamic countries. He adds that I grew up in Islamic countries and experienced the situation of women there directly.

He continues to explain that the statements mentioned were taken seriously out of context, and that some were not public, and thus not relevant to the case. And that the eight hours of recordings should be played to understand the context.

He proceeds to invoke three expert witnesses who will testify that I speak the truth:

- Wafa Sultan
- Hans Jansen
- Robert Spencer

10:53: The judge inquires if we are talking about Islamic extremism, or of Islam as such?

I explain that we are talking Islam as such, as defined by its scripture, and I quote Erdogan that there is no moderate Islam anyway.

The judge accepts playing of the tapes.

Then proceeds to ask about us being lied to 24 hours a day. I explain the concept of *taqiyya*. The judge says: "That is your interpretation." To which I respond: "No, this is the canonical interpretation."

Next question is: "Is Islam in a never-ending war with the West?"

I refer to history and newspapers to document that, and that *jihad* has at times been considered a pillar of Islam.

11:15: The "burqa ghost" story is related.

I took a photo of a woman in a burqa in Meidlinger Hauptstrasse, Vienna, and related this in my seminars. It is difficult to figure out why the public prosecutor finds this offensive, not to mention illegal. The defense asks about this. I explain a few things about freedom for women—all women—to decide for themselves.

A reference is then made to debates at OSCE,[2] where I discussed

---

2 Organization for Security and Cooperation in Europe.

child molestation, and said: Christian cardinals molest children in conflict with their religion; Muslims in line with theirs. As background the marriage between Muhammad and Aisha is related, as documented by several *hadith* authors.

Pedophilia is discussed, in light of Muhammad being the perfect example for Muslims, as stated in Qur'an 33:21. The *hadith* contain everything Muhammad ever did or said.

I explain what the *hadith* collections are, how they constitute an indispensable part of Islam, due to 33:21 and similar suras. And I emphasize that I am not making up statements, merely quoting canonical Islamic scripture.

11:34: The Judge opens a discussion if we're talking of "All Muslims" here.

I say no, for most Muslims do not know what is in the Qur'an, which is in a language (Arabic) they do not understand, and thus place their confidence in the imams for interpretations.

Here is my exchange with the judge:

Judge: "Is every Muslim a *jihadist*?"
Elisabeth: "No, not at all. But *jihad* is an obligation for Muslims."
Elisabeth: "Converts, not cultural Muslims, are problematic."
Elisabeth: "This is about the teachings of Islam, not about Muslims."
Judge: "You said Muslims in the seminars?"
Elisabeth: "Yes, in context that is needed to understand the relevance of this."
Judge: "What percentage of Muslims are *jihadis*?"
Elisabeth: "I do not know. Not the majority. One *promille* [per thousand] is enough to be a problem, though."

Then the quote about "Islam is s***" is debated. I point out that I was debating, using visual quotes, if it is legal or punishable to say "Islam is s***." Thus, what we are discussing here is the meta-question:

Is it illegal, or punishable, to debate the legality of saying: "Islam is s***"?

Update 12:06 (5:06am EST): The significant event at this point of the trial is the unwrapping of *'Umdat al-salik wa 'uddat al-nasik,* or *The Reliance of the Traveller.*

My defense lawyer goes through some points of the charges, asking me:

Lawyer: You said: "Muslims kill due to Islamic teachings. Christians also kill, but not due to their religious teachings." Are there not verses in the Bible that encourage killing?

Elisabeth: Not in the New Testament, and not actively used today.

The defense lawyer explains the death threats against Ayaan Hirsi Ali and the security she needs to live under.

Elisabeth tells about the killing of Theo van Gogh, and the Qur'an quotes used to justify that.

Lawyer: "Are there child marriages in Islamic countries?"

Elisabeth: "Yes, for example Saudi Arabia, Yemen, Afghanistan. Also the late Ayatollah Khomeini recommended pedophilia, and the current Iranian President Ahmadinejad recommends his teachings.

Elisabeth: According to Islamic law, these marriages are legal and justifiable.

Lawyer: Are corporal punishments, like chopping off of limbs, part of Islamic law?

Elisabeth: Yes, this is described for instance in *Reliance of the Traveller*.

[My defense lawyer and I have explained about the classical Sunni Islamic book *Reliance of the Traveller*, unwrapping a fresh copy in court.]

Update 12:40 (5:40am EST): The lawyer continues to ask me to explain various statements:

Lawyer: What is meant by "We are decadent"?

Elisabeth: That is the point of view of Islamic fundamentalists.

Lawyer: What is meant by "We do not want *shariah* here, full stop"?

Elisabeth: Free, secular societies is what we want.

Lawyer: What is meant by "Islamic law is not compatible with free societies, we need to understand this"?

Elisabeth: Islam is a whole, and this whole is not compatible with free societies like the Austrian.

Lawyer: Did you see any veiled Muslim men?

Elisabeth   (laughing): No, this is an obligation only for women.

Lawyer: You were referring to Paris, Brussels, Rotterdam. What is the meaning of that?

Elisabeth: This is a reference to the no-go zones, where shariah is effectively the law. There immigrant youths torch cars, throw stones at the police, etc.

Prosecutor: Are each and every one of these persons Muslims?

Elisabeth: The majority are.

Lawyer: What is meant when you say: "How many times have

we been told that Islam is a Religion of Peace?" Is this an incitement to hate or violence?

Elisabeth: I do not mean to incite hatred or violence. We need to be informed, make people aware, inform our politicians and write letters to the newspapers.

Lawyer: What is meant by "We do not want gender apartheid, polygamy"?

I explain polygamy in Islam, and the fact that this is a reality in Europe, today.

I finally discuss the First Amendment of the US Constitution, the absolute right to express ones' opinions, as a fundamental prerequisite for a sound democracy.

At this point, more people have arrived. There are 18 seats for the audience, 30-35 listeners total.

Final update 14:34 (7:34am EST): The remainder of the hearing has been postponed until January 18th, so it seems that my ordeal will be dragged out for at least several more months.

Below is the final report for the day:

> The *NEWS* journalist Veronika Dolna was called as a witness. Technicalities of her recording equipment were discussed by the judge, including the fact that of the first seminar, only half an hour was recorded.
>
> The judge inquired about some of the statements quoted being from breaks, not from the seminar proper. Only three to four persons heard those, not 32 or more, the criterion for a statement being "public." This is important for legal reasons, as only statements made to a large group can be punishable.
>
> The judge dug further into the methods of the journalist. Why did the journalist quote statements made in the breaks, not part of the lecture? The journalists says "For journalistic reasons." Also for dramaturgic reasons, that it makes for a more dramatic and catchy article.
>
> Further, the judge asked if it was made clear in advance that the journalist would be recording the seminars. She responded that she had not told anyone, as her work constituted "investigative journalism," a journalistic tool.
>
> The lawyer probed further into the issue of the quotes being part of the prepared seminar, or offhand comments in the breaks.
>
> Next, the events concerning the opera *Idomeneo* were discussed. The background is that the performance of this classical Mozart piece by Deutsche Oper Berlin, which was canceled due to Islamic pressure. The director had added decapitation of Buddha, Jesus and Muhammad

to the original play. Fear of unrest caused the play to be canceled. The well-known German magazine *Focus* had, in that context, written that we should under no circumstances cave in to pressure like this.

This rounded off the day after roughly three hours of hearings. Since there is a need to play the complete recordings (eight hours) from the seminars, the next hearing was scheduled for January 18th.

The proceedings had a serious breach of procedure: The journalist from *NEWS* had not been summoned as a witness, yet was permitted to take the stand. Witnesses are not permitted to be present at the hearings before they are summoned. The defense lawyer will look into possible consequences of this.

What an exhausting experience, one that I never wanted to go through again. Due to the adjournment I would have to do just that, but first I needed some rest to celebrate Christmas without having to think about the January trial date.

A few days before the January trial date, I penned the following:

With just a few days remaining before the next stage of my trial, I had two interesting encounters with two quite different friends. Both kept me thinking very hard even after we parted ways.

Allison is the mother of twin girls who went to kindergarten with my daughter. Allison and her husband are liberals in the sense of "live and let live." They have no connection with religion, any religion, and they believe that everyone should have the freedom to believe in whatever they want, to dress in any way they want, to eat whatever they want. We have had many a discussion about what I do and what I believe in, and although we are friends, they have always told me that they think that what I do is wrong in the sense that I am unfairly attacking Muslims.

Allison called me the other night. We talked, and when I told her that I was sad that she and her husband had chosen the United Arab Emirates for their next vacation, she answered that I was a radical. I asked, somewhat surprised, why she thought that.

"Well, I see the hatred in your face when you see a woman in a head-scarf on the street."

"What?" I answered. "How can you tell? Can you read my mind?"

In any case, I do not hate people, but I criticize the ideology that forces women to cover up, that takes away a woman's right to choose her life and her destiny, an ideology that enslaves women. I inform people about the contents of the Qur'an and am thus a "hate preacher." Or, in other words, by teaching the Qur'an I am preaching "hate." And people listening to me will feel hatred.

"But you also hate the woman; I can see that," she replied.

I then told her the following: "Allison, once again: how do you know that? Can you read my thoughts? Furthermore, your belief in 'live and let live' can only work if everyone adheres to it. But Islam does not call for 'live and let live.' In any case, you are actually saying what the prosecutor is saying, that this woman hates Muslims, hates Islam, incites other people to hate Muslims by feeling hatred towards Muslims. You should be hoping for a guilty verdict, because you believe you know what I feel."

She was shocked. Apparently I had nailed her. "No, not at all. I want to you to win, with all my heart. You need to win."

"But you're saying something very different, Allison."

"Well, actually I want you to win for your daughter's sake."

Note that she didn't say: I want you to win because you're right. Or: You have the right to your opinions, even though I may not agree with them. No, she said: For your daughter's sake.

"I want you to win because your daughter should not have to deal with a mother who was found guilty in court. She won't understand it."

We then decided to change the subject, but afterwards the conversation continued to linger in my mind. What had happened here? Was I wrong? I can only repeat myself for the umpteenth time that I do not hate Muslims (as a matter of fact, I do not hate anyone, period), but liberals do not believe people like me. No matter what I say or do, it seems they are projecting their own bigotries onto me. I am merely holding up a mirror. What they see is not my—non-existent—hatred, but their own.

The next day I met my neighbor and friend Samantha. During our neighborly small talk I told her that I was busy preparing for my case, and this prompted her to say in a near-whisper, "You know, I have been following your case, and though I wasn't always so sure about what you stood for I can tell you now that I think you're spot on. I admire you. I do not have the courage to do what you are doing, but you are doing the right thing. I also tell my friends that I think you are right and you need to be supported. They criticized you heavily before, but they are also starting to understand."

Not only did Samantha's words move me to tears, but I was amazed at her honesty in admitting that she had actually studied my words and found them to be the truth. And this is what I hope the court will also conclude after careful study of my arguments. One may not agree with my statements, but they are still true. No matter how painful the truth may be, it must remain what it is: the truth.

Day 2 of the trial – January 18, 2011

The Tundra Tabloids [a Finnish blog] reports that my lawyer and I are more than ready and willing to prove the truthfulness of everything spoken at the seminars, underlining that this is about the right to tell the truth without fear of legal punishment. For telling the truth can never be illegal in a free society, and the truth should always be the foundation for the defense and the aim for any court proceeding.

January 18, my husband's birthday. Instead of celebrating with him, I once again made my way to the courthouse with a heavy heart. As on the previous day, the events in the courtroom were live-blogged:

9:14: It's a hazy day in Vienna, and we're awaiting the start of the second hearing in the case against Elisabeth Sabaditsch-Wolff, who is charged with "Inciting hatred" and "Denigrating the teachings of a recognized religion" in her seminar to FPÖ about political Islam.

Update 9:50am (Vienna time):

Some 30 persons are present, including several journalists and Austrian television.

Defense hands over the translation of relevant parts of *Reliance of the Traveller*. The judge verifies basic personal facts about Elisabeth, then proceeds directly to playing the seminar tapes. Noise is quite audible in the recordings. This goes to the heart of our problems with terrorism and Islamic fundamentalism, and will be reproduced in part here.

First issue taken up in the seminar is the Muslim Brotherhood and its extensive political influence in Austria and Europe, and its desire to implement religious rule (*shariah*) where possible, and the use of terrorism to pursue this objective as well as the lamentable lack of strong, moderate voices from Islam.

The *hadith* is quoted, for it consists of what Muhammad did and said, the ideal for pious Muslims and the foundation for *shariah* law, which basically codifies Qur'anic commandments and behavior described in the *hadith* into what is today Islamic law.

You can hear Elisabeth say: "There is no Islam without *shariah*, that cannot be separated. *Shariah*-based societies have been known for many centuries, and still exist today. The aim is to establish an order of society similar to that Muhammad had decreed and exemplified. The ultimate aim of Islamists today remains the same: to implement *shariah* as widely as possible, ideally throughout the world. Sura 9:5 is an example of this:

Then when the Sacred Months (the 1st, 7th, 11th, and 12th months of the Islâmic calendar) have passed, then kill the *Mushrikûn* (see

V.2:105) wherever you find them, and capture them and besiege them, and prepare for them each and every ambush. But if they repent and perform *As-Salât (Iqâmat-as-Salât)*, and give *Zakât*, then leave their way free. Verily, Allâh is Oft-Forgiving, Most Merciful.
(*as-Salat* is Islamic prayer, *Zakat* Islamic tax.)"

10:00am: Brief update:

Next mentioned is *taqiyya*—the permission and/or obligation to lie towards non-Muslims when doing so will further the cause of Islam. The Qur'an, Bukhari and Muslim *hadith* scriptural references are given for this. Also described in detailed in *Reliance of the Traveller* chapter 8.

Dr. Rami interrupts, asking for a clarification of the relevance of this passage. There seems to be a difference from the transcript. PowerPoint presentations are brought out to clarify.

The playing of the tape continues; Elisabeth is heard saying: "The religiously-sanctioned lying is difficult for our politicians to handle. It is not clearly described in the Qur'an, is mainly based on *hadith*, drawn on Muhammad's tactics against his enemies."

Some discussion with the audience follows. References are made to a variety of Qur'an verses, and the principle of abrogation[3] in Islam.

Final update 11:12am:

Dr. Rami interrupts to point out that the quiet, factual tone of the seminar demonstrates that this is not hate speech, but an educational setting going through relevant documentation.

Dr. Rami also highlights the question from the first seminar, if it would remain legal to say "Islam is bull****", pointing out that this was not a statement of fact (visual "quoting" had been used by Elisabeth to indicate this). The relevant seminar recording is selected to be played next.

Back to the seminar tapes. Euro-Islam is discussed. "Muslims hate us." Elisabeth is heard saying: "Who here would dare go in the street with a sign: 'Islam is Bull****!'?"

The judge discusses the statement that the conduct of Muhammad is exemplary for Muslims, including the problem of Muhammad marrying a six-year-old girl, and what exactly that would be called today, if

---

3 The concept of "abrogation" in the Qur'an is that Allah chose to reveal *ayat* (a verse in the Qur'an) that supersede earlier *ayat* in the same Qur'an. The central verse that deals with abrogation is Surah 2:106: "None of Our revelations do We abrogate or cause to be forgotten, but We substitute something better or similar: Knowest thou not that Allah Hath power over all things?"
https://www.answering-islam.org/Authors/Farooq_Ibrahim/abrogation.htm.

not pedophilia.

Dr. Rami interrupts the playback, pointing out that the purpose of playing the tapes has been accomplished, namely demonstrating that the sessions were scholarly, thoroughly documented, and in no way constituted "incitement to hatred" or similar.

The judge adjourns the hearing, scheduling the next one for February 15th at 10:30.

[Reason for the adjournment, according to German-language sources:

The judge has introduced a new charge: denigration of religious teachings. Elisabeth's lawyer was not prepared for this.]

So, rather than the hoped-for verdict, the trial was adjourned until February 15th.

What happened?

On the first day of the trial the previous November, my lawyer, Dr. Rami, had insisted on playing the incriminating tapes that had been recorded without permission during my seminar. However, due to technical reasons the court was unable to play the tapes, and the task was postponed until the most recent court session on Tuesday January 18.

Instead of playing the entire four hours of tape, Dr. Rami decided after the first 45 minutes that the court had heard enough to prove that there was no incitement to hatred or anything else. Rather, it was very clear that the tone and setting of the seminar was one of sober respect.

It was thus a complete surprise when the judge—not the prosecutor!—proceeded to inform us that the charge of "denigrating religious teaching of a legally recognized religion" was added to the existing charges. My lawyer immediately demanded a postponement so that the defense could prepare a new strategy.

Although the charge of "incitement to hatred" carried a higher sentence, it was more difficult to prove. The added charge, however, now made a conviction—and thus the need for an appeal—more likely.

A new wrinkle in my case appeared a few days after the second day of my trial, when the Austrian newspapers reported that I could be heard on the seminar tape saying that "Euro-Islam is s***." This was a blatant falsehood—the tape clearly indicated that I said no such thing.

The story is that APA (Austria Press Agency) sent a young man to follow the proceedings, and he "misheard" me say "Euro-Islam is s**," when in fact I said "Euro-Islam is wishful thinking." The phrases in German are *Euro-Islam ist Scheiße* versus *Euro-Islam ist Wunschdenken*, so there was obviously no possibility that the reporter had confused two similar-sounding words—this was a malicious misquote.

My counsel immediately initiated a libel suit against all newspapers that had printed the falsehood.

One of my supporters, Maria Stückler, penned a letter to the editor of *Die Presse* about the newspapers' libel against me:

The Trial concerning the Islam Seminar: "The Muslim lies"

I was at the trial of Mrs. Sabaditsch-Wolff, but did not hear the statement: "Euro-Islam is s***." Rather, I remember [the statement] "Euro-Islam is wishful thinking." And the statement, "Islam is crap" only served to demonstrate how poor the situation for freedom of expression already is in Austria (as in all of Europe).

I also did not hear "the Muslim lies," but I did hear "we are being lied to 24 hours a day," and indeed with reference to and explanation of the principle of *taqiyya*, that is, legitimized lying to infidels. Countless statements attest that the representatives of Islam practice this principle: [saying] for instance, that the Qur'an forbids the beating of women, but in truth it commands men to do it—even on mere suspicion. Or that stoning has nothing to do with *shariah*, but everything to do with patriarchy, but Mohammed himself practiced it and Iran, for instance, still uses this punishment today. Or that Islam guarantees religious freedom, while in reality it provides the death penalty for apostasy. Or that Islam is peace and tolerance, but *shariah* declares the perpetual duty of holy war and massively discriminates against subjugated non-Muslims. Prof. Bassam Tibi (himself a Muslim) on the Christian-Islamic dialogue: "Blessed are the Deceived."

It is not Mrs. Sabaditsch-Wolff who alleges Mohammed's pedophilia, but the basic Islamic texts themselves: At the age of over 50, he married a nine year-old girl. And the Qur'an, too, in its regulations governing divorce, assumes as fact the marriage of pre-pubescent girls. Up to now, Islamic legal scholars from Morocco to Indonesia (including the NU as the largest Muslim organization in the country) have justified child marriages by reference to the example of Mohammed and to the Qur'an. In numerous Islamic countries, the law does not even recognize a minimum age. So if this statement represents a "derogation of religious teachings," then one can only say: "It is Islam and its Prophet themselves that are derogating Islam and its Prophet." Nothing demonstrates more clearly than this the relationship of Islam and common sense.

When the media spread untrue claims about critics of Islam, that then apparently falls under the category of freedom of the press. If someone states uncomfortable truths about Islam, however, it can happen that that person is accused by the media of hateful incitement.

The media should not forget that freedom of expression is the basis of freedom of the press, so much more so, as—according to "EU Framework Decision against Racism and Xenophobia"—truth is not a mitigating factor.

And human rights organizations should not forget that without freedom of expression, all other human rights are obsolete. It is high time for them to begin fighting against the hate-speech laws, which have entered the EU by the back door.

And the politicians should be reminded that human rights are not a political instrument which they can manipulate at will. Rather, they should respect them, and not criminalize them.
—Maria Stückler

Thank you, Mrs. Stückler, for these true words. While thankfully they were printed—this would be impossible nowadays—unsurprisingly, even back then they made no difference to public opinion.

It should come as no surprise to my readers that the judge ruled against me. In laymen's terms, while it was proven (in this separate court case) that I did not utter the words "Euro-Islam is shit," I have no right to be compensated because I said "so many other things that are very bad." According to the judge,

> She even made the presumptuous claim that Muslims rape their children because of their religion, and that this is absurd needs to be elaborated. [...] Because the defendant also said these words in another court case, while trying to prove these allegations by insinuating that according to Islamic tradition, Mohammed had an underage wife and consummated the marriage with her, *proves her Islamophobic frame of mind, which she tries to depict through her pseudo-religious knowledge* and which she tries to hide behind her alleged right to freedom of speech. Of course, she does not prove why her statements—without any historical connotation—and the obvious fact that *every founder of every religion is in general worthy of veneration* would lead to the deduction that Muslims "rape" their children due to their religion.[4] (Emphasis added)

The judge's reasoning is as incorrect as it is insidious. Like Judge Bettina Neubauer, this judge said it didn't really matter whether I had made the statement or not, because my sentiments amounted to the

---

4 Court case 113 Hv 69/11m, dated September 27, 2011. My own translation.

same thing. According to the judge, it is irrelevant that I never said those words, because I was already on trial for similar words. Moreover, he accused me of Islamophobia, an invented term intended to silence any discussion of Islam by non-Muslims and which carried no legal definition—a smart strategy, from his point of view, since he did not have to address the substance of my arguments. By throwing out my lawsuit, he stifled the debate. My only regret is that I never challenged the judge's reasoning in this respect.

Additionally, the judge accused me of "pseudo-religious knowledge," insinuating that only Muslims (and those with a university degree in Islamic theology) are capable of understanding Islam. This classic Muslim rationale does not belong in an Austrian court of law. Furthermore, according to the judge, I was trying to portray my views as my right, thanks to freedom of speech; however, I was unable to explain coherently why—if founders of religions in their own religions are venerated—I could make the deduction that Muslims for religious reasons sexually abuse children. Therefore, the lack of evidence was expected. And finally, that "every founder of every religion is worthy of veneration" is a patently false statement. First, basic knowledge of Islam would have helped the judge in this case: a devout Muslim does not venerate Mohammed; instead, the Qur'an[5] calls upon Muslims to emulate the prophet Mohammed in every way. Second, does the sentence "every founder is worthy of veneration" mean that I am, that everyone is, supposed to venerate Mohammed? And what if I don't? (I know the answer to that question, both from a Muslim and a non-Muslim point of view.)

Not content with simply brushing aside the fact that I never made the offensive statement reported in the media, the judge decided to psychoanalyze me from the bench. This is what passes for "justice" in Modern Multicultural Austria.

The psychoanalysis continued. Shortly after the second day of my trial, Carla Amina Baghajati, a prominent Muslim convert and spokeswoman for Islam in Austria, was interviewed by a women's monthly magazine.[6] One can learn a lot about the politically correct *zeitgeist* in Austria from the questions asked, and the responses by Ms. Baghajati provide insights into the strategies employed by Austrian Muslims when

---

5   Qur'an 33:21 "Surely there was a good example for you in the Messenger of Allah." *Towards Understanding the Quran*, Sayyid Abul A'la Mawdudi, UK Islamic Mission Dawah Centre, Birmingham (UK).

6   Amina Baghajati's interview is translated into English at *Gates of Vienna* Feb. 10, 2011. https://gatesofvienna.net/2011/02/a-dangerous-mindset/.

exploiting that *zeitgeist*. The interview is full of brazen assertions served up for the gullible readers. Here are few of them:

- I am suffering from selective perception.
- A fringe group is spreading dangerously superficial knowledge about Islam.
- No one knows what shariah really is.
- *Reliance of the Traveller* is not an Islamic law book that you can buy in the bookstore.
- Muslims are the ones who have chiefly been attacked and insulted in Austria.
- The latest research shows that Aisha at the time of the consummation of her marriage could not have been nine years old but was ten years older, that is, 19.
- Only if someone were in mortal danger if revealed as a Muslim would he be allowed to lie and say: No, I am not a Muslim.
- Muslims are against forced marriage in principle—all the more of children!

I am fascinated by what today would be called "alternative facts." And what is more irksome is that Ms. Baghajati gets away with her assertions, since any criticism would be equated with "hateful discourse" and bring accusations of "Islamophobia."

February 15, 2011

VERDICT: GUILTY ON THE COUNT OF DENIGRATION OF RELIGIOUS TEACHINGS, NOT GUILTY ON THE COUNT OF HATE SPEECH.

My recollections of this day up to the announcement of the verdict are non-existent; it's as if I wasn't even there. I have to rely on what was live-blogged that day. However, I do remember the following in slow-motion:

The judge shuffled the papers in front of her, pulled out a sheet and said to me:

"Please rise for the verdict."

"You are not guilty on the charge of hate speech. [...] You are guilty on the charge of denigration of religious teachings of a legally recognized religion in Austria." The judge continued:

Judge: The integration of Muslims is surely a question of particular public interest—you are allowed to be critical—but not incitement of hatred.

[judge states the permitted utterances]

The language used in the seminars were not inciting hatred, but the utterances regarding Muhammad and pedophilia were punishable.

"Pedophilia" is factually incorrect, since pedophilia is a sexual preference which solely or mainly is directed towards children. This does not apply to Mohammad. He was still married to Aisha when she was 18.

Did you understand the sentence?

[discontent in court]

I may have said, "I understand the sentence, but I do not agree with it."

Feeling my eyes bulging out of their sockets, I stared at the judge. Did she just argue that Mohammed married a six-year-old, consummated the marriage when she was nine years old and because she stayed with him until his death, i.e. until she was 18, this cannot be called pedophilia?

Judge Bettina Neubauer

The judge second-guessed the Qur'an by saying Aisha was 18. She evidently noted that Aisha was 18 years old when Mohammed died, which is factual. The implication is that because he did not divorce her after she became above legal age, he was not a pedophile.

She said it's not pedophilia, because Mohammed had no exclusive desire for underage girls; he wanted any female he could get his hands on. By implication, the child marriages so prevalent in hardcore Islamic countries cannot be legally categorized as "pedophilia," either.

I remarked angrily after the verdict when I saw the judge turning the corner outside the courtroom: "This is a sad day for my daughter and all girls."

Convicted for speaking out against sex with minors. How's that? Because I insisted that sex with minors is pedophilia, I am guilty of denigrating religious teachings. Well, that tells us all we need to know about Islam, doesn't it?

I was fined €480 (US$550), which on the surface looks "doable." But it really is a harsh sentence, in my view. I received a sentence of 120 "day fines" of €4 each because I did not have a job. Had I had a (well-paid) job, the day fine could have been as high as €100 or more per day. You do the math. In addition, the sentence was one third of the maximum sentence, and I was a first-time offender!

When posting about the case, many commentators used the following quote from *Alice's Adventures in Wonderland* because it so aptly describes the reality of my case:

> 'Let the jury consider their verdict,' the King said, for about the twentieth time that day.
>
> 'No, no!' said the Queen. 'Sentence first – verdict afterwards.'
>
> 'Stuff and nonsense!' said Alice loudly. 'The idea of having the sentence first!'
>
> 'Hold your tongue!' said the Queen, turning purple.
>
> 'I won't!' said Alice.
>
> 'Off with her head!' the Queen shouted at the top of her voice. Nobody moved.
>
> 'Who cares for you?' said Alice, (she had grown to her full size by this time.) 'You're nothing but a pack of cards!'
>
> At this the whole pack rose up into the air, and came flying down upon her: she gave a little scream, half of fright and half of anger, and tried to beat them off, and found herself lying on the bank, with her head in the lap of her sister, who was gently brushing away some dead leaves that had fluttered down from the trees upon her face.
>
> 'Wake up, Alice dear!' said her sister; 'Why, what a long sleep you've had!'
>
> —From Chapter 12 of *Alice's Adventures in Wonderland* by Lewis Carroll

Unlike Alice, I do not have the luxury of waking up from the surreal judicial drama into whose rabbit hole I fell.

Like the Queen and the King of Wonderland, the prosecution and the judge in my case apparently settled on the sentence long before considering a verdict. My trial was as nonsensical as that of the Knave. Like Alice, mine was the only voice of sanity in a courtroom full of madmen.

But the rabbit hole goes even deeper than that. The judge in the case, Bettina Neubauer, convicted me for saying that Mohammed was a pedophile. There's only one problem: I never said any such thing. As the transcript of my seminar demonstrates, I in fact said that "Mohammed had a thing for little kids," the plain facts of which even the judge was forced to accept.

In other words, the judge in my trial, acting on her own initiative, put words into my mouth and then convicted me for saying them.

If only The Hon. Neubauer were the Red Queen in a pack of cards!

If only we could all wake up from this feverish nightmare!

The irony of this entire ten-year legal ordeal is that I did, however, use the word "pedophilia" in my seminar, but only to describe what Susanne Winter had done to earn her own "hate speech" conviction.[7] I explained all of this in the following post:

In my seminar I described a conversation with my sister.

It was January 2007, I think, and my sister called me about the scandal Susanne Winter had caused by saying what she said. I told her that it was public knowledge that Mohammed had married a six-year-old and consummated the marriage when she was nine. I then said that if this isn't pedophilia, then what is?

She said, no, you can't say it that way, you have to word it differently, more diplomatically.

I said, well tell me how. She was silent—she didn't know.

What's important here is that I was recounting a story that happened before Winter had been convicted, and it was the only time on record that I actually used the word.

In all other instances I circumvented the word by saying "Mohammed had a thing for little kids," knowing that Winter had been convicted for saying what she said.

And still, Judge Bettina Neubauer called me a "repeat offender" and fined me heavily.

Here are the exact words for which I was found guilty:

---

7 Rabinowiz, Beila. "Austrian Politician Faces Jail For Remarks About Islam," *Pipeline News,* January 15, 2007.

7.   One of the biggest problems we are facing today is that Mohammed is seen as the ideal man, the perfect human being, the perfect Muslim. It is imperative for a devout Muslim to copy Mohammed. This is not according to today's standards or our way of life or laws. This is because he was a warlord, had had plenty of women, to put it this way, and he had a thing for children. And according to our standards he was not a perfect human. As a result we are faced with huge problems, because Muslims are in conflict with democracy and our value system.

[…] and when we speak about the Al-Bukhari collection of *hadith* you can be certain that this is recognized by all [Sunni] Muslims. And it is in Al-Bukhari where we can find the information about Aisha and sex with children.

8.   I remember talking with my sister — and I have recounted this story a few times already — about Susanne Winter's infamous talk. My sister called me on the phone, saying, "Oh my God, did you tell her that?" "No, it wasn't me, but you can find it in the books, it's not a secret." She: "But you can't say it that way." Me: "A 56-year-old and a six-year-old? What do you call that? Give me an example. What do you call it if not pedophilia?" She: "Well, you have to use a circumlocution, be more diplomatic." My sister is symptomatic. We have heard this so often: "Those were different times." I say, No, [this behavior] wasn't OK back then and it is not OK today. Period. And this (old men marrying young girls) is still happening today. This is never to be condoned.

The day after the verdict, my attorney sent me the following letter explaining in legal terms what the judgment meant.

> Gheneff-Rami-Sommer
> Attorneys at Law
> To: Mrs. Elisabeth Sabaditsch-Wolff
> February 15, 2011
> Elisabeth Sabaditsch-Wolff Trial
> 112 HV 144/10g, Regional Criminal Court Vienna
>
> Dear Mrs. Sabaditsch-Wolff,
>
> As you know, the main trial in the above-named case took place on February 15, 2011.
> After your supplemental interrogation, the requests for evidential interrogation of witnesses Wafa Sultan, Hans Jansen and Robert Spencer — previously not dealt with by the court — were rejected, because

the court of first instance perceived their statements to be valuations ("subjective assertions"), to the content of which the requested witnesses could contribute nothing. The request to question Ilse Albrecht was refused because she would only have been able to testify subjectively whether she was upset or angry at your comments on Mohammed.

In conclusion the welcome verdict was announced: You were exonerated of the charge of incitement according to § 283 StGB. The court found your statements on Islam permissible in the sense of Art 10 European Human Rights Convention, since according to this regulation criticism must be made in a provocative manner. Our arguments were agreed to in their entirety.

You were found, however, to have committed the offense of § 188 StGB (Austrian penal code; denigration of a legally recognized religion) because of your statements in the seminars of October 15, 2009 and November 12, 2009 about Mohammed and his sexual intercourse with nine year-old Aisha. The judge's basis for that focused on the circumstance that the offense of § 188 StGB is an abstract criminal threat, and therefore the mere aptness to cause offense was sufficient to qualify as the crime. What was incomprehensible was the judge's conclusion that Mohammed's sexual contact with nine-year-old Aisha was not pedophilia, because Mohammed continued his marriage to Aisha until his death.

Punishment was set at 120 per diem payments of €4, in total €480 or an alternative sentence of 60 days imprisonment.

Further, the costs of the trial must be paid.

The verdict does not have the force of law, since we as well as the prosecutor have announced the intention to appeal by reason of invalidity and because of the remarks about culpability and sentencing.

We have four weeks after receipt of the copy of the verdict to execute the appeal.

With warm greetings, I remain

Dr. Michael Rami

Take a deep breath and think about the implications of this letter. I was convicted for stating the plain facts: the prophet Mohammed had sex with a nine-year-old-girl. I never used the word pedophilia; I simply described in everyday language the prophet's... ahem... tastes.

The statements I made are not considered false by observant Muslims. They are written down in Islamic scripture, and are considered correct and authoritative by virtually every Islamic scholar and theologian.

These scriptural passages are not considered offensive to Muslims when they are recited in a mosque or a madrassa. Mohammed was the perfect man, so by definition his actions cannot be offensive. They are in fact exemplary. That is why Muslim men continue to marry little girls to this day.

My statements are offensive because they were made by a non-Muslim in public, and brought discredit upon Islam in the eyes of other non-believers. This offense is referred to as "Islamic slander" and is a grave violation of Islamic law. Under *shariah*, the penalty is death.

But it is only illegal under shariah.

The verdict had nothing to do with Austrian law, or European law. It was based solely on the unwritten laws of politically correct multiculturalism, which absolutely forbids the offending of Muslims.

This entire judicial farce was necessary in order to establish a *shariah*-based precedent in Austria. Whether the judge realizes it or not, her role in the case was to enforce Islamic law in the country formerly known as Austria. Welcome to the Caliphate.

The decision by the Vienna court did not go unremarked by the Austrian press, especially *Die Presse*. And not all coverage and opinion was politically correct: the take by Christian Ortner[8] on my case is incisive and refreshingly candid. I emphasize that this comment would not be published today.

Following Christian Ortner's second op-ed,[9] the final discussion on what transpired in the courtroom took place between Mr. Farid Hafez and myself.

Naturally, the Muslim side needed to counter these opinions with the Muslim point of view, and so sent an intellectual to do the job. Mr. Farid Hafez is a political scientist and who, along with another political scientist, is the co-editor of the yearly "Handbook of Islamophobia" in Austria.

I usually choose to ignore comments like those of Mr. Hafez. But in this case, I felt compelled to counter because he attacked me personally. Much to my surprise — and that of the Austrian Counterjihad — my comment was published right away. Knowing what we know about the

---

8 Ortner, Christian. "Why Does the Vienna Criminal Court Care About Mohammed's Sex Life?" *Die Presse*, Feb. 2011. English translation at *Gates of Vienna* https://gatesofvienna.net/2011/02/whose-law-rules-in-austria/.

9 Ortner, Christian. "There Is Freedom of Expression in Europe — So Long as Only the One Opinion Is Expressed," *Die Presse*, March 23, 2011. https://diepresse.com/home/meinung/quergeschrieben/christianortner/644646/In-Europa-herrscht-Meinungsfreiheit-solange-nur-eine-Meinung.

Austrian media, this is nothing less than sensational!

Next came the response from Farid Hafez. Hafez is a political scientist, teaches at the university, and is publisher of the *Yearbook for Research in Islamophobia*. Among other things, Hafez stated the following:

> What kind of philosophy does this woman represent when she messianically claims that she began her anti-Islam campaign for her daughter? Because in the end this daughter would be living in a country where burqas, and honor killing as well as genital mutilation will be considered cultural enrichment. It is beyond debate that this view of the world is sick. Let us assume that this is simply consciously-applied intelligence. Then we are talking about hostility to Islam as a strategy. That does not make things any better. Because this strategy must fall on fertile ground.
>
> Here is where the insanity becomes really obvious. It is about the delusion of Islamization which is used over and over by right-wing politicians. As the delusion of Jewish capital that ruled the world existed, so today the delusion of Islamization is being pushed.[10]

Die Presse surprised me by publishing my response.[11] However, the editors cut parts of my text, some of which were significant. Here it is in full:

Elisabeth Sabaditsch-Wolff, M.A.
Housewife and Mother

Critique of Islam: Not "sick" But Very Healthy!

Farid Hafez—a so-called expert on Islamophobia—is now commenting on me personally. That is fine, since until now my case has been completely ignored by the Austrian media following the motto, "Don't touch it with a ten-foot pole." Admittedly, I would find it preferable, and more significant, if Hafez dealt with the content of my many talks rather than launching *ad hominen* attacks against me. But he, like so many other Islam apologists, specifically avoids answering me and the many other critics of Islam with factual arguments. It is these very apologists who always switch from the factual to the emotional level, because they

---

10 Hafez, Farid, "When Freedom of Expression Is Confused With Incitement Against Islam," *Die Presse*, March 29, 2011.

11 Sabaditsch-Wolff, Elisabeth, "The Islamization of Europe Is No Delusion," *Die Presse*, March 30, 2011.

are so vulnerable through their own documents.

I assume Mr. Hafez is acquainted with the contents of the Qur'an, the Hadith and the Sira (the biography of Mohammed). I therefore also assume that he is acquainted with the over 200 Qur'an verses which explicitly call for hatred against and killing of so-called kuffar (Islamic designation for infidels, *ergo* non-Muslims) and are preached week after week in mosques. I further assume that Mr. Hafez knows the Doctrine of Abrogation which makes legally obligatory the replacement of several, older Meccan verses with later, substantially more hostile Medinan verses. Mr. Hafez, I am not "claiming" anything—I am simply proving the calls for violence by quoting from the Qur'an. Now, before I am accused of arbitrarily quoting out of context—There is no context in the Qur'an, since the chapters are arranged in order of their length and not according to connectedness. But of course Mr. Hafez knows all this quite well.

Mr. Hafez—like all other representatives of the Islamic religious community—does not go into all this. It is much simpler to ignore the content and instead smear and revile the messenger. That is true for me as it is for Geert Wilders. The turn of phrase "global crusader" reveals Mr. Hafez as someone who is very familiar with the language of the Organization of the Islamic Conference—the second-largest world-wide organization—for the OIC, which is the leader in affairs having to do with Islamophobia. It is of no interest to them that a phobia is an irrational fear, while critics of Islam have been dealing with the teachings of Islam for many years. There is no Islamophobia. There is only the fear of the Left and the Islamists that normal people will be informed about the true Islam.

Mr. Hafez further laments "this exclusion of people marked out as 'other' which has nothing to do with freedom of expression." And yet only three percent of Turks want to marry a local woman, while it is forbidden for Turkish women to marry non-Turkish men or infidels. This in contrast to 80 percent of Russian immigrants, who do not feel compelled to seek a "pure-faith" woman in their homeland. Who is excluding whom, Mr. Hafez?

And isn't honor killing in this context only the tip of the iceberg? When a father tells his son to cut off the daughter's head because she may have become too friendly with an "infidel," is that not a kind of "exclusion of the person marked out as other"? And in this context, let us not forget the preachers who week after week use Qur'an verses 7:166, 2:65 and 5:60 to designate Jews as apes and pigs and thus exclude them.

Among other things, Mr. Hafez questions my philosophy. I can explain it to him, because it is quite simple: I stand for absolute freedom of expression, democracy, universal human rights (as opposed to the Islamic human rights of the Cairo Declaration of 1990), pluralism, equality of man and woman. I ask you: what is reprehensible in that?

In closing, I thank Mr. Hafez for his remote diagnosis that my point of view is "sick." But I feel quite healthy.

This was the last time I was published in the mainstream media. Not once since have I been asked to weigh in on anything that has anything to do with Islam or the blatantly obvious Islamization, in particular following the great migration into Austria in 2015. The opposition was silenced. We have been shunned ever since.

The logical next step I took was to appeal the verdict.

CHAPTER TEN

The Appeal

Those who do not talk to each other sooner or later will fight each other.
—Wolfgang Hübner

G IVEN THE FLAGRANCY and blatant ignorance of facts of the verdict handed down by Judge Bettina Neubauer in February 2011, the question of not appealing was moot from the start. I also believed that this was a groundbreaking case, one that would someday turn into a landmark case. I never thought that I would ever lose; I was optimistic that justice would eventually prevail.

Before the appeals proceedings, the Austrian columnist Andreas Unterberger had a few things to say about my case.

> More and more often we are confronted by actions of the Austrian prosecutor's office—especially the troops of the BSA [Association of Social-Democratic Academics], active in the Vienna and Graz districts—that scare us to death. Are we living, at least, in the remnants of a country of laws? This worry is compounded by the fact that domestic justice is obviously controlled by people whose education is worse than spotty.
>
> A dramatic example of this is the case against Elisabeth-Sabaditsch Wolff, which is now entering its second trial. It is about the "crime" that the Islam expert and former collaborator of Alois Mock called—at an FPÖ seminar—the sexual congress of the Prophet Mohammed with a nine-year-old girl "pedophilia." Sabaditsch-Wolff was convicted because of that in the first trial. And the chief prosecutor's office of Vienna has the time for a pages-long defense of this scandalous verdict. (Yes, this is the same prosecutor's office that never took the time to

systematically follow up the suspicion of many experts that there were still more perpetrators in the Kampusch case—that is, one of the worst cases of child abuse in Austria.)

In commenting on the appeal, there is sharp language about the "alleged consummation of the marriage with the nine year-old wife." Which is scandalous in more ways than one. What normal human being who repudiates child abuse as one of the worst crimes calls a nine-year-old girl (who was "married" at age six) simply "wife"? Second, this consummation is only "alleged" for the prosecutor, but for the Islamic world, it is still today an example with legal implications. So we read literally in the (doubtless left-leaning) *Wikipedia* under the keyword "child-marriage": "The minimum age for girls to marry according to the provisions of Islamic schools of law is nine years. The schools of law orient on Mohammed's marriage to Aisha, which is said to have been consummated when Aisha was nine years old." Moreover, the prosecutor does not try at all to argue against the indicated age, which has been confirmed by all available sources. Like a tabloid, the prosecutor consistently says "alleged."

Of course, there are no film records of the sexual intercourse between Mohammed and that girl. But the fact that this—and above all, the traditionally handed down age of the "bride"—still serves Islamic lawmakers as a model is certainly far more serious than the exact date. Especially, when it is a question of analyzing Islam.

It is still more unbelievable that the prosecutor defends the judge's statement that child marriages were also widespread in the ruling houses of Europe. And for that reason, entering into child marriages is not the same as pedophilia.

It leaves you open-mouthed. In the first place, those historic child marriages were for purely dynastic reasons—not sexual (bad enough, but quite different from pedophiliac motives). They were intended to secure the power of two ruling houses. Thee is no such consideration in the Mohammed-Aisha "marriage."

Second, it is not known about any of these child marriages when they were consummated. Which is hard to visualize in the case of an eight year-old boy. And in Aisha's case, the criticism is directed more at the time of the consummation and less at the time of the "wedding," which took place in her sixth year.

Third, in these dynastic child marriages in European history, both partners were children. An enormous distinction from the age difference between the 53 year-old Mohammed and the nine year-old Aisha.

Fourth, most of these child marriages were administratively arranged. The children who were entered into marriage by their parents did not see each other before or at the "wedding," but years later (if at all). Mostly only ambassadors of the ruling houses were present at the marriage agreement.

Considering the state of the teaching of history, this all may be unknown to judges, and "chief" and "primary" state's attorneys. They are therefore that much more obligated to become acquainted with the facts, before writing such abstruse reasons into verdicts and replies to appeals.

The prosecutors' battle against Sabaditsch-Wolff is that much more astonishing when countless quite aggressive and totally fact-free instances of mockery of the Christian religion have played out with no legal complications. When necessary, the "freedom of art" was used as a shield.

Astounding, too, is the parallel verdict of a media judge against the woman: She had been accused by a left-leaning glossy magazine, which maintained that Sabaditsch-Wolff had said: "Euro-Islam is just [crap]." The judge had to admit in the verdict that this sentence was never spoken. Nonetheless, he exculpated the magazine in a scurrilous, meandering argument, by referring to the legally invalid verdict and because Sabaditsch-Wolff had spoken negatively about Islam. So leftist opinion terrorism has gone so far in the justice system that you cannot even defend yourself when words that have never been spoken are put into your mouth.

These accusations and verdicts are only imaginable when there is a political witch-hunt against everything that is right of center (in other words, against more than half of the population) and if someone wants to come to the aid of the politically slanted campaign of a glossy magazine supported by tax-paid ads. On the other hand, it would be absolutely inconceivable in a free constitutional state where freedom of expression and scientific facts are still valid.[1]

Once again, I was grateful to see so many friends and supporters present at the Appeals Court. Once again, I felt I was in the wrong place. I was no criminal and did not belong in a courtroom.

Below is the live-blog account of what occurred:

3:10am EST Elisabeth Sabaditsch-Wolff, Dr. Rami are present.

The court makes a summary of what the case is about: §188 appeal case. Denigration of legally recognized religion, specifically Muhammad.

---

1 Unterberger, Andreas, "All the Things That Judges and Prosecutors Don't Know," November 5, 2011, https://www.andreas-unterberger.at/2011/11/was-alles-richter-und-staatsanwaelte-nicht-wissen/
English translation at *Gates of Vienna*: https://gatesofvienna.net/2011/11/alleged-austrian-justice/. Reproduced by permission.

"The problem is that Muhammad is considered a perfect example for Muslim men, that is against our laws and public order. He had a great consumption of women, including minors, and in general behaved in ways contrary to modern law. That is all documentable from the Bukhari hadith. Former member of parliament Susanne Winter said similar things and was convicted.

A 56-year having sex with a nine-year-old, what do we call this, if not pedophilia?"

3:18 am EST Dr. Rami represents the Defense.

Demands acquittal. ESW is a harmless woman conducting seminars, which were infiltrated by a journalist from *NEWS* magazine. Thirty pages [of transcript] are obviously harmless, just a few out of context quotes are made controversial.

He underlines that a "hate preacher" would be someone standing in public places inciting hatred among thousands or millions, not a teacher in a small seminar.

"Denigration" implies that something *false* and negative is said about religious persons, like Jesus. Something true and negative, like Muhammad having sex with a girl aged 9, cannot constitute "denigration," and must thus not be punishable.

Dr. Rami quotes *Wikipedia*: "The wife of Muhammad, Aisha, entered the marriage at age six, which was consummated at the age of nine"

This is completely public knowledge already, repeating this cannot be punishable under the law.

That Muhammad, as Elisabeth put it, "had something for little kids" is simply another way to put it, yet carefully rewording the facts be cannot punishable either.

Also, it's important that we don't suppress discussion of these matters, put people in prison for discussing it.

9:21 CET, 3:21 am EST: The Public Prosecutor takes over for a few comments about in what detail the previous judge had gone into the precise definition of "pedophilia."

The Judge asks Elisabeth to take the floor for any comments pertaining to the written defense statement by Dr. Rami:

She says that she only spoke the truth, and "Telling the truth must never be punishable."

Dr. Rami adds details from Islamic sources:

Muhammad had at least nine wives, more according to other sources, as well as a variety of concubines and others.

The Judge calls a break, and says that the verdict will come no earlier than 10 o'clock.

Update 10:14 CET, 4:14 am EST: The Judge states:

The defense has made the factual details of the case very clear, it's an interesting case.

What we're dealing with here is only the verdict from the first court. The Judge is lecturing a bit about the legal mechanism of cases like this.

It's not the first time that Freedom of Expression is discussed in this court, nor at the European Court of Human Rights.

The Court has the obligation to clear up if there are objective mistakes in the first court. This is not the first case of its kind, far from it.

We don't need to go through all the details of the case in the courtroom, it's all written down in advance, and the Judge has read it. All the details are stacked up here [two 15-centimeter stacks].

The Defense made comments in order that the audience would understand the case. Otherwise not much of the case needed to be explained verbally.

If one only heard the Defense, it would seem incredible that one cannot legally speak the truth.

There is Article 10 of the Human Rights Convention, which of course is undisputed. This is valid both for pleasant and unpleasant information, including disturbing, shocking and hurtful information. The exercise of this right implies a duty as well, as duties are the flip side of the right. The exercise of this right implies responsibility and duties. Uttering false, harmful statements can be punishable. Protection of public order and basic values may require restrictions on exercise of free speech.

The Supreme Court of Austria has dealt with this in the case of Susanne Winter already. Muhammad married Aisha at the age of 56, and Winter called him "child molester." We cannot leave that Supreme Court decision out of consideration.

10:25 CET, 4:25 am EST: VERDICT UPHELD

As for the guilt, "Having something with children" is an excess of opinion that cannot be tolerated. It is a ridiculing that cannot be justified.

As for punishment, it can be lowered. 4 December 2009 – 20 December 2011 is a long time for the process.

First conviction is UPHELD!

After the verdict, there was commotion in the courtroom, with some spectators approaching the bench and verbally attacking the judge. I did not approve of this, though I could hardly blame them for their feelings. I had no more strength inside me; I was deflated and deeply saddened. My firm plans were not to pay the fine because to do so would effectively recognize the legitimacy of an unjust and tyrannical legal decision.

After the press conference at the premises of the Wiener Akademikerbund, when I was finally home alone, I cried for the first and only time. I wept for my daughter, her right to speak her mind freely, and I felt I had let her down.

The day before Christmas I published a message of thanks for my supporters. Among other thigs, I said,

> I must admit that I entered the courtroom with some cautious optimism. However, when I sat down to face the presiding judge, with another nameless judge on his left and right, I knew in my heart that the verdict once again had already been written, as it was from the day of my indictment.
>
> Let's be honest: from the very beginning we freedom-loving men and women, we who seek to defend democracy and universal human rights, never had a chance. The destruction of everything we stand up for is too far advanced.
>
> The appeals court verdict is interesting, but even more shocking that the first guilty verdict. The judge explained that while it is certainly within the law to say that "Mohammed had sex with a 9-year-old," calling this spade a spade is considered "excessive" and thus "denigrating." Imagine that you were no longer allowed to call a murderer "heinous" because you might be convicted of having an "excessive" opinion as a result.
>
> Here in Austria we are no longer permitted to name the crime committed by the founder of a religion, in whose name millions of young girls are married off and raped by their "husbands." This is an unbearable thought for me, as the mother of a young girl. And it is an unacceptable situation, one I shall fight till the very end.
>
> Paraphrasing Congressman Allen West's words: "I will remain steadfast in my opinions and loyal to my family and my beloved Austria."
>
> Finally, a word to Ms. Dolna, the journalist to whom I must be grateful for "exposing" me to the world. Ms. Dolna, I was told that you laughed when the verdict was announced. I say to you: "Father, forgive her for she knows not what she did."

Media reaction was unsurprisingly scant, with a short clip from the press conference and an editorial from *Kurier,* which is a pro-EU, pro-immigration daily in Austria. Thus it is quite surprising that the editor-in-chief actually understood the implications of the verdict against me.[2]

Unfortunately, I could not go through with my plans not to pay the fine. This is how I explained my decision:

> This past Thursday I asked the notary public in charge of my defense account to pay the now-infamous €480 I was fined for my words the Austrian state deemed "an excessive assessment."
>
> You will recall that I was adamantly opposed to handing over nearly €500 to the government. I still feel this way. And I am still willing to go to jail. However, the legal constraints imposed on me have forced me to change course, and hand over money to the very state that has prosecuted and criminalized me for speaking the truth.
>
> This is the story of what happened.
>
> The terms of the verdict required me to pay 120 "day fines" of €4 each, giving a total of €480, or spend two months in jail.
>
> What was omitted from the court's pronouncement was the fact that there is a step between the payment of the fine and going to jail: the bailiff would enter my family's apartment with a warrant in an attempt to collect something worth €480. This might be anything, from my laptop to jewelry to the sofa.
>
> Only if he were unable to make the necessary collection would I have to go to jail. In order to manage that, I would have to assault the bailiff—something that goes against my nature. So I really had no choice: I would have to pay the fine, one way or the other.
>
> I found out about all this only fairly recently. As a result, I made a quick decision: I would pay the fine, much as I hated doing so.
>
> My daughter's well-being was also factored into the equation. Although she was a beacon of strength during the trial, I noticed a gradual change in her. She was clearly suffering, and that is something that I as a mother could not accept.
>
> I believe in standing up for free speech, even if I put myself at risk. But I will not put my daughter at risk. The Austrian state has already victimized me. I will not permit them to victimize my daughter, too. It is my obligation as her mother not to do something that would scar her for life. If my daughter suffers, I suffer as well.
>
> Rest assured that I loathed paying that fine. I still strongly resent the state's decision to limit my freedom of speech.
>
> I will continue my protest. We are not giving up, but merely chang-

---

2 "A Verdict With Consequences: Islam defends itself against insults. Christian churches do not (yet)," *Kurier,* Dec. 21, 2011.

ing our tactics.

I ask you to continue to support me and my fight for the right to freedom of speech. By extension, I am fighting for the rights of everyone, including those who are unaware that their rights are under threat.

If we do not stand up for our freedoms, we will lose them. Therefore I will continue to stand strong.

With your help, freedom will prevail!

Dr. Maria Stückler once again composed another brilliant letter to the appeals judge who handed down the verdict against me:

> *Whether one tells the truth or not, it exists.*
> — Kurt Tucholsky
> *Appeasement is like feeding a crocodile in the hope of being the last to be eaten.*
> — Winston Churchill

Vienna, January 28, 2012

Dear [Judge]:

I protest most strenuously against the conviction of Mrs. Elisabeth Sabaditsch-Wolff according to § 188 criminal code for statements she made in the context of an Islam seminar in the FPÖ party-sponsored seminar.

This conviction represents a political abuse of § 188 criminal code and is an offense against the human right of freedom of expression. It is not Mrs. Sabaditsch-Wolff, but the actions of Mohammed himself which derogate him and his teachings. She was instead convicted because she spoke a truth that was very uncomfortable for the ruling party. It is no coincidence that FPÖ was also sitting in the defendant's seat.

If the judgment had had anything to do with justice and the defense of civil standards, then it could not have protected Mohammed—in view of the fatal effect of his example up to now—from "denigration." Quite the contrary! By protecting Mohammed from "denigration," Austrian justice denigrates itself.

The Decision

The Superior Court confirmed the verdict, although with a somewhat different reasoning. While the lower court regarded "pedophilia" as factually completely unjustified, the higher court judged the remark "liked a little something with children" to be an extreme evaluation. Only the isolated explanation that Mohammed had sex with a child was allowable.

In supporting the verdict, there was explicit reference to the Win-

174 ᴇ⌐⊃ *The Truth is No Defense*

ter case and the disposition of the European Court of Human Rights [ECHR]:

Dr. Susanne Winter was convicted by the superior court in Graz under § 188 criminal code on the basis of her statement that Mohammed in present understanding was a child abuser.

According to the ECtHR, the constitutional right of freedom of expression includes making shocking and insulting statements, but the practice of this right is tied to duties and responsibility—pre-eminently in connection with religious doctrine. Thus, there is the obligation to refrain even from true statements if they are baselessly insulting.

The example was given of mocking a handicapped person because of his handicap. The handicap is a fact, but the mockery is a baseless insult.

Political Justice

This example is so skewed that it says everything about the political character of the verdict. Here, indeed, criticism of and profession of contempt for a person (Mohammed) because of his action, which even according to *Austrian law* (!) is a crime, is placed on a level with mockery of an unfortunate (handicapped person).

The whole process of the trial—from the placing of the complaint to the justification of the verdict—show that this was a political process. Should any further proof be needed, it is provided by the systematic non-use of § 188 StG (*Strafgesetzbuch*, criminal law) in cases of mockery and ridicule of Christianity and its sacred figures.

Justifications of the verdict— rom thread-bare to crazy

Mrs. Sabaditsch-Wolff and/or Susanne Winter judged Mohammed with the designation pedophilia or child abuse just as they would any other person—that is, by his actions and not his claim, which is contradicted by them.

It is the action and not the designation that derogates Mohammed and Islam.

The "denigration" which makes both defendants "guilty" in the eyes of Austrian justice consists of truth, insofar as they called the deeds of Mohammed by their name "without regard to the person" (a pillar of European law, if I am not mistaken), and in so doing gave expression to a politically very uncomfortable truth.

And as far as the expression "liked to have a little something with children" is concerned, this was not said without reason. because Mohammed's behavior in this respect sets the norm even today. It legitimizes not only marriage with children, but sanctions pedophiliac behavior.

Islamic legal scholars from Morocco to Indonesia (among them the largest Moslem organization in Indonesia, NU, which is considered the "most moderate"), still sanction marriage to children. In many Islamic countries, there is not even a minimum age for marriage. And even where state law provides one, e.g., in Turkey, marriages to minor girls are not rare, And such cases are known in the Muslim communities in Europe and in the West in general.

So pedophilia itself in the strict sense can be pursued "legally." Furthermore, a Muslim may at any time put aside his wife with no grounds and even take several new ones. Both Shi'ites and Sunnis are acquainted with the "temporary marriage" and the time can be as short as desired. Islamic law, based on the sayings and deeds of Mohammed, does not put limits on pedophiliac abuse. Rather, it fosters it.

And the legal abuse of girls paves the way for the sexual abuse of boys.

Bottom line: Anyone who does not speak with scientific exactitude about Islam and its Prophet, uses language carelessly or goes so far as to measure his still normative acts and words by European standards and *Austrian legislation* (!) commits a crime in the eyes of *Austrian justice* (!)—cultural relativism to a tee.

Politically uncomfortable truths

Mrs. Sabaditsch-Wolff and Mrs. Winter were not found guilty because they denigrated the religious doctrines of Islam—the actions of Mohammed and the doctrines of Islam manage that themselves—but because they spoke extremely politically uncomfortable truths: that Islamic law (*shariah*) and therefore Islam contradict "our social standards and laws."

This conviction was intended to make an example, since Mohammed was guilty of quite different and far more uncomfortable acts: assassination, mass murder, campaigns of war and pillage, enslavement and slave trading, rape, extortion, etc. Anyone can read about this in the basic texts of Islam: Qur'an, *hadith* and *sira* (official biography of Mohammed).

All these are actions directed against non-Muslims, which are likewise justified in *shariah*, Islamic law. This is a law that has all the characteristics of a law of conquest and occupation, and claims a temporal and spatial universality as an allegedly "divine" law.

That this claim has lost none of its validity is directly demonstrated for us. Not small minorities, but great majorities speak for the dominance of *shariah*—in the Arab world in votes and in Muslim communities in Europe in polls. And the OIC (with its 57 member countries representing the entire Islamic world) has for years tried to impose upon the whole world the most important of all the conditions of *shariah* — "No one may criticize Islam, and each must honor it as the 'religion of peace and tolerance'" by Islamizing the UN human rights organization.

Islam is by no means only a religion. It is a political ideology with a totalitarian claim. Criticism of Islam is not just our right, but, from the standpoint of human rights, it is our duty.

A very uncomfortable truth for governing parties: They should accept responsibility for a completely irresponsible immigration policy and put an end to a mass immigration that has become a runaway process. It is no coincidence that in both cases the FPÖ is sitting at the defendant's table.

In the indictment, it is not against Islam, but against Sabaditsch-Wolff, that the charge of incitement is laid, by way of regulations directed against non-Muslims. When it became clear in the course of the trial that a conviction for incitement was not possible (in accordance with legal interpretation at the time), the charge was changed to denigration of religious doctrines. (§ 188 StG)

Bottom Line: Mrs. Sabaditsch-Wolff had to be convicted at all costs. If any further proof is needed, here it is:

Systematic refusal to prosecute denigration of Christianity

Invoking freedom of thought and art, the justice system regularly refuses to prosecute obvious derision and mockery of Christianity and its most sacred persons—derision and mockery which are devoid of any factual basis and far exceed any "excessive evaluation" to say nothing of criticism.

Such derision and mockery are also frequently propagated "publicly and legally" and sometimes even subsidized as "art." To give just a recent example: In December 2011, a so-called "Blasphemous Christmas Fair" took place for the second time in Vienna. A presentation explicitly targeting § 188 StG (*Strafgesetzbuch*, penal code), in the erroneous belief that it would protect Christianity. Radio ORF—legally financed by fees required of the public—reported on it precisely on Christmas Eve in its "cultural broadcast," Austria 1.

Bottom line: In abuse of §188 StG, the Austrian "rule of law" protects Islam and its Prophet from "denigration, but does not protect Christianity from derision and mockery. The more perverse and ominous the doctrines and the more intolerant the adherents of the religion in question are, so much greater is the protection of the Austrian "constitutional state." Truth as evidence is out of style and the door is open to extortion.

Iron Curtain Transformed Into Iron Hijab

Twenty years after the fall of the Wall, we must unfortunately confirm that the Iron Curtain did not fall, but moved west and changed to the Iron Hijab. Freedom of expression ends where Islam begins. Lies are already reasons of state and the law is a Potemkin Village. With this verdict, the Austrian "constitutional state" has become an accomplice of the OIC (Organization of Islamic Cooperation) and the enforcer of the most important of all *shariah* provisions—"No one may criticize

Islam and its Prophet. Everyone must worship him."

The Austrian "constitutional state" allegedly dedicated to human rights is protecting, of all people, a "Prophet" who treacherously had his critics murdered and thus delivered all his future critics to being shot down—up to the present day—Salman Rushdie (*The Satanic Verses*), Van Gogh and Ayaan Hirsi Ali (*Submission*), the Pope (*Regensburg speech*), Robert Redeker (article in *Le Figaro*), Kurt Westergaard (*Danish Cartoons*), Wilders (*Fitna*) — just the best-known.

Not only the Islam-critic, but also religious peace is threatened. This is a glimpse into the Islamic world, where state regulations on blasphemy have become a deadly weapon in the hands of Islamic fanatics and loosed a spiral of religious violence. A prime example is Pakistan where more than a thousand charges have been made since the introduction of state blasphemy regulations under Zia ul-Haq. Virtually all of them were made with complaints created out of whole cloth, which have become crazier and more absurd. But once in the crosshairs of the law and publicly exposed, the accused is under sentence of death even when set free.

Against this murderous background, the Austrian "constitutional state" has already made the preferring of charges an injustice.

— Dr. Maria Stückler

Only a year before, I was preparing for my final court appearance. Back then, I was still hopeful that some kind of legal sanity existed in this country. It was painful to be proven wrong and realize that—wittingly or unwittingly—Austria has become *shariah*-compliant. Even more irksome was the fact that I was literally forced to pay the fine of 480 euros.

I became more despondent when I considered the gulag-like United Kingdom, which was at the time resorting to the incarceration of those who defended democratic and liberal values while granting bail to criminals who rape, rob and reap the financial rewards of a country blinded by the illness of multiculturalism. It was and still is sickening to witness, and very frightening.

While we all watched in horror what transpired in the United Kingdom, Sweden and Norway, my brilliant and able lawyer was keeping the Austrian legal system busy, trying to convince those *shariah*-compliant legal experts in the justice system that they made a grave mistake.

On the home front, the court system was still forced to deal with the issue of whether the word "pedophilia" was being used with its exact scientific significance. On December 11, 2013, the case was handled in the Procurator General's Office, which had already ruled the case well-judged. My lawyer told me in advance that this was to be seen as a very positive sign, as the court could have thrown out the case in written form. So, we assumed that the case would not be thrown out. This left us with the following two possibilities: 1. I would be acquitted, or; 2. The case would go back to the lower courts. The main question to be discussed was the merit of what I had said. Did freedom of speech trump religious teachings? Another positive sign: my counsel had repeatedly endeavored to have the case tried in the media court. All motions were denied. This time, by chance, my case was allotted to the so-called media Senate. Moreover, it is very uncommon for the Supreme Court to deliberate as long as it did on my case (more than 1.5 years). A source familiar with the case thought the court may have wanted to avoid a conviction by the European Court of Human Rights. What was happening now would become the final decision, as we had appealed for an exceptional legal redress. By scheduling the hearing, the court appeared to have decided that this case needed more discussion.

Austrian Supreme Court

As if I hadn't had enough of courtrooms already, I again found myself sitting next to Dr. Rami in another court of law, this time facing the Supreme Court. Was I optimistic? Not really.

In the courtroom:

10:42:   We are now in the courthouse. The defense attorney Dr. Rami says that an acquittal is quite likely—but adds that live reporting from the court room is not quite doable.

10:44:   While there is a good chance the case will be over and closed here, today, there is a reason it would be better to lose:

If the case is lost in Austria, it would be taken to the European Court of Human Rights, where the chance to win is very good. And winning it at the ECtHR would have positive implications for free speech, including the right to criticize religion, throughout Europe.

10:45:   Elisabeth is getting ready for the court.

10:49:   The hearing is scheduled to last an hour. We cannot report directly from it, but will be taking notes and reporting right afterwards. The result first, of course!

11:51:   Bulk update coming below (Court is in recess):

The hearing is delayed due to the Public Prosecutor missing the 10 o'clock starting time. The Court starts with making a summary of previous proceedings, including the conviction of a €480 fine or 60 days in prison for violation of Article 188, denigration of a legally recognized religion.

The defense, Dr. Rami, presents his case, that since Elisabeth's statements are based in documentation, they cannot be punishable under the law, as it does not constitute denigration.

He refers to the case of Salman Rushdie and his book *The Satanic Verses*, which would also be shocking to the 1.5 billion Muslims in the world, and to the Danish Mohammad cartoons, which were explicitly meant to mock the beliefs of others. Those cartoons led to extensive riots and many deaths, a clear sign that Islamic forces seek to limit our freedom of expression, in particular as it pertains to Islam.

Dr. Rami also refers to two similar cases which led to acquittal, despite broad negative portrayals of religions, including stating "Christianity is permeated by anti-Semitism." What is on our desk today is benign compared to this. Further, the disputed statement (if Mohammad could rightly considered a pedophile or not) is a mere detail of a seminar about the foundations of Islam. And, as has been stated earlier, the idea that Mohammad was a pedophile makes sense in light of his having sexual relations to a minor (Aisha), as documented in Islamic scripture.

Finally, the whole point of freedom of expression is that it must be permissible to say things that cause offense, shock and unpleasant reactions among some listeners.

For the reason above, the Defense proposes that the Court deliver an unconditional acquittal.

12:05: **Conviction upheld!**

13:35: More information:

The Prosecutor held that it had no relevance that the statement in question was made during educational seminars. Further, the Prosecutor disagreed with the advertising of the seminars as being "historical science," and asserted instead that the intention of seminars was to defame Islam under a mantle of being "scientific."

As a comparison, she noted a case where somebody had asserted that microwave ovens cause severe damage to the quality of food and to public health, and had put skull warning stickers on the ovens. He was convicted for statements and actions that could not be justified by scientific methods.

Likewise, despite Islamic scripture and scholars being in agreement on the fact that Mohammad systematically had a sexual relationship with a minor (Aisha, aged 9), that is insufficient to deduce that Mohammad was a pedophile. Thus, stating so is unscientific and constitutes an impermissible excess of opinion.

The Court asks Elisabeth if she agrees with the presentation made by the defense, which she wholeheartedly confirms.

First decision of the Court: The case will not be returned to a lower court for retrial.

It is the opinion of the Court that defaming Mohammad was a primary purpose of the seminars, rather than the purported purpose of providing factual knowledge of Islam. Thus, the seminars have made no meaningful contribution to discussions that would be of public interest, but instead had a primary purpose of defaming Mohammad, an icon of a legally recognized religion.

[Reporter's note: Having seen the slides used in the seminars, I can say with certainty that Mohammad was not a primary topic of the lectures; the focus was on Islamic law and practice.]

The Court considers the case to balance freedom of religion against the right to free expression against freedom of religion, Articles 9 and 10 Human Rights Convention. However, there is a much narrower limit to value judgments concerning religion than concerning non-religious matters, and the notion that Mohammad may have been a pedophile constitutes an "excess of opinion," "of no public interest," as decided upon previously by the High Court.

The European Convention of Human Rights grants individual countries the right to interpret Article 10 (freedom of expression) as they see fit, and the Court holds that there are much tighter limits to freedom of expression on matters related to religion than on other issues.

Thus, the conviction for defaming a legally recognized religion is upheld.

Further, the Court considered the proportionality of the punishment relative to the crime of expression committed. The lower courts did not find unconditional imprisonment a necessity, but rather convicted Elisabeth a fine of €480, which is fitting in light of her low income, optionally converted into 60 days of prison. The Court considers this proportionate to the crime committed and upholds it.

My face shows my feelings

The conclusion to this court appearance was that my case was now proceeding in full force to the European Court of Human Rights because all of my options in the Austrian legal system were exhausted.

Dr. Rami and I discussed the case and its repercussions afterwards. For instance, the reader may remember that there were quite a few questionable occurrences during the trials. One example: According to the court, I should have been aware of the contents of the judgment against Susanne Winter, and therefore should have refrained from repeating her words.

So I am supposed to be informed by all judgments made in courts every single day. How ludicrous! Dr. Rami agrees:

"The appeals court has propounded a new fact for assessing guilt, namely the fact that 'the accused has paid no attention at all to the nearly identical situation in the judgment of the supreme provincial court in Graz, but rather obstinately denied it.' And yet, nothing was said about this verdict of the Graz court or the conviction of Dr. Susanne Winter in the statements of the accused, nor in the proceedings of the lower or the appeals court."

In addition, I was also "ambushed" during the trial when the judge introduced her theory of "pedophilia"—or the lack thereof in Mohammed's case: because royalty in the Middle Ages married off children, there is no proof of Mohammed's behavior being motivated by anything but love. The Procurator General's Office opined that all is well, but Dr. Rami disagrees:

"The procurator sees no breach of the ban on ambush (surprise), since the argument of the court that child marriages were widespread in Europe was not addressed 'as a fact decisive for guilt and subsumption, because this statement was not the object of the accusation.'

"The Procurator General overlooks the fact that she [Elisabeth Sabaditsch-Wolff] was convicted, because the court assumed she was not concerned with a factual debate, since she had accused Islam of child marriages even though such had been widespread in Europe.

"It is incomprehensible that the Procurator general discounts this mistake by the court, but a few pages later refers to precisely this passage by the court, according to which the accused was not concerned with a factual argument."

Finally, Dr. Rami told me he was studying everything about Islam in depth, and was doing everything in his power to win this important case. He added that the courts were probably very surprised at our tenacity.

The mainstream media—*Die Presse*— among other things, had this to say:[3]

> Sabaditsch-Wolff's attorney, Michael Rami, declared: "We are already prepared to fight the decision of the Appellate Court at the European Court on Human Rights and will fight this one too." To date, there is no decision at the European Court, nor can it be estimated when the case will be heard, says Rami.
>
> "It is not a question of whether the statements are considered good

---

3 "Islam Seminar: Lecturer Loses At Supreme Court," *Die Presse*, January 1, 2012.

or bad, but whether it is legally permissible to say such things." The basic right to freedom of expression, said the attorney, covers "also and specifically statements that are shocking." The attorney noted that Sabaditsch-Wolff's statements were "factually based."

As I wrote at the time:

The march through the Austrian court system has finally come to a conclusion, though not in the way we free speech activists had wished for the struggle to end. Free speech has died, and with it our right to criticize an ideology that masquerades as a religion while reaping the benefits, both material and spiritual, of the Austrian state.

Just a reminder to the readers:

Islam, along with Christianity of all denominations, Jehovah's Witnesses, Judaism, and Buddhism, has been a "legally recognized religion" in Austria since 1912. This entails the state, i.e. the taxpayer, shouldering the burden of religious education in schools and provides special tax breaks, among many other perks.

In order to achieve legal recognition, a religion must prove that its teachings are compatible with the precepts of the law. This is ideally done by providing the representative of the state (the minister of culture) with a translated copy of the religious teachings. All religious groups with legal status in Austria have done so; only one has not. Want to venture a guess as to which religious groups has been in arrears until this day?

As a result of this Law on Islam, one may not criticize religious teachings, even if the authorities do not know the contents of the Qur'an, the *sunna* or the *sira*, all of which make up Islam. And as a result, a conviction for "denigrating the religious teachings of a legally recognized religion" with respect to Islam constitutes enforcement of *shariah* law by the Austrian judiciary, even if they are unaware of this fact.

This is what occurred in my case. Back in late 2009, my seminars on Islam were infiltrated by a young (female) journalist and surreptitiously recorded. I was later reported to the authorities, who decided to put me on trial.

It is important to remember that there was never any victim, never anyone who felt any insult, no Muslims who complained, no imam who denounced what I had said. It was the state that took the case up in lieu of Muslims who "might be offended." Offended by my simply stating the words of the Qur'an and the *sunna* and musing about what these words might mean in the early 21st century in light of Qur'an 33:21, a verse that calls Mohammed *Al Insan al Kamil*, the man to be emulated by all devout Muslims for all times. That is what the Austrian legal system calls "denigration of religious teachings;" that is, it recognizes Mohammed's marriage and consummation of his marriage to Aisha when she was six and nine, respectively. This behavior—which is to be emulated and is being emulated every single day as evidenced by news stories reporting the deaths of nine-year-olds after giving birth—will always be unacceptable.

The freedom to call a spade a spade must not be infringed due to religious laws and sensitivities. Laws gagging free speech must be repealed here in the European Union. I still dream of a European-style First Amendment that will allow us to speak our minds. Yet I realize that there is a long way to go; we haven't even begun comprehending the magnitude of losing the right to free speech.

Do a survey on your own in the streets here in Europe. I am certain that most people will say: "Well, you should not have said what you said. If you had shut up, you wouldn't have been in trouble. And anyway, you can't say it that way." As my lawyer rightly argued all the way to the Supreme Court, you may not like what I said, but I must have the right to say it. Free speech means saying things that may shock someone. Free speech is not necessary so that citizens may hear speeches by the president or the weather forecast.

To sum up: after fighting for nearly four years all legal possibilities have now been exhausted—unsuccessfully. My case has been pending at the European Court of Human Rights in Strasbourg since February 2012, and will set an important precedent for the freedom to criticize religions and/or religiously-sanctioned conduct.

One final note: I will never cease fighting for my God-given right to free speech. Religious sensitivities must never trump freedom of speech.

Our tenacity now took us to Strasbourg, France. The destination was The European Court of Human Rights.

CHAPTER ELEVEN

Waiting for the European Court of Human Rights' Decision

A lie doesn't become truth, wrong doesn't become right and evil doesn't become good just because it's accepted by the majority.
—Booker T. Washington

Asking whether a statement is "covered by freedom of expression," means you have no clue what freedom means.
—Frank Martin

WITH THE AUSTRIAN SUPREME COURT justices' decision against my right to freedom of expression, I had exhausted my legal options in March 2014. The door to the European Court of Human Rights was now wide open. I petitioned the European Court for Human Rights (ECtHR) twice: once following my loss on appeal in December 2011 and once following the decision of the Supreme Court in December 2013. The European Convention on Human Rights requires that "all domestic remedies need to be exhausted … within a period of six months from the date on which the final decision was taken."

After the appellate court decision, I appealed to the Supreme Court and, because I could not anticipate whether the court would consider my case (which it wasn't required to), my attorney petitioned the ECtHR twice just to make sure, in a manner of speaking.

On December 25, 2015, I received the following communication from Mr. Rami, my lawyer:

Dear Mrs. Sabaditsch-Wolff:

As you know, we have entered an appeal of your criminal conviction at the European Court of Human Rights (ECtHR).

Enclosed is the communication received today from the ECtHR, indicating that it has now begun to deal with the content of your case. This is a large initial step, because the ECtHR has been dramatically overtaxed for years, and rejects most appeals as inadmissible, without any contextual examination.

A distinction must be made in the procedure of the ECtHR between the (formal) admissibility and the content merit of an appeal. The ECtHR decides on the content merit of an appeal only if it is formally admissible. Put simply, this is not the case if certain formalities (e.g. deadlines) are not satisfied, or if the appeal is obviously not justified.

Our appeal raises the following violations of rights:

Article 6, para 1 Human Rights Convention (HRC), because a) the Austrian courts blind-sided us with alleged "common knowledge" on the subjects of pedophilia and child marriages (keyword "unfair treatment") and b) the Austrian court session lasted too long.

Article 7, para 1 HRC, because the regulation in question of § 188 of the Austrian criminal code is too vague;

Article 10, para 1 HRC, because your conviction violates the basic right of free speech.

The ECHR has, without explanation, rejected your appeals concerning Article 6, para 1 and Article 7, para 1 HRC as inadmissible, but an examination of your arguments concerning Article 10, para 1 has begun. To this end, it has required the Austrian government to supply a position paper on your appeal, no later than April 8, 2016. When it arrives, we can comment on it. To avoid any misunderstanding: What has been said above does not mean that your appeal will be granted, only that the ECtHR will consider your argument that your right to freedom of expression (Article 10, para 1 HRC) has been violated.

[...]

Yours truly,
Dr. Michael Rami

EUROPEAN COURT OF HUMAN RIGHTS
COUR EUROPÉENNE DES DROITS DE L'HOMME

2 8. Dez, 2015

~~FRIST~~ BIS ....
AZ ....

T : +33 (0)3 88 41 20 18
F : +33 (0)3 88 41 27 30
www.echr.coe.int

GHENEFF-RAMI-SOMMER
Rechtsanwälte KEG
Floragasse 5
A - 1040 WIEN

FOURTH SECTION

ECHR-LE4.1aR
CS/WNP/nsc

18/12/2015

Application no. 38450/12
E.S. v. Austria

Dear Sir,

I write to inform you that following a preliminary examination of the admissibility of the above application on 16/12/2015, the President of the Section to which the case has been allocated decided, under Rule 54 § 2 (b) of the Rules of Court, that notice of part of the application should be given to the Government of Austria and that the Government should be invited to submit written observations on the admissibility and merits of the complaint concerning the alleged violation of Article 10.

You will find enclosed an information note to applicants on the proceedings after communication of an application.

The Government have been requested to submit their observations by 08/04/2016. These will be sent to you in order that you may submit written observations in reply on behalf of the applicant, together with any claim for just satisfaction under Article 41 (cf. Rule 60). **Please do not send any submissions before being asked to do so by the Court.** Any unsolicited submissions will normally not be included in the case file for consideration by the Court (Rule 38 § 1). Under Rule 34 § 4 (a), the Government have been authorised to submit their observations in German if they so prefer, but they must provide the Court with a translation into English or French no later than 06/05/2016.

The Government have been requested to deal with the question set out in the documents appended to this letter (Statement of facts prepared by the Registry of the Court and Questions to the parties).

The Government have also been requested to indicate by 08/04/2016 their position regarding a friendly settlement of this case and to submit any proposals they may wish to make in this regard (Rule 62). The same request will be made of you when you receive their observations.

.../...

EUROPEAN COURT OF HUMAN RIGHTS
COUNCIL OF EUROPE
67075 STRASBOURG CEDEX
FRANCE

COUNCIL OF EUROPE

CONSEIL DE L'EUROPE

COUR EUROPÉENNE DES DROITS DE L'HOMME
CONSEIL DE L'EUROPE
67075 STRASBOURG CEDEX
FRANCE

- 2 -

I would inform you that at this stage of the proceedings, according to Rule 34 § 3, all communications of applicants or their representatives shall as a rule be made in one of the Court's official languages, English or French.

I wish to inform you that the President of the Section has decided not to disclose the applicant's identity to the public and that the Government have been informed of the fact that the applicant has been granted anonymity and of the consequence this entails for any documents submitted to the Court. In connection with the above decision, the President of the Section has also made a ruling to the effect that any documents deposited with the Registry in which the applicant's name appears or which could otherwise easily lead to her identification shall not be made accessible to the public (Rule 33 § 1).

As regards the remainder of the application, the President of the Section, sitting in a single-judge formation (assisted by a rapporteur as provided for in Article 24 § 2 of the Convention), declared it inadmissible.

Having regard to all the material in his possession and in so far as he has jurisdiction to examine the allegations made, he considered that the conditions of admissibility provided for in Articles 34 and 35 of the Convention were not fulfilled.

This decision is final. It is not open to appeal before the Grand Chamber or any other body. The Registry cannot provide you with any further information about the single judge's decision. This information has been communicated to you in accordance with Rule 52A of the Rules of Court.

Yours faithfully,

F. Aracı
Deputy Section Registrar ·

Encs: Statement of facts and Question
       Information note

After that letter, I had to wait. And wait. And wait.

My lawyer had warned me that the process would take many years and that we would have to be very patient, but six years? Yes, that is how long the court waited to decide on what freedom of speech means in Europe.

The ensuing years, until the final verdict, were characterized by raising funds to offset my legal fees and expenses, and developing a greater awareness of the gravity and the consequences of the case at hand.

There was never any question that I would not be in a position to cover the costs of fighting the charges laid against me, but nor did I feel I should. This case was not about me but about the right to speak one's mind freely; therefore, I believed the legal costs needed to be shouldered by as many people as possible.

The raising of funds presented a great personal challenge. First, the group of prospective donors in Austria and Germany was extremely limited, due to the latent lack of interest in the subject matter, as discussed in previous chapters, and the fact that fundraising has little to no tradition in Europe. Traditionally, most Europeans do not set aside funds to donate to their favorite causes; thus, the necessary budgets are simply unavailable. From the beginning of my court case, I was acutely aware of this situation, and I knew I would never be successful in raising the needed funds in Europe. Nevertheless, the German human rights group Bürgerbewegung Pax Europa (Citizens Movement Pax Europa) was instrumental in supporting me in Germany, for which I am very grateful.

Second, I needed to ensure that the donated funds were properly administered. Under no circumstances did I ever want to be accused of getting rich at the expense of others. I therefore requested the assistance of a notary, who set up an escrow account specifically for any donations earmarked for my legal expenses. I never had any personal access to this account.

I always knew that I needed to look to my contacts and friends in the United States and their extraordinary generosity. The main driver for this fundraising was the website *Gates of Vienna* (GoV), which had supported me from Day One, that "dreary day in November 2009." GoV instantly initiated a donation drive called "Elisabeth's Voice," while other friends set up the website "SaveFreeSpeech.org," informing allies about my fight for freedom of speech in both English and German and providing information on how to donate. This was complemented by my frequent travels around the United States, where I spoke to countless groups about my case. These organizations included, but were not limited to, ACT! For America, ACT! For Canada, Tea Party groups, American Freedom Alliance, The United West, Ahavath Torah Congregation (in Stoughton, MA), the Institute on Religion and Democracy, the Center for Security Policy, Middle East Forum, and The Lawfare Project. It was the smaller and larger donations from the many attendees at these venues that made all the difference. To all who contributed, I am sincerely grateful for your standing up for Europe's freedom of speech. Thank you for caring about what happens in Europe.

As I said in one of my speeches:

> You may think that what happens in Europe doesn't matter to you here in America. But our present is your future. What is happening in Europe will happen here in just a few short years. (Speech delivered for

ACT! For America in Orlando, FL; May 2014)

And, as British journalist and filmmaker Katie Hopkins has so aptly warned Americans:

Do not let yourself fall as we have fallen!

Throughout all the years of waiting for the ECHR to decide the fate of Europe's freedom of speech, I met countless amazing and brave Americans who exhibited not only a deep love of their country but also cared about the fate of Europe. I always thank them for taking time out of their busy schedules to listen to what I, an Austrian citizen, had to say. They could have been doing a million different things at those times, and so I respect them for choosing to come out and pay attention to a warning from Europe.

I noted why I persisted in speaking out, even as my legal battle continued:

> After my conviction, I could have let discretion be the better part of valor. I could have kept my head down. I could have avoided public appearances, and shut my mouth about Islam.
>
> But that's not in my nature — it's not who I am. I vowed NOT to stop speaking freely about the danger posed by Islamization. My personal story serves as an instructive example about the erosion of freedom in Europe.
>
> [Speech delivered at different venues during November 2017]

Oftentimes, the events I spoke at began with the American Pledge of Allegiance, which gives me shivers every time I listen to its powerful message. The Pledge was then followed by a rendition of the "Star-Spangled Banner" and, upon my request, "God Bless America." What a beautiful and moving way to set the stage for my own message!

While all of my speeches raised my case, it was usually embedded in an overarching theme. There was always something going on in Europe that warranted a stern warning to Americans. I also tried to explain what motivated me to continue this uphill battle. The answer was quite simple:

> I took on this job for the sake of my daughter. I looked around at what was happening to my country—burqas and honor killings and female genital mutilation, all the wonderful "cultural enrichment" that

comes with *shariah*—and thought about the kind of world she will have to live in when she grows up.

She is six years old now. What will the streets of Vienna be like when she is sixteen? Or twenty-six? Or thirty-six?

How can I live with myself if I do not at least try to prevent my country from surrendering to Islam?

This is not a job that any of us would have chosen to do, but it is the job that has been chosen for us. Our children and our grandchildren will never forgive us if we fail to act now, while successful action is still possible.

[Speech entitled "Shut Up, America!" delivered at the launch of The United West, March 6, 2011]

I will continue to speak the truth, no matter what. I owe as much to my daughter, and her children and children's children. No matter the final outcome, I want her to be able to say: "My mother did everything she possibly could."

[Speech delivered at different venues during, April 2016]

Silence is not an option.

Nothing will keep me silent. I am adamant that my daughter and my daughter's daughters shall never live as Islamic chattel.

["Death Can Be Silent—The Present State of Free Speech in the U.S., Europe and Beyond," delivered at Ahavath Torah Congregation, Stoughton, MA, June 2013]

In the summer months of 2015, I, along with millions of fellow Europeans, watched speechlessly and helplessly as an unknown number of people entered the territory of the European Union. *Wikipedia*, not known for its right-wing bias, explained the events as follows:

The European migrant crisis, also known as the refugee crisis, is a period beginning in 2015 characterized by rising numbers of people arriving in the European Union (EU) from across the Mediterranean Sea or overland through Southeast Europe. It is part of a pattern of increased immigration to Europe from other continents which began in the mid-20th century and which has encountered resistance in many European countries. Immigrants from outside Europe include asylum seekers and economic migrants. Most of the migrants came from Muslim-majority countries in regions south and east of Europe, including the Greater Middle East and Africa.

Having made my way to the border area between Austria and Slovenia in November 2015, and having witnessed the illegal entry of thousands of people—mostly young men—I described the dramatic impact of this migration into the countries of Europe as follows:

> For the past nine months Austria and the rest of Western Europe have undergone a profound transformation, one that will inevitably change the face of Europe permanently. I refer, of course, to the migration crisis, which began in earnest last summer, and is continuing as I speak to you. As the weather warms up and spring gives way to summer, we may expect the crisis to intensify even further. More than a million immigrants arrived in Austria and Germany via the "Balkan route" last year, and at least as many are expected to come this year—probably significantly more.
>
> These migrants are generally referred to by our political leaders and the media as "refugees," but this is hardly the case. Not only are most of them from countries where there is no war to flee from, but they are also overwhelmingly young Muslim men, of fighting age. In other words, the current crisis is actually an instance of Islamic *hijra*, or migration into infidel lands to advance the cause of Islam. The *hijra* goes hand in hand with *jihad*—once enough Muslim migrants have settled in the target country, violent *jihad* can begin.
>
> It should be quite clear by now that the *jihad* phase has already begun in Western Europe. The most recent instances were the massacres in Paris and Brussels, which were acts of *jihad* carried out by Muslims. Some of the terrorists were in fact "refugees" who had pretended to be "Syrian" and came in with the migrant wave.
>
> And all of them were fighting *jihad* in the way of Allah, as instructed by the Qur'an.
>
> I could take up my entire time slot tonight talking about the European migration crisis, and never do more than scratch the surface. However, I'd like to discuss one aspect of the crisis that is very important: the manipulation by the mainstream media of the news about the migrants.
>
> A single example from a beach in Turkey will help give you an idea of what is going on. In other words, the media people knew exactly what was going on. They knew the true story. They knew that the police were being professional, acting with restraint, and were never violent. Yet they decided to publicize a misleading photograph and describe it dishonestly.
>
> The image that sparked Western interest in the crisis was the widely-publicized photograph of the dead toddler on the beach in Greece. That photo is an example of media manipulation. Not about the fact of the baby's death, but what was done with his little body once he was dead. There is now ample evidence that the body was moved and

arranged in place so that the most heart-wrenching photo could be taken. Furthermore, the father of the child was not a poor helpless refugee trying to escape to freedom, but an accomplice of the people smugglers who piloted the boat, who irresponsibly brought his family with him.

In any other line of work this sort of non-professional behavior would be grounds for dismissal, and possibly even prosecution for fraud or libel. But not for journalists working for *Der Spiegel* or *Le Figaro* or *The Guardian* or CNN. To them, the media narrative is more important than the truth. And the media narrative was (and is) that poor innocent refugees were being brutalized by evil fascistic police in Hungary.

Those facts about the incident never made it into public consciousness. Not like the image of the pitiful corpse at the edge of the waves—that's the kind of story that the Western media love to dish out, especially when it promotes the media narrative. It's also the kind of story that Western audiences love to lap up—it's what *Gates of Vienna*, the website I'm associated with, calls "Dead Baby Porn."

Dead Baby Porn tugs the heartstrings of well-meaning Westerners. It reinforces all their presuppositions about current events. It gives them a vicarious frisson about the poor, suffering child. And, in their response, it makes them feel morally superior when they join the clamor to open their country's borders to the unfortunate "refugees."

The media feed the public a steady stream of photos and videos that feature pitiful migrant women and children. We see them looking through the razor wire towards "freedom," weeping, cooking their food over a campfire, and being pushed back by border guards. Yet these images are so misleading that they constitute disinformation.

The ugly fact is that the overwhelming majority of the "refugees" are healthy young men who either have no wives and children, or left them behind to seize the opportunity for *hijra* into Europe. They come from Afghanistan, Morocco, Eritrea, Albania, and Pakistan, but they acquire forged or stolen Syrian passports so that they become "Syrian" and thus qualify for VIP status in the flood of refugees.

We are being deliberately manipulated. The Western public is being manipulated into supporting the migration of fighting-age Muslim men into Europe. They are being manipulated into joining the crowd of starry-eyed people holding up "Welcome Refugees" signs in European train stations. And they are being manipulated into paying for all of it through their donations to various NGOs whose mission is to aid the "refugees."

Yet their donations do not cover the entire cost. It's a very expensive proposition to send refugees from Anatolia to the Greek islands, and then through Macedonia, Serbia, Croatia, Slovenia, and Austria to Germany. It's not just the payment to the people-smugglers who take them across a few miles of the Aegean and dump them just off the beach on Lesbos, although that is expensive enough. From there they are carried by ferry to the mainland, housed, clothed, and fed. When they continue their journey, they ride on buses and trains almost the entire distance—they walk only a few hundred yards to cross each border, getting out of a bus in one country and boarding another one in the next.

This is yet another way in which you, the Western public, are being manipulated by the media. All those photos and videos of endless columns of refugees walking along dusty roads carrying their children and pathetic belongings—those are not representative of the migrants' journey. A typical shot would show hundreds of young men sitting on buses with air conditioning and upholstered seats. But you don't see many of those, do you?

Someone is paying the costs of all this. Public donations cover only a small portion of the billions of dollars paid out to transport migrants. The governments of the countries involved pay some of the cost. And the European Union pays some of it. And there are multiple indications that George Soros and is Open Society Foundations are bankrolling a lot of the process, including the printing of maps and helpful instructions for the "refugees" in multiple languages.

Make what you will of all of this. No matter what their motives are, the internationalists who push for global governance and a borderless world are expending vast amounts of money to fool the European public and move millions of Muslim immigrants into Western Europe. Europe will become more "diverse," whether it likes it or not.

And if, as a consequence, terror attacks have to kill hundreds or thousands of people, and women have to be gang-raped, why, those are just unfortunate side-effects.

You can't make an omelet without breaking eggs, you know. Especially white European eggs.

[…]

When taken together, the events I've described tonight paint a picture of a Europe that is careening over the multicultural cliff. The traditional cultures and nations of Europe are being deliberately deconstructed so that a borderless society with no national identities can be constructed on top of the ruins.

And a borderless Europe is simply a precursor to a borderless global society. This future entity is commonly referred to as the "New World Order" or "global governance," and it is intended to be an unaccountable worldwide system of management and control modeled on the United Nations. A totalitarian behemoth—to paraphrase what George Orwell said: "If you want a vision of the globalist future, imagine a boot stamping on a human face—forever."

Paradoxically, even as [the European countries] close their borders to more immigrants, these countries are cracking down harder on domestic dissent on the topic of immigration and Islam. In Germany and Britain, people are being arrested for posting messages that criticize immigrants or Islam on social media. Police in Berlin recently raided ten residences after their occupants had voiced anti-migrant sentiments on Facebook. A man in Belgium spoke negatively about Muslims who celebrated the Brussels massacre, and was immediately visited at his home by three policemen, who requested that he refrain from such criticism in future.

If European countries are now determined to keep out future migrants, why are they cracking down on citizens who criticize immigration?

The short answer is: there are millions of immigrants already here. Hence they must be placated. If criticizing them makes them angry and causes them to take to the streets in violent demonstrations, then criticism of them must be outlawed.

I don't need to tell you that most of these millions of immigrants are Muslims. That's why criticism of Islam must be vigorously suppressed. Notwithstanding the much-trumpeted status of Islam as a "religion of peace," Muslims in Europe are notoriously prone to violence, and are always ready to take to the streets at a moment's notice. They may begin with loud chanting and signs that say "behead those who insult the prophet," but they more than likely will escalate rapidly to throwing rocks, assaulting the police, burning cars, vandalizing property, and other forms of general mayhem.

No, it's better (and easier) to silence the critics of Islam, in the hope that mob violence may be postponed for a just little while longer.

Exceptions to the general repression may be found in EU member states of the former East Bloc. It seems that people who survived decades under communism are less susceptible to the tyranny of political correctness. Led by Prime Minister Viktor Orbán of Hungary, President Miloš Zeman of the Czech Republic, and Prime Minister Robert Fico of Slovakia, an alliance of resistance known as the Visegrád Group which was formed in Central Europe after the fall of the Iron Curtain. Not only do these countries allow dissent on the issue of Islam, their political leaders among the foremost Islam critics—what they say into the microphones in their state broadcasting studios is the same thing that prompted the prosecution of Geert Wilders, Tommy Robinson, and myself.

Nowadays, those former communist dictatorships host the freest speech in Europe.

(Speech delivered in various venues, April 2016)

Note this part:

> The short answer is: there are millions of immigrants already here. Hence they must be placated. If criticizing them makes them angry and causes them to take to the streets in violent demonstrations, then criticism of them must be outlawed.

ACT! For America honored me by naming one of their awards after me. I was deeply touched by the gesture.
With me in the photo is Valerie Price, a fearless leader of ACT! For Canada and a great friend.
(NB Valerie gave her consent to be named and pictured.)

This eerily portended the ECtHR ruling that would be handed down two and a half years later. It is this reasoning that was used by the court to uphold my conviction in an Austrian court. The ECtHR in effect outlawed criticism of Islam in order to "keep the peace."

In August 2016, I detailed the effect that "The Great Migration" has had on freedom of speech in Europe:

> Thank you for inviting me to speak here in Los Angeles tonight. It's a privilege to be here, and a privilege to be in the USA. A place where I can speak my mind and say what I think, without fear of being arrested and prosecuted.
>
> Speaking your mind is your right under the First Amendment. But Europeans do not have that right. Yes, once upon a time free speech was granted to us as our privilege, but that privilege has since been withdrawn.
>
> The government giveth, and the government taketh away.
>
> All across Western Europe, from Sweden to Britain to Germany and Austria, citizens are being singled out and harassed for what they say. They are being put under surveillance by the State. They lose their jobs. They are being prosecuted. When they are convicted, they are fined, and sometimes even sent to prison.
>
> By now you're probably wondering what it is that people are saying that gets them in so much trouble with the State.
>
> Are they fomenting insurrection?
>
> Are they threatening to assassinate their political leaders?
>
> Are they inciting violent rebellion?
>
> No, it's nothing so exciting as that. Ordinary, peaceful Europeans who just happen to love their countries are being targeted for criticizing multiculturalism. They are being threatened with legal action for questioning their countries' immigration policies.
>
> In Modern Multicultural Europe, you are simply not allowed to object to Islamization.
>
> You've probably heard of the so-called "European refugee crisis," which has been underway since the beginning of last summer. Europe is being inundated with immigrants from the Middle East and Africa, most of them Muslims. During the past year, upwards of a million migrants entered Germany. Germany alone!
>
> Sweden, France, Belgium, the Netherlands, Italy, and Austria have also seen a huge surge in immigration from the Third World. As a result there has been a rapid spike in the crime rate in all these countries. Especially crimes against women and girls—harassment, groping, molestation, and rape. Public swimming pools in Germany have become notorious as hunting grounds for young Muslim males who prey on

women, little girls, and little boys. The horrible fact is that molestation and rape have become everyday occurrences in German swimming pools.

And, I don't have to tell you about the terrorist attacks:

- The "truck *jihad*" in Nice on Bastille Day.
- The ax attack on the train near Würzburg.
- The shooting massacre in Munich.
- The priest who had his throat slit in a Normandy church while celebrating Mass.
- The surgeon who was threatened with beheading in Troisdorf.
- The suicide bomber in Ansbach.

On and on and on.

This is why conscientious Europeans are objecting to immigration. This is why ordinary citizens are questioning the wisdom of allowing Islam into Europe.

And this is why the State is cracking down on free speech, because there must be no criticism, no questioning, and no objections to Islamization.

Many Americans became aware of the migration crisis only in the last year, since the photo of the dead toddler on the beach appeared in the media and German chancellor Angela Merkel publicly welcomed all the Middle Eastern "refugees" into Europe. However, the crisis has actually been underway for a long time. It simmered slowly for several decades, going mostly unnoticed except by those whose neighborhoods gradually turned into no-go zones. About ten years ago it started bubbling rapidly, boiling harder and harder every year. And now the lid is about to blow off the multicultural pot.

The European establishment, for reasons best known to itself, has decided not to address the systemic problem represented by Muslim immigration, but rather to suppress any and all criticism—or even discussion—of the issue. As far as the elites are concerned, the policy has been decided. It has been fixed in place, and there's no going back.

The fact that most Western European countries will have Muslim majorities in fifty years is of no concern to our leaders. They and their families live in gated communities far from the mean streets of the *shariah* zones, where gang violence has become the norm. They will never have to experience the joys of multiculturalism directly. Why should they care?

This is the backdrop behind the crackdown on free speech in Europe.

Ten years ago there were hardly any prosecutions for "hate speech." Five years ago there were several dozen such cases, including my own.

I used to bring a list of them when I came to the States so that I could read out the names at gatherings like this one.

This year there are too many to count—never mind naming them. Hundreds, perhaps thousands of people have been warned by the police, detained, arrested, prosecuted, or convicted. The UK may boast the greatest numbers, but people have been arrested in France, Belgium, the Netherlands, Denmark, Sweden, Finland, Germany, Switzerland, and Austria. For several years all the "hate speech" convictions resulted only in fines or suspended sentences, but in the past two years at least two people—Dan Park in Sweden and Tommy Robinson in England—have done prison time, actual prison time, for exercising their right to free speech.

That's what it has come to in Europe. This is no longer the twilight of freedom—full night is upon us.

The same fate awaits you here in America if your country continues on its present course. "Refugees" are being resettled here, too—a hundred thousand of them this year, if President Obama has his way. And criticism of Islam will become illegal, if Hillary Clinton has her way. Not over there somewhere, but right here in the Land of Liberty!

Europe's present will be America's future, if people fail to wake up and see what is being done to them.

If we step back and take the long view of events, what is happening now in Europe is part of a time-honored strategy in Islam. It's called the *hijra*, the "migration," and it's one of the primary ways in which Islam is spread.

First Muslims make *hijra* to infidel lands, and then, when they are present in sufficient numbers, they wage violent *jihad* against the infidel order. After the non-believers have been subdued, and the Muslims are ascendant, *shariah* law is established and formerly infidel territory becomes part of the Islamic State. The new, fully Islamized addition to the Caliphate will eventually be as vibrant and advanced as Bangladesh, Yemen, and Somalia.

Here's how it used to work in the past: Small groups of Muslims, maybe a clan or two, would move into a non-Muslim area and establish themselves. They would be unobtrusive, non-confrontational, and fully observant of local laws. Eventually other Muslims would join them, and the Islamic enclave would become larger and larger. All the while they would be building mosques—which were not at all like churches or synagogues, but rather like weapons storehouses and command centers where plans for the coming *jihad* were laid.

When their numbers were sufficient, the peaceful veneer was removed. They initiated small-scale raids and incursions against their neighbors. They burned down farms and villages, looted houses, and took slaves. Eventually, a full-scale war would be launched, and the new territory would be annexed to the Islamic *ummah* greater community. After that a migration to the next neighbor in line began, and the whole process was repeated.

Such is the tradition, as laid down in Islamic scripture, the Qur'an and the *hadith*. But the current *hijra* into Europe has a slightly different twist: The leaders of Western European countries and the European Union have invited the Muslims in. They are helping them to migrate, and are paying their way. They have facilitated their passage across the Mediterranean Sea onto the shores of southern Europe and transported them to their destinations in northern Europe.

After the closing of the "Balkan Route" through the countries of southeastern Europe, there are even as of yet unconfirmed reports that migrants are being flown into Germany on charter flights in the dead of night.

There can no longer be any doubt: Our political leaders have become traitors to their own people. This is especially true of the unelected and unaccountable leaders who run the totalitarian apparatus of the EU in Brussels. Immigration policy is being shoved down the throats of the member states, without any regard for the opinion of the national governments or the European people.

The elites of the EU are enacting the famous poem by the German poet and playwright Bertolt Brecht before our very eyes: they are abolishing the people and appointing another.

As my good friend Fjordman says: "This is the greatest organized betrayal in Western history."

As I mentioned earlier, activists are being arrested and prosecuted all over Europe. Geert Wilders, the leader of the Party for Freedom in the Netherlands, is the most prominent example. I also mention Dan Park in Sweden and Tommy Robinson in England. Other examples are Jussi Halla-aho in Finland, Michael Stürzenberger in Germany, and Lars Hedegaard in Denmark.

My English friend Paul Weston was arrested for publicly quoting Winston Churchill's words about Islam! That's how bad it is.

[I describe my case in detail.]

While my case was officially tried under "Denigration of religious teachings of a legally recognized religion," I maintain that it was in fact a classic prosecution of "hate speech," a criminal offense. But "hate speech" laws are particularly pernicious to free speech because they:

1. Include a significant subjective element, and they focus on the perception of the listener. Perception becomes reality.

2. Do not necessarily require a falsehood. The case against me focused on the insult, even though the court established that Mohammed married Aisha when she was six years old and consummated the

marriage when she was nine years old. When "hate speech" is the issue, truth is no defense.

3. Rarely require a victim. In my case, there was no victim, only an unidentifiable group of alleged victims.

Regardless of the formal wording of the charge, the case against me was a classic "hate speech" case, targeting me for what I think and say.

And now I'll describe a typical day in the life of Elisabeth Sabad-itsch-Wolff:

I begin my morning by reading newspapers—both tabloid and "serious." Not a single day goes by without reports of Chechen and Afghan gangs beating each other up, of Afghan and/or Syrian "young" men groping or raping girls as young as ten; of old ladies being attacked and knifed by refugees.

I sigh in relief, because finally the newspapers are willing and able to report the perpetrators' identities. Previously, it was "a man" or "a youth," even though everyone knew what that meant: a young, testosterone-rich immigrant boy-man. One of these high-spirited youngsters excused his rape of a young girl by saying to the judge: "I haven't had sex for four months."

In Germany, this type of excuse gets a monster off with community service.

Or another excuse: "I didn't know I wasn't allowed to kill my wife." Off you go with another light sentence! All the while, ethnic Germans and Austrians are severely punished for criticizing the effects of Mrs. Merkel's disastrous "welcome refugees" policies.

This may help you understand why I, as the mother of an eleven-year-old, worry all the time. Every morning, when I kiss my daughter good-bye, I hope and pray she returns in one piece, unscathed, smiling rather than in tears. She is armed with an alarm attached to her key chain. Will it suffice in the event of...? I hardly dare to imagine the possibilities.

There's no doubt that my worries reflect real dangers. One need only open the daily newspapers. Or read pertinent websites such as *Gates of Vienna*.

My neighbor was attacked by an Afghan refugee while riding the tram. He slashed her jeans with a knife until they were torn to shreds.

These are the things we must not discuss in public. Or, if we do, we must disguise the fact that the violence and violation are perpetrated by Muslim immigrants.

And above all, we must not allow our feelings about such matters to become known. Our public face must register nothing but approval for the disastrous immigration policies that have inundated our country with feral savages.

It's 32 years late, but 1984 has finally arrived! We all love Big Brother!

The totalitarian crackdown against freedom of expression has enlisted so-called European values such as tolerance, anti-discrimination and diversity. The insistence on upholding these high-minded abstractions is one of the reasons for European weakness in the face of Islamic terrorism.

As the combination of *hijra* and *jihad* lays waste to most of Europe, public officials are busy putting down even the slightest hints of dissent by European citizens.

Last fall, as the Great Migration Crisis unfolded in Germany and the rest of Europe, German Justice Minister Heiko Maas announced that laws against "hate speech" would be strictly enforced against people who criticized immigrants and immigration policy on social media. Chancellor Angela Merkel later enlisted Facebook, Twitter, and other internet giants to help her crack down on such "hate speech."

Mrs. Merkel and Mr. Maas delegated the task of monitoring the web to Anetta Kahane, a former Stasi (East German secret police) informer, and her NGO, the Amadeu Antonio Foundation.

The pressure was increased further last month, when police raided the residences of at least sixty people who were suspected of posting "agitation" against immigrants on the Internet. Justice Minister Maas told the public:

> "The resolute action of investigative authorities should motivate everyone to think before getting creative on Facebook... Everyone should take that to heart before opening his mouth."

In other words, all those people were arrested or investigated as a warning to everyone else.

The law under which malefactors are being prosecuted is Section 130 of the German criminal code, which requires the prosecution of anyone who "incites hatred against a national, racial, religious group or a group defined by their ethnic origins." Such crimes may be punished by three to five years in prison.

The German Ministry of the Interior recently said on Twitter: "We condemn 'hate speech,' whether liable to prosecution or not. Everyone may exercise free speech, but it must be factual and without any attacks." It is no longer judges and the law who decide what kind of speech may or may not be disseminated; it is consultations among groups like Kahane's outfit, privatized and informal, that decide.

Jesus characterized the Pharisees as "hypocrites" and—even worse—"a brood of vipers." Would Heiko Maas demand that Jesus be prosecuted for "hate speech?"

To quote Fjordman again: "We live in an age of madness, where common sense is being branded as extremism, and betraying your nation is hailed as a great moral achievement."

Geert Wilders insists that Europe must enact an equivalent of the First Amendment to the US Constitution. Without such formal constitutional protections, European citizens are vulnerable to the whims of the State, which has assumed increasingly totalitarian powers for the suppression of dissent.

A First Amendment for Europe would remove those powers from the State and return them to the people, where they rightfully belong. In order for this to happen, Europeans must awaken from seventy years of slumber and realize what is happening to them. They must remember that their liberties are not in fact granted to them by the State, but are God-given. Any government that attempts to usurp them is, in fact, tyrannical.

As argued by the Colombian representative during the adoption of the International Convention on the Elimination of all Forms of Racial Discrimination (ICERD):

To penalize ideas, whatever their nature, is to pave the way for tyranny, for the abuse of power; and even in the most favorable circumstances it will merely lead to a sorry situation where interpretation is left to judges and law offices. [...] [I]deas are fought with ideas and reasons; theories are refuted with arguments and not by resort to the scaffold, prison, exile, confiscation or fines.

A large part of the problem, of course, is the tyrannical European Union, a monstrous, bloated supranational entity that has usurped the prerogatives of its member states. European nations are increasingly fettered by the mandarins of Brussels, who dictate from afar the most important policies, including immigration policy. [...]

Polls indicate that doubts regarding immigration policy and the saving of the euro are now deeply ingrained in European society, despite all the propaganda and the different political parties' views on this matter. A majority of Germans (and Austrians) fear rising crime, Islamization, and *Überfremdung*, translated roughly as alienation of state and people.

[...]

Up until now, the many pieces of the political puzzle — crime, Islamization, the rising number of ethnic slums—have not been assembled by the populace into a finished picture of this crisis. The aims of the totalitarian-utopian EU project have not been detected. People remain unaware that the ultimate goal is the obliteration of Germans and Europeans as historical subjects.

When the worst crises occur—when Islamic terror attacks make the streets run with blood—there is a brief period of apparent solidarity.

But everything soon returns to "normal" and the Powers That Be continue tightening the screws on domestic dissent.

Those who said "*Je suis Charlie*" only a year ago are now fighting "hate speech" with increasing ferocity.

At the national political level, dissident parties that support national sovereignty and want to limit immigration are reviled and demonized in the media. Various administrative procedures are implemented against them to reduce their effectiveness.

In Sweden, the postal service refuses to deliver mailings sent out by the Sweden Democrats. Supporters of the party are hounded by violent leftists and sometimes lose their jobs.

In Britain, United Kingdom Independence Party (UKIP) supporters may lose custody of their children.

In the Netherlands, the leader of the Freedom Party (PVV)—the most popular party in the country—has been put on trial for "hate speech" three times.

In France, the leader of the National Front was subjected to a criminal investigation for her remarks about public street prayers by Muslims.

In Austria there are calls to disenfranchise people who vote for the Austrian Freedom Party (FPÖ).

Like Hillary Clinton, European opponents of free speech want to redefine "incitement." If something you say about Islam upsets Muslims, and then while they are upset they riot and rape and loot and burn cars, then it is you who are responsible for their violence. Limiting your speech is thus necessary, because "hateful" speech is causatively connected with violence.

Using this sort of logic, the truth can be considered "hate speech." Discussing verifiable facts about Islam—its doctrines, its history, the behavior of Muslims in the name of Allah—may upset Muslims and incite them to become violent. This proves that "hate speech" has occurred, regardless of the truth of what was said. And it means that your right to utter such truths may be restricted.

The enforcement of a "hate speech" regime thus leads to the denial of the obvious: we deny the origin and meaning of the most evil occurrences around the globe.

A Syrian refugee kills his pregnant girlfriend? Keep quiet; otherwise you will be guilty of "hate speech."

A Tunisian man kills innocent children by running over them with a truck on the streets of Nice? Better not say or write anything about the reasons for this madness if you want to keep your job and stay out of jail.

And so we refuse to articulate a message of resistance against the evil we see around us.

Our political and social leaders have granted us free speech with buts. "Yes, we have freedom of speech, but…"
How many times have you heard this?

"I believe in free speech, but drawing cartoons of Mohammed is taking it too far."
"No one is a stronger supporter of free speech than I am, but that doesn't mean someone should be allowed to insult another person's religion."

Once you apply a "but," free speech ceases to be a right. Instead it becomes a concession to be rationed out by someone in authority, who decides where the "buts" will fall.

You cannot have freedom with "buts." You cannot have half-freedom, part-time freedom, contingent freedom. You cannot declare your support for free speech, but only defend those parts of it that you like or that meet your preferred standards.

The First Amendment of the US Constitution provided a clear unambiguous commitment to free speech, thereby setting a global gold standard for civil liberties that is still unequaled anywhere in the world, more than 200 years later.

This is what I have set my sights on for Austria and Europe. Now, before it is too late, we need to reclaim our right to speak freely.

Our time is short in Europe. Please keep us in your prayers.
[Speech delivered at various venues during August 2016]

One of my playing fields was the world's largest regional organization the Organization for Security and Cooperation in Europe (OSCE). In July 2009, my colleagues Henrik and Harald joined me at what would be a decade-long fight, sometimes even a battle in the diplomatic plenary, for freedoms and Western civilization at the OSCE. In 2017, I described our foray into the diplomatic world as follows:

In addition to my public-speaking engagements, my activism for the past eight years has also focused on the infiltration and subversion of a trans-national organization known as the Organization for Security and Cooperation in Europe—the OSCE. Many of you have probably never heard of the OSCE, or have only a vague awareness of it. It doesn't get much public attention except when it sends observers to monitor elections in someplace like Ukraine. Yet it's quite significant in other respects, as I will explain in a moment.

For the past ten or fifteen years the OSCE has been steadily and quietly infiltrated by Islamic organizations. Its policies and decision-making processes have gradually been compromised, so that it is now a virtual mouthpiece for the Muslim Brotherhood and Turkish Islamic fundamentalists.

In a word: It has been Islamized.

The transformation of the OSCE is a strange tale of international diplomacy, honest activism, corruption and mandatory lies—all mixed together.

The OSCE has its roots in the fight against communism during the Cold War, specifically the Helsinki Accords of 1975. Back then, it was called the Commission on Security and Cooperation in Europe (CSCE). It was created to uphold the human rights commitments of nations in the region, particularly those of the East Bloc. The communist countries signed on, thinking the CSCE was simply another paper entity that they could ignore with impunity. They didn't realize that being publicly held to account for its human rights record would prove a major embarrassment to the Soviet Union. They had no idea that, by joining the CSCE, they would be contributing to the peaceful collapse of communism in Eastern Europe and the USSR.

The CSCE could rightly claim a share of the credit for prompting the push towards *glasnost* that eventually dissolved the U.S.S.R. With its headquarters in Warsaw, where memories of Soviet repression remained fresh, the OSCE managed to hold onto its mission for more than a decade after the Iron Curtain disappeared from Europe. However, lacking its original *raison d'être*, the OSCE became subject to "organizational drift." It was ripe for infiltration and exploitation by any group with a definite agenda.

Islam is exactly such a group. It has its agenda, as laid down in its foundational scriptures, and it has patience, zeal, and energy.

Here in the 21st century freedom faces a foe no less formidable than Communism. This new enemy attacks us on a multitude of fronts, including international institutions established to defend freedom and democracy. By subverting such institutions until they become meaningless, Islamic operatives open the floodgates to the introduction of *shariah* into our societies, without any meaningful resistance.

But they didn't count on us joining the fray. By "us," I mean the transatlantic Counterjihad. The larger culture brands us "Islamophobes," but I prefer to think of us as the Resistance. We resist the erosion of our fundamental freedoms. We resist the encroachment of *shariah* law in our society. And we resist the Islamization of our culture.

Back in 2009, we learned that our civil society organizations could simply register at OSCE, walk into the conferences, and begin speaking the plain, simple, reasonable truth. And since the OSCE cannot agree on anything unless all participants agree, a few dissident voices can nip bad ideas in the bud. So we went there to do just that.

First, we destroyed a so-called "NGO Roundtable" of leftist confusion, to the explicit regret of the moderator. Then, we infuriated the Turkish delegation by suggesting that Muslims sign up to abandon terrorism, racism, and other evils; that earned us some real enemies, but the Holy See (representing the Vatican) really liked what we did that day. At the same time, we directly observed the Muslim Brotherhood's infiltration of the U.S. government, and the influence of the Organization of Islamic Cooperation (OIC) in the American delegation. Scary games, indeed.

Encouraged by having spoken the truth, I went one step further in November 2009 and quoted the passage in the Qur'an that permits men to beat their wives, which elicited a very angry reaction in the plenary. "Religion has nothing to do with violence towards women." Shortly after that, my now-famous trials and tribulations in the Austrian courts began.

Other topics we have brought up over the years include the Cairo Declaration of Human Rights in Islam another word for *shariah*, the need to discredit the OIC-promoted concept of "Islamophobia," and the lack of proper definitions of numerous terms that are frequently spoken or written at the OSCE. We also outed one of the Muslim Brotherhood infiltrators, Salam al-Marayati, forcing the US government to come to his defense.

Once you understand how to phrase things, you can politely provoke quite outrageous responses. One such case was at the so-called "Security Days," a meeting held in Vienna in 2015, where we simply asked "Can the truth ever constitute 'hate speech'?" To our surprise, we got a clear response: "Since the truth can hurt, the answer is 'Yes.'"

The OSCE Representative for Freedom of the Media actually accepted that concept!

A particularly acute problem is what we have labeled "new forms of censorship," in which governments force private corporations to censor conservative or Islam-critical voices, often under pressure from Islamic organizations. Those governments then wash their hands and deny any accusation of censorship.

A recently-enacted German law is particularly noxious in this regard: It criminalizes criticism of Islam or immigration on social media. The journalist and activist Michael Stürzenberger is a case in point. Mr. Stürzenberger—who is a freedom fighter if there ever was one—was prosecuted for posting a historically accurate photo from World War Two on Facebook. The photo showed a Nazi official extending a warm greeting to the Grand Mufti of Jerusalem, Haj Amin al-Husseini. The photo was the truth, and nothing but the truth. Nazi leaders, including Adolf Hitler, had indeed warmly welcomed the Grand Mufti to Germany. But the truth is no defense where Islam is involved: the photo was insulting to a religious or ethnic group; therefore it violated the law. Michael Stürzenberger was convicted and sentenced to six months in prison. His conviction is currently being appealed.[1]

Yet the OSCE remains unconcerned about such egregious violations of human rights. Discussions at OSCE conferences have become dominated by left-wing multicultural cant. We were bombarded with progressive jargon—"diversity," "tolerance" and "inclusion." "Gender-" this, that, and the other. The ubiquitous cry of "racism!" And all the phobias—"homophobia," "transphobia" and of course "Islamophobia."

We're simple people who don't understand all that. We understand clear-cut, basic ideas such as "freedom of expression," "freedom of assembly" and "civil liberties," not complex constructs straight out of the Saul Alinsky *Rules for Radicals* playbook.

Our plain-spoken common sense disturbs the complacency of an organization that otherwise rests solidly in its own constructed "narrative" of universal tolerance, non-discrimination and other forms of mandatory ignorance. It's not that we seek to violate their unwritten rules; we just don't see them. That's because we're loyal to the original intentions of the OSCE. We defend classical democracy and old-fashioned liberty.

Our stubborn insistence on sticking to the original mission of the OSCE made us somewhat unpopular with the Moderators. As a result, they have investigated their options for keeping us out. They'd like to forbid our attendance, but the rules are clear: Any non-terrorist NGO has the right to participate at the OSCE, and we will keep doing that.

The most recent OSCE conference we attended was in Warsaw back in September. The sessions were particularly confrontational: We had a strong team of very principled people speaking out against censorship, *shariah* and other evils. This drew many rebukes from the Moderator for not being "sufficiently tolerant"—and when we challenged that, we were told in clear prose that it is not permissible to associate any particular religion with terrorism. That is, the mandarins who now run the show at the OSCE have ruled that a particular element of dogma must NOT be disputed, and insist that no evidence that might contradict it will be allowed.

Everyone who understands the historical facts about Islam, Islamic law, and terrorism will immediately realize that this constitutes a mandatory lie. And that's what we were up against in Warsaw: systemic, institutionalized untruth.

But just as a single light can dispel a thousand years of darkness,

---

1 Mr. Stürzenberger has since been acquitted of this charge. http://www.pi-news.net/2018/02/landgericht-muenchen-islamfaschismus-freispruch-rechtskraeftig/ (in German).

simple voices of reason can cut through the fog of a thousand minds lost in confusion. We've observed that our work discourages our enemies and encourages our allies. Slowly, incrementally, we are having an effect. This is why we go there, and this is why we'll keep going there.

In all honesty, sometimes the wait for the decision of the ECtHR felt interminable; sometimes my patience was seriously tested. When, for example, in August 2016, the European Centre for Law and Justice was permitted to weigh in on my behalf, my lawyer and I were almost certain that a verdict was imminent. At that point, I just wanted the ordeal to be over, whatever the court's decision. I was sick of speculating about how the court would decide when I knew for a fact that what I said in the fall of 2009 was nothing but the truth. But, as I would soon learn, the truth is no defense.

CHAPTER TWELVE

The European Court of Human Rights—or Wrongs?

The masses have never thirsted after truth. Whoever can supply them with illusions is easily their master; whoever attempts to destroy their illusions is always their victim.
—Gustave Le Bon, *The Crowd: A Study of the Popular Mind* (2009).

I NEVER KNEW what hit me. I was in the midst of saying good-bye to my dying mother when—true to fashion—I was informed by a friend about a news release. (See Appendix A.)

The shock about this terrible and terribly wrong verdict was compounded by the death of my mother only hours later. Thankfully, with the help of a good friend, I was able to release the following statement:

On Thursday, 25 October 2018, the European Court of Human Rights ruled that my conviction by an Austrian court for discussing the marriage between Prophet Mohammed and a six year old girl, Aisha, did not infringe my rights of freedom of speech.

I was not extended the courtesy of being told of this ruling. Like many others, I had to read it in the media.

The ECtHR found there had been no violation of Article 10 (freedom of expression) of the European Convention on Human Rights and that right to expression needed to be balanced with the rights of others to have their religious feelings protected, and served the legitimate aim of preserving religious peace in Austria.

In other words, my right to speak freely is less important than protecting the religious feelings of others.

This should ring warning bells for my fellow citizens across the continent. We should all be extremely concerned that the rights of Muslims in Europe NOT to be offended are greater than our own rights, and mine as a native European Christian woman, to speak freely.

I am proud to be the woman who has raised this alarm.

I am also optimistic. Since giving my seminars in Austria in 2009, we have come a very long way.

Ten years ago the press labeled me a "confused doom-monger" and I was compared to Osama Bin Laden. Now, Islam is being discussed in every sphere of life and people are waking up to the reality of a culture so opposed to our own.

The cultural and political threat posed by Islam to Western societies is now widely recognized and discussed. It is fair to say European society, as well as the political realm, is undergoing an enlightenment, as it is more awake than ever to the need to defend our own Judeo-Christian culture.

I believe my seminars in 2009, and subsequent work have contributed to strong pushback against an Islamic culture which is so at odds with our own. And note with interest that only one sentence out of 12 hours of seminars on Islam was a prosecutable offense. I assume the remaining content is now officially sanctioned by our Establishment masters.

It is obvious to me that public education and discourse on the subject of Islam can have a fundamental and far-reaching impact, even if our state or supra-national authorities try to stifle or silence it, in order to appease a culture so foreign to our own.

This fight continues. My voice will not and cannot be silenced.

Elisabeth Sabaditsch-Wolff

Apart from a short statement taken from the ECtHR press release, the Austrian mainstream media ignored me, as expected. There was one very thoughtful guest commentary in the semi-conservative Austrian daily *Die Presse*;[1] there was no other mainstream analysis of the verdict.

Given that there was still one, albeit very remote, chance to appeal this verdict, I immediately traveled to the United States to inform my supporters about the verdict and to raise funds; the appeal would be very expensive.

Upon my return, I wrote the following, published in *Gates of Vienna*:

---

1 Schöllhammer, Ralph, "A New Form of Censorship is Spooking Through Europe," *Die Presse*, November 19, 2018.

Oppression

Oppression is felt differently in different places and at different times. There are degrees to the level of one's feeling of oppression. I know what I'm talking about: I've experienced it numerous times in my life. Let me explain.

When I lived and worked in Kuwait in the late 1990s, I already felt somewhat caged. I always like telling the story of how in pre-Amazon days I would visit Kuwait's bookstores and marvel at the censorship imposed by the Kuwaiti (likely religious) authorities. There was little to no variety in the books I could buy, and many of those that made it onto the bookshelves were hopelessly outdated. For a committed bookworm like I am, this was an oppressive feeling.

Oppression in Kuwait manifested itself not only in the lack of knowledge in the form of books, but also in the prohibition of alcohol and pork. Freedom to me means the freedom to live, eat, read, think, and speak as I wish. In Kuwait I was unable to eat, drink or read what I chose. I want to make my own choices, just as I do not choose to eat dog or roaches, but should be free to do so.

So, when I boarded a plane to Dubai or Oman I always breathed a sigh of relief. Mind you, freedom is always relative. Compared to the United States, Dubai is still a repressive society, but the contrast with Kuwait's situation is staggering: parties, booze, pork, and other "vices," as long as you as a non-Muslim follow certain rules. If not, and you are caught, you'd better have your passport and a fast airplane at hand or you'll wind up in jail. Just check your local sob stories in the papers.

Fast-forward a few years to Tripoli, Libya. Seldom have I felt more caged, more jailed than in Tripoli at the beginning of this century. There was no way to spend money or free time, both of which were at hand in some abundance: no shopping centers like in Kuwait or Dubai to spend one's hard-earned shekels—pardon, dinars—no movie theaters, even if censored, no decent restaurants, no beach clubs. Just a lot of socialism, Islam and sand.

So driving those three hours from Tripoli across the border to Tunisia was a relief: freedom!—to a degree, of course. Not the kind that I was looking for, but at least I was able to breathe freely, buy some beer and enjoy a beach club on the island of Djerba.

And so it was when I finally left the Arab world that I thought I had left Islamic-style oppression behind me. I settled in Vienna, my hometown, hoping to regain the freedom to move about, to eat what I wished, to read as much as I could (thank you, in this case, to the Internet and Amazon), to dress as I wished, to speak my mind, in short, to live my life in freedom. You see, one only realizes what freedom means when it has been taken away. In our circles, this statement is considered a platitude. It's not really, however. And this is what I felt during my recent travels to the United States.

Living in today's Europe, I never fully realized just how constricted my freedom has become in recent years. Of course, I KNOW that my freedom is being reduced on a daily basis by the European Union's useless and annoying data protection regulations, which were tightened to the extreme this year, but I never really felt it as strongly, as overpoweringly, as I did at the end of this year. I actually found myself breathing a deep sigh of relief upon entering the United States, knowing that what I would be telling Americans would be protected by the United States Constitution and its First Amendment. One really does speak a different language if one doesn't have to self-censor all the time.

And that is what we do in Europe; we just don't realize it. Even I don't. But I recognized the stark difference as I viewed my European self from an American perspective. Believe me when I tell you that I am still in shock, even if I am at the forefront of my fight for the restoration of freedom of speech in Europe. But never have I felt this level of despair at the loss of my personal freedom as well as a profound fear of the future for my daughter.

As the year draws to a close, what can we do, what can you do?

Well, it depends on where you reside.

For those who live in Europe—and I am one—there is currently little hope. I really don't know what else to tell Europeans. How do you explain the loss of a fundamental right to someone who never realized he had that right to begin with, who never knew he even needed this right? Who needs free speech to buy the latest model iPhone? Or the latest plasma TV? So what's the use of free speech, then?

And why would you care about the impact of the European Court of Human Rights' verdict against me, but also against every European's right to express his views on a religion?

And finally, knowing what could happen to you, seeing what happened to me, or to Tommy Robinson, or to Michael Stürzenberger, or to all the other nameless victims of a repressive speech regime, would you really want to become active? No, I do not fault you for remaining silent and idle. But I do ask you to donate. A few euros here, a couple of dollars there will make all the difference to those on the front lines.

And now to readers in the United States: Hear our pleas for help. Remember your guaranteed freedoms, protect them, fight for them, and don't forget your brothers and sisters in Europe. You've saved Europe before and I guarantee you'll have to do it again.

Listen carefully to what I recently discussed in the United States. I've been warning for a decade now, and I will continue my warning. Come see me and talk to me. Watch my videos. Read *Gates of Vienna*. Support *GoV* and Vlad Tepes financially. At the end of the day, we can't fight for your freedoms without your dollars. It's as simple as that.

My Christmas wish is that one day I can travel to the US and talk to my audience about the restoration of freedom of speech in Europe. I want to be able to breathe the above-mentioned sigh of relief upon entering my beloved Austria, and thank God for the ability to live in a country that recognizes my right to express my views without being hauled before a judge.

January 2019 was characterized by hard work for the very last chance I had to rectify this travesty of justice. I had to petition the Grand Chamber of the ECtHR within three months of the publication of the initial judgment, and so my lawyer, assisted by experts from Alliance Defending Freedom International,[2] was tasked to complete this crucially important project. The deadline was January 25, 2019, and it was successfully met. The "Request for referral of the case to the Chamber of the European Court of Human Rights (Article 43 ECHR)" was delivered to the ECtHR in Strasbourg, France.

This photo was taken during the filing of the very last appeal at the ECtHR. The appeal was ultimately and finally rejected.

Once again, we had to wait and exercise patience. Until March 21,

---

2 https://adfinternational.org/, ADF International is a faith-based legal advocacy organization that protects fundamental freedoms and promotes the inherent dignity of all people.

2019, when a terse press release from the ECtHR shattered our last hope for the exercise of free speech in Europe. Buried in a number of other decisions announced in the press release was my case—request for referral rejected.

And so it ends.

Gates of Vienna reported this on March 21:

The Grand Chamber of the ECtHR Refuses to Hear ESW's Appeal

Back in January Elisabeth Sabaditsch-Wolff filed an appeal of her "hate speech" conviction with the Grand Chamber of the European Court of Human Rights (ECtHR). The Grand Chamber has now refused to hear her appeal (the announcement of the decision comprises one line in this press item from the Court).

This was the last avenue of appeal open to her—her conviction had been upheld by the Austrian Supreme Court, and then (after five long years) the ECtHR. There is no higher judicial authority to which she can appeal; her case is now officially closed.

As you can imagine, Elisabeth was hit hard by the news. Here's the note she sent out to the supporters who helped her pay the (very expensive) legal costs of the appeal:

I am sorry. I did all I could.

Since the current Austrian government is disinterested in doing anything about this tragedy, I am herewith ceasing my work in Austria. I grateful to everyone who supported me in the past decade.

Thanks to the a new project called "Encounter Truth" I will now spread the truth to the American people, at least, to those who still believe in Free Speech, in the First Amendment. There is much work to be done: we all know how much the First Amendment, how much free speech is currently under attack in the United States.

My lawyer's words:

'I do not need to stress that I consider this decision to be completely wrong and a serious blow to freedom of expression.'

Please pray for Austria, for Europe.

Henrik Raeder Clausen who has worked with me for many years, had this to say about European "justice:"

Elisabeth lost her appeal to the European Court of Human Wrongs —ehm, Rights. The Grand Chamber summarily dismissed the appeal. €45,000 in legal expenses and much hope lost, with the stroke of a pen.

She is of course deeply disappointed by the outcome. This means that the verdict from October stands unchallenged, with no further route for appeal. Thus, the European Court of Human Rights has introduced a "Right not to have religious feelings hurt," which is as important as Freedom of Expression, if not more.

One has to wonder what kind of imbeciles are now taking care of the highest human rights authority in Europe?

For Elisabeth, this marks the end of her work in Europe. She has good connections and major plans to work in the United States.

Another reason for her change of focus is that the CSPI [Center for the Study of Political Islam] people have won the battle for influence with the Austrian politicians. They have convinced the Austrian politicians that "Political Islam" is the problem, not Islam as such. From a legal perspective, this will lead to a law against "Political Islam," while the law on Islam as such (which Elisabeth and Christian Zeitz have struggled to get fixed) will remain unchanged.

A third reason for her ceasing all work in Austria is that her contacts in government let her down when it came to her case at the European Court of Human Rights. When she asked for a public statement of support, the Freedom Party [FPÖ] simply responded: "No. We do not want to offend our coalition partner [ÖVP] with a freedom of expression problem."

We also discussed our participation at OSCE.[3] We've been there for ten years now, hopefully getting to the hearts and minds of people present there, inspiring them to do the Right Thing. We probably caused severe harm to the organization as such, by using it for its intended purpose, thereby disturbing the leftist imbeciles now in charge of what used to be a very fine legacy. Our guess is that the usefulness of going there is spent, but we'll not make a final decision just yet.

Things are changing rapidly. The political madness, which we believed could be cured with rationality and reason, seems to survive just about any attack we have thrown at it. In fact, the madness seems to grow ever more pervasive, despite the efforts of good people left and right.

My take: This will get pretty chaotic. So-called "extremist forces" will come into play, now that the moderate ones have been systematically ignored, harassed and persecuted for a decade. Prayer and meditation make sense. Struggling to inspire brave, rational behavior among the press and politicians no longer does.

---

3 Organization for Security and Cooperation in Europe.

Conclusion

Jesus said: And you will know the truth, and the truth shall set you free.
—John 8:32

The end is just a little harder when brought about by friends.
—Jesus Christ Superstar

THE LEGAL BATTLE for what I believe is my God-given right to express myself freely lasted for ten years of my life. As I explained throughout this book, the path leading me to fight for free speech was clear from the day I first attended kindergarten in New York and subsequently moved to Tehran, from the time I studied the United States Constitution in 8th grade in Chicago to the months and years I spent in Kuwait and Libya. All of these stops in my life were chips that had already fallen into place when I received my summons to stand trial starting in November 2010.

I was neither the first nor the last to be prosecuted for speaking the truth. Many have faced judges before me, great names like Italian journalist Oriana Fallaci, who sadly had to fight for her health and succumbed to her illness before she could fight for her freedom of speech. Many more brave men and women are currently resisting the imposed hate speech regime; they are being dragged through costly trials, thereby oftentimes losing their livelihoods and their reputations. More often than not do families break apart as a result.

What made my case exceptional was my ability to fight the grave injustice and—what I believe—is the error of the initial judgment handed down in February 2011 and reaffirmed all the way to the European Court of Human Rights. No one else before me has done this, though I fervently hope that one day someone will follow in my footsteps and perhaps even succeed.

⁊

Dymphna, one of the proprietors at the website *Gates of Vienna* and a friend for life,[1] summed up my journey more succinctly than I ever could:

> When I think of Elisabeth, certain words come to mind: indomitable, of course. Smart. Sassy. Generous. Loyal. A fiercely partisan momma, whose overarching fight is for the future of her child and the next generation. The traits I envy most? Elisabeth's determination and her focus. She never forgets why she's here and what her goal has become.
>
> Sometimes I wonder if Elisabeth ever would have wandered into the minefield of the Counterjihad if she hadn't been a mother, if she hadn't been concerned for the future of the country she'd be leaving to her child. I remember well the irony in her reply when someone asked her (I forget who) what she'd be doing if she weren't in this fight. One part of her answer resonated for me: she said she'd have been planning another baby instead of trials and jail. How sad, to have to sacrifice her family hopes for this undertaking. Certainly it was never her intention to be hauled into court on hate speech charges back when she started her lectures on Islam.
>
> Like so many of us, Elisabeth had no idea of the treachery of the leftist consensus media or the elites who run things. Those are the malign, self-satisfied folks who set her up. She'd never have been charged in the first place were there not so many opportunistic "jornolists" who make their living via the entrapment of those who are willing to stand and up tell the truth.
>
> Remember Malvolio's speech in *Twelfth Night* when he talks about fame? In the second act, he priggishly bloviates —
>
> > …some are born great,
> > some achieve greatness, and
> > some have greatness thrust upon them.
>
> Unlike poor old Malvolio, Elisabeth really is in that third category, those who weren't looking for the limelight but found it shining relentlessly in their general direction anyway. Being a wonderful mixture of enthusiasm and simplicity, she has used the platform she's been thrust upon to make common cause with others who speak out for the rights we take for granted in the US, though ours are under ever-more chill-

---

1 Dymphna, to whom this book is dedicated, passed away while I was writing this book.

ing attacks.

Thank you, Dymphna, for your unwavering support. I couldn't have said it better.

You may be surprised to read that I bear absolutely no grudge against *NEWS* magazine or Ms. Dolna. I simply look at her career—she is apparently now working for a Vienna-based Catholic weekly newspaper and has her own blog—or the even trashier *NEWS* magazine with notoriously low readership numbers and I know that even if viewed only from this perspective, everything is just all right.

However, there is so much more to say about these past ten years.

First, there are the fantastic friends, supporters and allies I have made, men and women whom I immensely admire and respect, patriotic organizations like ACT! for America, ACT! for Canada, and The United West, which as soon as they found out about my troubles with the law, stood behind me, supporting me both financially and in getting the word out. In particular, the ACT! national conference in 2013 is one I will always remember because I was honored to present the first annual "Elisabeth Sabaditsch-Wolff Profiles in Courage Award" to heroes like Allen West and Valerie Price. Rep. Louie Gohmert and Rep. Michele Bachmann sought me out for discussions about my case and the situation in Europe when they visited Vienna, and also when I came to Washington DC. Both have been very supportive, as have Rep. Trent Franks, General Thomas McInerney and the recently deceased Admiral James "Ace" Lyons.

Secondly, I have been given the priceless opportunity to speak at venues not only all over the United States, but also Canada, Europe and Israel. Certainly unintentionally, *NEWS* and Ms. Dolna released a genie in a bottle, and for this I will always be grateful. I was able to say what needed to be said at a time when no one was willing to address the massive elephant in the room. I paved the way, I trekked part of that yellow brick road, and though this walk was a challenge at times, I do not regret one arduous yard I walked, for there were and still are many formidable companions. I thank them for standing and walking by my side. You were truly the wind beneath my wings. I could not have flown without you.

As already mentioned in a previous chapter, simultaneous to my battle for free speech, my friends Henrik and Harald and I began attending meeting held at the Organization for Security and Cooperation in Europe, the largest international security organization in the Western

Hemisphere (born out of the Cold War), and of which the United States is a founding participating State. What my esteemed colleagues and I experienced at the OSCE is for another book to be written; suffice it to say that I did not hold back at these conferences. In September 2015, I chastised the entire plenary about their attempts to silence and suppress truth by introducing the concept of thought-crimes and hate crimes, reproduced here in its entirety. I echoed President Ronald Reagan:

Tear down the walls of un-free speech!
Working Session No. 12
Specifically Selected Topic: Combating Hate Crimes and Ensuring Effective Protection against Discrimination
OSCE/ODIHR, Warsaw, Poland
29 September 2015

What we are witnessing today is the implementation of ever-more restrictions to our freedom to speak our minds. We should not be addressing hate speech but free speech!

Who among the participating States back in the 1980s, at the height of the Cold War, with freedom and communist oppression opposing each other, would have dreamed that we would one day be attending OSCE meetings discussing speech restrictions?

Who among the participating States back in the 1980s would have dreamed that one day we would have to tell our children to hold back their opinions in school for fear of repercussions?

Who among the participating States back in the 1980s would have dreamed that one day we would be confronted with legislation governing thought-crimes?

Who among the participating States back in the 1980s—fighting for the forces of freedom: freedom of thought, freedom of speeches, freedom of expression against the forces of darkness—could have foreseen that this day would come?

You, the participating States of the OSCE, were once instrumental in tearing down the walls of oppression, leading the way to freedom, the freedom to speak one's mind openly and without fear of repercussions. You have failed. By even discussing so-called hate crimes—which are nothing other than the destruction of the free marketplace of ideas—the OSCE has returned to the dark ages of oppression.

Will we sit here in the coming years discussing whatever has been allowed by OSCE participating States? How much farther will the corridor of what is "acceptable" speech be narrowed?

Bürgerbewegung Pax Europa [the German NGO that I represent] calls on the OSCE to tear down the walls of tyranny of thought-crimes! Only a free marketplace of ideas guarantees vibrant societies.

I am grateful that my public speaking allowed me to travel to places I had never been before and always wanted to visit. Israel was and still is one of these places. And so my trip to Israel in December 2010 was a dream come true because I had always wanted to visit Israel, the bulwark of freedom and democracy in the Middle East. Not only was I able to see first-hand how dangerous it is for Israelis to live in cities such as Ashkelon and Ashdod due to their proximity to the Gaza Strip and the Palestinians' inclination to send greetings to their neighbors, but I was deeply moved touring Yad Vashem in Jerusalem, where my friends and colleagues signed the guest book as follows:

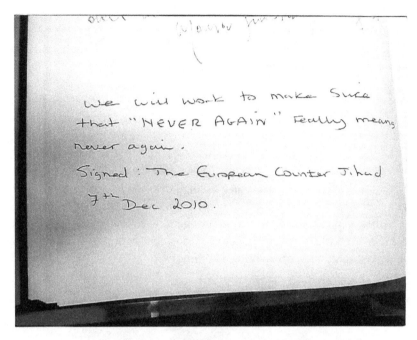

We will work to make Sure
that "NEVER AGAIN" Feally means
never again.
Signed : The European Counter Jihad
7th Dec 2010.

On the final evening in Jerusalem, I observed the following in my speech:

Israel is on the front lines of the very same war. Israel is surrounded by the barbarism and backwardness and destitution that awaits us all if we continue to surrender to the evil forces that would destroy Western Civilization. We have only to look at what has happened to Lebanon over the last fifty years to see the future that awaits a modern "multicultural" Europe.

And we only have to look a few kilometers to the south of this spot to see what Israel would be like if it were not inhabited by the Jews. A satellite photograph of the Gaza Strip reveals something telling: when you move a bit south from Ashkelon, or a bit west from Sderot, the rich and productive landscape of Israel abruptly ends and the vast wasteland of Gaza begins. This wasteland extends further south into Egypt, east into Jordan, and north into Lebanon.

Israel is an oasis of civilization in a desert of barbarism.

This is why Israel is so important to the struggle against the Great *Jihad*. Anyone who is committed to resisting Islamization will find in Israel a natural ally.

This is not a matter of Left and Right. *Shariah* has no respect for any of our political parties. It does not recognize the very foundation on which our diverse political structures rest.

Make no mistake about it: the fight against *shariah* is a fight to save civilization itself.

To discover the future of Europe and Israel if the door is not closed against expansionist Islam, examine what remains of Zoroastrian Persia, or Buddhist Afghanistan, or Christian Syria.

This is what awaits us if we do not act now. Our great civilization will be replaced by poverty and despotism and degradation.

Speaking at the Ahavath Torah Synagogue

Not only did I speak in Israel for the first time ever, but I was also invited to address the congregation of Ahavath Torah in Stoughton, MA, by my close friend and ally, Rabbi Jonathan Hausman. It was an emotional moment for me:

I've never been to a synagogue before—although I have visited many mosques! I'm humbled to stand here before you. Thank you, Rabbi, for inviting me and giving the me the opportunity to exercise my freedom of speech.

He and I have a connection: his paternal grandmother was an Austrian, and if his English weren't so good, we would be able to get by in Yiddish and German.

[W]hat we say here tonight is still quite legal—for now, anyway. Until Bill Killian [US Attorney for Eastern Tennessee] reaches his goal of removing First Amendment protections from the criticism of Islam, our right to say these things is guaranteed by the United States Constitution. I'm not so lucky—I don't have such a guarantee in Austria. Danes, Britons, Swedes, and Germans also lack that protection.

But you, as Americans, still have the privilege of the First Amendment.

The time to use that privilege is now, while you still can.

The free speech movement depends on people like you. We cannot expect our leaders or our media to preserve our freedoms—it's up to us.

I'll close with a quote from a well-known Swedish *samizdat* writer who writes under the pseudonym Julia Caesar. She has dedicated her life and her writings to exposing what has been done to her country without the consent of its people. In a recent essay called "We Changed Our Lives," she writes:

We knew that no human being and no political system building their existence on lies could last forever.

We knew the truth always wins.

We knew the truth can break through quickly.

We knew the truth can take a long time and sometimes breaks through with violence.

We knew the truth had been replaced with new systems of lies.

We used to think about the orchestra playing onboard the sinking Titanic. We thought that the musicians perhaps felt a little better than those who ran around on deck in a state of panic. And we had no choice, for that matter. We simply couldn't manage to watch our country going down.

Ladies and gentlemen, we have no choice. And time is short. The ship is closing in on the iceberg while the orchestra plays and dancers glide across the floor under the party lights.

It's not just Sweden that's going down, or the United States, or Austria. The entire Western world is steaming full speed ahead towards that iceberg.

Silence is not an option.

Nothing will keep me silent. I am adamant that my daughter and my daughter's daughters shall never live as Islamic chattel.

It is our responsibility—the responsibility of all of us—to do what we can now, while change is still possible.

In September 2014, I was invited once more by Rabbi Hausman at Ahavath Torah Synagogue to discuss the worrying rising anti-Semitism in Europe. Because this an even more timely topic today, I am reproducing my speech in its entirety, and I stand by every word:

Most of you have already heard of what is commonly called "the new anti-Semitism" in Europe. In the past ten years or so anti-Semitism has risen to a level not seen in Western Europe since the fall of the Third Reich. However, what you may not know is that the new Jew-hatred is expressed mainly by European Muslims—the "New Swedes," the "New Germans," the "New Austrians," and so on. Those wonderful denizens of Modern Multicultural Europe.

It must be stated clearly: the rising anti-Semitism in Europe is IS-LAMIC anti-Semitism. Dr. Andrew Bostom has chronicled this history of Islamic anti-Semitism, which is as old as Islam itself. Jew-hatred is sanctioned, and even mandated by the Qur'an and the sayings of Mohammed. There is no Muslim community in Europe, not even the most "mainstream," that is not rife with Jew-hatred. *Mein Kampf* and *The Protocols of the Elders of Zion* are best-sellers among Muslims wherever it is legal to sell them, and where it is not, they are underground favorites in Islamic communities.

And Muslims in Europe have allied themselves with the Left. A few years ago, during anti-Israel demonstrations in Belgium, socialist politicians marched alongside supporters of the Palestinians while the Muslim participants chanted: "*Hamas! Hamas! Jews to the gas!*"

The news media would have Jews be afraid of "right-wing" parties is Europe, which they often equate with "neo-fascism" or "neo-Nazism." Nothing could be further from the truth: it is among the socialists, who sold their souls to forge an alliance with Islam, where the expressions of Jew-hatred are the loudest and most frequent.

Yes, anti-Semitism exists among native Europeans. There's no denying that. But true anti-Semites, those who are obsessed with Jew-hatred as a primary political motive, are few in number. Their political parties are generally considered a joke in most countries. They are marginal at best. They have no large following, and they do not win elections.

There are two exceptions, however. The two most significant Jew-hating parties are Jobbik in Hungary and Golden Dawn in Greece.

The former was able to flourish in a former East Bloc country, where pre-war attitudes were preserved by communism like a fly in amber. The latter developed out of the despair and chaos of economic ruin in the most destitute country in Europe—much as the National Socialists did in Germany during the Great Depression.

The anti-*jihad* parties are frequently equated with Jobbik and Golden Dawn, but the two factions bear no resemblance to each other. Islam-critics appeal to a different demographic. Anti-Semitic parties and groups eventually tend to form alliances of convenience with Muslims, due to their common interest in destroying Israel and exterminating Jews.

In contrast, the anti-*jihad* parties support Israel, promote civil liberties, and generally espouse a classical liberal philosophy. Examples include the PVV in the Netherlands, the Danish People's Party, the Sweden Democrats, and the Lega Nord in Italy. What they all have in common is their opposition to Islamization and mass immigration.

The Flemish separatist party Vlaams Belang is widely demonized as being "neo-Nazi" or "neo-fascist." Yet it is one of the only truly free-market parties in Europe, and it is the ONLY party that defended Jews on the floor of the Flemish parliament during the violent anti-Israel demonstrations in 2009. The smear against Vlaams Belang is one of the most unjust and outrageous media operations of the past twenty years—and, given the leftist sympathies of the mainstream media, that is really saying something.

The attempt to convert anti-*jihad* parties into "right-wing extremists" was a deliberate operation, a false "narrative" created by the left and the mainstream media to demonize and marginalize Europeans who resist Islamization.

I stand here in support of Israel, and in solidarity with Jews everywhere. To paraphrase Douglas Murray:

All across Europe there is a new hatred in the air, but it is also the old one. The people on the streets of Paris, Berlin, London, Amsterdam and other cities across Europe include the descendants of some of those who fought against, fought for, allied or collaborated with the evil regime which spurred this hatred on last time. But most of the perpetrators are not those people. Most of them are of immigrant backgrounds. In Britain, these are mainly from the Indian sub-continent (predominantly Pakistan); in France and the Netherlands, they are from North Africa; in Germany and Austria, largely from Turkey.

Everyone in Europe can see this, but no one wants to identify it.

We live in so much fear of being identified as "politically incorrect." We are rightly disgusted by racism of any kind. And yet here we see—and nowhere more clearly than in Germany—the new racist nightmare for Europe. We thought we had gotten rid of anti-Semitism in Europe. We thought we had made it totally unacceptable. And yet here Europe has imported millions of people who fail in varying degrees to assimilate. Many of those people now look as if they have taken up the exact same hatred we all hoped we had left behind.

These are dark days in the Middle East. But they are darker days in Europe. Whether we deal with this renewed evil or not will be the challenge of this generation.

Let me say this clearly: I unconditionally support Israel's right to exist. It is the only democracy in the Middle East, no matter what the Leftists on both sides of the Atlantic argue.

I also believe there is no meeting Hamas or Fatah halfway. Amos Oz, certainly not known for his conservative opinions, recently said: "Even a man of compromise cannot approach Hamas and say: 'Maybe we meet halfway and Israel exists only on Mondays, Wednesdays and Fridays.'"

The truth is, we are all living in Israel. It's just that some of us haven't realized it yet.

I say it again, echoing Douglas Murray: We are all Israel.

Sadly and shamefully, in the decade since I gave this speech, the situation has dramatically deteriorated, chiefly due to the 2015 influx of mostly Muslim migrants, prompting Jews all over Europe to once again abandon their countries and make their way to Israel.[2]

In the past ten years, the number of friends and colleagues who have been silenced or forced into hiding for fear of their safety has risen dramatically. I can no longer count them on the fingers of my hand; I would now have to resort to pages of names if I were to tell you about their fate. One of the latest—of the more prominent casualties—is a former German radio and television presenter known for his flippant humor. Until June 30, readers of his Facebook page could enjoy his so-called "*Elmis Moin Briefn,*" a German wordplay on "morning briefing," in which he would irreverently comment on the latest madness in Germany and the world. On July 1, 2019, he posted the following on his Facebook page:

---

2 British journalist Katie Hopkins has reported on this in her video essay, "HOME-LANDS." https://www.youtube.com/watch?v=orTAUMMWd-A.

Elmis moinbrifn
July 1, 2019

Dear readers and fans of "*moinbrifn*"! Yes, the rumors are true. As of today, I'm stopping my daily "brifn" on Facebook. Really a mistake, with far more than 3,000 likes per post and 55,000 followers and a reach of 60,000 readers. But I do not want to be dependent in the future on the capricious whims of a social platform. It is true that this time Facebook has banned me for another 30 days for hate speech. I used a common term for criminal immigrants, sounding much like a precious metal.[3] I thought that was far more harmless than, for example, "riff-raff." A court decided that this term is hate speech. From there, it is only a small step to [being accused of] rabble-rousing, and I do not care to go along with that.

I'm concerned at the development in Facebook. More restrictions of freedom of expression will follow. We are developing slowly but surely to a kind of German Democratic Republic 2.0, and there are those who are working at it. Successfully, as can be seen! An affair like "brifn" lives on daily events and continuity, and that just cannot be, with continuous interruptions by psychopaths. I am considering a weekly "brifn" but I cannot promise.

I myself am in the last decade of life and there are more important things in life than constantly being patronized by idiots. This country is faltering to its end and patting itself on the back as it does. I can still half-heartedly make humorous comments about it, but unfortunately, I cannot change it. The point of no return has long since been passed.

This intentional, uncontrolled immigration will bring us misery a thousand-fold, of that I am certain. Just as certain as an apeman who believes he can blockade a highway, because his sister is marrying her cousin.

Well, I am grateful for the many nice comments on the "brifns" and I am especially gratified by support, sent by messenger, from people who were not able to "like" my essays, because it would have risked their jobs. It was there that I gave daily observations on the situation in my homeland, which seems to have gone completely off course. And that does not just apply to open-air swimming pools. For instance, when a funding drive for —in my opinion—an obvious people smuggler who has broken every international law of the sea, brings in far more than a million euros, something is wrong in our society. She should be locked up and lose her captain's commission. And that will never happen.

Naturally, I will continue to comment occasionally on the politicos the day, but then, a thirty-day ban won't be so annoying. I hope for

---

3 He referred to "migrants" as "pieces of gold" (*Goldstücke*).

your understanding.

My researches have depressed me. They have deprived me of any prospect of a good outcome for the German population. We will lose this immigration war.

What a former journalist said is true: "The era of Merkel has settled like a tombstone on this land!" (R.I.P.). There is something to that.

Now I am going to make a round in the woods on my e-bike!

To all fans: Take care of yourselves! Protect your daughters! Be healthy!

That's a wrap

ELMI (Your favorite xenophobe)

If you think that what happened to me or Elmar Hörig or many others in Europe could never take place in the United States because your speech is protected by the First Amendment, think again. As Robert Spencer, eminent Islamic scholar and a man I am allowed to call friend, argues succinctly:

> Remember back in 2009, when Barack Obama declared in Cairo: "I consider it part of my responsibility as President of the United States to fight against negative stereotypes of Islam wherever they appear." Obama is no longer President, but the idea that the U.S. government should be solicitous of Islam in a way that it is not of Judaism, Christianity, Hinduism, Buddhism, or any other religion is still very much with us.
>
> Remember also when Hillary Clinton, then Secretary of State, spoke at an Organization of Islamic Cooperation (OIC) conference in Istanbul on July 15, 2011. Clinton said that she wanted to "applaud the Organization of Islamic Conference and the European Union for helping pass Resolution 16/18 at the Human Rights Council."
>
> Resolution 16/18 called for the nations of the world to ban "defamation of religion," a euphemism for criticism of Islam, since no one anywhere minded when other religions were criticized. Clinton explained in order to circumvent the First Amendment and render criticism of Islam unacceptable in the American public square, "we are focused on promoting interfaith education and collaboration, enforcing anti-discrimination laws, protecting the rights of all people to worship as they choose, and to use some old-fashioned techniques of peer pressure and shaming, so that people don't feel that they have the support to do what we abhor."
>
> Clinton was declaring her intention, and presumably the policy of the Obama administration, to stigmatize speech, to the extent that people would be afraid to cross what former OIC Secretary General Ek-

230 *eo* *The Truth is No Defense*

meleddin Ihsanoglu had called "red lines that should not be crossed."

Even before Clinton spoke these fateful words, these techniques she recommended had been used by media and academic elites, whose agenda was difficult to distinguish from that of the Obama administration. In the eight years since she spoke them, these techniques have been perfected: honest analysis of the motivating ideology behind *jihad* terror is universally stigmatized as "Islamophobia," and those who have dared to engage in such analysis are defamed as "hate group leaders" by the Southern Poverty Law Center (SPLC), in reports that are repeated in the establishment media as if they were neutral and objective. The "peer pressure" and "shaming" of those who speak honestly about the *jihad* threat is now reflexive, automatic, and even internalized by many not only on the Left, but also among conservatives: the Conservative Political Action Conference (CPAC) has not allowed an open discussion of this issue for years, and establishment Republicans for the most part eagerly toe the "Islamophobia" line and happily make common cause with deceptive and cynical "moderate Muslims" of questionable intentions.[4]

To add insult to injury, our politicians and governmental-subsidized non-governmental organizations like the Southern Poverty Law Center (in the US) or Hope Not Hate (in the UK) are members of the Global Ministry of Truth, telling us that Islam is a religion of peace hijacked by a Tiny Minority of Extremists."' They are forcing truth upon us, thereby preventing us from seeking truth and knowledge. They try to silence us at international forums. And they attempt to silence opposing opinions by "de-platforming" us, essentially cutting us off from information-giving and information-receiving by shutting down Twitter accounts, Facebook accounts and other social media presence. It is as if we never existed. We are gone and, according to the Ministry of Truth, the world is a better and more peaceful place for it. Except for the continued terrorist attacks. Except for the continued hatred exhibited by the faithful of a certain religion. Except for the lack of diverse opinions.

Do you want to live in a world like that?

I closed my 2017 speech, and I will close this book, with the following words:

I'd like to read you the text of a placard that was posted on walls and lamp posts in Warsaw during the Polish National Independence Day march on November 11, 2017. The anonymous author was allud-

---

4 https://gellerreport.com/2019/03/islamophobia-criminal-offense.html/.

ing to the famous piece written by the German dissident, Pastor Martin Niemöller. The text of the placard was translated by a Polish member of our [translation] team:

> When the refugees came, I didn't protest — they were poor refugees.
>
> When they established mosques, I didn't protest—they have the right to pray.
>
> When they introduced Halal food in schools I didn't protest—they can only eat what the Qur'an allows them to.
>
> When they carried out attacks I didn't protest—it's only a small group of radicals, which doesn't represent true Islam.
>
> When they raped women I didn't protest—rapes occur in every culture and religion, and they have nothing to do with Islam.
>
> When they demanded *shariah* zones I didn't protest—they need their own space, and we live in a free country.
>
> When their MPs took their seats in parliament I didn't protest—they're almost half the population now and have a right to be represented.
>
> When they introduced *shariah* law, it was too late for me to protest.

I strongly urge you to continue your fight for free speech, and your resistance to Islamization.

This is a civilizational struggle that we CANNOT afford to lose.

Just keep reminding yourself: "If not me, who? If not now, when?"

Finally, please continue your support in whatever way you can. This is about all of you as much as it is about me. This is about our future.

Never give up.

Never give in.

Never surrender.

ANALYSIS

BY ROBERT SPENCER

ESW WAS RIGHT ABOUT MUHAMMAD. SO WHY WAS SHE PERSECUTED?

I N OCTOBER 2018, according to the Turkish publication *Daily Sabah*, the European Court of Human Rights (ECHR) ruled that Elisabeth Sabaditsch-Wolff's "criminal conviction and fine for her statements accusing the Prophet Muhammad of pedophilia did not breach her right to free speech."[1]

The Court claimed that "the applicant's statements had been likely to arouse justified indignation in Muslims" and "amounted to a generalization without factual basis." What's more, the Court added, Sabaditsch-Wolff's statements "were not phrased in a neutral manner aimed at being an objective contribution to a public debate concerning child marriages."[2]

The statements in question came from a November 2009 seminar, which the socialist magazine *NEWS* secretly recorded and then had Sabaditsch-Wolff charged with hate speech.[3] This is the first problematic aspect of the ECHR's ruling: Sabaditsch-Wolff made her statements in a private seminar, and never intended them to be a "contribution to a public debate concerning child marriages" at all. *NEWS* published them

---

1 "Insulting Prophet Muhammad not 'free speech,' ECtHR rules," *Daily Sabah*, October 25, 2018.

2 Ibid.

3 Soeren Kern, "A Black Day for Austria," *Gatestone Institute*, December 26, 2011.

without her consent.

The other, and more significant, problematic aspect of the ECHR's ruling is that Sabaditsch-Wolff hadn't actually engaged in any "hate speech;" her lectures were largely made up of quotations from the Qur'an and other Islamic sources. If these were "likely to arouse justified indignation in Muslims," the fault lay in those texts, not in Sabaditsch-Wolff. Yet in February of 2011, Sabaditsch-Wolff was found guilty not only of hate speech, but of "denigration of religious beliefs of a legally recognized religion."[4] Sabaditsch-Wolff was duly found guilty of the latter charge.[5]

Sabaditsch-Wolff was guilty, Judge Bettina Neubauer explained, because she had said that Muhammad, the prophet of Islam, "had a thing for little girls."[6] This supposedly constituted denigration because while Muhammad consummated his marriage with a nine-year-old girl when he was fifty-four, Islamic sources did not record that he ever showed any interest in other prepubescent girls, and also had adult wives at the same time, so it was false and defamatory to say that he was a pedophile.

It is indeed true that marrying young girls was not all that unusual for Muhammad's seventh century cultural context, but the only reason why the question of Muhammad's marriage to a child has any relevance today is because of Muhammad's status in Islamic theology Muhammad is the supreme example of conduct (cf. Qur'an 33:21). The noted Muslim scholar Muqtedar Khan of the Center for the Study of Islam and Democracy explains:

> No religious leader has as much influence on his followers as does Muhammad (Peace be upon him) the last Prophet of Islam....And Muhammad as the final messenger of God enjoys preeminence when it comes to revelation—the Qur'an—and traditions. So much so that the words, deeds and silences (that which he saw and did not forbid) of Muhammad became an independent source of Islamic law. Muslims, as a part of religious observance, not only obey, but also seek to emulate and imitate their Prophet in every aspect of life. Thus Muhammad is the medium as well as a source of the divine law. [7]

---

4 Ibid.

5 Ibid.

6 Ibid.

7 Dr. Muqtedar Khan, "The Legacy of Prophet Muhammad and the Issues of Pedophilia and Polygamy," *Ijtihad*, June 9, 2003.

If Muslims "seek to emulate and imitate their Prophet in every aspect of life" and he did indeed marry a child, then some Muslims are likely to marry children. This is a question of facts that can be objectively established: first, whether Islamic texts indeed attest that Muhammad married a child, and second, whether any Muslims imitate him in this.

Hadiths—reports of Muhammad's words and deeds that are normative for Islamic law when deemed authentic by Muslim scholars—record that Muhammad's favorite wife, Aisha, was six when Muhammad wedded her and nine when he consummated the marriage. These *hadiths* come from several of the *hadith* collections that Muslim theologians consider to be the most reliable: the as-Sahih as-Sittah, that is, the authentic and trustworthy ones (sahih means "sound" or "reliable"). These include, in order of their importance and general reputation for reliability, Sahih Bukhari, the most respected and authoritative *hadith* collection, compiled by the imam Muhammad ibn Ismail al-Bukhari (810–870); Sahih Muslim, by Muslim ibn al-Hajjaj (821–875); the Sunan of Abu Dawud as-Sijistani (818–889); As-Sunan as-Sughra, by Ahmad ibn Shuayb an-Nasai (829–915); the Jami of Abi Isa Muhammad At-Tirmidhi (824–892); and the Sunan of Muhammad ibn Maja (824–887). Abu Dawud as-Sijistani, for example, reportedly traveled to Arabia, Iraq, Khurasan, Egypt, Syria, Iran, and elsewhere collecting *hadiths*. One respected imam, Zakariya bin Yahya as-Saji, declared: "The Qur'an is the foundation of Islam and Sunan Abu Dawud is its pillar." Another, Ibn al-Arabi, added: "There is no need of acquaintance of anything after acquiring the knowledge of the Qur'an and of Sunan Abu Dawud."[8]

The most respected *hadith* collection, Bukhari's, began in a dream, according to Dr. Muhammad Muhsin Khan, a Saudi Islamic scholar and Qur'an translator. Dr. Khan writes that Bukhari dreamed he was "standing in front of Prophet Muhammad having a fan in his hand and driving away the flies from the Prophet." The imam interpreted this dream as a divine sign that he would "drive away the falsehood asserted against the Prophet." Accordingly, he spent his life attempting to distinguish authentic *hadiths* from forgeries. According to Islamic tradition, Bukhari traversed the Islamic world collecting stories about Muhammad's words and deeds—fully 300,000 of them.[9] Ultimately he rejected

---

8 Abu Dawud, *Sunan Abu Dawud, English Translation with Explanatory Notes*, translated by Ahmad Hasan, Kitab Bhavan, 1990, v.

9 Muhammad Muhsin Khan, introduction to *Sahih al-Bukhari*, 18–19, in Muhammed Ibn Ismail Al-Bukhari, *Sahih al-Bukhari: The Translation of the Meanings*, translated by Muhammad Muhsin Khan, Darussalam, 1997, 18-19.

nearly 293,000 of them as fabricated, or at least impossible to evaluate as to their reliability. He chose and published 7,563 *hadiths*, certifying them as reliable, though these included repetitions; in all, he included 2,602 separate *hadiths* that he deemed authentic. Even these run to nine volumes in a modern-day English/Arabic edition published in Saudi Arabia.

The imam Muslim ibn al-Hajjaj was Bukhari's disciple. Born in Nishapur in what is now Iran, he is said to have traveled to Arabia, Egypt, Syria, and Iraq to collect *hadiths*. According to Islamic tradition, he also collected 300,000 *hadiths*, of which he preserved 4,000 as authentic in his Sahih. Most Muslim scholars consider his collection, as well as that of Bukhari, to be almost entirely reliable; Muslims raise virtually no question about the authenticity of traditions that appear in both *Sahih Bukhari* and *Sahih Muslim*—of which there are many. One Internet-based introduction to Islamic faith and practice, which assures readers that "nothing on this site violates the fixed principles of Islamic law," sums up the prevailing opinion among Muslims: "Sahih Bukhari is distinguished with it's [sic] strong reliability." It adds that the imam Muslim chose the *hadiths* that he included in *Sahih Muslim* "based on stringent acceptance criteria."[10]

The assertion that Muhammad married Aisha when she was six and consummated the marriage when she was nine is found in the collections of Bukhari, Muslim, Abu Dawud, Ibn Majah, and an-Nasai. In some of these collections it is found multiple times, which indicates that the compiler of the *hadith* collection received the *hadith* from different sources; the multiplication of sources is considered to be an attestation of authenticity.

These *hadith* are quite clear and specific about Aisha's age:

> The Prophet wrote the (marriage contract) with Aisha while she was six years old and consummated his marriage with her while she was nine years old and she remained with him for nine years (i.e. till his death) (Bukhari 7.62.88).

Another tradition has Aisha herself recount the scene:

> The Prophet engaged me when I was a girl of six (years). We went to Medina and stayed at the home of Bani-al-Harith bin Khazraj. Then I got ill and my hair fell down. Later on my hair grew (again) and my

---

10 "Hadith & Sunnah," www.islamonline.net.

mother, Um Ruman, came to me while I was playing in a swing with some of my girl friends. She called me, and I went to her, not knowing what she wanted to do to me. She caught me by the hand and made me stand at the door of the house. I was breathless then, and when my breathing became all right, she took some water and rubbed my face and head with it. Then she took me into the house. There in the house I saw some Ansari women who said, "Best wishes and Allah's Blessing and a good luck." Then she entrusted me to them and they prepared me (for the marriage). Unexpectedly Allah's Apostle came to me in the forenoon and my mother handed me over to him, and at that time I was a girl of nine years of age. (Bukhari 5.58.234).

The facts of the issue are repeated in other collections:

Narrated Aisha: 'A'isha (Allah be pleased with her) reported that Allah's Apostle married her when she was six years old, and he (the Holy Prophet) took her to his house when she was nine, and when he (the Holy Prophet) died she was eighteen years old. (Muslim 16.84.1422)

Muhammad was at this time fifty-four years old. Below are just some of the other *hadiths* attesting to Aisha's age.

Aisha (Allah be pleased with her) reported: Allah's Messenger married me when I was six years old, and I was admitted to his house at the age of nine. She further said: We went to Medina and I had an attack of fever for a month, and my hair had come down to the earlobes. Umm Ruman (my mother) came to me and I was at that time on a swing along with my playmates. She called me loudly and I went to her and I did not know what she had wanted of me. She took hold of my hand and took me to the door, and I was saying: Ha, ha (as if I was gasping), until the agitation of my heart was over. She took me to a house, where had gathered the women of the Ansar. They all blessed me and wished me good luck and said: May you have share in good. She (my mother) entrusted me to them. They washed my head and embellished me and nothing frightened me. Allah's Messenger (may peace be upon him) came there in the morning, and I was entrusted to him. (Muslim 16.81.1422)

Narrated Aisha, Ummul Mu'minin:
The Messenger of Allah married me when I was seven or six. When we came to Medina, some women came. according to Bishr's version: Umm Ruman came to me when I was swinging. They took me, made me prepared and decorated me. I was then brought to the Messenger

of Allah, and he took up cohabitation with me when I was nine. She halted me at the door, and I burst into laughter. Abu Dawud said: That is to say: I menstruated, and I was brought in a house, and there were some women of the Ansari in it. They said: With good luck and blessing. The tradition of one of them has been included in the other. (Abu Dawud 43.161.4933)

It was narrated that Aishah said: "The Messenger of Allah married me when I was six, and consummated the marriage with me when I was nine." (an-Nasai 26.184.3379)

Aishah said: "The Messenger of Allah married me when I was six years old. Then we came to Al-Madinah and settled among Banu Harith bin Khazraj. I became ill and my hair fell out, then it grew back and became abundant. My mother Umm Ruman came to me while I was on an Urjuhah with some of my friends, and called for me. I went to her, and I did not know what she wanted. She took me by the hand and made me stand at the door of the house, and I was panting. When I got my breath back, she took some water and wiped my face and head, and led me into the house. There were some woman of the Ansar inside the house, and they said: 'With blessings and good fortune (from Allah).' (My mother) handed me over to them and they tidied me up. And suddenly I saw the Messenger of Allah in the morning. And she handed me over to him and I was at that time, nine years old." (Ibn Majah 3.9.1876)

With so much attestation to Muhammad's child marriage, how can it possibly be "hate speech" or denigrating to Muslims to say Muhammad was a pedophile? The definition of a pedophile is "a person who is sexually attracted to children." Given his marriage to Aisha, in what way does Muhammad not fit this definition?

Another attestation to the accuracy of what Sabaditsch-Wolff said is the fact that because Muhammad is the supreme example for Muslims to emulate, child marriage is accepted in large swaths of the Islamic world. Turkey's directorate of religious affairs (Diyanet) said in January 2018 that under Islamic law, girls as young as nine can marry.[11]

Other Islamic authorities have also stated that child marriage is acceptable:

> "Islam has no age barrier in marriage and Muslims have no apology for those who refuse to accept this" — Ishaq Akintola, professor of Islamic

---

11   "Turkish child marriage religious document sparks anger," *BBC*, January 3, 2018.

Eschatology and Director of Muslim Rights Concern, Nigeria[12]

"There is no minimum marriage age for either men or women in Islamic law. The law in many countries permits girls to marry only from the age of 18. This is arbitrary legislation, not Islamic law." — Dr. Abd Al-Hamid Al-'Ubeidi, Iraqi expert on Islamic law[13]

There is no minimum age for marriage and that girls can be married "even if they are in the cradle." — Dr. Salih bin Fawzan, prominent cleric and member of Saudi Arabia's highest religious council[14]

"Islam does not forbid marriage of young children." — Pakistan's Council of Islamic Ideology[15]

And so in April 2011, the Bangladesh Mufti Fazlul Haque Amini declared that those trying to pass a law banning child marriage in that country were putting Muhammad in a bad light: "Banning child marriage will cause challenging the marriage of the holy prophet of Islam, [putting] the moral character of the prophet into controversy and challenge." He added a threat: "Islam permits child marriage and it will not be tolerated if any ruler will ever try to touch this issue in the name of giving more rights to women."[16] The Mufti said that 200,000 *jihadists* were ready to sacrifice their lives for any law restricting child marriage.

Article 1041 of the Civil Code of the Islamic Republic of Iran states that girls can be engaged before the age of nine, and married at nine: "Marriage before puberty (nine full lunar years for girls) is prohibited. Marriage contracted before reaching puberty with the permission of the guardian is valid provided that the interests of the ward are duly observed."

According to journalist and historian Amir Taheri in *The Spirit of Allah: Khomeini and the Islamic Revolution* (pp. 90-91), Iran's Ayatollah

---

12 "Islam has no age barrier for marriage — MURIC Director, Akintola," *Punch*, March 6, 2016.

13 "Iraqi Expert on Islamic Law Calls to Allow Young Girls to Get Married: In Islamic Countries, Girls Get Their Periods at the Age of 8-10. Westerners Criticize the Prophet Muhammad for Having Sex with His 9 Year Old Wife, But Allow Fornication with Underage Girls," *MEMRI*, March 14, 2008.

14 Raymond Ibrahim, "Islamic Law: Girls Can Be Married 'Even If They Are In The Cradle,'" *VIE*, December 29, 2014.

15 "Laws prohibiting underage marriage not Islamic: Council of Islamic Ideology," from *The Nation* (Pakistan), March 11, 2014.

16 "Islamist leader threatens of waging Jihad," *Weekly Blitz*, April 20, 2011.

Khomeini himself married a ten-year-old girl when he was twenty-eight. Khomeini called marriage to a prepubescent girl "a divine blessing," and advised the faithful to give their own daughters away accordingly: "Do your best to ensure that your daughters do not see their first blood in your house." When he took power in Iran, he lowered the legal marriageable age of girls to nine, in accord with Muhammad's example.

In light of all this, the conviction and fine of Elisabeth Sabaditsch-Wolff should be vacated. She was not speaking publicly and her statements were not inaccurate. Truth ought to be an adequate defense.

—Robert Spencer, director of *Jihad Watch* and author of over two dozen books on Islam, Muhammad, Islamic history and modern Islamic terrorism.

ANALYSIS

BY CLARE M. LOPEZ

The Great Purge: An Ongoing Threat to Freedom of Speech

FOR A LONG TIME, we Americans felt safe and protected by the First Amendment to our Constitution. It explicitly promised that Americans would remain free of any U.S. governmental infringement on the right to free speech and a free press (among others). The classic example of the 1st Amendment in action was the 1977 decision by the Supreme Court in the *National Socialist Party of America v. Village of Skokie, 432 U.S. 43* case that upheld the right of the National Socialist Party of America to march freely and openly in the street, despite the revulsion that most Americans, including Supreme Court justices, must feel about the Nazis' hateful antisemitic ideology. Likewise, the 1989 Supreme Court decision in the *Texas v. Johnson, 491 U.S. 397* case invalidated prohibitions on desecrating the American flag—an act that sickens every true patriot, but once again, a ruling that upheld our constitutional right to freedom of speech (including 'expression'), however offensive that speech or expression may be. The one clear exception to this right is the immediate incitement to violence, which remains prohibited by law. Libel and slander, which are based on the utterance of falsehood with malicious intent and result, are also illegal under U.S. law.

With even such hateful and offensive expressions, as demonstrated in the two cases above, protected by our Constitution's Bill of Rights guarantee to freedom of speech, we Americans believed the 1st Amendment virtually inviolable...until the turn of the 21st century, that is. Beginning with the attacks of 9/11, which led to the massive infiltration of our national security leadership and every agency of the U.S. government by the forces of the Islamic *Jihad* (with the U.S. Muslim Brotherhood in the vanguard), which have progressively censored honest analysis of *jihadist* ideology. In a matter of years, decades at most, we see here in America the same subtile stifling of free speech, most especially of any speech that accurately describes Islam, *jihad*, or Islamic Law (*shariah*), that brave champions of liberty in Europe, like Elisabeth Sabaditsch-Wolff, have experienced coming down over them in recent times.

We had already seen the steady march of Islamic Law across vast swaths of the earth, where most of the rights guaranteed under our American Bill of Rights are savagely trampled; and we had also watched with dismay the steady erosion of such freedoms in Western Europe, the cradle of Western Civilization. The liberty-crushing animosity to free speech that is intrinsic to all tyranny, but specifically to those Islamic and Marxist elements now overwhelming Western Europe, was somehow allowed to seep into the societies of once-fierce defenders of liberty. Country after country (elites following elites), increasingly embraced a willingness to muzzle their own countrymen who try to speak truth about the influx of people whose world view is antithetically opposed to the philosophy of John Locke, John Stuart Mill, and Alexis de Tocqueville, among other great European liberal philosophers.

With not only our Constitution and Bill of Rights, but two oceans to guard us and our freedom, re-enforced by our perceived victory in the Cold War, we Americans relaxed a bit too much in the years after the collapse of the Soviet Union in 1991. For it was exactly during the following decade that the insidious influence of Islamic Law—incredibly—began to expand in a serious way throughout every sector of American society. Yes, the Egypt-based Muslim Brotherhood had long before spread its tentacles abroad, especially in Western Europe, before, during, and after WWII. Few Americans realized that President Dwight D. Eisenhower himself had welcomed a Brotherhood delegation, led by Saed Ramadan (son-in-law of the Brotherhood's founder, Hassan al-Banna), into the Oval Office of the White House in 1952. In fact, the penetration had begun even earlier, as the wartime OSS (Office of Strategic Services) and its successor, the CIA (Central Intelligence Agency), picked up the remnants of the Nazis' old Brotherhood networks—and for the same purpose: to work against the Soviet Union.

But thanks to an understandable Cold War focus on communism's physical encroachments in countries across the world, but with lesser attention paid to its methods of ideological infiltration, lessons that might have been learned about Islamic information operations were either neglected or quickly forgotten. And so it was that by the time of the 1980s war to oust the Red Army from Afghanistan, there was hardly anyone around who might have urged caution against arming, backing, funding, and training an army of *mujahedin* there. In any case, opposition to the Soviets was the single-minded focus of the Reagan administration—admittedly with good reason and to ultimately successful effect.

The most unrecognized side effect of our tight-focused campaign to defeat the USSR, though, was the reality that during the Cold War, few if any, of America's senior officials acquired any understanding about the doctrine, law, or scripture of Islam—the centuries-long history of *jihad* against the West (including the Barbary Pirates' depredations against a nascent U.S.) having long since been forgotten. The fact that *jihad fi sabilallah* in emulation of the life of Muhammad had never ceased, but continued its inexorable advance against ancient Jewish communities and what used to be known as 'Christendom,' steadily wiping out any who refused to accept the domination of Islam across vast swaths of the Middle East, North Africa, Southwest Asia, and beyond, was no longer taught in European or American schools. It wasn't (yet) forbidden to teach such things: it was just not considered a priority. And thus did entire generations of American diplomatic, intelligence, and military officers rise to rank, entirely bereft of the realization that another lethal enemy of Western Civilization already had penetrated our defenses and insinuated itself deep inside our society, seeking to destroy it.

How did this happen? How did we get from Locke, Mill, and de Tocqueville to the Great Purge? In short, it happened because the Islamic Movement and its hard left, communist/Marxist allies had a plan and we didn't and still don't.

That plan uses the tried-and-true information operations tactics of communism and Marxism and, for the Islamic Movement, *dawah*. *Dawah* is an Islamic information operation which aims first and foremost to establish Islamic institutions, indoctrinate the non-Muslim population, and counter "the prejudices of Judeo-Christians against Islam," as Muslim Brotherhood (*Ikhwan*) scholar Shamim A. Siddiqi wrote in his 1989 *Methodology of Dawah*. In that blueprint document, available in English, online, Siddiqi explained how *dawah* is a gradual process, geared to the pace possible to maintain without jolting the host population into a counter response. The process of *dawah*, like Marxist infiltration, involves the establishment of a beachhead in every sector of society: academia, the courts, faith communities, government, media, military, social society, and the workplace.

That process was outlined in detail in a document seized by Swiss authorities at the villa of Joseph Nada, a senior Muslim Brotherhood operative, in November 2001, which has come to be known as "The Project." It is a 14-page plan dated 1 December 1982, that outlines a "flexible, multi-phased, long-term approach to the 'cultural invasion' of the West," according to Patrick Poole, a counterterrorism and Muslim Brotherhood expert. Taking a deliberately different approach than the terrorism favored by al-Qaeda and other kinetic operators, the Brotherhood understood that a progressive infiltration of the structures of Western society would achieve the same ends without the violence that would elicit an overwhelming legal and military response from the intended targets. Perhaps the key bullet point from "The Project" document is the one that recommends "using deception to mask the intended goals..." This *dawah* process and such deception, combined with an onslaught of millions of Muslim migrants allowed into Europe in the early 21st century, are what has now assaulted every institution of Western Civilization still extant there, and paved the way for the indictment, legal prosecution, and conviction of truth-tellers like Elisabeth Sabaditsch-Wolff.

The first Muslim Brotherhood front organization established in the U.S. was the Muslim Students Association (MSA), on the Urbana-Champaign campus of the University of Illinois in 1964. Fifty-five years later, there are hundreds of MSA chapters at colleges, universities, high schools, and even middle schools across the country. Hundreds, even thousands more front groups followed, including the HAMAS-affiliated Council on American Islamic Relations (CAIR), the Islamic Circle of North America (ICNA), Islamic Society of North America (ISNA), Muslim American Society (MAS), Muslim Public Affairs Council (MPAC), the North American Islamic Trust (NAIT), and so many more—many of them named by the Justice Department as unindicted co-conspirators in the 2008 Holy Land Foundation HAMAS terror funding trial.

None of this is secret or classified information. Every bit of it is openly available online. So, how have so many in America's leading institutions, including the national security leadership of the U.S. government, been deceived into accepting them and their propaganda and even incorporating it into official policy?

It's called Information Dominance.

Recall the wording from the Brotherhood's 1991 "Explanatory Memorandum," which stated that it would "sabotage [our] miserable house by [our own] hands." This is exactly what is happening. Lacking a factual training foundation in the basics of the Islamic canon and its 1400-year history of conquest and subjugation, America's leaders in every important field representing the pillars of support of our society were too easily fooled into accepting a counterfactual understanding of Islam and the nature of the Muslim Brotherhood. With nothing and no one to counter that propaganda, it has been our very leaders—academics, lawyers, ministers, priests, rabbis, police chiefs, sheriffs, and officials at every level of government—who are now the enforcers of the Brotherhood's narrative on their own students, flocks, and subordinates. Ensuring and controlling the flow of information thus became the front line of the Islamic Movement's attack against the Western world, including right here in the U.S.

One of the earliest and most important targets of the Brotherhood campaign to shut down free speech about Islam in America was the U.S. Intelligence Community (IC). It was not long after 9/11 that efforts began to scrub IC documents dealing with counterterrorism of accurate language about Islam. Jim Guirard, the well-meaning but misguided founder of the True Speak Institute, allowed himself to be influenced by deceitful input from the Muslim Brotherhood and then, in turn, succeeded in misleading senior U.S. government (USG) officials into adopting politically correct but entirely inaccurate terminology. Those officials' failure to execute their professional duty to "know the enemy" led first to a garbled lexicon of Arabic-language vocabulary and subsequently to the literal removal of words like *"jihad,"* "Muslim," "Islam," *"shariah,"* or "caliphate" (all used in the 2004 9/11 Commission Report) from official USG usage.

By the time the FBI published its Counterterrorism Lexicon in 2008, such words were entirely gone. In quick succession, the Department of Homeland Security (DHS), the National Counter Terrorism Center (NCTC), and the State Department all instructed their employees to refrain from using such words to describe the enemy threat. The lame excuse was that using such words might somehow confer undeserved religious credibility on terrorists or, worse yet, alienate so-called 'moderate Muslims,' whom they somehow deemed important to the Global War on Terrorism (itself a misnomer). By 2012, at the urging of clearly-identifiable Muslim Brotherhood associates used as advisors by the U.S. government as well as Local Law Enforcement (LLE), the entire

Executive Branch of the USG was busy purging all training curricula government-wide that described the linkage between Islamic doctrine, law, and scripture—and—Islamic terrorism. All instructors knowledge-able in these subjects likewise were purged and barred from teaching inside the USG. People literally began losing their contracts and their jobs if they were accused of using non-approved, albeit accurate, language about the enemy, the enemy's ideology, or the enemy's threat doctrine. This was truly *Catastrophic Failure: Blindfolding America in the Face of Jihad*, as the title of Islam scholar Stephen Coughlin's 2015 book termed it. As I wrote in my April 2013 essay for the Gatestone Institute on Brotherhood penetration of the USG, "If the officials whose professional responsibility it is to implement countermeasures based on the enemy's threat doctrine are not allowed even to speak the words that explain that ideology that drives the enemy's hatred, there is no chance these officials will be able effectively to direct a national security strategy. And that, of course, is the whole point."

Today, under the Trump administration, although the saturation of the USG by advisors and employees associated with the Muslim Brotherhood has lessened somewhat, there still has been no reversal of the Great Purge. Accurate training curricula about Islam and the Brotherhood have not been restored to the White House or Cabinet Departments, the IC, National Security Council, or military service academies and staff colleges. Instructors like Steve Coughlin, Bill Gawthrop, John Guandolo, Robert Spencer, Bill Warner, and others have not been reinstated, contracted, and funded to begin the mammoth task of education about the Islamic Movement's enemy threat doctrine. Moreover, the spread of Islamic *dawah* throughout the ranks of the federal bureaucracy, LLE, and the US. Bureau of Prisons (where Muslim chaplains are overwhelmingly *Ikhwan* trained and credentialed) has in no way been confronted, much less reversed. Worst of all, because the senior levels of official U.S. national security have failed so abjectly in their duty to "support and defend the Constitution against all enemies, foreign and domestic," the spread of Brotherhood influence and propaganda continues to proceed unimpeded throughout all sectors of American society.

Impossible to have been foreseen by our Founding Fathers, it is not only government that has violated our Constitution and participated in the erosion of our 1st Amendment right to free speech, but the enormously influential big tech companies like Apple and Google that today dominate online platforms like Facebook, Twitter, YouTube, and others. Largely because the Brotherhood and other Islamic Movement operatives, and also the treasonous agents of Marxism, have been allowed to run rampant, to infiltrate, indoctrinate, and co-opt on our college campuses, among faith communities, in Hollywood and Silicon Valley, and within police and sheriffs' departments, society, and the workplace, there is now a powerful and dangerous alliance that has been struck between the growing ranks of communists and Marxists on the one hand, and the forces of the Islamic Movement on the other—a Red-Green Axis—united in demands to shut down free speech in this country. Each of these liberty-crushing tyrannies, the Islamic and the Marxist, knows that freedom of speech and press is the linchpin of a free society. The ability of the individual citizen to speak and write freely without fear of censorship, persecution, or prosecution is the most critical of all our First Things Principles, because that right ensures the survival of all the rest: equality of all in human dignity before the rule of man-made law, government by consent of the governed, protection of minorities, etc. Our enemies know this and that is why we see the freedom of speech under such concerted attack all across the West, even here at home, with increasing attacks on the 1st Amendment.

Islamic Law (*shariah*) is utterly antithetical to the U.S. Constitution as well as the spirit of all Judeo-Christian-based Western Civilization. All one has to do is lay a book of *shariah* side-by-side with the Declaration of Independence, the U.S. Constitution, and especially its Bill of Rights to see how impossible it is to reconcile them. Both Marxists and the Islamic Movement know they can never prevail against them by way of a frontal attack. So, they have joined forces (for the time being) to assail these foundational documents and the freedoms upheld in them by using the very liberties guaranteed by our laws against them. Slick, sophisticated, and improbably successful, the agents of the Red and the Green adopt strategies calculated to appeal to those not well-versed in their own faith or freedom. Terms like "incitement to hatred," "denigration of religious beliefs," and "Islamophobia" are flung at those like Elisabeth Sabaditsch-Wolff who speak truth about Islamic doctrine, history, law, and scripture. In Western Europe, such things already are crimes that are actually prosecuted in court.

We, the children of the Enlightenment; the descendants of Athens, Rome, and Jerusalem; the lucky inheritors of Western Civilization and the Westphalian system of nation state sovereignty, are at a turning point. Menacing forces of tyranny seek to obliterate all trace of individual liberty and national sovereignty from the face of the earth because the objective of each is global domination—and that perverse objective cannot succeed as long as any independent, free-thinking, free-speaking individual or any nation of free people remains alive to counter them. This time, though, it is not with artillery, planes, and tanks that the dark ones come against us. It is with civilizational *jihad, dezinformatsia,* and stealth. America's military might and technological prowess are second to none in the world. The principles of our founding documents and foundational principles have brought more freedom and opportunity to more people than anytime or anywhere else in the history of the world. But we are not very good at recognizing, acknowledging or countering the sly sophistication of today's enemies of freedom. Those enemies are operating primarily on the Information Battlefield. And so must we, if the light of Western Civilization is not to go dark on our watch.

We can and we must do this with information operations of our own that begin with knowing the enemy. The Great Purge must be reversed with classes, education, information, and training. Political correctness must be abandoned. A public-private partnership must once again fund and support those who speak truth about the enemy threat doctrine, whether Islamic or Marxist. Civics and appreciation for factual American history must return to the classroom. American citizens at every level of society must work hard to be both informed and engaged.

Upon this depends the fate of Western Civilization. It is our responsibility to make sure the light of that Civilization continues to burn brightly for generations to come.

—Clare M. Lopez is Vice President for Research and Analysis at the Center for Security Policy, a Washington, D.C., think tank focused on national security issues. She is an expert on matters related to Islam, *jihad, shariah,* the Muslim Brotherhood, and the Middle East, especially Iran, and the author, co-author, and editor of numerous books and articles on these subjects. She is widely published and featured frequently in broadcast, Internet, and print media.

ANALYSIS

BY STEPHEN COUGHLIN

On the Road to Serfdom

Again, the evil practices of the last and worst form of democracy are all found in tyrannies . . . Hence tyrants are always fond of bad men, because they love to be flattered, but no man who has the spirit of a freeman in him will lower himself by flattery; good men love others, or at any rate do not flatter them. Moreover, the bad are useful for bad purposes . . . Another mark of a tyrant is that he likes foreigners better than citizens, and lives with them and invites them to his table; for the one are enemies, but the others enter into no rivalry with him.[1]
—Aristotle, *Politics*, Book V, Part XI, 350 BC, 227.

O N OCTOBER 25, 2018, the European Court of Human Rights (the ECtHR) announced judgment on the appeal of Elisabeth Sabaditsch-Wolff, an Austrian citizen, on her conviction in an Austrian court for her "criminal conviction for disparaging religious doctrines" in contravention of her "right to freedom of expression under Article 10 of the Convention (for the Protection of Human Rights and Fundamental Freedoms[2])."[3] The ECtHR ruled against Sabaditsch-Wolff:

1 Aristotle, *Politics*, Book V, Part XI, , 350 BC, trans by Benjamin Jowett, Oxford Clarendon Press, 1908, 227.

2 Article 10, Convention for the Protection of Human Rights and Fundamental Freedoms as amended by Protocols No. 11 and No. 14, Rome, 4.XI.1950, Council of Europe, 4. (Hereafter, Article 10) https://rm.coe.int/1680063765.

3 Procedure 3, Case of *E.S. v. Austria*, Application no. 38450/12, Judgment,

- The Court found in conclusion that in the instant case the domestic courts carefully balanced the applicant's right to freedom of expression with the rights of others to have their religious feelings protected, and to have religious peace preserved in Austrian society.[4]

From the start, sensitivities notwithstanding, it is important to point out that the statements that lead to Sabaditsch-Wolff's conviction are true and well-established.[5] Yet, the ECtHR suggests that Sabaditsch-Wolff was making a value judgment in the absence of facts[6] even as the ECtHR opinion documents her accurate reference to an Islamic authority, Bukhari,[7] for the points she made when accurately describing a behavior that Austrians historically disfavor both culturally and criminally. There is no controversy to the fact of child marriage or that it is being permissively imported into Europe. Just a sampling:

Strasbourg, 25 October 2018 (Final March 18, 2019), European Court of Human Rights (Fifth Section). (Hereafter, *E.S. v Austria*). https://hudoc.echr.coe.int/eng#{"itemid":["001-187188"]}.

4   Press Release Issued by the Registrar of the Court, European Court of Human Rights, October 25, 2018, "Conviction for Calling Muhammad a Paedophile is not in Breach of Article 10," Judgment *E.S. v Austria*, [The judgment is available only in English] (Hereafter, ECtHR Press Release).

5   ¶13. The statements which the court found incriminating, *E.S. v Austria*, states: "2. The most important of all *hadith* collections recognised by all legal schools: The most important is the Sahih Al-Bukhari. If a *hadith* was quoted after Bukhari, one can be sure that all Muslims would recognise it. And, unfortunately, in Al-Bukhari the thing with Aisha and child sex is written . . . II./ I remember my sister, I have said this several times already, when [S.W.] made her famous statement in Graz, my sister called me and asked: "For God's sake. Did you tell [S.W.] that?" To which I answered: "No, it wasn't me, but you can look it up, it's not really a secret." And her: "You can't say it like that!" And me: "A 56-year-old and a six-year-old? What do you call that? Give me an example? What do we call it, if it is not paedophilia?" Her: "Well, one has to paraphrase it, say it in a more diplomatic way." My sister is symptomatic. We have heard that so many times. "Those were different times" – it wasn't okay back then, and it's not okay today. Full stop. And it is still happening today. One can never approve of something like that. They all create their own reality, because the truth is so cruel . . ."

6   ECtHR Press Release; "The Court reiterated that it has distinguished in its case-law between statements of fact and value judgments. It emphasised that the truth of value judgments was not susceptible to proof. However, a value judgment without any factual basis to support it might be excessive."

7   ¶13. The statements which the court found incriminating, *E.S. v Austria*, states: "2. The most important of all *hadith* collections recognised by all legal schools: The most important is the Sahih Al-Bukhari. If a *hadith* was quoted after Bukhari, one can be sure that all Muslims would recognise it."

- "Muslim Woman [in the UK] Defends Child Marriage" SOCO Films, YouTube, February 14, 2019.
- "Sharia Expert Defends Child Marriage," JanSobieski1629, YouTube, March 29, 2008.
- "Saudi Cleric Muhammad Musa Al-Sharif Defends the Marrying Off of Under-Age Girls in Saudi Arabia: Atheists, Christians, and Fornicators Are Responsible for Human Rights Treaties," *MEMRI, 2010.*
- Majid Rafizadeh, "An 8-Year-Old Bride," *Gatestone,* December 15, 2018.
- Soeren Kern, "Britain's Underage Muslim Marriage Epidemic," *Gatestone,* October 15, 2015.
- Gilgamesh Nabeel, "Early Marriage Figures for Iraq are Startling. Child Advocates worry it could Rise even More," *PRI,* August 13, 2018.

As important, in an era of uncontrolled immigration of undocumented men from territories demonstrating strong ISIS influence, it continues to be broadly reported that ISIS leverages the licitness of forced child sex and marriage in its day-to-day operations:

- Asaad Hanna, Syrian Girls Forced to Marry ISIS Fighters, *Al-Monitor,* May 13, 2014.
- Troup Buchanan, "ISIS Justifies Capture and Sexual Enslavement of Thousands of Yazidi Women and Girls," *Independent,* October 13, 2014.
- "Iraq: ISIS Escapees Describe Systematic Rape," *Human Rights Watch,* April 14, 2015.

Talk about the sanctioned predation of girls. Talk about a (real) war on women. And yet, the ECtHR would silence a woman, in fact the mother of a daughter, for daring to articulate her concerns on this phenomenon. To no-one's surprise, the sampling of print media provided above could be extended for pages. For anyone with 30 seconds on Google (or better yet DuckDuckGo), there is no difficulty in finding ubiquitously available supporting material that validates the same statements that Sabaditsch-Wolff made that the ECtHR suggests are "based on manifestly untrue facts." The claim is ridiculous. While the topic may be sensitive for some, as the sampling of citations from prominent Middle Eastern media suggests, this is a familiar concern in the Muslim world as well. It simply cannot be said to be so obscure as to require an expertized knowledge in order to arrive at an informed opinion as the ECtHR suggests when expertizing Sabaditsch-Wolff for the purpose of crucifying her on that imputed expertise.[8] The ECtHR opinion's characterization of Sabaditsch-Wolff oozes the ridicule it harbors against ordinary citizens.

So, what does the ECtHR mean when stating "that Mrs S. must have been aware that her statements were partly based on untrue facts and apt to arouse indignation in others"?[9] Which material facts are "manifestly" untrue?[10] While the ECtHR opinion suggests much, it actually says very little. Yet, if Sabaditsch-Wolff's statements are correct, and they are, why should it matter that others are being allowed to use them as pretext for becoming "indignant" in anticipation of violence with the passive support of the state—just as with Antifa? Come to think of it, maybe informed Europeans should be concerned that the state is shutting down a citizen's free expression because others are being allowed to use them as pretext for becoming "indignant" in anticipation of violence with the passive support of [that same] state—just as with Antifa.

The ECtHR's reasoning is tortured in its vagueness. For those who truly value freedom of expression, the ECtHR Press Release raises more questions than it answers. Why, for example, is a citizen's right to free expression over-burdened by conditions that render the right unattainable for all but elites and the highly educated? From the Release:

- "They [Sabaditsch-Wolff's argument] had not been made in an objective manner contributing to a debate of public interest (e.g. on child marriage)"[11]

  o If a person chooses to exercise her right to free expression by defending an Austrian value ensconced in history, in tradition, and in law when expressed in Austria, why should she be obligated to submit those views to a dialectical process of cultural negation (the Frankfurt School's strategy of *Aufheben der Kultur*) when her interest is precisely in defending them from such a court mandated process as a condition of exercising that right? Just like Marx and Hegel, *Auf-*

---

8 ¶53; , *E.S. v Austria*, states: "The Court notes that the applicant described herself as an expert in the field of Islamic doctrine, already having held seminars of that kind for a while."

9 Appendix A: ECtHR Press Release.

10 *E.S. v Austria*, for example, at ¶ 55; "Moreover, the applicant was wrong to assume that improper attacks on religious groups had to be tolerated even if they were based on untrue facts (see paragraph 35 above). On the contrary, the Court has held that statements which are based on (manifestly) untrue facts do not enjoy the protection of Article 10."

11 ECtHR Press Release.

heben is also a German import.

• "She failed to neutrally inform her audience of the historical background, which consequently did not allow for a serious debate on that issue."[12]

> o Freedom of expression is the freedom to advocate. The ECtHR seems to demand the overburdening of free expression by making it contingent on the peculiar Hegelian notion that one must explain the whole before one can speak of particulars. For example, it would be like requiring someone to explain the entire concept of soccer, down to its specific sports kinesiology, before being able to tell the person next to him that someone just scored a goal so as not to confuse the listener who may think it a hockey goal even as the discussion takes place at the soccer pitch that both are attending every time any scoring drive is discussed. Sabaditsch-Wolff is not an academic and makes no claim to be one. Her private citizen comments were scaled to her audience and to the environment to make the points she intends to make. The court demands that she have advance training in Middle Eastern studies as a condition of her speaking her mind on the status of predation among immigrants in Austria. Free expression that is obligated to provide historical and cultural context on every point made, and made only on condition that it be conducted in a neutrally phrased debating forum, is no free expression at all. In fact, it purposefully over-burdens the right, rendering free expression a nullity. This holds true for the other implied demand; that free expression is over-burdened by the requirement that all expression be parsed, including every sentence, word, and phrase.

The vagueness of the ECtHR's reasoning follows a surfacing pattern of enforcement based on judicial fiat where the court's saying it is so, makes it so. This follows "hate speech" memes that are being weaponized in international forums like the United Nations (UN), the Organization for Security and Co-operation in Europe (OSCE), and the European Union (EU). The vagueness of the ECtHR opinion is patterned after other "hate speech" sleights of hand that conceal the deliberate emptiness of speech suppression reasoning underlying "hate speech" efforts. The calculated obfuscation involved in this process enables the smoke screen that provides the state the operating space to abuse its power when imposing its will on its own citizens - for any reason or no reason at all.

---

12   ECtHR Press Release.

Hence, even as the UN General Secretary Antonio Guterres spoke of the need to step up international efforts to suppress "hate speech" at the June 18, 2019, "United Nations Strategy and Plan of Action on Hate Speech,"[13] the Special Advisor on the Prevention of Genocide at that same forum was clear that "hate speech is a very grey area for which no international legal definition yet exists" in circumstances where, as of May 2019, the UN is on record as acknowledging that "there is no international legal definition of hate speech, and the characterization of what is 'hateful' is controversial and disputed." Push past the deliberate vagueness of the ECtHR's opinion, and one can see that the real authority for upholding Sabaditsch-Wolff's conviction is the *de facto* enforcement of "hate speech" standards. There is something totalitarian about the arbitrary prosecution of citizens for hate speech in circumstances where the state knows that the term has no definition.

Strangely, this is precisely the same characterization one hears about "Islamophobia." Actually, it's not strange at all. At the 2013 OSCE Side Event "Education Initiatives and Approaches for Addressing Anti-Semitism and Intolerance against Muslims"[14] in Warsaw, Poland (an event Sabaditsch-Wolff personally attended), the architect of the Islamophobia strategy signaled Marx's "Eleventh Thesis" from Marx's 1845 *Theses on Feuerbach*[15] that "the philosophers have only interpreted the world, in various ways; the point is to change it," when admitting that Islamophobia "terminology is difficult," that "terminology is important and we have the wrong terminology," and that "we need language to change the world." Should anyone be shocked that the "hate speech" and "Islamophobia" narratives are joined at the united front level or that they tag-team in their assault on citizens like Sabaditsch-Wolff? This is the intended design behind ECtHR enforcement of such judgments against private citizens like Sabaditsch-Wolff.

By design, "hate speech" standards afford the state the authority to declare that saying $2 + 2 = 4$ constitutes hate speech when demanding its citizens say, "$2 + 2 = 5$." The intended effect of the ECtHR's opinion was not simply to silence Sabaditsch-Wolff, it was also to send a chilling effect on the speech of all Member State citizens of the EU who

---

13 https://www.un.org/sg/en/content/sg/statement/2019-06-18/secretary-generals-remarks-the-launch-of-the-united-nations-strategy-and-plan-of-action-hate-speech-delivered.

14 https://d.tube/#!/v/vladtepesblog/QmStwfxYUeTqgE53F6g9hb94HZi3zpEZ-Z48bRRTep3mk52.

15 https://www.marxists.org/archive/marx/works/1845/theses/theses.htm.

would deign to speak unauthorized truth. As such, the ECtHR imposed what U.S. First Amendment jurisprudence considers the worst form of speech suppression, *prior restraint*. As *Black's Law Dictionary* states, "prior restraint on speech and publication are the most serious and least tolerable infringement on First Amendment Rights." As such, *Black's* continues, "Any system of prior restraints of expression bears a heavy presumption against its constitutional validity, and the Government has a heavy burden of showing justification for imposition of such a restraint." The ECtHR opinion cannot bear the weight of such a presumption. There is no hyperbole here. As we learned at a separate OSCE event, this time in Vienna, in May 2015, at the forum on "Promoting Dialogue to Prevent Readicalization and Violent Extremism," an event Sabaditsch-Wolff also attended, we were told that speaking the truth can constitute "hate speech." At the event, "How can the Media help Prevent Violent Radicalization that Leads to Terrorism?," the panel was asked a series of specific questions on whether speaking something known to be true can constitute hate speech:

- "Truth can constitute hate speech because sometimes truth is difficult."

- "Sometimes when you report on facts and these facts point out a community, then it can be a source of hateful speech. So, your question was 'Does that mean that hiding the truth can be a means to tackle hate speech?', I would answer, 'Sometimes it is and sometimes we do by not saying the entire truth.' Does that mean that hiding the truth would be a means to tackle the hate speech I would answer sometimes it is and sometimes we do by not saying the entire truth. It sometimes takes the form of the political correct."[16]

This is the *de facto* standard the ECtHR used to convict Sabaditsch-Wolff; she spoke of actions known to be happening and accurately associated them with a community that the state protects from such scrutiny. This explains why the ECtHR opinion, and all such related opinions, are so deliberately vague. Her conviction continues a process designed to reduce Europeans from citizens to subjects on the road to

---

16   At the Night Owl Session "How can the Media help Prevent Violent Radicalization that Leads to Terrorism?," at the OSCE Security Days forum on "Promoting Dialogue to Prevent Readicalization and Violent Extremism" in Hofburg, Vienna, Austria, May 21, 2015, at 10:48 and then at 11:10. https://d.tube/#!/v/vladtepesblog/QmUGN-69SE9AxzYi52MUH7DnnduTxeKPCrZCqYuBrRQys9.

a planned neo-post-modern serfdom. This is not hard to see. As Hayek wrote in *The Road to Serfdom*, "One need not be a prophet to be aware of (the) impending dangers"[17] this poses to free peoples. The ECtHR opinion against Sabaditsch-Wolff, and many more like them, are the "hate speech" altars on which the veneer of freedom of expression is sacrificed, exposing the built-in contradictions of Article 10. Contradiction you say? How is that? While Section 1 of Article 10 appropriately states the oft quoted,

- "Everyone has the right to freedom of expression. This right shall include freedom to hold opinions and to receive and impart information and ideas without interference by public authority and regardless of frontiers,"[18]

Section 2 so conditions that "right" that it converts it to something that becomes little more than a revocable privilege granted by the state. The language of Article 10, read in totality, is simply a revocable privilege:

- 2 The exercise of these freedoms, since it carries with it duties and responsibilities, may be subject to such formalities, conditions, restrictions or penalties as are prescribed by law . . . [19]

In looking at the extraordinary efforts the EU, the ECtHR, and Austria are willing to undertake to suppress the voice of a lone citizen activist, a concerned mother no less, one cannot help but see in their actions the warning Hayek posed in the depths of World War II:

- "It is not difficult to deprive the great majority of independent thought. But the minority who will retain an inclination to criticize must also be silenced. Public criticism or even expressions of doubt must be suppressed because they tend to weaken pubic support . . . If the people are to support the common effort without hesitation, they must be convinced that not only the end aimed at but also the means chosen are the right ones . . . When the doubt or fear expressed concerns not the success of a particular enterprise but of the whole social plan, it must even more be treated as sabotage.[20]

---

17 F. A. Hayek, *The Road to Serfdom*, George Routledge and Sons, LTD, London, 1944, 1.

18 Article 10, 4.

19 Article 10, 4.

20 F. A. Hayek, *The Road to Serfdom*, George Routledge and Sons, LTD, London,

But to what end? Why would Europe seek the suppression of its own citizens? In choosing the road to serfdom, Austria rejected Hayek in favor of Coudenhove-Kalergi. From the *New York Times*,[21] to *My-Europe*,[22] to *Political Thoughts-The Magazine*,[23] Coudenhove-Kalergi is considered a founding father of the European Union. Yet Coudenhove-Kalergi hated European nations, hated the European people,[24] and harbored strange racial views that envisioned the breeding of ethnically European peoples out of existence.[25] What if understanding current events is as simple as recognizing that Coudenhove-Kalergi's ethos is the driving force behind the EU? It would certainly clear things up even as it demystifies.

In accepting Hayek's wisdom, Europe could have shaken itself from the death grip Hegel holds over it. For almost two centuries, Europe has suffered under a dialectical delusion that sees the world divided along a binary that compels the destructive drive to the absolute, the *Drand nach dem Absoluten*. While Europe remains captured in this binary, it oscillates between being so in love with itself, it must destroy the other, or so in love with the other that it must destroy itself. Neither pole ad-

---

1944, 118-119.

21 https://www.nytimes.com/1972/07/29/archives/count-coudenhovekalergi-dies-i-founded-the-paneurope-union.html.

22 https://my-europe.org/articles/richard-nikolaus-count-coudenhove-kalergi/.

23 pol-check.blogspot.com/2015/06/practical-idealism-by-richard-nicolaus.html.

24 Richard N. Coudenhove-Kalergi, *Pan-Europa*, Pan-Europa Verlag, Wien (Vienna), 1923, 23; "Europe as a political concept (*Begriff*) does not exist. The part of the world that bears this name harbors a chaos of peoples and states, of the powder chamber of international conflicts, a retort of future war. The European question and the European hatred contaminate the international atmosphere and are constantly disturbing the most peaceful parts of the world."

25 R. N. Coudenhove Kalergi, *Praktischer Idealismus*, Pan-Europa Verlag, Wein-Leipzig, 1925., 22-23; "Inbreeding strengthens the character, weakens the mind—crossing weakens the character, strengthens the spirit. Where inbreeding and crossbreeding meet under favorable circumstances, they testify to the highest human type, combining the strongest character with the keenest spirit. Where, under unfavorable circumstances, inbreeding and mixing meet, they create degeneration types with weak character, dull mind. The man of the distant future will be a hybrid. The present races and castes will fall prey to the overcoming of space, time and prejudice. The Eurasian-Negroid future breed, externally similar to the ancient Egyptians, will replace the diversity of peoples with a variety of personalities. For, according to the laws of inheritance, diversity grows with the difference of the ancestors, and with the monotony of the ancestors, the uniformity of the descendants. In inbreeding families, one child is like the other, because they all represent one common family type. In mixed-race families, the children differ more from each other: each forms a novel variation of the diverging parental and pre-parental elements."

mits a sane middle; it's a binary, it can't.

For those seeking Hayek's path to freedom, it is obvious that one does not have to be a "fascist" or "racist" to recognize the insanity of the Left's destruction of its own people any more than they are Communists for warning of the predatory activities of Nazis when they seek the annihilation of the other. Both are unhealthy extremes that of necessity and design must result in complete nihilizing destruction. Societies that think this way have fallen from the median way. The opposite of Fascist is not Communist, nor vice versa. Rather, they both represent the twin poles of the same nihilizing binary that always seeks the destruction of the object of its attention. The opposite of the dialectical delusion is the abandonment of it, detoxifying from it, and assuming a non-predatory world view. As long as Europe remains captured by its Hegelian obsession, Europe will always occupy one of the two poles and hence, will always pose a threat to either itself or to others. It is infectious. It has infected the world. It has its death grip on America as well. More people have died due to strife from this dialectical binary than quite possibly all the wars in the history of the world combined.

For the victims of this binary, it hardly matters whether the courts that suppress them come from one pole or the other. Whether it's the self-loathing ethos or the "other"-loathing, they will still be deprived of rights by a state that claims such authority. In Sabaditsch-Wolff's case, the state is overseeing the importation of an "other" for the purpose of imposing it on its own national population in order to suppress it under the rubric of "pluralism." As such, the only thing Sabaditsch-Wolff is guilty of is expressing her concerns in the context of an Austrian world view, among Austrians, in Austria. For Austria, the Left seeks to *"Aufheben der Kultur!"*[26] It is in this context that one should not forget that Sabaditsch-Wolff was not prosecuted by Muslim immigrants but rather by European courts wielding policies that seek the destruction of Austrian identity, among Austrians, in Austria. Coudenhove Kalergi would understand.

When a people, a nation, are forced to suppress their own culture from within their own culture in the name of an imposed "other," terms like "tolerance" do not reflect the tolerance of one people to that of the "other," but rather reflect the mandates of Marcuse's repressive tolerance. The ECtHR reasoning leading to Sabaditsch-Wolff's conviction is in lock-step with Marcuse's "Repressive Tolerance" norms such that

---

26 Destroy the Culture!

"tolerance" means the deliberate intolerance of all existing social orders, including Austria's, "pluralism" means imposing a hostile group on a target group for the purpose of nihilizing it, and "hate speech" is the deliberate application of "might makes right" regimes by states empowered to decide who is to be targeted, by what, and why. This is the process Sabaditsch-Wolff got caught up in when she was convicted. (For an explanation of Marcuse's "Repressive Tolerance," see *Re-Remembering the Mis-Remembered Left.*[27])

As the citizens of Europe slowly wake up to the realization that Europe is well along the path of its own destruction, they would be well served to take Hayek's observations to heart:

- "We are ready to accept almost any explanation of the present crisis of our civilization except one: that the present state of the world may be the result of genuine error on our own part and that the pursuit of some of our most cherished ideals has apparently produced results utterly different from those which we expected."[28]

Sabaditsch-Wolff's conviction should be a call to action by all discerning citizens that their rights, in fact their very identities, are being purposefully targeted for destruction by their own leadership elites and by their own leadership. She was convicted by a court for saying things known to be true. One should be extremely suspect of discussions on free expression in speech regimes that allows for the criminalization of speech known to be true, while still insisting on its being free expression. This raises the question Bertrand Russell posed in the context of the same dialectical nightmare that continues to haunt Austria: "Do the citizens exist for the sake of the State, or the State for the sake of the citizens?" For Austria, and for all the people of Europe, this is a question that can no longer be put off.

—Stephen C. Coughlin, Esq., is an attorney, decorated intelligence officer and noted specialist on counter-terrorism, ideology and associated issues as they relate to terrorism and subversion.

---

27 https://unconstrainedanalytics.org/report-re-remembering-the-mis-remembered-left-the-lefts-strategy-and-tactics-to-transform-america/.

28 F. A. Hayek, *The Road to Serfdom*, George Routledge and Sons, LTD, London, 1944, 8.

ANALYSIS

BY GRÉGOR PUPPINCK

The European Centre for Law and Justice (ECLJ), of which I am the Director, is a non-governmental organization (NGO) dedicated to the promotion of life, family values, and the freedoms of expression and religion before international institutions, such as the Council of Europe and the United Nations (UN). The ECLJ intervenes in many cases with the European Court of Human Rights (ECHR), through a mechanism called *"third-party intervention."*[1] We do not represent one or another party to the dispute as advocate or adviser, but we share our legal expertise to the Court.

In the *E.S. v. Austria* case, the ECLJ was the only third-party intervener at the Court. We also intervened in the press, because the case became more political than juridical. A civilizational challenge was at stake in this case.

Our juridical intervention at the European Court of Human Rights

In our intervention, we reminded the Court that freedom of thought, conscience and religion, and freedom of expression are complementary; they serve one another in their interactions, although this interaction can sometimes be difficult. Without freedom of thought and conscience, there is just no message to convey, and without freedom of expression, it would be impossible to share and change one's convictions.

---

1 The written observations of the ECLJ can be read in full on our website (https://eclj.org/). They are also summarized by the Court in the judgment itself: ECHR, *E.S. v. Austria,* no. 38450/12, 25 October 2018, § 38.

In a famous case, the Court held that freedom of expression "*is applicable not only to 'information' or 'ideas' that are favourably received or regarded as inoffensive or as a matter of indifference, but also to those that offend, shock or disturb the State or any sector of the population.*"[2] It also applies to "*controversial*" statements.[3]

However, the Court also considers that "*whoever exercises his freedom of expression undertakes 'duties and responsibilities' the scope of which depends on his situation and the technical means he uses.*"[4] The Court thus usually accepts the legitimacy of restrictions of freedom of expression against "*provocative portrayals of objects of religious veneration*"[5] that are "*gratuitously offensive to others,*" when such portrayals can be regarded as a "*malicious violation of the spirit of tolerance, which must also be a feature of democratic society.*"[6] The Court also considers that it is legitimate to protect beliefs, and finds the criminalization of blasphemy acceptable when it sanctions a "*high degree of profanation,*"[7] especially against obscene portrayals that have "*a very aggressive sexual connotation*"[8] likely to have an impact on the views of believers (e.g. public display). The Court distinguishes obscenity, which generally has a sexual connotation,[9] from debates.[10] We concluded from the case law, and our own appreciation, that the propagation of gratuitously offensive and unnecessary obscenities can be restricted; the rest should be tolerated.

Elisabeth Sabaditsch-Wolff's case was not about defending a right to the expression of blasphemous obscenities, but to preserve the faculty of telling the truth and denouncing errors, even if it displeases others.

Of course, comparing the union of Muhammad (56 years old) to Aisha (9 years old) to pedophilia may be intended to provoke a neg-

---

2 ECHR, *Handyside v. the United Kingdom (Plenary)*, no. 5493/72, 7 December 1976, § 49.

3 ECHR, *Lehideux and Isorni v. France [GC]*, no. 24662/94 23 September 1998, § 52.

4 ECHR, *Handyside*, op. cit., § 49.

5 ECHR, *Otto-Preminger-Institut v. Austria*, no. 13470/87, 20 September 1994, § 49.

6 Ibid., § 47.

7 ECHR, *Wingrove v. the United Kingdom*, no. 17419/90, 25 November 1996, § 60.

8 See: Gérard Gonzalez, « Les excès de la liberté d'expression et le respect des convictions religieuses selon la Cour européenne des droits de l'homme », *RDLF*, 2015, chronique n°10.

9 For example: ECHR, *Otto Preminger*, op. cit.; *Wingrove*, op. cit.; I.A v. Turkey, no. 42571/98, 13 September 2005.

10 ECHR, *Giniewski v. France*, no. 64016/00, 31 January 2006.

ative value judgment, but that is not enough reason to make this presentation (even generalized) a wrongful judgment of values. Elisabeth Sabaditsch-Wolff's statements questioned Mohammed's sexuality, but they were not obscene. They were based on real events that enable one to reasonably establish a link with pedophilia. They made reference to facts, and "*it is an integral part of freedom of expression to seek historical truth.*"[11] The denial of "*established historical facts*"[12] may be condemned, but not their reminder—even if they were unpleasant.

Moreover, Mrs. Sabaditsch-Wolff's statements were intended to contribute to a "Basic knowledge of Islam," which is clearly a question of public interest. The case law of the Court usually protects statements touching a "*question of indisputable public interest in a democratic society.*"[13] Islam cannot be excluded from the scope of the debate of ideas on the grounds that its whole set of doctrines has an important religious dimension. Islam also has social, political and historical dimensions that must be freely discussed. Muhammad was also a political figure who continues to exert a strong influence; hence, it should be widely possible to criticize him within the context of a political debate.[14] The facts criticized by Elisabeth Sabaditsch-Wolff are directly related to the on-going practice of marriage of prepubescent girls in countries influenced by Muslim culture.[15]

Certainly, one can condemn remarks that directly incite to violence against a religious group, but not those which, although reasonable, are likely to provoke the concerned religious group to violence. Otherwise, the limits of freedom of expression are being set by the violence of "believers." In this case, not only did Mrs. Sabaditsch-Wolff's statements not incite to imminent violence, but they did not even create a real disturbance to the public order.

For all these reasons, we considered that Elisabeth Sabaditsch-Wolff's statements were part of her right to freedom of expression, under Article 10 of the European Convention of Human Rights.

Beyond this case, we explained to the Court that Article 188 of the

---

11 ECHR, *Chauvy and others v. France*, no. 64915/01, 29 June 2004, § 69.

12 ECHR, *Garaudy v. France*, (Dec.), no. 65831/01, 24 June 2003.

13 ECHR, *Giniewski*, op. cit., § 51.

14 ECHR, *Lingens v. Austria*, no. 9815/82, 8 July 1986.

15 According to the United Nations Population Fund (UNFPA), between 2011 and 2020, 50 million girls under 15 years old are estimated to be married. This phenomenon is also marginally present in Europe.

Austrian Criminal Code,[16] criminalizing the denigration of religious doctrine would have a "chilling effect," which would develop into a sense of insecurity obstructing free debate. As highlighted by the three dissenting judges in the *I.A. v. Turkey* judgment: "*Such a risk of self-censorship is very dangerous for this freedom, which is essential in a democracy, to say nothing of the implicit encouragement of blacklisting or 'fatwas'.*"[17] If obscenity and incitement to violence must be censored, such should not be the case of mere criticism.

A political and worrying Chamber's judgment

The fifth section of the European Court of Human Rights, to everyone's surprise, accepted the arguments of the Austrian courts and validated the conviction by a unanimous judgment on October 25, 2018. The seven European judges considered that Elisabeth Sabaditsch-Wolff did not so much seek to inform the public objectively than "*demonstrate that Muhammad was not a worthy subject of worship.*"[18] In support of this conviction, the Court held that insinuating that Muhammad was a "*paedophile*" would be a "*generalisation without a factual basis*"[19] on the grounds that he continued his relationship with Aisha for several years and had also married older women. According to the Court, these remarks were "*likely to arouse justified indignation*" of the Muslims and constituted "*a malicious violation of the spirit of tolerance, which was one of the bases of a democratic society*" capable of "*stirring up prejudice*" and "*putting at risk religious peace.*"[20] These remarks could therefore be condemned for inciting religious intolerance.

Rarely a judgment of the Court has been criticized so unanimously. Most Western commentators—both conservative and free-thinkers— were shocked by this decision. I wrote articles and was interviewed in the main French newspapers, magazines and information websites. I

---

16 Article 188 of the Criminal Code – "Denigrating religious doctrines:" "*Whoever, in circumstances where his behaviour is likely to arouse justified indignation, disparages or insults a person who, or an object which, is an object of veneration of a church or religious community established within the country, or a dogma, a lawful custom or a lawful institution of such a church or religious community, shall be liable to a prison sentence of up to six months or a fine of up to 360 daily rates.*"

17 ECHR, *I.A*, op. cit., Joint Dissenting opinion of Judges Costa, Cabral Barreto and Jungwiert.

18 ECHR, *E.S. v. Austria*, no. 38450/12, 25 October 2018, § 52.

19 Ibid., § 57.

20 Ibid.

denounced the fact that the only true reason for this decision is the fear of Muslims.[21] This judgment allows the muzzling of criticism of Islam in the name of *living-together*. This goes against Western modernity, which, on the contrary, requires Islam to be subjected to historical criticism, without fear of upsetting the beliefs of its followers or even of provoking tensions. This decision of the ECHR would have justified the conviction of the cartoons of Charlie Hebdo, but also of Voltaire's book on Muhammad. Whereas the Court's logic rests on the absurd dogma of the equality of religions, I am convinced that it is urgent to criticize and compare religions in the light of their contributions to the good of humanity.

I also revealed that Al-Azhar University, Pakistan and the Arab press welcomed the Court's judgment, which allowed them to justify their own repression of freedom of expression in religious matters.[22] These statements are not surprising; in fact, the Organization of Islamic Cooperation (OIC)—gathering 57 Muslim States—has fought since 1999 in order to obtain an international ban on *"defamation of religions,"* that is to say on blasphemy.[23]

The Observatory of Islamophobia of the prestigious Al-Azhar University in Cairo, the highest authority of Sunni Islam, expressed its support of the Court's decision and described it as *"courageous."*[24] It saw in it a general condemnation of *"blasphemies against the Prophet"* contributing *"to reduce the problems of Islamophobia"* while *"the number of Muslims in Europe could reach 14% in 2050."* Accordingly, the Secretary General of the largest world federation of Koranic schools (10,000 madrassas), Qari Hanif Jalandhari, saw in this decision *"a very important step"* and asked the United Nations to elaborate global legislation *"condemning anyone who commits a blasphemy against divine books or sa-*

---

21 Grégor Puppinck, « Délit de blasphème : « La CEDH n'est pas Charlie ! » », interview by Paul Sugy, *Figaro Vox*, 26 October 2018. Cf. the expression *"I am Charlie"* following the Islamic attack in the satirical newspaper Charlie Hebdo in January 2015.

22 Grégor Puppinck, « Blasphème contre Mahomet : Al-Azhar et le Pakistan se félicitent de la décision de la Cour européenne des droits de l'homme », *Valeurs actuelles*, 1er mars 2019.

23 ECLJ, Grégor Puppinck, « Lutter contre la diffamation des religions », Rapport en réponse à la consultation du Bureau du Haut-commissaire aux droits de l'homme des Nations Unies sur le suivi par la France de la Résolution 7/19 du Conseil des droits de l'homme du 27 mars 2008 sur « la lutte contre la diffamation des religions », Rapport soumis en Juin 2008 et actualisé en juin 2010.

24 See the website of the Observatory of Islamophobia of Al-Azhar University (Article published on 30 October 2018): http://gate.ahram.org.eg/News/2029268.aspx.

cred persons of all religions."[25] In the Arab press, this judgment was also greeted with enthusiasm and presented as a *"historical decision,"* or as *"a victory for the Islamic world after the crisis of the cartoons published several times by several European newspapers."*

Pakistan's Prime Minister Imran Khan *"welcomed the recent decision of the European Court of Human Rights not to authorize acts of profanity under the guise of freedom of expression."*[26] Addressing the President of the European Parliament, he expressed *"the hope that European countries will comply with the decision of the European Court and take measures to strengthen respect for religions and interreligious harmony."* He also expressed the *"serious concerns of the Government and people of Pakistan regarding the blasphemous caricatures of the Holy Prophet, stressing the need to redouble efforts in European countries to avoid such provocative incidents; to raise awareness of the religious sensitivity of Muslims, especially the respect of the Prophet Muhammad."* Indeed, in Pakistan, in addition to the emblematic Asia Bibi case, about 1,500 persons were accused of blasphemy between 1987 and 2016 according to the Centre for Social Justice, and more than 70 persons were murdered since 1990 on such crime allegations. In 2017, a thirty-year-old man was sentenced to death for allegedly *"insulting Prophet Muhammad"* on Facebook.[27] Prime Minister Imran Khan declared again, in June 2018, before an audience of imams, his will to *"support and defend article 295c"* of the Penal Code which punishes by death or life imprisonment anyone who *"defiles the sacred name of the Holy Prophet Muhammad."*[28]

The decision of the Court and all these reactions led us to fight in favor of a referral at the Court.

The dashed hope for a referral to the Grand Chamber

After the Chamber judgment was delivered, we recommended to Elisabeth Sabaditsch-Wolff's lawyers to request a referral of the case to

25 "EU court lauded for upholding verdict against blasphemy," *The Nation* (Pakistan), 27 October 2018.

26 Government of Pakistan, Ministry of Information, Broadcasting & National Heritage, Press Information Department, "Prime Minister Underscores the Importance of Respecting Religious Sentiments of all," Press release No. 70, 13 November 2018.

27 Sune Engel Rasmussen, "Pakistan: man sentenced to death for blasphemy on Facebook," *The Guardian*, 11 June 2017.

28 Memphis Barker, "Imran Khan criticised for defence of Pakistan blasphemy laws," *The Guardian*, 9 July 2018.

the Grand Chamber. This most solemn formation of the Court is composed of seventeen judges and its judgments are final and cannot be appealed against. Requests for referral are accepted on an exceptional basis (5% of the cases), when the Court considers that what is at stake is *"a serious question affecting the interpretation or application of the Convention or the Protocols thereto or a serious issue of general importance."* The Grand Chamber can then sometimes reverse the prior judgment of the Chamber. A reversal had been obtained in some cases in which the ECLJ intervened.

We hoped that the Court would accept to re-try the *E.S. v. Austria* case in the Grand Chamber. Indeed, the judgment of the Chamber stood out clearly from the Court's case law. Previously, the Court had established the principle that freedom of expression protects words that *"offend, shock or disturb"*[29] and that freedom of religion does not confer the right *"to see religion protected from negative comment."*[30] Moreover, it had recognized that believers had the obligation to *"tolerate and accept the rejection by others of their religious beliefs and even the propagation by others of doctrines hostile to their faith."*[31] On that basis, the Strasbourg judges guaranteed the freedom of expression of anti-religious messages. Last year, it gave its protection to the famous *"Pussy Riot,"* a punk band condemned in Russia for organizing a *"performance"* in the choir of the Moscow Cathedral with cries including *"shit, shit, shit L***."*[32] It also held that Lithuania could not sanction the dissemination of blasphemous advertisements presenting Christ and the Virgin Mary as tattooed and lascivious junkies.[33] Thus the Court protected obscenity against Christian symbols in Lithuania and Russia.

However, in 2018, the European Court did precisely the opposite: it censored the criticism of Islam, with *E.S. v. Austria*. The fact that rational criticism of religion is less protected than antireligious obscenity seems particularly unfair. That is why we encouraged the Grand Chamber to reconsider the judgment on *E.S. v. Austria*, in order to clarify its case law. In a high-level seminar organized by the ECLJ at the Council of Europe on freedom of expression in religious matters,[34] several speakers

---

29 ECHR, *Handyside*, op. cit., §49.

30 https://eclj.org/free-speech/echr/la-cedh-reviendra-t-elle-sur-la-condamnation-dune-personne-qui-avait-taxe-mahomet-de-pedophilie.

31 ECHR, *Otto-Preminger-Institut*, § 47.

32 ECHR, *Mariya Alekhina and others v. Russia*, no. 38004/12, 17 July 2018.

33 ECHR, *Sekmadienis Ltd. v. Lituania*, no. 69317/14, 31 January 2018.

34 ECLJ, "New challenges to the Freedom of Religion in Europe in the Light of the

pointed out the inconsistency of this recent case law, which gives an impression of "double standards" depending on whether the offended believers are Christians or Muslims. Obscenity and incitement to violence must be censored, but not criticism.

The appeal to the Grand Chamber was supported by the 62,000 signatories of the ECLJ petition for the right to criticize Islam in Europe. Twenty French personalities also co-signed a tribune I wrote for the defense of the freedom of expression in religious matters. Among them were former Muslims, Catholic researchers and intellectuals, feminists and non-religious writers. The signatories included Waleed Al-Husseini, Rémi Brague, Chantal Delsol, Zineb El-Rhazoui, Annie Laurent, Boualem Sansal, Pierre-André Taguieff and Michèle Tribalat. All of them, for their job, research and private reflection, need to benefit from extensive freedom of expression about religion, especially about Islam. According to the tribune, these personalities consider that the Chamber judgment of October 25, 2018, violated the freedom of expression of Mrs. Sabaditsch-Wolff. Our tribune was concluded by the following statement: "*we wish to express to the Court our attachment to reason-based debate, whether political or scientific, and the right to criticize religions. The future of our civilization is at stake.*"[35]

Seized with an "appeal," the European Court could have corrected its previous judgment; it has chosen not to do so and has even granted it the authority of a "*key case*" intended to enlighten all national jurisdictions. The unfair judgment against Elisabeth Sabaditsch-Wolff was thus not accidental but indicates a new orientation of the Court.

A distorted "religious peace" to the detriment of truth and justice

The Court did not give any reason for refusing to refer the case to appeal. We are thus left to making conjectures. I see it as a shift towards multiculturalism, willing to sacrifice freedom of expression to the demands of *living together* and multiculturalism. Such a judgment renounces the ideal of truth-based justice and prefers the arbitrary one of "*tolerance.*" In doing so, it is the judge who decides what can be said according to his own conception of *living together* and to his fear of the reactions of those who might feel offended by these remarks. The ideal of "*religious peace*" promoted by the judgment of the Chamber is ap-

---

Recent Judgments of the ECHR" seminar organized at the Council of Europe, 13 December 2018.

35 ECLJ, "Defend the right to criticize Islam," petition of 61,615 signatures.

pealing, but its price is the freedom to speak the truth. It implies that any statement, even true, is condemnable as intolerance and incitement to violence as soon as threatening people declare themselves offended in their religious feelings.

Of course, it is true that peace is the greatest good of society; and it is therefore right that, in order to preserve it, the authorities must sometimes limit individual freedoms. But society must be well threatened to sacrifice even the freedom to speak the truth; or then, not believe in it anymore. "*What does the truth matter towards peace?*" relativists from all sides will say. If truth does not exist, then, indeed, freedom of expression is of little value, and a mandatory "*tolerance*" should be imposed upon all. True peace should not be reduced to the superficial absence of violent conflict, and it is vain to pretend to establish it on lies or relativism.

The European tradition teaches that there is no lasting peace without truth and justice. Because Europe is the heir, since ancient times, of a civilization that identifies God with truth and love, and not with arbitrariness and force, we place those at the top of our values and do not conceive that truthfulness could offend God or society. Seeking the truth and knowing God are one. This is certainly the origin of our attachment to rational research and criticism. We want a society in which "*Love and faithfulness meet together; righteousness and peace kiss each other*" (Psalm 85:10). Righteousness and peace, which characterize the ideal of every society, need both love and truth.

Elisabeth Sabaditsch-Wolff told the truth. She is criticized above all for having done so in a "*malicious*" way, that is to say, without love. What do we know about it, and is it justice's role to assume one's intentions? Moreover, to make this reproach is to forget that the denunciation of evil, to protect society, beneath its apparent roughness, is an act of love.

—Grégor Puppinck, PhD, is Director General of the European Centre for Law and Justice (ECLJ).

ANALYSIS

BY CHRISTIAN ZEITZ

Order, Freedom and Cultural Self-Defense

Why Islamization does not come under natural law and how
the "Austrian approach" can safeguard religious peace

translated by John Melville Harris

Section 1
Opinion diktat, muteness and cultural self-abnegation in the face of Islam

ISLAM IS NOT TO BE DISCUSSED, for such is invariably associated with the risk of "insulting" Islam and Muslims.

Questions are not to be posed about the nature of Islam, for the deposit of faith and the "doctrine" are the "internal affairs" of Islamic religious societies. To be especially eschewed, are questions and remarks which might infer a lack of "respect" toward Islam or Muslims, for respect is considered a central category of multicultural social cohesion.

Muslims are not be treated differently from indigenous citizens, for "anti-discrimination legislation" expressly prohibits unequal treatment, even though people are unequal and behave very much unequally. Headscarves, billowing garments—raven-black or brightly colored as in *1001 Nights*—beards, kaftans and crakows are by no means to be adduced as grounds for "discrimination" in the allocation of positions in the workplace, because equal treatment of the unequal is a European dogma.

The strategic self-separation of Muslims through numerous ritual-istic, special provisions (prayer rites, ablutions, dietary regulations, fast-ing, etc.) leads perforce to the desynchronization of daily life, hence to a constitutional disparity between Muslims and members of the host societies. That this leads to increasing social segregation is, however, extolled as the attainment of "cultural diversity," and this likewise is a dogma of the European Union which is beyond any criticism.

How this separation is expected to harmonize with the professed political guiding principle of the "integration" of newcomers is nowhere taken up for detailed discussion. Presumably it suffices to claim that Is-lam is an "enrichment" for the senile European culture. It therefore de-serves "admiration" and must be defended against any rejection.

Non-Muslims are absolutely forbidden to research Islam and to teach or lecture on it, for only Muslims trained as imams have the right to impart Islam. They alone are entitled to the sovereignty of interpre-tation over what concerns Islam. In general, Arabic is claimed as the language of revelation. The Qur'an is said not to be translatable into an-other language without loss of meaning or danger of distortion; at best, it can be re-narrated. Whoever has not mastered the Arabic language of the Qur'an is forbidden from the outset to make (critical) statements about Islam.

Dialogue, however, is an obligation, since inter-religious dialogue is a correlate of the multi-religious society. We must continually "be in conversation!" However, the dialogue must be limited to the ever re-current establishment of points by which all religions are said to be the same; in particular, that we all worship "the same God." A discussion which gives expression to the divergent concepts of different religions and their possible incompatibilities with Islam *vis-à-vis* the constitu-tional state is deemed unacceptable and under no circumstances is it to be characterized as "dialogue."

Even though we have no right to research Islam, to ask critical ques-tions about it, or to reject certain elements of Islamic doctrine as cultur-ally foreign or threatening, despite not really knowing anything about Islam and not being permitted know anything, we must nevertheless grant the followers of Islam unrestricted freedom to practice their cult, for there exists, after all, the "fundamental right to freedom of religion." Without knowing content-wise to what end Islam and its followers are being given "freedom," the countries of the West are at the same time relinquishing every residue of preference for the tenets of their own religious background; for after all, there exists an obligation to the "religious neutrality of law and justice."

In any event, refusal to accept the claims of Islam and its institutional representatives is considered an expression of "Islamophobia." Depending on the way they are deployed, these claims range from demands that Islam be "respected" and recognized for its peaceable quality and enriching effect, through demands for an Islam-compatible food supply in public institutions like schools and hospitals, up to requiring that daily rhythms be adjusted to those of the Islamic cult system, including the elimination of Christian symbols from the public sphere. To reject these claims, which are manifestly components of a strategy for transforming the ensemble of epochal cultural conditions of daily life [*Alltagskultur*], is considered "Islamophobic;" that is, it is considered a symptom of a state of mind to be found somewhere between mental illness and a criminal disposition.

There are those who prove that certain verses from the Qur'an and the *hadith* place narrow limits on the project of "liberal renewal;" they refer to the dogmatic calls for the killing of unbelievers, the prescribed enmity toward Christians and Jews, the inferior position of women, the instruction to conduct raids and the imperative to collect tribute from non-Muslims, the standardization of corporal punishment, the mandatory provision for retributive justice or blood vengeance as well as the ritualization of all daily life down to the last detail. Whoever provides such documentation is reflexively delegitimized with the claim that he is "wresting quotations from their context."

And should the Qur'an-faithful *Irhabis* (literally, "terrorists") act according to instructions and take implacable measures in order to "strike terror into the hearts of unbelievers," the professional "Islam understanders" in the Western mass media are the first, aside from the professional functionaries of the Islamic institutions, to protest that violence and murderous terror have nothing to do with the "true Islam," hence "nothing to do with anything."

Whoever is skeptical in the face of such guidelines is reassured by the prospect of Islam's putative "reformability." After all, Islam, until today, has had a much shorter period of development available to it than, for example, Christianity, and therefore ought not to be judged too harshly. A phase of "enlightenment," hence an unfolding of "liberal Islam"—also fondly identified with the trademark of "Euro-Islam"—is impending, especially if Islam is not brought into contempt with "stereotypes," thereby hindering the unfolding of its peaceful potential.

Given the foregoing, the elites of the Western countries are eagerly at pains to lessen the burden of *jihad* for potential actors of a violent precursor to Islamization, in that they knock the intellectual weapons used to fight the radical antithesis of this Western cultural order from the hands of those who are prepared to fight for its centuries long, organically grown custom- and tradition-based ethic for daily living [*Alltagsethik*].

Freedom of opinion [*Meinungsfreiheit*] is the key resource for the defense of a society which rests on voluntary cooperation, the economic success of the many and on the spiritual pre-eminence of the individual. For such a society builds on the culture of civil non-violence and can therefore not be defended by physical aggression, but only by unconditional freedom of speech [*Freiheit des Wortes*]. Freedom of opinion is the right to say what is right, but also to say what is false. For only competition among opinions decides what "truth" is in a secular constitutional state.

The use of a criminal code for opinion offenses [*Meinungsstrafrecht*] is the *ultima ratio* for the termination of freedom of opinion. Criminal laws governing opinion when selectively applied have a particularly disastrous effect in the battle for truth. This currently pertains to all Western countries in the field of conflict between the fundamental rights to freedom of opinion and freedom of religion, in that the two norms are being applied asymmetrically, so that Islam and its unlimited practice are continually protected and defended against criticism; Christianity, by contrast, is exposed to contempt.

In Austria, the criminal law governing opinions is standardized by what constitutes offenses under the "Disparagement of Religious Doctrines" [*Herabwürdigung religiöser Lehren*] and "Incitement to Hatred" [*Verhetzung*], criminal codes § 188 and § 283 respectively. While attacks on Christianity over the past three decades have not led to a single conviction (no Christian church has ever found fault with this), complaints are not only regularly brought against criticism of Islam, or even against the mere naming of objectively demonstrable Islamic faith contents, but punishment is also imposed. Elisabeth Sabaditsch-Wolff, to whom this essay is dedicated with the admiration of the author for her commitment and work, was convicted because she thematized Mohammed's sexual consummation with the nine-year-old Aisha, which is very well documented in the *hadith* literature, and emphasized the normative sig-

nificance of Mohammed's actions as a model for all Muslims. Many other Islam critics have followed her as victims of the justice system.

But the carrying-on of the politicized justice system in critical areas
is not the endpoint of the development. The redefinition of any unwelcome expression of aversion as a "hate crime" opens the door once and
for all to official and judicial despotism. Regardless of the basis of action,
every form of aversion is to become the object of criminal prosecution,
although it is impossible by legal means to distinguish hatred from mere
displeasure. And unlike what constitutes "Incitement to Hatred," the
asymmetrical effect favoring Islam is not merely a question of selective
application by the judicial system, but one of the legal conception itself:
in the description of what constitutes an offense, the protection against
"hatred" already applies only to minorities, their religion and culture,
migrants or immigrants as well as to those subject to "racist" persecution, but never to the indigenous majority and their culture or their national heritage. This way, and not otherwise, is how the OSCE[1] will have
it. They have been advancing this project for many years. So too will the
relevant European organizations have it this way, such as the EU Fundamental Rights Agency and the ECRI;[2] and likewise those European
states (which have already singularly distinguished themselves on this
question), pursue and conceive of the matter in the same way. Deserving special mention in this connection is Germany with its "Network
Enforcement Act" [*Netzdurchsuchungsgesetz*], a law of spying and denunciation. As well, there is France, which is currently (summer 2019)
on the point of finalizing a similar legislative proposal.

Overall, Germany is definitely the one country, which has not only
already carried out the unlimited welcoming culture for seekers after
full-maintenance who are arriving from all over the world, but she has
also gone the furthest in hurrying along the dismantling of the remnant
of democratic-constitutional structures. The totalitarian intent of the
political elites, and the downright fascist quality of the particular meta-
political climate which they control, can be appreciated by referencing
the manifest drawing-room social acceptability of recent statements by
individual senior-level representatives of the system, and which have
stood without any consequences whatsoever. For example, the secretary

---

1 Organisation for Security and Co-operation in Europe.
2 European Commission for Racism and Intolerance: the Council of Europe's independent human rights monitoring body specialised in combating anti-Semitism,
discrimination, racism, religious intolerance and xenophobia.

general of the largest German governing party (CDU[3]), Peter Tauber, announced the following on 19 June 2019: one must now think of ways to deny certain fundamental rights to "right wing extremists" (which would include, for example, people, who in connection with mass immigration, speak of "losing control of the country"). Taking the matter somewhat further is the demand of the Bavarian politician, Tobias Himpenmacher (*die Linke Partei*),[4] who considers a "central lodging for integration-reluctant neo-Nazis" to be necessary; that is, the erection of concentration camps, so that those who wish to live together "in freedom and tolerance" will no longer be disturbed (*Donauwörther Zeitung*, 7 July 2019).

It can reasonably be assumed that this is by no means the end point of the development, for as Clausewitz says: "War drives to the ultimate extreme."

The commitment to freedom of opinion is no orchid discipline from the field of constitutional law; it is not the hobby of old, idiosyncratic pedants who are unable to accept that freedom of consumption, sexual intercourse and supranational capital transactions do not entirely define the characteristics of the liberal constitutional state. Freedom of opinion is entirely coextensive with the foundation of liberal democracy as such. If the idea of "governance by the people" is ever to have any kind of meaning and any kind of real underpinning, the decision-making processes of the people—whether it be elections or issue-related plebiscites—must follow from the guaranteed prerequisites for all rational problem-solving mechanisms. The prerequisites for all rational decision-making are: identification and naming of the problem, the disclosure of the proposed variants of solutions to the problem, the evaluation of the effects or consequences of implementing any problem-solving proposal, the (subjective) assessment of the effects or consequences in each case, and finally, the possibility of making a conscious decision on one of the proposed problem-solving mechanisms.

In (real) democracy, participation and majority voting are indispensable at each decision-making stage. And the instrument that makes both participation and the majority vote possible is freedom of opinion. This is central to the entire mechanism of democracy, and not just at the stages of assessment and decision, which describe so to speak the subjective component of the decision-making process. Rather, freedom

---

3　Christian Democratic Union [*Christlich-Demokratische Union*].

4　The Left Party.

of speech is also crucial for mastery of the objective components of the above-mentioned (democratic) decision-making process; specifically, for identifying and naming problems and for assessing the possible solutions and their consequences. In democracy, nothing is "true," nothing is "objectively correct," which has not been exposed to the chalybeate bath of the competition of divergent opinions. And in order for its function to be capable of fulfillment, competing opinions must not be exposed to any restrictions, or at least to only extremely mild ones. If we should have learned anything from Sir Karl Popper, then this!

In recent years, the social and political reality of Western countries has been deriding this fundamental understanding mercilessly. As early as the first stage of the above-mentioned decision-making process, it has completely destroyed freedom of opinion and its organically associated freedom of speech. It is in every way factually demonstrable and objectively provable that: the mass influx of people from the Third World has substantially changed the demographic fabric of European and American societies; mass migration is in part favored and reinforced by specific decision-makers or "influencers;" in virtually all Western states, the Muslim share of the population has grown, in some cases drastically in recent decades; the daily cultural, customs and traditions and character of the urban districts dominated by Muslim communities have changed drastically; and, in the wake of these kinds of processes, a substantial deterioration among the affected indigenous population has occurred, whether it concerns security, the degree of self-determination or the modalities of everyday dealings with one another. But in the countries of the West it is increasingly impossible, meaning it is frowned upon, or actually even forbidden, to characterize these processes as "population exchange," "planned migration," "Islamization" and "loss of control over the country."

Persons or associations who use these forbidden expressions to describe the changes highlighted here are not just scorned and loathed as "right-wing populists," "right-wing extremists," "racists" or "Nazis"— more than that, in many countries, they are politically and socially marginalized; they are registered, observed, monitored and prosecuted by secret services and constitutional protection agencies; and in any event, excluded from political decision-making. As for an assessment and evaluation of different possibilities for dealing politically with the above mentioned changes or the problems arising from them, it never even begins to reach that point. It follows that there can be no talk at all of the peoples' participation in the fundamental decisions which bear upon the above-mentioned changes and the ways of dealing with them. Is there a single country in the world, in which the people throughout the decades decided or co-decided on mass immigration and the acceptance of ongoing Islamic influence on everyday life?

The abolition of freedom of opinion is therefore equivalent to the transformation of democracy into a totalitarian dictatorship. That this is not being carried out by people with peaked caps and jackboots and on the basis of an hierarchically enforced central plan, but rather through the systemic co-operation of diverse agencies based on the decentralized deployment of an extensive set of potent instruments and with reference to the all-encompassing multicultural ideology, does not matter. But it is precisely this systemic [*systemische*] quality of contemporary totalitarianism that should be the focus of objective analysis. The system-analytical approach must also remain in the forefront in understanding the essential characteristics of the various societal structures in which human coexistence has been brought about over the last centuries and millennia, and which finally in recent decades have fallen victim to an asymmetrical ideological warfare.

Every organism possesses an immune system that enables it to survive even under adverse conditions. That is also valid for social systems which strive to defend their identity and functional effectiveness against external attacks and internal disturbances. This ability is always based on three requisite competences: (1) to identify, apprehend and verbally name the attacks or disturbances, (2) to understand and analyze—in their real, material presence [*Wesenheit*]—the method of operation of the attacks and their effects, and (3) to combat the attacks and disturbances in a system-compliant way, that is, to solve the problems associated with them without in the process harming or endangering the inner constitutional structure [*Verfasstheit*] and construction principles of the system itself.

The first, or immediately preceding section of this essay corresponds to the first of the three named competences and seeks to describe the loss of ability to apprehend and name the problem: the anxiety about "insult," "discrimination," "prejudices" and "stereotypes;" the anathema of "Islamophobia" and "impiety;" the fetish of "diversity," "multi-colored tolerance" [*Buntheit*] and "multicultural coexistence;" the imposition of "dialogue;" the acceptance of the Muslim sovereignty of the interpretation over Islam and the non-disclosure of its dogmas of faith as "internal affairs;" the whitewash of "nothing has anything do with anything;" and finally, the tabooing of criticism of the Islamization process under the banner of securing the "fundamental right to freedom of religion" have led to muteness, liquidation of freedom of opinion, incapacity for truth and to the complete paralysis of the powers of self-defense.

The second of the three above-named competencies of social systems (protection against attack), requires the ability to apprehend and understand the method of operation of external attacks. This, in turn, presupposes an understanding of both the functional principles of one's own social system as well as the specific nature of the aggressor and his repertoire of action. It would be reasonable for a second section of this essay to tackle precisely this analytical task.

However, theoretical presuppositions for such a step in the work are extensive and would far exceed the scope of this short essay. Also they have yet to be undertaken in an adequate way elsewhere in the relevant literature, since the positivism dominating the social sciences today is standing in the way of an adequate treatment. For that reason, only two points can be made here in a few lines—apart from that, those interested are directed to works of the author that are now being prepared for publication. First, reference should be made to the necessary cultural history of human communities in conjunction with a theory of the significance of religion for countries and societies; and secondly, the nature of Islam, or the nature of a societal order based on Islam should be developed and contrasted with a Christian enculturated social order. The following points are only hypotheses at this point, but they offer an idea of the direction "the journey" of an elaborated presentation of this analysis must take:

1. All social formations are the product of an enculturation of religious concepts.

2. Each social formation is part of a cultural framework, which, for its part, stands in systematic interaction with the respective ruling religious form.

3. A cultural framework and the social formation embedded in it define a stage of civilization. This stamps, completely, the underlying mentality [*Wesen*] of the human mind [*Geistes*].

4. Civilizational stages are separated from one another by cultural thresholds. The cultural framework of a given stage of civilization, as a rule, incorporates into itself the knowledge [*Wissen*] of the previous stage.

5. Religions are quasi-organic systems; that is to say, they are wholes [*Ganzheiten*], whose subsystems cannot be changed arbitrarily,

deformed or substituted for each other.

6. Islam enculturates a social order which differs systemically from any which Christianity has brought about. The former is structurally incompatible with the latter.

7. The exercise of the Islamic religion reproduces its order. It can therefore be tolerated in a society informed by Christianity only under restricted conditions.

The third above-mentioned competence, the ability to fight against disturbances within one's own culture-system and combat attacks on it in a system-conforming way, corresponds to the second section of this essay. It should be kept in mind while reading it that the political and legal measures suggested form only one important element of a strategy which is as much a comprehensive as it is an efficient, yet nevertheless peaceful and constitutional way of dealing with the problem of Islamization.

If a final preliminary remark regarding the following section might still be permitted, the means and methods that should be brought to bear to defend against Islamization must not jeopardize the essential features of the system itself or destroy the guiding principles of its blueprint. That means that the defense and the quest to preserve a constitutional state and social order based on individual freedom and the moral order of the West against the totalitarianism of an Islamic social order must not be achieved by means outside of the constitutional and Christian moral traditions. The late Austro-Hungarian Habsburg monarchy created a framework of this kind with the development of the concept of the "state-church law" [*Staatskirchenrecht*], whereby the first Western law dealing with Islam was brought about. This "Austrian approach" has been developed further. The chance of providing long-lasting religious peace with it has been squandered by the forces of cultural socialism and still awaits political implementation.

Section 2
Islam as socio-cultural threat to the West and the answer is the "Austrian School of Islamology"

The Islamization of the West and the policy of the elites

In the face of the enormous dislocations which have arisen for Western societies in recent decades owing to the increasing impact of Islam on social reality, there have been more or less meaningful discussions about the political management of this phenomenon. Considering what the present analysis has sought to show, the invariably suggestive question posed, as to whether or not Islam "belongs" to this or that particular Western country, must be regarded as an exceptional absurdity. Particularly following the experiences with the mass migration of persons who, since 2015, have been emigrating "on Allah's path," the opinion is now established in the destination lands for "refuge-and asylum-seekers" that Islamization has nothing to do with "cultural enrichment."

The question of an adequate reaction to the existing pressure of Islamization and its consequences has already reached into the daily politics of practically all Western countries. In response to this, an abstract concept, which is to say, a political concept has been established, which many decision makers have eagerly taken up: that of "political Islam." Within a few years, this idea has found its place in analytical debate as well as in everyday politics.

Although the concept is quite widespread, and indeed counts as somewhat established, there is little agreement among those promoting this concept, or at least they are not clear among themselves whether the concept has to do with classification for "different types of Islam" or whether it is a tactical political maneuver, a mere verbal cipher.

The fact is, there is a distinction to be made among different "versions" of Islam, which, with the aid of various adjectives, is quite popular whenever one ought not to criticize Islam as such, or is unwilling to do so. "Political Islam" is then equated with "radical Islam," which is categorically differentiated from "moderate Islam." The latter is considered "good" and compatible with the order of the West; the former is evil and culturally incompatible with it. This view slides easily, and hence very frequently in practice over into the model of thinking which holds that "political Islam" is a misuse of "religious Islam" by political power brokers acting in their own interests. Accordingly, "Islam" itself thereby becomes the victim of extra-religious machinations. "Political Islam" is then the projection screen for all evil, which must be combated in its own right in order to protect Islam itself. Why something which is in itself good only becomes "bad" by virtue of being pursued "politically" cannot yet be explained.

In any event, the truth is, there are various forms and degrees by which Muslims or Islamic communities exercise their religion. As supposedly obvious evidence, there is the penchant for pointing to the intensity, penetration, totality or universality with which Islam has been practiced historically or would have a cultural impact in diverse geographical regions. Also in this connection, one likes to refer to the many denominations, law schools and dynastic modalities of implementation. But of course, as with every other religion, this argument must result in there being as many different "Islams" as there are practicing Muslims. The idea, as one can see here, falls hopelessly short in the fundamental inability up to now of all the adherents of the concept of "political Islam," as well as those of every other adjectivally circumscribed type of Islam, to distinguish, or be capable of distinguishing the substance of this religion, its core domain, from its accidental admixtures.

The very deserving Bill Warner, apart from his journalistic activity of combining the academic with the popular, makes the definitional standard for a "political Islam" the criterion of whether a given Islamic (Qur'anic) content concerns itself with the treatment of "infidels" or not. Others, such as the Islam critic, Ayaan Hirsi Ali, take into account the activity of political or proto-political institutions like the Muslim Brotherhood, upon whose—partly violent—agitation hangs the proof of "political Islam" or its distinguishability from its completely harmless little brother. And the governments of some countries and many of their respective political parties and advisers have been working for a considerable time on a "law against political Islam," pursuant to which violent machinations "in the name of Allah" might be prevented and the disquieted public calmed.

However, the facets of admittance to the idea of "political Islam" are as multifarious as the concept itself. It is irredeemable, meaningless and counterproductive. It is hopeless to attribute all the unwanted, conflict-ridden characteristics of Islam to a political homunculus in order thereby to rescue the "true Islam" as an awe-inspiring religious form. The construction of a "political Islam" is quasi the conceptual brother of the visionary wish for a "Euro-Islam" or a "liberal Islam." The latter rests upon the same methodological operation and hence on the same conceptual fallacies, as a result of which one imagines he can in any desired manner choose, assemble and combine the components of Islam with Islam-alien elements, thereby achieving reconciliation with modernity.

The Phantasm of "Political Islam" and its destructive consequences

The phantasm of "political Islam" vanishes definitively and irrevocably into thin air when one researches the possible relational field between "Islam" and "politics" at an essential, more basic level. An in-depth consideration of the sequence of steps to the secular order shows that politics is the product of a relatively late phase in the modern development of culture. Politics is not simply some form, or even any form of societal interaction that aims at power or governance. It is the product of the complementarity among those great institutions or cultural components which underwent their formation only within the European and American sphere of the nineteenth century. On the other hand, the ruling principle and essence of Islam dates from a stage in the socio-cultural development of humanity lying several thousand years in the past (not just 1,400 years), a period into which the Islamic cultural order is ultimately pressing to return again. Everything in Islam is religion, everything is communal order, everything is culture and everything represents the totality of Islam in its access to all spheres of human life.

All imperatives, interdicts, and paradigmatic representations of the Islamic revelation, the way of life of the Prophet Mohammed as exemplar, and the quasi-historical events of the alleged period of emergence of Islam as we know them from the Qur'an, *hadith*, and biographies of the Prophet; all of these attest to the following all too clearly: what is "political" about the law of retribution, about polygamy, about the despotic capriciousness of Allah, about the rites and purification prescriptions, about the headscarf and the different versions of *jihad*?

Islam is true reality, not because it is "political," but because it is a comprehensive and universal pattern for the socio-cultural coexistence of human beings.

"Political Islam," by contrast, is the product of analytical desperation and an alibi-like political populism.

Nevertheless, the question remains as to how one can explain the actual variability of Islamic communal formations, the broad spectrum in the application of Islamic imperatives, the enforcement of Islamic cultural patterns as well as the radicality of their protagonists if not by the existence of different "versions" of Islam. The answer can be given in the present paper with only a hint as to the directional thrust of continuing work. In Austria, a research paradigm has been established over the course of the past decade which calls itself the "Austrian School of Islamology." It inclines toward the methods of the "Austrian School of Economics," the insights of the sociology of religion as well as the fruits of thought from the field of cultural philosophy.

The notion that there are numerous "versions" of Islam manifesting themselves in denominations, law schools, dynasties and local and regional expressions among others—"there is no such thing as the Is-

lam..."—rests on an intellectual fallacy of empirical reductionism. This
error looks only at snapshots of various cultural constellations and per-
sists in the consideration of static, situational patterns.

The methodological approach of the "Austrian School of Islam-ology"

In contrast, the "Austrian School" understands Islam as a living organism, as an internally consistent whole—a system which continually tends towards homeostatic equilibrium whilst carrying out adaptive
motions, adopting thereby morphologically diverse forms and traits.
Everything whose "genetic code" consists in the holistic composite of
Qur'an, *hadith* and the biographies of the Prophet must be understood
as Islam. Islam's entire repertoire of conditions, its developmental stages
and the variants thereof are rooted in this "genetic code." To this repertoire of conditions belongs a corresponding repertoire of actions, which
arise from the Qur'anic doctrinal imperative, the archetypical formation
of Allah's characterological representation as well as the exemplar-ef-
fect of the Prophet's mode of behavior. The individual elements of the
Qur'anic doctrine of action have different grades of validity under different external conditions, because they rest on specifically formulated
and contextualized imperatives which take into account the respective
situational contingencies. The ritual component and the symbolic world
of Islam have similar relation-induced effects. Taken in their synthesis,
these elements provide the Islamic organism with a high level of functional application and plasticity.

This is indispensable for the survivability of Islam under changing
economic, demographic, technical and geopolitical conditions; for owing to the complete absence of a productive economic ethic, Islam is
dependent on the consumption of foreign, extra-Islamic real and cultural capital, which exposes it to the danger of cultural and ideological
"impurity." Therefore, the Qur'anic principle of "*razzia*," acquisition of
tribute and capital consumption must of necessity correspond to the
cyclical sequences of the spread of religious radicalization, combined
with the retarding effect of the consolidation or enrooting of the deposit of faith on the one hand, and religious "tolerance" and "readiness
to compromise" on the other hand. The ever-recurring violent conflicts
between different denominations and other game variants of Islam are
also to be understood as part of this cyclical process.

The organic holism of Islam cannot be grasped with a momentary inspection. Those who abandon themselves to the illusion of point-in-time referenced comparisons of the configuration of diverse Islamic communities in disparate territories must perforce embrace the idea of different "versions of Islam," which amounts to different concepts of Islam. Snapshots of situational patterns can, at best, say something about the "real Islam" on a specific date. Whoever, on the other hand, wishes to research Islam in its wholeness, must study the pattern of its process-structure in its timeline if he is to understand the laws of the one and unique Islam-organism. This is definitely also a precondition for the ability to deal proactively and adequately with the dangers and consequences of Islamization from the perspective of a destination country of Muslim migration or from the standpoint of a host country with a growing Islamic population.

The content of the final section of this small work is also linked to the approach of the "Austrian School of Islamology." This explores the question of how the secular state enculturated in Christian monotheism should deal with Islam and Muslims.

The failure of policy

In recent decades, the overwhelming majority of Western states have seen a massive increase in the Muslim share of the population. Initially, after the Second World War, it was barely noticeable; from the 1960s, it was insidious, yet noticeable owing to the labor migration; then it took a sudden leap by virtue of decisive, massive geopolitical events like the "Bosnian War" and the collapse of the Soviet Union in the 1990s; finally, it increased explosively in consequence of the mass migration and asylum crisis as of 2015. Overtop of this demographic interfacing, progressive Islamization followed by and large rampantly; that is, Islam had an increasing effect on the customs and traditions of the everyday culture; and Islamic communities became increasingly important in the politics of the affected countries. That means that the political sector possesses no well-ordered strategy for dealing with this phenomenon, and there is even less of a specific juridical infrastructure for how the Islamic religion is implemented. The latter is carried out exclusively on the basis of general freedom of religion in the respective countries and with reference to the relevant international standards of general human rights. Specific problems arising from individual followers of Islam who have attracted attention, or with particular radically acting Islamic institutions, are dealt with at best on the basis of general criminal or administrative law.

With that, the problem appears to be settled for most political decision makers. Attitudes of resignation among critics, or even their capitulation, are accordingly widespread in everyday political life.

The Austrian Islam Act

The only country that represents a striking exception on this question—at least theoretically—is Austria. There are two historical reasons for this: first, the specific form of contact with the Bosnian Muslims at the end of the centuries-long confrontations of the Danube Monarchy with the Ottoman Empire; and second, the unique tradition of the Austrian, so-called state-church law [*Staatskirchenrecht*], which, through the Recognition Act of 1874, formulated the admission requirements for newly constituted faith communities in a very concise way. The first factor owes its effect to the Emperor, Franz Josef, who wished to shape relations with his Bosnian subjects within an economically prospering milieu and a culturally beneficial setting. The second factor rests on the deeply rooted Austrian tradition of thought that a matter is only well regulated if there is a legal substrate for it.

It was these two factors which led to the drafting and adoption of the world's first "Law on Islam." And it is almost unbelievable that to this day Austria is the only country in the world where there is a law concerning Islam of this kind.

After the final repulse of the Ottoman expansion into the Balkans by the European peacekeeping power of the Austrian-Hungarian Habsburg monarchy, Bosnia-Herzegovina became an Austrian protectorate in the course of the Congress of Berlin in 1878. Only in 1909 was Bosnia admitted to the Austro-Hungarian Monarchy, when it was formally placed under the administrative control of the Hungarian Ministry of Finance. In 1910, Kaiser Franz Joseph formalized its admission by decreeing a special constitutional status. The monarchy conferred upon the country a remarkable economic boom, undertook a singular effort to maintain religious peace and endeavored to preserve the societal structures which were in many respects tied to the Muslim elites. As a special sign of equal rights, Islam was accordingly to be granted the status throughout the realm of a legally recognized religious community [*Religionsgemeinschaft*]. Grounded in a knowledge which was by no means inconsiderable, a parliamentary special commission was instituted specifically for the purpose, and it evaluated the possible consequences of such a recognition. After some three years of work, the Commission finally recommended that legal recognition be implemented. This occurred with the "consent of both houses of the *Reichsrat*" to the Law on Islam of 15 July 1912.

In its concept as a special law [*Sondergesetz*], which took into account the individual characteristics of the Muslim community and in many respects granted it special accommodation, this was nevertheless a provisional arrangement which allowed the Muslims lengthy time limits for constituting a formal institution and for the qualifying of their religious officials. Because of the First World War, and owing to the circumstance that in its aftermath, for decades Islam no longer had any relevance in the territory of what henceforth became the small state of Austria, the law was never really transformed into a condition of religio-legal normalcy. Since then, many deficiencies and inadequacies in dealing with the "real Islam" have been slipping into Austria. These difficulties, however, with the increasing Islamic presence in the Europe of the 21st century, have been proving ever more pressing.

The initiative for renewal of the Islam Act and the political failures

The exponents of the above-mentioned "Austrian School of Islamology," who were formed from the circles within the Association of Vienna Academics [*Wiener Akademikerbund*] in the first decade of the 21st century, took the opportunity to launch the project for a renewal of the Islam Act and complete the intellectual preparations for it. For present purposes, the basic reflections are taken from the insights summarized in this work as follows:

* Religion is veritable reality. It shapes the cultures, societies and countries in which it is embedded.

* The exercise of religion, through its adherents, reproduces the very order which came into being through the cultural stamp of that same religion.

* Christian monotheism and Islam enculturate completely different social and political orders which are incompatible and cannot be combined with each other in essential points.

* An order condensed from Christianity can therefore not accept, as "equally entitled options," the societal building blocks of a societal or political order arising from Islam.

* The dogma of the "religious neutrality of the state" is therefore a contradiction in terms and is incompatible with the legitimacy which

every polity has in defending itself against enforced change.

*   Although tied to certain risks, the order of the secular constitutional state must accept the freedom of individual religious practice, even in the case of foreign cults (to be understood only within the framework of general laws), if it is not to fall into self-contradiction.

*   The constitutional state can and must, however, regulate or restrict in a specific way collective/corporate implementation of religious practices whenever these arise mandatorily out of the constitutive characteristics of a religion.

This set of principles leads almost of necessity to a solution approaching a specific form of Islam Act. The Austrian law governing religion is for that reason designed as the "State-Church Act," for it is obligated to the conviction that a well-ordered form of corporate enforcement in the area of religion in a secular constitutional state is only possible if the state stands *vis-à-vis* a legal personality bearing the responsibility for religious practice and its possible consequences. This affects Christianity automatically, because it exists by definition as a Church (or churches). Owing to its historical genesis and its history of revelation, Islam has no knowledge inherent to itself out of which institutions of this kind can arise. If there is a will to grant corporate religious freedom to Islam, this must be brought about, *uno actu*, by the constitution of a legal personality responsible for the community. For only within the symmetry of freedom and responsibility can religious peace be preserved within a national community.

The Islam Act follows this ruling principle by virtue of it being, in essence, a law governing the recognition of a religious society and the conditions constituting it. This approach was already extant in the Islam Act of 1912, but was not sufficiently implemented, so that a constitutionally satisfactory foundation for enforcement of the law did not exist, and over the course of decades this situation ran completely out of control. The result of this deficit was the spread of an uncontrolled growth of Islamic institutions, activities and events which changed the day-to-day cultural customs and traditions, all resulting from decades-long seepage processes [*Sickerprozessen*] which neither the political nor administrative levels were in a position to manage.

In the meantime, in the small country of Austria, around four hundred mosque facilities have been established, which are instituted on the basis of civil law governing associations, and within which collective, Islamic enforcement of religion is conducted. These mosques have nothing to do formally with the IGGÖ (Islamic Religious Authority of

Austria), which was recognized and established by virtue of the Islam Act, operates as the "official representative" of Islam, conducts "inter-religious dialogue," functions as a contact for politicians and media, enjoys state privileges, and claims financial endowments for religious instruction and other activities. The mosque associations are almost exclusively embedded in the opulent framework of the ethnicities, national backgrounds or tribal connections which are shouldering them, and they also draw financial maintenance from this edifice. In connection with these unofficial mosques there is also the widespread influence of the radical institutions such as the Muslim Brotherhood, the Turkish Milli Görüs as well as Salafist networks. Through them in particular, even recruitment for Islamic State (ISIS) terrorism has been carried out.

All of this was already sufficient justification in its own right for demanding a renewal of legislation on Islam in Austria. But only the pressure of the accelerating migration flow during 2014 and 2015 and the resulting change in "public opinion" tipped the balance in favor of tackling this project in the sphere of real politics. To this purpose, representatives of the "Austrian School of Islamology" have raised the already longstanding demands for reform and have specified concrete proposals. As expected, this mobilized the indignation of professional Islamic activist communities—"enjoy your last days of freedom!" And out of the usual mixture of culpable ignorance, opportunism, political patronage and lack of principles, the Austrian political sector passed the "Law on Islam 2015," which has completely failed in its purpose. Despite intense discussions and warnings of a factual nature being given within the pre-parliamentary as well as the parliamentary sphere, a legal text was railroaded through; and although nominally containing portions of the experts' demands, it was nevertheless legally (deliberately?) so inadequately laid out, there were such obvious, predeterminable weak points, that an implementation according to the sense of its objectives is impossible.

In effect, the "new Law on Islam" has even exacerbated the mechanism for the rampant spread of Islamic communities, the absence of enforceable responsibility as well as the influence of radical, often foreign forces. As an example, one need only make reference here to the fully official and formally implemented legislative act, pursuant to which the ethnic-Bosnian associations have been subordinated to the decision-making power of the Grand Mufti of Sarajevo, who in turn is solidly under Saudi Arabian influence.

The wretched appearance of four members of the government's turquoise-blue coalition (ÖVP/FPÖ) at a press conference on June 8, 2018, must be rated an exceptional blunder. They wholeheartedly announced the dissolution of mosque associations and the deportation of foreign imams. After a few months, they were forced to recognize that all measures foundered on the inadequate principles for implementation of the Islam Act—exactly as the critics had already predicted on the day of the press conference.

Indispensable measures for cultural self-defense in all countries of the West

It therefore remains the task henceforth to continue the implementation of the proposals of the "Austrian School of Islamology," in Austria and in all other countries, who wish to take seriously the battle against a rampant Islamization and the resulting total transformation of their inherent cultural substance. Among the set of proposed measures, the most important for implementation are the following:

a.   That there be disclosure of the basic tenets of faith in the interests of enforcing the right of the general public to be informed about the teaching contents, views and goals of all religious communities. Such disclosure is the precondition for a serious test of compatibility with state law and would also be necessary for securing any kind of meaningful inter-religious dialogue or dialogue between the state and religious societies.

b.   That the collective enforcement of the religious practice of Muslims be restricted to religious societies recognized by the state, and that this be tied to the requirement for the dissolution of associations where the Islamic religious life escapes any kind of transparency *vis-à-vis* the public and deprives the competent state authorities of any access.

c.   That the foreign financing of operations involving religion be prohibited pursuant to the postulate that each Austrian religious society has independent viability (i.S. § 6 of the Recognition Act or perhaps § 2 of the Orthodox Act), with the objective, as well, of minimizing the radicalizing influence of foreign states and organizations not operating in accordance with human rights.

The political and legal way of dealing with Islam up to now has been marked by the illusion that Islam is "a religion like any other" and therefore the "state-church law," which developed in connection with the Christian churches and denominations, can be applied more or less automatically and unchanged to the laying of a legal framework for the state to use in dealing with Islam. This illusion has proved to be a mistake, for the religio-legal and political relationship of the state to Islam has up to now been relying on quasi-ecclesiastical characteristics of Islam which it does not exhibit, but would have to possess in order to communicate in a legally binding way with authorities and civil society, without special constructs and formalisms, and in order to be capable of assuming responsibility for the actions of its adherents.

Political policy makers are being called upon to quickly and determinedly come to grips with the implementation of a project that ensures religious peace, for the momentum of the consequences of this influx of Muslim migrants, and the consistent wish of radical Islamic states and organizations to use as many of them as possible to man outposts for their religious and power-political interests, admits of no further delay.

—Christian Zeitz is Director of Research at the Institute for Applied Political Economy in Vienna.

THE AUSTRIAN LAW ON ISLAM

BY CHRISTIAN ZEITZ

AND

ELISABETH SABADITSCH-WOLFF

T HE AUSTRIAN LAW on Islam is unique in all of Europe, perhaps even worldwide: Islam, along with other major religions such as Catholicism, Protestantism, the Jewish faith, Buddhism, and others, is granted a special status within the legal system. Not only that, but the taxpayer also foots the bill for imams, religious education, and other matters. (This also concerns all other legally recognized religions.)

The original law was necessitated by Austria-Hungary's annexation of Bosnia-Herzegovina at the beginning of the 20th century: the incorporation of Hanafi Muslim soldiers into the Austrian army demanded that the Hanafi school of Islam be legally recognized. Little did the authors of the law know that nine decades later this very law would be the cause of so much discussion.

The main point of discontent has always been the lack of disclosure of the tenets of the faith by the Islamic Faith Community, as demanded from and adhered to by *all* other faith communities. Thus, official Austria does not know what faithful Muslims believe. This has resulted in the ridiculous situation that numerous Islam-critics have been convicted for "denigration of religious beliefs of a legally recognized religion" while the state has no idea what these teaching comprise!

After the final repulse of the Ottoman expansion in the Balkans by the European forces of the Austro-Hungarian Habsburg monarchy, Bosnia and Herzegovina were made protectorates of Austria by the Berlin Congress of 1878. Not until 1909 were they accepted into the Austro-Hungarian monarchy. In 1910, this acceptance was formalized by a special status conferred by Emperor Franz Joseph. The monarchy was affording the land a respectable economic prosperity, and was at pains to preserve the religious peace as well as the social structures frequently linked with the Muslim elites. As a special mark of equality, Islam was therefore to be awarded the status of a legally recognized religious community throughout the entire empire. This took place "with the agreement of both Houses of the Imperial Assembly" in the Law on Islam of July 15, 1912.

Recognition as a religious society [*Religionsgesellschaft*] in the sense of Article XV of the Constitution [*Staatsgrundgesetz*] of 1867 was granted to the adherents of Islam—restricted, however, to the "Hanafite Rite." This group had the "right of collective practice of religion" restricted to recognized churches and religious societies. "The external legal relationships of the adherents of Islam" are to be settled by statute, once "the foundation and existence of at least one religious community [*Kultusgemeinde*] has been achieved" (§1). The "doctrines of Islam, its institutions [*Einrichtungen*] and customs, shall enjoy… protection unless they are in contradiction to the laws of the state." (§6)

The law was definitely regarded and enacted as a transitional solution and emergency measure in the face of the verified, temporarily tolerated incapacity of the adherents of Islam to conform to the requirements for approval of recognized religious societies. This follows unquestionably from the text and protocols of the parliamentary commission appointed to evaluate the justification and reasonableness of a law exclusive to Islam. The commission invokes the general regulation on admission of a recognized religious society, which had been standardized in the Recognition Act of 1874 and which is valid to the present day.

The Law on Islam was revised in March 2015, unsuccessfully and with disastrous consequences for Austria. What follows is the analysis of the Vienna Association of Academics (*Wiener Akademikerbund*):

The Law on Islam—A Black Day for Austria

Yesterday, after long discussions, the new Law on Islam was passed in the Austrian National Assembly. The new act is a revision of a law from 1912 and was intended to be a great advance. What resulted is somewhere between half-baked and counterproductive. It misses the central point and is *de facto* unenforceable. Christian Zeitz, academic director of the Institute for Applied Political Economy, was involved intensively beforehand with both the law and the material. If Austria had enacted his insights, they would at least be one step further along.

But neither the expertly qualified critics nor the much publicized "broad base" had a say. The entire parliamentary opposition—albeit for various reasons—voted against it. And so what was decided was neither helpful nor beneficial, or, as Christian Zeitz foresaw:

The Law on Islam—Project of a Constitutional Attempt to Deal with Islam—Is at the Point of Collapse

On January 13th, the government template for the Law on Islam was the object of vigorous debate in the constitutional committee of the National Assembly. In the framework of hearing the testimony of experts, specialists familiar with the subject matter worked out the weaknesses of the draft law that the government was hoping to have rubber-stamped by the entire chamber. I myself concentrated on the formal defects of this legislative approach and on the fact that it completely ignores the reality of Islam and its representative institutions in Austria. With the implementation of this law, the Islamic organizations would receive even more privileges. Even more significant: with this law, the rampant, creeping Islamization of our land will be protected against any national supervision or control and against any timely attempt to prevent a progressive radicalization in government agencies. Neither the Minister of Culture, Josef Ostermayer, nor his staff, were able to counter these doubts.

What happened? What does the background of this awkward matter look like? Why is this legal matter of such great relevance for the social and political situation in our country? Where does it go from here?

In 1912, four years after Bosnia-Herzegovina had been incorporated among the legal entities of the Danube monarchy, the Emperor signed a law in Austria that was a worldwide first, in which the "followers of Islam" were legalized as a recognized religious community. For the hundred-year jubilee in 2012, a "time-appropriate" Law on Islam was foreseen, which was to have portrayed the actual situation in "multi-religious Austria." At first, extended negotiations with the IGGiÖ, which sought an expansion of its rights (its own university faculties, state-compensated spiritual directors in the army, Islamic ministry in hospitals and prisons, Islamic cemeteries, Islamic provisioning in public facilities with Islam-compatible "halal" foods) delayed the project. Also because of that delay, however, three of the most important requirements advanced by citizens for years as causing concern for the maintenance of secular, liberal order and religious peace in the land were accepted. They are:

1. The obligation to make public the articles of faith in the Islamic communities. Such an obligation is necessary to make possible the repeatedly invoked "inter-religious dialogue." Even more, it is indis-

pensable to being able to determine what elements of the "doctrine of Islam" are not compatible with the laws of Austria. Actually, the Law of 1912 already requires such a procedure. For there are certainly reasons to assume that substantial portions of especially the Islamic social and legal system (*shariah*) are not compatible with the laws of an enlightened constitutional state. It is a particular scandal that there are critics of Islam who have been convicted of "derogation of religious doctrines," which doctrines, however, have not been revealed by anyone, anywhere.

2. The banning of the financing of Islamic religious enterprises (mosques, *et alii*) by foreign sources. This regulation would be especially important because the experience of recent decades, both in country and out, shows unmistakably that radicalization of Muslim communities frequently results from investment ("mosque-building") and personal expenditures for religious officers ("imams") by foreign institutions that are interested in bringing about a radical form of Islam. Saudi Arabia is especially active in this area, as is the Turkish religious authority with its Austrian branch ATIB (*Avrupa Türk-Islam Birliği* [Union of Turkish-Islamic Cultural Organizations in Europe]).

3. The necessary dissolution of mosque and prayer groups which have been established in a rampant, unmanageable process in recent years, and have overspread all of Austria with a dense net of 460 such institutions. The reality of the practice or pursuit of a religion in completely unaccounted-for organizations is incompatible with the idea of a legally recognized religious society which is responsible for its actions and its practitioners and therefore enjoys legal protection and privileges.

These three requirements were included in the ministerial draft for the new Law on Islam which was published on October 2nd of last year (2014). There was an instant storm of outrage from Muslim functionaries and their political and media protectors. The new Islam law would manifest a "general suspicion," would "discriminate" against Muslims, and make Muslims "second-class citizens," and therefore unworthy of constitutional protections and human rights.

The defects of the draft law disappeared in the propaganda storm produced by Islamic functionaries, who had one more opportunity to demonstrate their high dudgeon at being insulted and play once more the role of victim. And this assures that the requirements mentioned will not be enacted and/or be enforceable, and thus the same, unsatisfactory and dangerous make-up of Islam in Austria remains not only untouchable, but totally legally secured and therefore preserved forever. The actual make-up of Islam is a bizarre twofold enterprise: the legally recognized IGGiÖ (Islamic Faith Community in Austria) manages state-financed Islamic religious education and political public works, for which it receives pubic donations, meanwhile not being responsible for one single mosque or religious community. The 460 Islamic organizations, on the other hand, manage mosques, sponsor Friday sermons and generally take care of the practice of the Islamic faith, by serving Muslims at the grassroots level, thus defining everyday Islam in the country.

The draft law is snarled up by connecting the dissolubility of the organizations on the basis of their "doctrine" to that of a legally recognized religious society. There is not sufficient space here for a detailed analysis of this thorny matter and a demonstration of the consequent effects of the faulty legislative construct. This was done in the course of a detailed presentation by the Wiener Akademikerbund. The fact is that the organizations, according to this law, cannot be dissolved. This is tragic, since the requirements of "transparency" and "foreign financing" cannot be applied to the sponsors of the mosques and Islamic religious enterprises.

This problem, which seems to be merely an academic-juridical one, is of eminent significance for social co-existence, maintenance of our own culture and religious peace in the land. It affords a glance into the daily Islam-relevant reporting of the media, in just recent days. Three relevant examples:

In an interview conducted by the magazine *PROFIL*, with Dr. Fuat Sanac, president of IGGiÖ (Number 3 2015, of January 12, 2015), he denies the existence of the death penalty for blasphemy in Islamic states as well as the endorsement of suicide attacks by the highly influential Islamic legal scholar, Yusuf al-Qaradawi. "Islam is not political." "Islamic scholars must never cease to emphasize that the actions of terrorists are absolutely un-Islamic." And then a much-quoted mantra of all Islam sympathizers: "Killing a single person, according to the Qur'an, is the same as killing all of humanity."

It is worthwhile to quote the appropriate verse from the Qur'an: "Therefore we have commanded the children of Israel that anyone who kills a person other than for vengeance or if he [the person killed] has committed some mischief here on earth, then it is as if he [the killer] had killed all of humanity..." (Sura 5:32). Fuat Sanac suppressed the important second part of the verse. This, in fact, is one of the bases for Islamic blood revenge/right of vengeance. This becomes specific just one verse later where the consequences of the "mischief on this earth" are foreseen: "But the reward of those who rise up against Allah and strive only to bring ruin upon the earth shall be that they are killed or crucified or have their hands and feet chopped off on opposite sides, or that they shall be expelled from the land." (5:33) This is not the place to deal with the question of whether the methods of IS in Iraq are different in any detail from this Koranic imperative. The question to ask is, why Sanac so consistently (and repeatedly) misrepresents the details of his faith. And exactly that is the point.

How is it possible to advance a beneficial co-existence, let alone a respectful interchange, with representatives of a religious community which consistently refuses to offer any vaguely true information about its beliefs, and on the contrary, replies to any serious reappraisal with drop-dead arguments? The implementation of "disclosure of the elements of faith" would be an unconditional prerequisite for creation of a common base for Muslims and non-Muslims in a community of Austrian values.

In the January 19th, 2015, issue of *Kurier*, Muslim functionaries are upset about Minister Kurz's insistence on oversight of activities in Islamic religious enterprises. The omnipresent press representative of the IGGiÖ, Carla Amina Baghajati, speaks of "an intervention in the internal affairs of recognized religious societies." This is yet another archetypical demonstration of the confusion in the Law on Islam! To what recognized religious society does Baghajati refer? As already noted, the IGGiÖ does not manage one single mosque. NONE of the managing organizations of Islamic religious enterprises are recognized religious societies, and they have nothing to do with IGGiÖ, in that they neither operate under its auspices nor are they (able to be) internally supervised—and this completely regardless of whether they are "aid organizations" or not. President Sanac himself stated this unambiguously in August 2014. So the IGGiÖ will either assume the role of spokesman and protector of all of Islam in Austria or, when necessary, distance itself from individual institutions that are not in good order.

This second quotation from the media is firm evidence of the necessity of dissolving the rank proliferation of mosque organizations, as is indeed suggested but not made possible in the draft Islam law. The above example illustrates why this requirement is of such political importance. One pillar of a functional and just religious law is the equality of coverage of rights and duties as well as responsibility and supervision, by which a legally recognized and privileged religious society should be characterized. The shabby hare-and-tortoise game between religious society and proliferating organizations undermines this pillar and must, in the long run, damage or destroy any trust between the Muslim community and the majority society.

So it is of the utmost importance not only in the interests of the indigenous Austrians, but of at least the integration-ready Muslims, that the requirements mentioned here be made legally actionable and be politically enacted by a properly established Law on Islam. Integration-ready Muslims in Austria have a right to be informed clearly by the state community they wish to belong to, what elements of the Islamic doctrine cannot be carried out here. Indeed, we do not just have a "general suspicion" but the general knowledge that *shariah* in its entirety is not compatible with the law, customs and moral concepts of Austria (see, e.g., right of revenge, bodily punishments, inequality of women, polygamy and discrimination against "infidels"). It is an expression of the dishonesty and failure of the political elite to have consistently suppressed this obvious truth until this day.

So it is no wonder that the Muslim functionaries of the next generation—after no resistance to implementation of the Islamic legal concepts—are becoming increasingly more offensive in their demands. The third media quotation shows this vividly. In the commentary of the *Standard* newspaper of January 23rd, the front woman of the MJÖ (Muslim Youth of Austria), Dudu Kücükgöl, denounces the "daily, Islam-hostile exaggerations of populist political discourse," the "public paranoia," the "legally prescribed discrimination" and the effect of "crude Islamophobic think tanks." She demands "not just equality," but "attention from the state," which no doubt means this is not just a question of "religious freedom" but of the realization of political-Islamic demands. And in this sense, it is about the maintenance and buildup of the necessary instruments.

As an exemplar of the academically educated female Muslim in Austria, Kücükgöl sees already that the new Law on Islam would protect these instruments, and that she is only deploying the old saw about the "scandalous draft for a new Law on Islam" as a calculated distraction. She knows very well that the Law on Islam will go aground on its own goal of "dissolution of the organizations," if only their exponents employ the proper "wording" in reference to their self-understanding.

But the Austrian federal government does not see what Kücükgöl has recognized. The new Law on Islam in its present form is unenforceable, will have no effect and is, at best, intended as a sedative for a public that has become extraordinarily insecure.

In conclusion, for the Wiener Akademikerbund, which has long advocated a constructive religious law, the challenge is as follows. A correction of the religious law is necessary, with the goal of restricting the rampant growth of mosques, ensuring the responsibility of Islamic religious societies for the beliefs they represent, and preventing the increase of radical influence on the Islamic scene in Austria through foreign financing. From a legal-technical perspective, there would be no problem in accomplishing this, if the necessary political will can be found, and there is still time to bring the capacities of all constructive powers to bear. The Austrian federal government must be challenged not to push such important material through parliament as a prestige project. A good Law on Islam is one of the absolute last chances to preserve a permanent religious peace in Austria.

The transition from scientific analysis and analytical insights to solutions based on practical policy measures has always been a sensitive issue. The lack of contact between the advisory "theorists" and the "practical politicians" often precludes the effective implementation of even the most outstanding solutions. But in the case of the Law on Islam in Austria, that must not be a problem. The representatives of the "Austrian School of Islamic Studies"—namely the Vienna Akademikerbund and its friendly institutions—have for a long time intensively advised numerous top-level decision-makers in the political sector. This concerns in particular the competent representatives of the recently dissolved ÖVP-FPÖ coalition government, which was in office since the beginning of 2018. However, this did not stop them from announcing a package of measures that contained all the rookie mistakes on the Islam matter without much ado. A few hours after the bombastic presentation of these measures, therefore, the Wiener Akademikerbund heavily criticized and predicted that none of the announced measures would actually be implemented. And until the dissolution of the government in June 2019, just as predicted, not a single measure was indeed enforced. The government left behind the same Islamic law rubble heap that it started out with and in the subsequent election campaign indulged in the usual irrelevant and inconsequential phrases about "political Islam." Below is the essay with the criticism of the government press conference of June 8, 2018, and the corresponding forecasts that have come true to this day.

Bombshell in Ramadan
Why the PR-effective measures announced by the government will only function in part, and why the Islam Law must therefore be reformed immediately.
by Christian Zeitz

Whatever else happens, June 8, 2018, will enter the political history of the Republic of Austria. At an unusual hour—8:00 a.m.—the government presented a package of measures and intentions intended to halt abuses and subversive activities which have become established in parts of the Islamic community. With statements from Chancellor Kurz, Vice Chancellor Strache, Chancellery Minister (*ergo* Cultural Affairs Minister) Blümel, as well as Interior Minister Kickl, this intention was presented with a display of personal presence and determination unequaled in the Second Republic. Publicly making the theme "State and Islam" an inter-ministerial *causa prima* is noteworthy and deserves great approbation. The enormous resonance in the media (from the tiny Austrian town of Perchtoldsdorf to Washington) justifies the government in its public act just as does the agreement of the ordinarily carping opposition parties. Both of these things signal especially that by far the greatest portion of the Austrian population is finally fed up with the appeasement, indeed circumventive lying, about certain conditions and events inside the Islamic community, and is no longer willing to accept the obviously increasing threats to public security, the rule of law and everyday culture.

The representations of government members, taken separately, were doubtlessly heading in the right direction. Kurz: "The idea of the Islam Law (2015) was to prevent foreign political influence by abolishing foreign financing (of Islamic Communities)." Strache: "It is about opposing radical political Islam. Hate preaching and the abuse of religious instruction for the purposes of indoctrination must be stopped." Blümel: "Illegal mosque enterprises must be banned and, if necessary, closed. The Department of Cultural Affairs must check the conformance to the law of these institutions." Kickl: "ATIB (Turkish-Islamic Union for Cultural and Social Cooperation in Austria) is breaking the law. Imams are being financed from outside the country. Various activities in the associations can be classified by the government as politically radical."

The government has announced the following steps as immediately in prospect or already in process:

1.   Closing of a mosque in the 10th district in Vienna, where the "Wolf Salute" is used, representing the ideology of the Grey Wolves. The mosque is illegal. Even the IGGiÖ (Islamic Faith Community in Austria) reported this mosque to the competent authorities.

2.   Dissolution of the "Arabic Cultural Community," which had a "Salafist background" and would therefore represent political Islam. A decision from the Department of Cultural Affairs for dissolution is imminent.

3.   Repeal of current legal status of (ATIB-) imams, and/or refusal of restructuring and/or extension, because they are financed from abroad, which would be contrary to the ban on foreign finance. There are eleven present cases, altogether ca. forty.

4.   The Department of Cultural Affairs is charged with supervision of mosque establishments with regard to possible further instances of foreign financing (considering any possible evasive arrangements), as well with inspecting activities which could violate the principles of the "basic alignment of state and society in Austria." Among these are cer-

tain activities in youth work ("war reenactments in kindergarten").

5. The investigations may result in further closings of mosques and other facilities.

At first glance, the measures appear convincing and sensible. Hardly anyone in Austria would not want them to be successful. The question is whether and to what extent their execution is realistic. This depends primarily on the foundation for legal action the authorities authorize. In this connection, the ministers named or referenced the following laws to the following responsible authorities:

· The Islam Law, 2015. Primary responsibility lies with the Department of Cultural Affairs, which is a subordinate division of the Office of the Federal Chancellor.

· The Settlement and Residence Law, administered by the Ministry of the Interior.

· The Associations Law, administered by the provincial organizations authorities under the Ministry of the Interior.

Before the tenability of the grounds or enforcement and the likelihood of implementation of the announced measures are investigated, the following should be noted:

In recent years, the authorities have made several attempts to stem the steady proliferation of the Islam sector, the radicalization of many of its protagonists and the interlacing with the political aims of domestic and foreign organizations and players. Among them were very similar attempts to those now being announced. It is true that they were not as effectively publicized nor as supported by a massive political will as is now the case. In fact, however, none of these attempts has had any effect. Rather, diversion and shifting of activities to various, increasingly numerous institutional substrata and the real pressure—both political and external—on the authorities to cooperate in diverse compensatory measurements have always led to the Islam sector being strengthened and stabilized and even increased by such attempts at "enforcement through the Rule of Law."

This—at least in the view of those who wanted to defend the secular state—was one of the reasons for the initiative to renew the Islam legislation, which ultimately led to the Islam Law of 2015. This is regarded by the government as the most important resource in implementing the desired goals. That is precisely the weak point of the project. However much the government is to be praised for its enormous initiative, its estimation of the level of instrumentality must be seen as extremely unrealistic.

Necessary support for this determination in the following analysis must largely be confined to assertions, since presentation of the complex, logistical, institutional, Islam-specific and political structure that would have to be understood cannot be accomplished in this limited space. Please be assured that the relevant analysis does exist. Here, then, is an extraction of it:

The longstanding originators of renewing the Islam Law had, almost a decade ago, proposed three principles which were to re-order the Islam sector in accordance with the interests of the Republic, and secure the maintenance of religious peace in the land:

1.   The obligation to reveal the principles of faith (including German translation of the Qur'an and *Ahadith*), in order to have a standard for judging compatibility with the laws and customs of the country.

2.   Dissipation of the uncontrolled proliferation of religious facilities whose quantity and content evade any government control and any responsibility by virtue of being a legally recognized religious community.

3.   The ban on financing of Austrian Islamic institutions by foreign nations or organizations ("foreign financing"), to close off radicalizing influence from outside Austria.

The Islam Law of 2015 appears to have conformed to these proposals. At any rate, this is the case only on a nominal, terminological level, while the specific logistical construction has a precisely opposite effect:

Ad 1.   Transparency in the Islam Law was so standardized that it represents no obligation to the state, but is an "inner affair," because it is issued as part of its "constitution." (§ 6) The Department of Cultural Affairs, accordingly, has accepted a seven-page, completely vacuous pamphlet as "doctrine" of the IGGiÖ, in which slavery is whitewashed, and it is utterly tentative to external parties.

Ad 2.   On the basis of apparently meaningless subordinate clauses (in §8), alongside the religious community and the "cultural communities," the associations too are admitted as support institutions for mosques. Thus even the proliferation of mosques is still protected by being outside legal authority by means of the connectivity of the "cultural communities."

Ad 3.   The ban on "foreign financing" in the Islam Law is, first, only indirect ("financial independence," § 6 Abs. 2) and, second, not applicable to associations. The consequences of the Islam Law are so absurd that the authorities (the Department of Cultural Affairs and the authorities governing associations) officially allowed (had to allow?) the establishment of Bosnian mosques in Austria under the (Saudi Arabian-dominated) religious authority RIJASET in 2016.

Among the deficiencies already noted is a fact that is clearly unknown to the appropriate, responsible (political and administrative) bodies. That is, the Islam Law of 2015 canceled the determination in the Islam Law of 1912 that "Islam" itself is "a legally recognized religion." This now standardizes the conditions for acceptance of Islamic religious communities. However, since these religious communities (by the 1988 decision of the Constitutional Court) no longer have a claim to sole representation, other groups can assume religious freedom in whatever legal form they choose and, when necessary, claim that they represent a doctrine which deviates from the IGGiÖ. And when no law excludes this organizational format, this is a possible form.

Using the legal framework described, the actual make-up of the Islam sector in Austria has taken the following form:

The Islam sector's "umbrella" is the legally recognized religious society IGGiÖ. It is the "political player" in Austria, takes care of public relations, does the "inter-religious dialogue" for appeasement, organizes religious instruction and makes demands of the state. "Under" it are "cultural communities," which by law are simultaneously members of IGGiÖ and "persons of the public sector." Many of these, founded by third-level institutions—the mosque associations—are, on the one hand, under the cover of the IGGiÖ and to be left in peace, and on the other hand, able to develop their own ritual life without interference. This system could also be called "Islam's holding company."

The IGGiÖ is deeply political. Its "high aristocracy" is divided between two spheres of influence—the Arabic and the Turkish. The latter divides again into the realm of ATIB (subordinate to the Turkish religious authority *Dijanet*) and the "Islamic Federation" (*Milli Görüs*). The many small ethnically and nationally associated mosques are arranged under the umbrella of the IGGiÖ in one way or another. The "Arabic cultural community" under criticism and facing dissolution is, with altogether ten mosques, not exactly a part of the Arabic sector of the "IGGiÖ high aristocracy." On the contrary, it is not at all a constituent part of the Muslim Brotherhood Network in Austria. This "Arabic cultural community" is not under the dominion off the IGGiÖ and is therefore open to elimination. The same is true for the dissolution-vulnerable "Nasim Abu Mosque" in the 10th district, which is a spinoff of the "Grey Wolves" and therefore not sanctioned by the leadership of the IGGiÖ.

On the basis of the legal and institutional relationships sketched out here, there are a number of possibilities for thwarting or evading the measures or regulations announced by the government. Not only the affected cultural communities and associations, but the IGGiÖ too, has made some unambiguous announcements in this regard. A reliable prognosis of developments in the next months (and years) can be undertaken without extreme risk of error.

Any such should be preceded by three comments:

1.   In the rationale for the intended measures (especially for dissolution), reference is made to § 4 section 3 of the Islam Law, in which there is mention of a requisite "positive basic attitude toward the society and state." First, however, this is only a criterion for acceptance (and not for dissolution) and, second, it has no relevance at all for the question of the associations. Furthermore, the concept "basic attitude" is not a juridical one, but at best an interpretive criterion. It is important at this point to warn against endowing this concept with a juridical category. As the concept "hate" already has, this could become an arbitrarily deployed weapon against (political) critics of all kinds.

2.   The concept "Salafist positions or views" is also ill-suited as a criterion in the search for "grounds of dissolution." This is the revenge of the years-long, all-too-casual treatment of important concepts in public discussion of Islam. And meanwhile, "Salafist" has become everyday terminology for "terrorist." Although Islamic terrorism is not infrequently inspired by Salafist activists, the connotation is nonsensical. Salafism is, after all, just the extra-territorial variant of (Saudi) Wahhabism; and that is a political branch of Hanbalism. The Hanbalist school of (religious) jurisprudence is nothing less than one of the four Sunni schools of jurisprudence presented by the Islamic religious community as recognized schools of thought, which also had to be recognized by the Department of Cultural Affairs. So-called "Salafism" also does not fit the formal "dissolution criterion."

3.   Finally, certain relevant modes of behavior and events are presented as facts which would be legal grounds for dissolution. Re-creation of warlike slaughter by small children in kindergarten may certainly offend the cultural sensitivity of the average Austrian, but it is not grounds for dissolution. What law is it supposed to be breaking? It may perhaps reflect what some understand as "political Islam," but it can no more be dealt with legally than all the previously-mentioned concepts. That is, there is no "political Islam," because, among other things, there is no "non-political Islam." Could it seriously be maintained that the Islamic interdicts least compatible with Western social order—such as

blood feud, polygamy, and wife-beating (Sura 4, 34)—are expressions of a "political" concept? Instead of pursuing the phantom of "political Islam," the legal regime in which the state communicates with the Islamic sector should make clearer to Muslims what elements of the Islamic belief cannot and must not be realized/enacted in Austria. Not now and not ever.

After all the intellectual preparations, now is the time to venture a qualitative prognosis for execution of the measures announced by the government.

1.   The chances of dissolving the "Arabic cultural community" are good. It can only exist as a cultural community if it is accepted by the faith community as a component of itself. Since it is regarded by the IGGiÖ as an insubordinate foreign body, its removal is as good as certain. However, this does not apply to the mosque associations that belong to it, which will presumably organize anew and quite differently. Furthermore, the authorities must beware of becoming no more than accessories of the IGGiÖ.

2.   The mosque associations cannot at this time legally be dissolved, except those that appeal the decision as a kind of mobile warfare, and found a new association. It is important here that the law on association, which is its sole basis for implementation, contains no provision against associations that practice religion, and no ban on financing from out of the country.

3.   The negative disposition of original application procedures or extension procedures in regard to residence permission for imams will function—although modestly. But mosque complexes have manifold possibilities of channeling foreign donations. A Turkish imam paid by an Austrian legal entity can hardly be reproached for receiving no income in the sense of the Settlement and Residence Law, even if financed indirectly from foreign sources (of which he can be ignorant). The *Dijanet* (Turkish religious ministry) has 117,000 employees, of which some can be sent to Austria in rotation, and indeed in such quick succession that the authorities in Austria do not come close to creating a basis for enforcement.

The thinking expressed in this analysis is in no way in service of criticism of the government's intentions per se, or meant to relativize. On the contrary, appreciation for an initiative like that of the current coalition government cannot be expressed fully enough. Critical remarks help to create a realistic view of the amount of success that such a project might achieve under present conditions. And they are useful above all for insight into the unconditional necessity of re-ordering the legal basis of the Republic's dealings with Islam, its collective implementation and its institutions. Only such a re-ordering can improve the prospects of success.

The Islam Law of 2015, contrary to its public image, is a more than insufficient basis for implementation. But its present condition is by no means immutable. The rudiments of an effective reconstruction have been discussed in detail and are ready to hand. In its coalition agreement, the government has already decided to revise the Islam Law. It should begin.

Revise the Islam Law—now, and not sometime!

Analysis of Press Coverage in the U.S., Europe and Islamic Media

By Henrik R. Clausen and Christine Brim

Writers who reported on Elisabeth's case faced a quandary: how to write about the prosecution of a teacher for raising a question about Mohammed's consummation of marriage with nine year old Aisha, without incurring legal penalties or terrorist threats to themselves. Those penalties could be significant in both Europe and the U.S.

Starting with the death *fatwa* against Salman Rushdie in 1989, writers and public officials who criticized Islamic doctrine or practices were variously given death sentences, stabbed to death, shot to death, shot at resulting in the death or wounding of bystanders, attacked with an axe, and with bombs, and with grenades, firebombed, banned from entering the UK, sued and prosecuted for hate speech and discrimination against religious feelings (repeatedly and in numerous countries), fined, imprisoned or given suspended prison sentences, subjected to innumerable terrorist threats and plots, blacklisted and denied access to banking and payment services, and forced to go underground or to live in safe houses with security details. They lost their jobs, their writings were deplatformed, their books were removed from bookstores and their speaking engagements were shouted down by rioters.

This was the state of "free expression" in the 21st century for U.S., Canadian, Australian and European writers and elected officials such as Ayaan Hirsi Ali, Georges Bensoussan, Pierre Cassen, Stéphane "Charb" Charbonnier, Steve Emerson, Oriana Fallaci, Pim Fortuyn, Pamela Geller, Jussi Halla-aho, the Charlie Hebdo staff, Lars Hedegaard, David Horowitz, Michel Houellebecq, Carsten Juste, Jesper Langballe, Marine

Le Pen, Ezra Levant, Molly Norris, Flemming Rose, Salman Rushdie, Mark Steyn, Elisabeth Sabaditsch-Wolff, Daniel Scot, Robert Spencer, Michael Stürzenberger, Christine Tasin, Theo Van Gogh, Lars Vilks, Wafa Sultan, Kurt Westergaard, Geert Wilders, Susanne Winter and so many others worldwide. A chronology of this expanding authoritarianism is appended to the end of the chapter.

A growing body of authoritarian law in Europe, discussed elsewhere in this volume, made criticism of Islam subject to prosecution for hate speech, incitement or denigration of a religion—all charges leveled at Elisabeth when she was first prosecuted in 2010. In the U.S., the Constitution's First Amendment offered better protection for free expression, but private corporations, universities and associations worked assiduously to constrain criticism and factual reporting on Islamic doctrine and practices. In America if you quoted or criticized Islamic doctrine, you wouldn't be prosecuted by the state, but you could go broke, get fired, be silenced online and in print, or be on the receiving end of a death sentence *fatwa* or a terrorist attack, with little or no protection from law enforcement.

This was the environment in which Elisabeth and her legal team worked for a decade to educate the European and American public about her case, from 2009 to 2019.

Efforts to censor U.S. journalists writing about Islamic issues had started less than a month after the September 11, 2001, terrorist attacks. On October 6, 2001, the Society for Professional Journalists published their first set of politically correct rules for reporting on Islam in their "Guidelines for Countering Racial, Ethnic and Religious Profiling."[1] Reporters were told to "Use language that is informative and not inflammatory," without any guidance as to what would be "inflammatory," who would be inflamed, or why this caution was needed in covering Islamic news more than other topics. The Society of Professional Journalists "Guidelines" inspired other U.S. guidebooks such as the 2014 Carnegie Corporation-funded "Islam for Journalists,"[2] which provided far more detailed instructions for reporters on how to write (and not write) about Islam. By 2017, the Society for Professional Journalists was offering grants to local chapters to partner with the Council on Amer-

---

1 https://www.spj.org/divguidelines.asp.

2 https://www.foxnews.com/us/journalists-guide-to-islam-called-cave-in-to-political-correctness and https://www.researchgate.net/publication/286449318_Islam_for_Journalists_A_Primer_on_Covering_Muslim_Communities_in_America.

ican Islamic Relations (CAIR)[3] for day-long "Muslimedia" conferences to train reporters on what was permitted in reporting on Islam.[4]

These initiatives in 2001 by the leading U.S. professional association of journalists to prevent reporters from using "inflammatory" language anticipated the terms used against Elisabeth in an Austrian court in 2011, ten years later: her language was "capable of arousing justified indignation" and included "critical statements regarded by believers as extremely insulting and provocative." All these terms, emotional and vague—"inflammatory," "insulting and provocative" and so on—prompt the question as to why a society should expect its journalists to self-censor, rather than expecting the "believers" to tolerate criticism.

By the time the ECtHR issued its final decision in October 2018, even sympathetic media reports on Elisabeth's case tended to focus on the legal issues of censorship and free expression, while stipulating that her statements were, indeed, inflammatory or provocative. Many writers, however committed they were to free expression, took care to deplore her statements on Mohammed. Reporters often included a disclaimer of sorts in their articles: they would write about her case, but they didn't want under any circumstances to be aligned with her opinions.

Despite the chilling effect of this intimidation, both conservative and mainstream outlets published numerous detailed and often widely-circulated articles on Elisabeth's case, focusing on the legal issues and applicability of the ECtHR decision. Their primary audiences were the activists, political analysts, legal experts and legislators who were concerned about the precedent being set for free speech in Europe and in the U.S.

U.S. Media

After years of waiting for the ECtHR decision, U.S. media coverage greatly increased once the verdict was released on October 25, 2018, upholding the earlier decision of the Austrian Supreme Court against Elisabeth's right to free speech.[5] Elisabeth's team had less than three months

---

3 "CAIR was designated as a terrorist entity by the United Arab Emirates in 2014. The FBI and Justice Department suspended contact with CAIR in 2008 because of the group's links to terrorism, and the Anti-Defamation League has labeled CAIR an anti-Semitic group with ties to terrorism." For more detail, see the Investigative Project on Terrorism's 2019 report on CAIR: https://www.investigativeproject.org/7981/ipt-releases-cair-in-a-nutshell-report.

4 https://spectator.org/muslimedia-wants-you-to-think-its-moderate/.

5 https://hudoc.ECtHR.coe.int/eng#{"itemid":["001-187188"]}.

to draft their final appeal for the ECtHR to reconsider and to educate the public and policymakers in Europe and the U.S. on the consequences of this final loss of her defense of free speech. Aware of the deadline and the importance of the case, a number of mainstream and conservative magazines and news sites reacted swiftly to the ECtHR verdict.

Some publications may also have seized on the case as an opportunity to push back against the efforts to censor criticism of Islamic doctrine and blasphemy laws, efforts that had expanded since the case began in 2009.

Perhaps the most hostile report on the case, in that it was utterly deferential to the Court's opinion, was by *The Wall Street Journal's* German correspondent Bojan Pancevski in an article entitled, "Europe Court Upholds Ruling Against Woman Who Insulted Islam: Human rights court says disparagement of religious doctrines such as insulting the Prophet Muhammad isn't protected by freedom of expression."[6]

The Hollywood Reporter in their article, "European Court Won't Tolerate Blasphemy as Free Speech," actually provided more practical insight. *THR* worried, "The next time that any Hollywood studio wishes to distribute a film or television show in Europe that makes a sacrilegious statement, such expression may not necessarily be legally protected."[7] *THR* also noted the possibility that individual countries had some autonomy in deciding what was blasphemy, stating, "While nodding to the importance of context—the situation in a particular country—and affording some discretion for local authorities to evaluate whether statements are likely to disturb the religious peace, the European Court sees impermissible blasphemy here."

Commentary Magazine published Iranian-American journalist Sohrab Ahmari's analysis in "The Day Free Speech Died in Europe."[8] Ahmari saw the case in the broader context of European elites' overreach: "But notice the unstated premise here: The ECHR is suggesting that discussing the history of Islam and the psychology of its founder for their own sake is not in the 'public interest.' The court is arrogating to itself and the individual European states the power to decide which topics Europeans are permitted to debate and on what terms."

---

6 https://www.wsj.com/articles/europe-court-upholds-ruling-against-women-who-insulted-islam-1540580231.

7 https://www.hollywoodreporter.com/thr-esq/european-court-indicates-blasphemy-wont-be-tolerated-as-free-speech-1155530.

8 https://www.commentarymagazine.com/foreign-policy/europe/the-day-free-speech-died-in-europe/.

The Washington Examiner, a weekly online and print magazine in Washington, D.C., published an op-ed that pointed out the internal il-logic of the ECtHR decision, a criticism shared by several other U.S. and European authors. The piece, memorably entitled, "European Court of Human Rights: Sorry Charlie Hebdo But You Had It Coming,"[9] stated "I'm having a difficult time squaring the ECHR's acknowledgment that it's fair to criticize organized religion with its argument that 'presenting objects of religious worship in a provocative way capable of hurting the feelings of the followers of that religion could be conceived as a mali-cious violation of the spirit of tolerance.' 'It's OK, but only when it's not OK' is not exactly solid, ironclad legal reasoning—in fact, it's meaning-less drivel, bound to be misinterpreted, misused, and abused in future cases."

The biweekly print and online magazine *National Review* featured an article by legal expert and Fox News commentator Andrew McCar-thy entitled, "In Europe, Free Speech Bows to Sharia,"[10] noting: "It is thus *verboten* to say things that might upset Muslims. Particularly offensive is mention of Islam's many doctrinal tenets that make us cringe in the 21st century—approbation of child marriage, violent *jihad*, the treatment of women as chattel, the duty to kill apostates, and so on. That these tenets are accurately stated, supported by undeniable scriptural grounding, is beside the point. Or as the ECHR put it, reliance on scripture could be classified as 'an abusive attack on the Prophet of Islam, which could stir up prejudice and put at risk religious peace.'"

In a historically-informed and wide-ranging article scorchingly critical of the Court's decision, Graeme Wood's piece in the venerable American monthly magazine *The Atlantic* entitled, "In Europe, Speech Is an Alienable Right," noted: "Having sex with a child isn't pedophilia, in other words, if the child's prepubescence is not your biggest turn-on, or if you also have sex with adults, or if you continue having sex after the child reaches maturity. (Am I alone in finding the Austrian court's reasoning offensive? Muhammad lived in late antiquity, when January-December marriages were common. The Austrian judges have no such excuse. A decade ago, Austria was laboring to shed its reputa-tion as the 'land of sex dungeons.' I don't think 'land of narrowly defined pedophilia' is much of an improvement.) On this basis, the court said

---

9 https://www.washingtonexaminer.com/opinion/european-court-of-human-rights-sorry-charlie-hebdo-but-you-had-it-coming.

10 https://www.nationalreview.com/2018/10/free-speech-sharia-european-court-of-human-rights-ruling/.

E.S.'s statements were 'untrue facts,' and fair game for prosecution."[11] *The Atlantic* published a second critical article a week later by Simon Cottee, Senior lecturer in criminology at the University of Kent, entitled "A Flawed European Ruling on Free Speech."[12] Both articles were identified as part of "The Speech Wars," a project supported by the Charles Koch Foundation, the Reporters Committee for the Freedom of the Press, and the Fetzer Institute.

Erik Voeten, a professor at Georgetown University's School of Foreign Service, published a contrarian and carefully reasoned analysis of the case in *The Washington Post* on October 29, arguing that the Court's decision was not as influential as other reports were claiming, and in fact showed the Court's deference to national laws. In his article "American pundits think Europe has just introduced a blasphemy law through the back door. They're wrong," he stated, "Many European countries, including Austria, have blasphemy laws on their domestic books. The question then is: If states have such laws, should they be overruled by an international court? The human rights court has become extremely reluctant to interfere with state laws on sensitive domestic issues.... To be clear, the point is not that the judgment was necessarily legally or morally correct. Instead it is that, contrary to a large body of U.S. commentary, the main lesson from this judgment is not that the court is handing a victory to Islamism and undermining free speech. Instead, the ruling provides further evidence that the court thinks that it can no longer manage these highly sensitive issues at the European level."[13]

The Economist, like several other mainstream publications covering the story, noted the contrast with the Irish striking down their blasphemy laws in the very week that the Court decision upheld Austria's very illiberal blasphemy laws. In "Blasphemy bans are struck out in Ireland and reinforced in Austria," *The Economist* wrote, "The Austrian verdict, upheld by the ECHR, went far beyond the principle that in some circumstances, blasphemous acts (like burning a holy book on the street) might be a public-order offence. Nor did it focus on the question of whether people were, in practice, offended. It implied that in any con-

---

11 https://www.theatlantic.com/ideas/archive/2018/10/its-not-free-speech-criticize-muhammad-echr-ruled/574174/.

12 https://www.theatlantic.com/ideas/archive/2018/10/europe-rules-against-free-speech/574369/.

13 https://web.archive.org/web/20181216054232/https://www.washingtonpost.com/news/monkey-cage/wp/2018/10/29/american-pundits-think-europe-has-just-introduced-a-blasphemy-law-through-the-back-door-theyre-wrong/.

text whatever, merely expressing an "incorrect" or unbalanced view of a religious matter (from the viewpoint of the religion concerned) could be a punishable offence. For free-speech advocates this was a big step backwards."[14]

The Gatestone Institute is a New York City-based non-profit think tank that reports daily on security and human rights issues. Its influence is notable; the former Chairman of the Gatestone Institute, John Bolton, became President Trump's National Security Advisor. Gatestone published dozens of articles on Elisabeth's case, including several articles in the three month period before the January, 2019 deadline for her final appeal.[15] Authors of those articles were European policy experts such as Soeren Kern—"European Human Rights Court Backs Sharia Blasphemy Law,"[16] Douglas Murray—"The EU's Dangerous New Confidence Game,"[17] Judith Bergman—"The European Court of Human Rights Submits to Islam,"[18] Denis MacEoin—"European Court of Human Rights Blasphemy Laws: Where a Word out of Place Can Cost Your Life,"[19] and Saied Shoaaib—"The European Court of Human Rights Does Not Deserve Its Name."[20] Gatestone writers were among those resolutely unintimidated by efforts to silence the public policy debates about Islamic doctrine.

One of the most insightful examinations of the case came from the *Spectator's* Dominic Green, writing in the now-defunct *Weekly Standard* on November 5. In "Europe's Dangerous Blasphemy Laws Are Ripe for Exploitation," Green noted that the old blasphemy laws intended to protect Christian doctrine were now being invoked to protect Muslim beliefs from criticism: "In practice, in the demography of native births and immigration, and in activist confidence in the public square and courts, Islam is now the growing edge of European religion. So it should not surprise that Muslim activists are invoking semi-dormant European laws like Article 10 of the Austrian code, which intends to prevent dis-

---

14 https://www.economist.com/erasmus/2018/10/29/blasphemy-bans-are-struck-out-in-ireland-and-reinforced-in-austria.

15 https://www.gatestoneinstitute.org/search.php?cx=014255815713646959106%3Af-cvl99skesi&cof=FORID%3A9&ie=UTF-8&q=Elisabeth+Sabaditsch+Wolff&sa=Search.

16 https://www.gatestoneinstitute.org/13204/european-court-human-rights-sharia.

17 https://www.gatestoneinstitute.org/13262/eu-confidence-game.

18 https://www.gatestoneinstitute.org/13301/european-court-human-rights-islam.

19 https://www.gatestoneinstitute.org/13377/european-court-human-rights-blasphemy-laws.

20 https://www.gatestoneinstitute.org/13533/european-court-human-rights.

order by 'safeguarding religious peace and protecting religious feelings.'" Discussing the consequences of the Court decision, he concluded "After the ECHR ruling, the status of free speech in Europe on matters of religion is conditional upon which religion you are discussing and which state you are discussing it in…Europeans should annul their antique blasphemy laws to preempt abuse by a sectarian minority. The alternative, as evinced by Europe's past and recent history with blasphemy laws, is the curtailment of expression, inquiry, and even physical liberty."[21]

The online news site *jihadwatch.org* ran a two-part series on the case by Hugh Fitzgerald, "Does Europe Still Have Free Speech?"[22] Fitzgerald commented, "The European Court of Human Rights has performed a grave disservice in allowing the 'indignation' of Muslims to limit the freedom of speech of islamocritics in the advanced West. We have a perfect right to know the contents of the Qur'an, and about Muhammad's life as recorded in the *hadith*, and to make our own judgements, and freely speak our own minds about the texts and teachings of Islam and the morality of Muhammad's acts. In Europe, he is not yet the Perfect Man and Model of Conduct. The sanitized version of Islam that the European Court of Human Rights now seems determined to promote, lest something be said that causes Muslims to become violent, will only contribute to the outrage, and sense of despair, among Europeans…"

Journalist Marc Steyn is a best-selling author of several books[23] on the increasing peril of Islamic doctrine to free speech and the rule of law. In a lengthy November 5, 2018 article, "Rationalizing Our Surrender,"[24] he noted that he had covered the case back in 2011[25] and had met Elisabeth in person, adding "It should hardly be necessary to state that freedom of speech except for 'statements which hurt others' and do 'not contribute to a debate' or 'approach the topic in an objective manner' is not freedom of speech at all, but merely-narrowly construed state-regulated speech. And in Europe the courts are perfectly cool with that."

Human rights activist and best-selling author Phyllis Chesler's piece

---

21   https://www.washingtonexaminer.com/weekly-standard/european-court-blasphemy-free-speech-isnt-what-it-used-to-be.

22   https://www.jihadwatch.org/2018/10/hugh-fitzgerald-does-europe-still-have-free-speech-part-one and Part 2 https://www.jihadwatch.org/2018/10/hugh-fitzgerald-does-europe-still-have-free-speech-part-two

23   Lights Out, America Alone and After America: https://www.steynstore.com/page1.html.

24   https://www.steynonline.com/8969/rationalizing-our-surrender.

25   https://www.steynonline.com/4409/gagging-us-softly.

in the online *Tablet Magazine*, "The New Censorship: Is this the return of the Thought Police?"[26] presented Elisabeth as one of several free speech defenders in Europe, noting that, "What all these European dissidents have in common is that they've dared to express their (positive) views about Israel, and their (less than positive) views about Islam, Islamism, Muslim immigration, Islamic gender and religious apartheid and *jihad*. Although Islam is not a race, such ideas are considered racist even if they are true, perhaps especially if they are true."

In the short time before the final appeal to the ECtHR had to be filed in January, 2019, Elisabeth made a final push to raise awareness in the U.S. about the verdict's imminent threat to free speech. The venues for her presentations ranged from major radio programs to local talk shows, small gatherings to conferences of hundreds of attendees. Her speeches included presentations to the Independence Institute in Denver, the Fredericksburg Tea Party in Texas,[27] the American Freedom Alliance in Los Angeles[28] and others in New York City and Washington, DC. Her radio interviews included Colorado radio host Michelle Morin,[29] Secure Freedom Radio,[30] the Eric Metaxas radio show on the Salem Media network,[31] Debbie Georgatos's radio show in Dallas,[32] 710KNUS Radio,[33] the Christian Reporter News with Kat Rowoldt,[34] CounterPoint with Gary Jenkins on the Gospel America Network,[35] and the Fox News program with Judge Jeannine Pirro.[36]

European Media

Americans and others familiar with the US Constitution's First

---

26 https://www.tabletmag.com/jewish-arts-and-culture/culture-news/276879/the-new-censorship.

27 https://www.youtube.com/watch?v=cFKCGrNULao.

28 https://www.youtube.com/watch?time_continue=3&v=pkTGqCQ_yHc.

29 https://www.michellemorin.org/have-europes-blasphemy-laws-become-the-modern-day-concentration-camp/.

30 https://www.centerforsecuritypolicy.org/2018/12/03/a-warning-from-europe/.

31 https://www.metaxastalk.com/podcast/wednesday-december-12-2018/.

32 https://americacanwetalk.org/hr-2-cruise-interview-with-austrian-elisabeth-saba-ditsch-wolff/.

33 https://www.podbean.com/media/share/pb-w4khn-a045c2?utm_campaign=w_share_ep&utm_medium=dlink&utm_source=w_share.

34 https://www.youtube.com/watch?v=mxDHBy0KciA.

35 bit.ly/2GITRXA.

36 https://nation.foxnews.com/10-minute-justice-jeanine/.

Amendment will notice an authoritarian trend in some European main-stream media's coverage of Elisabeth's case, as they adopted, uncritically, the limited concept of freedom espoused by the ECtHR. German and Austrian media were especially eager to accept the Court's constrained view of freedom of expression. Reporters readily and obediently went along with the Court's assumption that freedom of speech applies only to specific areas, opinions or forms of expression, rather than being an inalienable right with only well-defined restrictions (such as fraud, in-citement to violence and the like).

Legal decisions over the past two decades have changed the mean-ing of "Freedom of expression" substantially, from a natural right to a right granted—or in Elisabeth's case revoked—by State authorities, on grounds that freedom "could stir up prejudice" or "excess of opinion."

In the early years of the case, only the Austrian daily *Der Standard* reported on it in Austria. On December 29th 2011, *Der Standard* wrote a detailed article about the second verdict, quoting the verdict penned by Judge Leo Levnaic-Iwanski:[37]

> *Bei dieser Aussage leuchte doch "deutlich ein Wertungsexzess" [...] Würde man "isoliert" erklären, dass Mohammed "Sex mit einem Kind hatte" würde das wohl nicht unter Strafe gestellt. Aber die von Saba-ditsch-Wolff vorgenommene "Verbrämung der Aussage", komme einer Verspottung gleich und sei daher zu verurteilen.*

> (This statement can be considered a "very obvious excessive opin-ion" [...] If one explained in an "isolated way" that Mohammed "had sex with a child," this would not be punishable. However, Sabad-itsch-Wolff's "dressing up of her assertion" amounts to denigration and is thus punishable.)

The article also reported from the ensuing press conference, where Elisabeth stated, "This is a black day for Austria." Elisabeth's lawyer Dr. Rami was quoted stating that this constituted a severe violation of the fundamental right to freedom of expression, a case that he would pursue further to the European Court of Human Rights.

Der Standard reported briefly on the verdict at the third Austrian court instance, quoting Dr. Rami:

---

37 https://www.derstandard.at/story/1324170300225/fpoe-islam-semi-nar-urteil-zur-geldstrafe-bestaetigt-sabaditsch-wolff-will-kaempfen.

"Wir sind bereits beim Europäischen Gerichtshof für Menschenrechte wegen des OLG-Urteils und werden auch diese Entscheidung anfechten." Bis dato liege keine Entscheidung des EGMR vor und es sei nicht abzuschätzen, bis wann dies der Fall sein wird, so Rami. "Es geht nicht darum, ob man die Äußerungen gut oder schlecht findet, sondern darum, ob es rechtlich zulässig ist, derartige Dinge zu sagen."[38]

("We are already at the European Court of Human Rights for the OLG judgment and will challenge this decision." So far, there is no decision from the ECtHR and it can not be estimated until when this will be the case, Rami said. "It's not about finding the remarks good or bad, but about whether it's legal to say things like that.")

A special case in Austria was the magazine *News.at*, who initiated the case by reporting Elisabeth's seminars as "hate speech." During 2010 the magazine published a handful of articles to support that view. It reported from the court hearing on January 18th, 2011, noting that:

Die Richterin sah im Falle eines Schuldspruches wegen Verhetzung zusätzlich den Tatbestand auf 'Herabwürdigung religiöser Lehren' erfüllt. Verteidiger Michael Rami beantragte daraufhin eine Vertagung der Verhandlung. Sie wird am 15. Februar fortgesetzt.[39]

(The judge saw in the case of a guilty verdict for incitement in addition the facts on 'degradation of religious teachings' met. Defender Michael Rami then requested a postponement of the trial. It will continue on the 15th of February.)

After that—silence. One would expect the magazine to follow up on a case that it initiated. The magazine did not make it clear that the charge of "hate speech" was readily dismissed by the Judge after listening to a few minutes of the recordings from the seminar. The magazine reported nothing further on the case, as it went through Austrian courts and the ECtHR.

While the case was largely ignored by the media while underway in Austria, the final verdict from the European Court of Human Rights was widely reported. The primary source was an October 26, 2018 *Deutsche Welle* article titled "Calling Prophet Muhammad a pedophile does not

---

38 https://www.derstandard.at/story/1388650338417/sabaditsch-wolff-blitzte-auch-bei-ogh-ab-gericht.

39 https://www.news.at/a/prozess-islam-seminar-justiz-fp-vortragender-verhetzung-286619.

fall within freedom of speech"[40] which reported "The Strasbourg-based ECHR ruled that Austrian courts carefully balanced the applicant's right to freedom of expression with the right of others to have their religious feelings protected, and served the legitimate aim of preserving religious peace in Austria…It also found that even in a debate it was not compatible with freedom of expression 'to pack incriminating statements into the wrapping of an otherwise acceptable expression of opinion and claim that this rendered passable those statements exceeding the permissible limits of freedom of expression.'"

The ECtHR decision also attracted the attention of numerous legal experts across Europe, many of whom were far more critical than the German and Austrian media. In *The Telegraph*, Tim Stanley wrote an opinion piece titled "European courts risk corroding free speech to create special status for Islam,"[41] where he compared the failure to defend our fundamental freedoms with the resentment against political elites that led to Brexit, noting "And this latest judgement is a classic example of unelected judges going well beyond their job description to shape social policy. Yes, the ECHR isn't the EU, but this is the sort of thing that motivated Euroscepticism in the UK and paved the way to Brexit. But were the Austrian court and the ECHR right to criticize her, as they did, for confusing pedophilia and child marriage? The judges implied a distinction between the two that most of us utterly reject. Europe's courts risk creating a new status for Islam that could appear to rope it off from criticism, a status that is bound to fuel jealousy and resentment, and won't be good for anyone in the long-run."

France's newspaper *Le Figaro* ran an interview with Gregor Puppinck with the title (translated) "Blasphemy offense: 'The ECHR is not Charlie!'"[42] Puppinck, Director of the European Center for Law and Justice (ECLJ), commented that "This decision is also very serious because it puts the objectives of 'mutual tolerance' and 'peaceful coexistence' on freedom of thought and expression in religious matters. It allows the muzzling of the criticism of Islam in the name of living together. It goes against Western modernity, which requires, on the contrary, to subject Islam to historical criticism, without fear of upsetting the beliefs of its

---

40 https://www.dw.com/en/calling-prophet-muhammad-a-pedophile-does-not-fall-within-freedom-of-speech-european-court/a-46050749.

41 https://www.telegraph.co.uk/news/2018/10/27/european-courts-risk-corroding-free-speech-create-special-status/.

42 http://www.lefigaro.fr/vox/religion/2018/10/26/31004-20181026ARTFIG00232-delit-de-blaspheme-la-cedh-n-est-pas-charlie.php.

followers and even provoking tensions."

The French think tank Institut Montaigne assessed the case's possible impact on France, in "Blasphemy in France and in Europe: A Right or an Offense,"[43] observing that "[t]he word 'blasphemy' mostly disappeared from European legislation, yet it has been translated into secular terms, which has often made it possible to perpetuate its condemnation by other means. In fact, a comparative approach to these different legislations demonstrates the extreme polysemy of the criminal lexicon around this issue."

Several other legal NGOs found the case of particular interest, and all found the ECtHR's legal reasoning, as one tactfully put it, "flawed"— or as others stated, sophistic, disturbing, ill-defined, troubling and absurd.

The Brussels-based political magazine *New Federalist* of the 30,000 member Young European Federalists NGO was appalled by the decision, stating "If this decision were to be confirmed, it would highlight a significant regression in the breadth of freedom of expression. This ruling could prove to be problematic, notably regarding scholars' freedom of research in religious sciences in countries where the crime of blasphemy still subsists. Citizens of these countries should drastically mobilise themselves, not only for the repeal of these provisions such as in Ireland but also to state that 'blasphemy is a part of human rights, not good habits,' as articulated very well by André Comte-Sponville in his *Dictionnaire philosophique*. What will the European Court of Human Rights think of the conviction of Christ to crucifixion for blasphemy against Judaism as well? Will it still look for a proportionality between the sanction and the need to ensure 'social and religious peace'?"[44]

A website for the *European Journal of International Law* ran a detailed, carefully reasoned analysis highly critical of the Court's decision by Marko Milanovic, Professor of Public International Law at the University of Nottingham School of Law, entitled "Legitimizing Blasphemy Laws Through the Backdoor: The European Court's Judgment in *E.S. v. Austria*."[45] Milanovic notes the Court's sleight of hand in changing the meaning of terms in its decision: "Look carefully what happens here: 'religious peace' and 'religious feelings', which are not mentioned as le-

---

43 https://www.institutmontaigne.org/en/blog/blasphemy-france-and-europe-right-or-offense.

44 https://www.thenewfederalist.eu/echr-you-shall-not-blaspheme-against-religious-prophets.

45 https://www.ejiltalk.org/legitimizing-blasphemy-laws-through-the-backdoor-the-

gitimate aims for the limitation of the freedom of expression in Article 10(2) of the Convention, become such under the guise of 'protecting the rights of others'.…'Religious peace' is then defined not simply as an absence of violence—which the applicant's statements were not held to provoke in the first place—but as some more nebulous idea of peaceful co-existence. Then, finally, a person's religious feelings are neatly subsumed under the person's rights, i.e., I have a right for my religious feelings not to be hurt. And all this, right or wrong, is simply taken by the Court at face value, without any kind of critical reflection."

Professor Steve Peers, University of Essex wrote at length on the case at the *EU Law Analysis* website, finding both merit and a great deal of incoherence in the Court's decision: "…it's odd that the Court however fails to consider the absence of any complaint by a Muslim organization as such, given that its reasoning turns on the importance of the objective of ensuring religious peace. Its distinction between marrying one child and a preference for children in general comes across as sophistry. And its concern that anyone could have attended the political seminar overlooks the broader context of an Internet full of critics of Islam: if the problem is a forest, does it make sense to prosecute an individual tree?"[46]

Emmanouil Bougiakiotis of the United Kingdom Constitutional Law Association, the UK's national body of constitutional law scholars affiliated to the International Association of Constitutional Law, wrote a comprehensive dissection of the Court decision's failings in "*E.S. v. Austria:* Blasphemy Laws and the Double Standards of the European Court of Human Rights"[47] Bougiakiotis commented that "The ECtHR's case law on the issue of blasphemy laws has never convincingly explained why the feelings of religious believers are protected under Article 9 of the Convention or why the feelings of other kind of believers are not. Obviously religious beliefs are, by far, not the only belief protected under Article 9… That said, this judgment seems to take things one step further. First of all, all courts heavily relied on the intention of the speaker not being to contribute to a debate on the matter but to defame Muhammad and to show him to be unworthy of worship. However, it is

---

european-courts-judgment-in-e-s-v-austria/.

46 http://eulawanalysis.blogspot.com/2018/10/freedom-to-insult-balancing-freedom-of.html.

47 https://ukconstitutionallaw.org/2018/11/22/emmanouil-bougiakiotis-e-s-v-austria-blasphemy-laws-and-the-double-standards-of-the-european-court-of-human-rights/.

rather peculiar that this should make a difference. Would a well-intentioned defamatory speech be protected under Article 10?"

The London legal website on intellectual property issues *IPKAT. com* focused on the technical applications of the precedent in the case with their article entitled "Criminal conviction over disparaging religious doctrines not a violation of freedom of expression: potential IP implications of the latest ECtHR ruling."[48] In addition to noting possible application to trademark censorship, IPKAT remarked that "This latest ECtHR decision is substantially in line with the approach taken in *Sekmadienis Ltd v. Lithuania*, a case whose national proceedings related to advertisements using Jesus look-alike models and phrases referring to him. The difference between the two cases is that, while in *Sekmadienis* the expression found to be against public morals was arguably used in a humorous context, here the intent of the applicant was to criticize."

The Dutch news and opinion website *The Post Online* published a review of the Court's decision by criminologist Bart Collard at Leiden University, entitled "In Europe there is no room for hurtful truths about Islam; Freedom of religion no longer needs to be protected separately."[49] Collard concluded that only political and legislative solutions could counter the bad precedents set by the decision: "The Netherlands must be clear in what it wants from Europe: removal or adaptation of Article 9 of the ECHR, so that freedom of religion is no longer protected separately, but falls under Article 10 of the ECHR (freedom of expression)."

Denmark Media

In Denmark, leading legal experts immediately took up the case. While the Free Press Society reported on the case as always,[50] an opinion piece by Morten Messerschmidt (MEP for Danish People's Party) in the Danish daily *Ekstra Bladet*[51] was widely read and discussed.

Messerschmidt, who holds a degree in law, noted that if the Islamic prophet Mohammad were alive today, his conduct would send him directly to prison, in the US even sentenced to several centuries behind bars. The problem presented by the Court's decision is that Is-

---

48 http://ipkitten.blogspot.com/2018/11/criminal-conviction-over-disparaging.html.

49 https://tpo.nl/2018/11/11/in-europa-is-geen-plaats-voor-kwetsende-waarheden-over-de-islam/.

50 https://www.trykkefrihed.dk/katastrofal-dom-fra-menneskerettighedsdomstolen.htm.

51 https://ekstrabladet.dk/opinionen/mortenmesserschmidt/messerschmidt-feje-dommere-fedter-for-islam/7383268.

lamic fundamentalists consider the behavior Elisabeth questioned to be model behavior, even today. Messerschmidt noted that giving in to such demands for "respect" constitutes "pandering to Islam" and "yielding ground to a brutal desert religion."

In his article, Messerschmidt went on to call the verdict "scandalous," as it restricts our right to relate facts that we discover, to hold and voice opinions about them, and to discuss them. The supposed rights claimed by the ECtHR to "have religious feelings protected" and the "justified demand to preserve religious peace" lead Messerschmidt to call the verdict "entirely political." In conclusion, he states that this is further proof that the European Court of Human Rights has lost its reason to exist, and should be ignored.

Jacob Mchangama, manager of the independent legal think tank *Justitia*,[52] took a similar position. In an opinion piece in the conservative daily *Berlingske*, he called it "absurd" that criticism of a person long dead could be considered criminal, and reasserted the fundamental requirement of a free society to discuss such matters freely, without needing to fear state intervention and punishment.

Flemming Rose, now a Senior Researcher at CATO Institute and formerly editor at the *Jyllands-Posten* during the 2006 Mohammad cartoon crisis, also commented on the case at *Berlingske*.[53] He noted that the verdict effectively constituted a conviction for blasphemy, and that this played right into the hands of Islamic fundamentalists. He argued that creating a "right to have religious feelings protected" is legal nonsense, that the right to hold and voice opinions on such matters is fundamental, and thus that the European Court of Human Rights had fundamentally mismanaged its task in defending our inalienable rights.

A somewhat different position was taken by Malthe Hilal-Harvald, Ph.d. student of Law at the University of Copenhagen. In a piece at *Altinget.dk*,[54] he argued that the verdict as such is correct, in part because the primary purpose of the ECtHR is to determine whether national law is applied correctly, in part because (in his opinion), the right to freedom of expression can be restricted if unrest is feared, or in order to protect religious feelings. In spite of this, Malthe Hilal-Harvald concluded that

---

52 http://justitia-int.org/berlingskehvad-er-sandheden-om-muhammed/.

53 https://www.berlingske.dk/kommentatorer/den-europaeiske-menneskeretsdomstol-fremmer-religioes-intolerance. See also https://quillette.com/2018/10/30/upholding-the-jihadists-veto/ by both Flemming Rose and Jacob Mchangama.

54 https://www.altinget.dk/artikel/forsker-maa-man-kalde-profeten-muhammed-for-paedofil.

the case was a missed opportunity to stand up for individual rights.

The debate in mainstream and specialist media motivated Martin Henriksen (Danish People's Party) to ask the Danish Minister of Justice Søren Pape for a guarantee that the ECtHR would not lead to a reintroduction of the blasphemy law that Denmark had previously abolished.[55] This guarantee was given in writing on November 27th, 2018.

As Jacob Sullum wrote in 2015, "Sacrilege may upset people, but it does not violate their rights. By abandoning that distinction, avowed defenders of Enlightenment values capitulate to the forces of darkness."[56]

Islamic Media

The ruling from the European Court of Human Rights attracted immediate attention in Islamic countries. Many media outlets reported on it, though in a more uniform manner than we saw in Western media. Two interpretations dominated the headlines, both expressing satisfaction with the verdict: One was concerned with insulting Muhammad, and the second with upholding Islamic blasphemy law.

Daily Sabah, a government-aligned Turkish daily, published a detailed report on October 25th 2018. The article, titled "Insulting Prophet Muhammad not 'free speech,' ECtHR rules," presented the verdict as a positive change compared to the setbacks that Islam had suffered under the conservative Austrian government formed in 2017: "Defaming the Prophet Muhammad exceeds the permissible limits of freedom of expression, ruled the European Court of Human Rights, upholding an Austrian court's decision. The European Court of Human Rights (ECtHR) ruled Thursday that an Austrian woman's criminal conviction and fine for her statements accusing the Prophet Muhammad of pedophilia did not breach her right to free speech. The ECtHR also underlined that it classified the 'impugned' statements as an abusive attack on the Prophet of Islam, which was capable of stirring up prejudice and putting at risk religious peace....Religious beliefs must be subject to criticism and denial, the ECHR observed, but when statements about religions went beyond critical denial and were likely to incite religious intolerance, states could take proportionate restrictive measures, the court said."

The article was highly critical of Austria's current government, very different from that in power when Elisabeth's case was first prosecuted in 2010. "Austria, a country of 8.8 million people, has roughly 600,000

55 https://ditoverblik.dk/vil-muhammed-dom-indskraenke-retten-til-at-kritisere-islam/.

56 https://reason.com/2018/10/25/european-court-womans-defamation-muhamma.

Muslim inhabitants. Lately, it has emerged as the leader of Islamophobia among European countries. The coalition government, an alliance of conservatives and the far right, came to power soon after Europe's migration crisis on promises to prevent another influx and restrict benefits for new immigrants and refugees. In April, Austria's far-right Chancellor Sebastian Kurz threatened to close one of the biggest mosques in Vienna and urged municipal authorities to be stricter regarding state subsidies for Muslim organizations in the city."[57]

Media that reprinted the *Daily Sabah* story included *Malaysia Today, Anadolu Agency, Al Arabiya, Daily Times, AboutIslam.net* and more. *AboutIslam.net* added a challenge to the story of Aisha presented in the traditionally accepted *hadith* and biography of Mohammed: "'A'ishah, the mother of the faithful, was the only virgin that the Prophet (peace and blessings of Allah be upon him) ever married. Professor Jasser Auda, a Visiting Professor of Islamic Law at Carleton University in Ottawa and a Founding and Board Member of the International Union of Muslim Scholars, said that lady Aisha married Prophet Mohammad (peace be upon him) when she was 16 or 17, and not 9 years old."[58]

The web site *Islam21C.com* reported on the case with some context from Austria and this conclusion in agreement with the verdict: "The court's decision follows common sense and decency, yet will undoubtedly upset many on the far-right and so-called 'liberals' that routinely appeal to 'free speech' to spread falsehoods and attack disadvantaged minorities—ironically the very objectives for the introduction of free speech laws in the first place."[59]

The other interpretation seen in articles from Islamic countries emphasized that the European Court of Human Rights had upheld Islamic blasphemy law over Western ideals of free expression. Examples of this view include October 26 articles in the Pakistani *Dawn.com*[60] news site and Indian *Siasat.com*[61] news site, expanding on an AP story. *Siasat* stressed the significance of the verdict by calling it "historic."

The online magazine *Life in Saudi Arabia* featured a more indepen-

---

57 https://www.dailysabah.com/europe/2018/10/25/insulting-prophet-muhammad-not-free-speech-ecthr-rules.

58 https://aboutislam.net/muslim-issues/europe/insulting-prophet-muhammad-isnt-free-speech-eu-rights-court/.

59 https://www.islam21c.com/news-views/court-rules-insulting-the-prophet-%EF%B7%BA-is-not-free-speech/.

60 https://www.dawn.com/news/1441388.

61 https://www.siasat.com/news/blasphemy-not-freedom-speech-europe-

dent analysis of the case and its consequences. The article set out by mentioning the problem that there has been several cases where non-Muslims have publicly criticized Islam and its founding figure Muhammad. The article considered the legal process and in particular the ECtHR decision a welcome turn away from many events harmful to Islam. And while the article does have a few factual errors, the conclusion is clear. Going forward, this will serve as a template for Islamic organizations in their efforts to stifle and stop criticism of Islam.

The Saudi article, entitled "European Courts convict a woman for insulting Prophet Muhammad S.A.W,"[62] stated that "Some Non-Muslims openly insult Prophet Muhammad S.A.W: There have been multiple incidences where non-Muslims have openly insulted the Islamic Prophet Muhammad S.A.W. When the Muslims raised their voices in the favor of their Prophet, they were told that it is their right to freedom and speech and thereby no or little action was taken against such people. However, tables were turned in 2009 when a woman named Mrs. S., who holds an Austrian nationality, came forth holding two seminars on defaming and insulting the Islamic Prophet Muhammad S.A.W....A good precedent has been set. All the Muslims living in Austria and the rest of Europe should know about this case. We know that once the precedent is set, the courts, later on, are bound to follow it unless the circumstances suggest otherwise. In this regard, any Muslim organization in Europe can take into court any or all the people who commit or intend to commit any blasphemous act against Prophet Muhammad S.A.W in the name of freedom of expression."

This interpretation—that the European Court of Human Rights accepts and upholds the Islamic understanding of blasphemy—is likely to be the template for interpretation of "Human Rights" in Turkey, Saudi Arabia and other Islamic countries. This is in line with the 1990 "Cairo Declaration of Human Rights in Islam", and is likely to be used to defend Islamic interests in Europe going forward by Muslim plaintiffs citing any remaining blasphemy laws in European nations.

That interpretation certainly was cited by Pakistani Prime Minister Imran Khan in his November 20, 2018 speech,[63] in which he asserted "We talked to the OIC, and our foreign minister raised this issue in the U.N. for the first time, and something happened that had never hap-

---

an-court-1425047/.

62 https://lifeinsaudiarabia.net/blog/2018/10/28/european-courts-convict-a-woman-for-insulting-prophet-muhammad-s-a-w/.

63 https://www.memri.org/reports/pakistani-pm-imran-khan-says-no-mention-je-

pened before. The European Union's Human Rights Court [sic] said for the first time that you cannot hurt somebody's religion under the pretext of freedom of speech, and especially it said that you cannot blaspheme against Muhammad's honor. We want the countries of the world to sign a convention which will be called the International Convention on Preventing the Defamation of Religions, which means that freedom of speech cannot be used as a pretext to hurt the world's 1.25 billion Muslims."

Stories left untold

Unfortunately, the media in Islamic countries did not address the public policy issue raised by Elisabeth's statements: the widely recognized problem of child marriage at the age of menarche or younger permitted in incorporated law in many Muslim-majority countries. Nor, for that matter, did the media in the U.S. or Europe address those issues. But the question of child marriage is in fact a subject of attempted reforms worldwide, especially in Muslim-majority countries—although many Islamic jurists still cite the example of Mohammed and Aisha as a barrier to those reforms. A leading NGO, Girls Not Brides, a global partnership of over 1000 civil society organizations from over 95 countries, constantly reports on the efforts to stop child marriage and the obstacles to those efforts in Muslim majority countries, among others, since the organization's start in 2011.[64] Girls Not Brides is meticulous in its treatment of child marriage as a global problem, but it recognizes the particular problems with reform under Islam: "Religious texts are open to interpretation, which can be used to condone child marriage. Customary and religious laws often allow to marry at a young age. In Lebanon for example, Shiite girls can marry at 9, Catholic girls at 14, and Israeli girls at 12. Deference to religious customs over the protection of girls' rights has stalled progress. In 2016 in Pakistan, the Council of Islamic Ideology demanded the withdrawal of a bill to raise the minimum age of marriage, considering it blasphemy."[65] Such issues were directly germane to the substance of Elisabeth's statements on Islamic doctrine, but were ignored by most reporters.

Another NGO, Women Living Under Muslim Laws (*Femmes Sous*

---

sus-history-announces-intl-anti-blasphemy.

64 https://www.girlsnotbrides.org/?s=Islam.

65 https://www.girlsnotbrides.org/can-religious-leaders-best-allies-end-child-marriage/.

Lois Musulmanes)[66] with representatives in over 70 countries, has taken strong initiatives against child marriage. WLUML published an article in 2011 after the Muslim Brotherhood took over Egypt entitled, "Egypt: 'They want to marry us at nine years old. Are these really the kind of men we want to run our country? Paedophiles?'"[67] which noted that under Muslim Brotherhood leader Morsi, "The new constitution has swept away recognition of women's rights and left the door open to the legalisation of perhaps Egypt's most crippling social issue—underage marriage. Draft legislation that would allow the legal age of marriage to be lowered from 18 to 13 has been drawn up, while clerics within the Muslim Brotherhood have indicated that marriage at the age of nine for girls is acceptable." In 2014, they posted an article on the proposed Iraqi constitution in "Iraq: Don't Legalize Marriage for 9-Year-Olds," noting "The pending legislation would restrict women's rights in matters of inheritance and parental and other rights after divorce, make it easier for men to take multiple wives, and allow girls to be married from age nine… and even allow girls younger than nine to be married with a parent's approval."[68] The article noted that the lowering of the marriage age was justified by Islamic doctrine: "The draft law, called the Jaafari Personal Status Law, is based on the principles of the Jaafari school of Shia religious jurisprudence, founded by Imam Jaafar al-Sadiq, the sixth Shia imam."

Many Muslim-majority countries have laws that assert a *de jure* age of marriage at 17 or 18 years of age. But these laws typically allow an exception for the girl's guardian, or *wali*, to contract for her in a marriage with the bridegroom at a much younger age in a child marriage, as noted by University of Kansas Law School's Raj Bhala, Rice Distinguished Professor, in his comprehensive *Understanding Islamic Law*.[69]

Statistics on age of marriage in Muslim-majority countries such as Afghanistan are unreliable, as observed by Nadjma Yassari and Hamid M. Saboory in the authoritative *Sharia Incorporated: A Comparative Overview of the Legal Systems of Twelve Muslim Countries in Past and Present*. They note that Afghanistan's civil code specifies a marriageable age of sixteen for girls, but "dilutes in the meantime the effect of its own

66 http://www.wluml.org/node/5408.

67 http://www.wluml.org/news/egypt-they-want-marry-us-nine-years-old-are-these-really-kind-men-we-want-run-our-country-paedo.

68 http://www.wluml.org/action/iraq-don't-legalize-marriage-9-year-olds.

69 Bhala, Raj, *Understanding Islamic Law (Shari'a)*, Lexis Nexis Group, New Providence, NJ, 2011, pages 872-873, Section 33.03 "Authority of Legal Guardian (Wali)."

provision by providing that a 'valid marriage contract may be concluded by the contracting parties themselves, or by their guardians and representatives.' The law, thus, falls short of addressing abusive exercise of the power of guardianship whereby parents, brothers and uncles often impose their will on minor, and even adult, boys and girls." The authors note that even though the civil code requires marriages to be registered, "in most parts of the country, marriages are neither certified nor registered. Only 5 percent of the marriages have been registered..."[70]

As the Islamic media observed with great satisfaction, the ECtHR decision will help to silence discussion of controversial issues in Islam— such as the widespread occurrence of child marriage that many Muslim women reformers are valiantly trying to bring to the world's attention.

Immediate Consequences of the Court's Decision

On March 19, 2019 the ECtHR announced it would not accept Elisabeth's final appeal to reconsider her case, stating that her request for referral was rejected and the October 25, 2018 judgement was final. The ECtHR decision was in line with broader trends in international institutions —though not in the institutions of all European countries—toward greater censorship of speech critical of Islam.

On January 18, 2019, one week before Elisabeth's final deadline to submit her appeal, United Nations Secretary-General Antonio Guterres had tasked his Special Adviser for the Prevention of Genocide, Adama Dieng, to "present a global plan of action against hate speech and hate crimes on a fast-track basis."[71] Three months after Elisabeth's appeal was rejected, on June 18 2019, the UN Secretary-General received what he had requested: a "UN Strategy and Plan of Action on Hate Speech"[72] ready for implementation. The definition of "hate speech" in the UN Plan of Action was dangerously all-encompassing: "In the context of this document, the term hate speech is understood as any kind of communication in speech, writing or behaviour, that attacks or uses pejorative or discriminatory language with reference to a person or a group on the

70 Yassari, Nadjma and Saboory, Mohammad Hamid, "Sharia and national law in Afghanistan," in the book *Sharia Incorporated: A comparative Overview of the Legal Systems of Twelve Muslim Countries in Past and Present*, edited by Jan Michiel Otto, Leiden University Press, Leiden Netherlands, 2010, pages 302-303.

71 https://www.un.org/sg/en/content/sg/press-encounter/2019-01-18/secretary-generals-press-conference.

72 https://www.un.org/en/genocideprevention/documents/UN%20Strategy%20and%20Plan%20of%20Action%20on%20Hate%20Speech%2018%20June%20SYNOPSIS.pdf.

basis of who they are, in other words, based on their religion, ethnicity, nationality, race, colour, descent, gender or other identity factor. This is often rooted in, and generates intolerance and hatred and, in certain contexts, can be demeaning and divisive."

In Judith Bergman's analysis of the new censorship framework, "UN Launches All-out War on Free Speech,"[73] she notes, "In the wake of the launch of Guterres' action plan, Pakistan has already presented a six-point plan 'to address the new manifestations of racism and faith-based hatred, especially Islamophobia at the United Nations headquarters."

That six-point plan from Pakistan for the UN on Islamophobia echoed the language of the Austrian decision against Elisabeth's right to criticize Islamic doctrine. Proposed by Pakistan's Permanent Representative to the UN Maleeha Lodhi, the plan demanded that "Governments need to adopt legislation to address the issue … tech companies must prevent digital technologies and social media platforms from becoming channels for inflammatory content, incitement and negative stereotyping."[74] As Bergman wrote, "The UN's all-out war on free speech is on."

However, these international efforts to censor free speech may confront stronger political opposition in individual countries than in the past—certainly more than in 2009 when Elisabeth's case started with her two seminars. The best-laid plans of European and international institutions may be blown off-course by events that they themselves initiated, with the rapid increase in immigration from Muslim-majority countries launched by Germany and the European Union in 2015. In response, Populist and conservative parties were elected to governments across Europe, in Italy, the U.K., Hungary, Poland, Czechia, major cities and regions in Spain and Germany, and most significant for Elisabeth's case—Austria. The 2019 political climate in many European countries was more Eurosceptic, more critical of immigration, and more supportive of free speech (even speech critical of Islam) than in 2009 when Elisabeth's case began. Rather than submitting to international or European institutions, many countries demonstrated a marked preference to set their own national policies. An all-out attack on free speech was undoubtedly re-launched by the U.N. and other international and Islamic institutions, but citizens in European nations were also forming political parties and electing governments to fight back.

The contrarian view of the consequences of Elisabeth's case may be

73 https://www.gatestoneinstitute.org/14516/united-nations-free-speech.

74 https://www.thenews.com.pk/print/489762-pakistan-proposes-plan-at-un-to-address-faith-based-hatred-islamophobia.

accurate in the long-run, if national governments summon the political will to protect free expression and eliminate blasphemy laws. The ECtHR repeatedly noted its deference to the national courts: "In exercising its supervisory function it is not the Court's task to take the place of the national authorities, but rather to review under Article 10, in the light of the case as a whole, the decisions they have taken pursuant to their power of appreciation, particularly whether they based their decisions on an acceptable assessment of the relevant facts."[75] The fight for free expression could return to the political arena in each country, with that devolution of authority reaffirmed by Elisabeth's case.

Yet the arbitrariness of the ECtHR's decision, its bad logic and worse bias, were still unchallenged after the final rejection of Elisabeth's appeal. This problem has not gone unnoticed and both legal experts and legislators are considering their next steps.

In December 2018, the European Centre for Law and Justice co-organized a seminar at the Council of Europe: "New challenges to the Freedom of Religion in Europe in the Light of the Recent Judgments of the ECHR." The seminar was organised "with the view to concentrate on the issue of the latest developments in the European Court of Human Rights case law related to the respect of religious beliefs. In the context of existing collisions between the freedom of religion (Article 9) and freedom of expression (Article 10) the necessity of striking the right balance in this field remains of utmost importance… aimed at elaborating proposals for a better consistency in this sphere and thus guaranteeing more effective protection of freedoms of religion and expression in the Council of Europe Member States."[76]

In a more recent June 2019 article by legal scholar Hanna Wiczanowska in the peer-reviewed *Torun International Studies Journal* of Poland's Nicolaus Copernicus University, the author looked at Elisabeth's case as well as others to derive clearer ECtHR standards to preserve free speech. Her analysis, "Searching For Common European Standards Regarding Blasphemy: Analysis Of Italian, Irish, Austrian Regulations In The Light Of The ECtHR,"[77] recommended a greater commitment to "recognizing the importance of protecting the artistic freedom for the democratic society."

In the long run, Elisabeth may win on the principles in her case, as it

---

75   https://hudoc.ECtHR.coe.int/eng#{"itemid":["001-187188"]}.

76   https://eclj.org/religious-freedom/echr/new-challenges-to-the-freedom-of-religion-in-europe-in-the-light-of-the-recent-judgments-of-the-echr.

77   https://apcz.umk.pl/czasopisma/index.php/TSM/article/view/TIS.2019.002/17838.

continues act as a catalyst for legal reformers and national governments to protect free speech.

State Prosecutions and Terrorist Attacks Against Journalists and Elected OfficialsWho Criticized Islamic Doctrine in the 21st Century

The following is only a partial list of the dozens of lawsuits, prose-cutions, terrorist threats, terrorist attacks, fines, and imprisonments of writers and elected officials who have criticized Islamic Doctrine in this century in the U.S., Canada, Australia and Europe.

In 1988 Salman Rushdie published his novel *The Satanic Verses*, in-spired in part by the life of Muhammad. In 1989 Iran's Ayatollah Ruhol-lah Khomeini issued a *fatwa* ordering Muslims to kill Rushdie, resulting in numerous bombings in bookstores and other places. More money was added to the bounty on Rushdie in 2016.[78]

In 2002, Dutch politician Pim Fortuyn was assassinated to silence his criticism of Islam.[79]

In 2002, four Muslim organizations filed a complaint against author Michel Houellebecq for stating that Islam was "stupid" and "dangerous" in an interview. Although the court acquitted Houellebecq, it refrained from doing so on free speech grounds.[80]

In 2002, Pakistani Christian convert Daniel Scot was prosecuted for anti-Islam speech in Australia. His 2004 conviction was overturned in 2006.[81]

In 2002, journalist Oriana Fallaci was sued over *The Rage and the Pride* in a French court and accused of violating anti-racist laws. The case was dismissed on a technicality.[82]

In 2004, Dutch politician Ayaan Hirsi Ali and Theo Van Gogh pro-duced a film critical of Islam entitled *Submission*, and Van Gogh was assassinated later that year.[83]

---

78 https://www.theguardian.com/books/2016/mar/02/pen-condemns-renewed-fat-wa-on-salman-rushdie-satanic-verses.

79 https://www.economist.com/europe/2002/05/09/the-political-legacy-of-pim-for-tuyn.

80 https://www.legal-project.org/issues/european-hate-speech-laws.

81 http://law.emory.edu/eilr/content/volume-28/issue-1/comments/can-i-say-that-blasphemy-law.html.

82 https://www.washingtontimes.com/news/2005/may/24/20050524-100551-2231r/.

83 https://www.nytimes.com/2004/11/03/world/europe/dutch-filmmaker-an-islam-

In November 2004, two attackers armed with grenades tried to assassinate Dutch politicians Geert Wilders and Ayann Hirsi Ali. Both elected officials were given protective security details by the Dutch government.[84]

In 2005, the *Jyllands-Posten* Muhammad cartoons controversy began after the Danish newspaper *Jyllands-Posten* published 12 editorial cartoons on 30 September 2005 including a cartoon by Danish cartoonist Kurt Westergaard. Al Qaeda would later publish a hit list including *Jyllands-Posten* editors Carsten Juste and Flemming Rose.[85]

In 2006 Oriana Fallaci again stood trial, this time in Italy, for "defamation of Islam." She died later that year before the case was resolved. [86]

In 2006, Ezra Levant, publisher of the *Western Standard* magazine, ran an article on the Danish cartoons of Mohammed with photos of the cartoons. "Hate speech" complaints were filed with the Alberta Human Rights and Citizenship Commission, resulting in "a 900-day investigation by no fewer than 15 government bureaucrats and lawyers for the thought crime of publishing news 'likely to expose a person to hatred or contempt.'" Levant spent $100,000 on legal fees before the commission dropped the charges.[87]

In 2007, the Canadian Islamic Congress filed complaints with the Canadian Human Rights Commission, Ontario Human Rights Commission (OHRC) and British Columbia Human Rights Tribunal (BCHRT) against *Maclean's Magazine* for articles on Islam including several by author Mark Steyn. All complaints were dismissed in 2008.[88]

In 2008, Kurt Westergaard, the *Jyllands-Posten* cartoonist, was the subject of a terrorist plot stopped before he could be attacked.[89]

In 2008, actress Brigitte Bardot was convicted and fined on charges of inciting racial hatred for her criticism of Islamic practices for butchering animals. This was the fifth time she had been fined for criticizing

critic-is-killed.html.

84 https://www.nytimes.com/2004/11/11/world/europe/dutch-police-seize-2-in-raid-on-terror-cell-after-a-siege.html.

85 https://www.theatlantic.com/international/archive/2016/03/flemming-rose-danish-cartoons/473670/.

86 https://www.theguardian.com/world/2006/jun/13/books.italy.

87 https://www.macleans.ca/news/canada/human-rights-racket/

88 https://www.macleans.ca/news/canada/five-years-two-tribunals-a-raft-of-secret-hearings-a-supreme-court-challenge-how-the-battle-for-free-speech-was-won/

89 http://news.bbc.co.uk/2/hi/europe/7240481.stm.

Islamic practices since 1997.[90]

In 2008, Geert Wilders launched his film Fitna, critical of Islamic doctrine. Efforts to try Wilders for hate speech faltered in 2007 and 2008, but in 2009 a court ordered prosecutors to bring him to trial. He was acquitted in 2011. In 2016 he was tried again and convicted of "inciting discrimination and hatred" but no fine was imposed. An appeal was ongoing in 2019.[91]

In 2009, Austrian elected official Susanne Winter was convicted with a fine and suspended prison sentence for criticizing Islam and stating that "'In today's system' Mohammed would be considered a 'child molester.'"[92]

In 2009, Helsinki, Finland City Council Member Jussi Halla-aho was convicted by the District Court of disturbing religious worship for writing in 2008 that Mohammad was a pedophile, referencing his marriage to Aisha and raising the question of pedophilia in Islamic doctrine. He was fined 330 euros. In October 2010, the Appeals court upheld the decision, as did the Supreme Court in 2012. The latter added the charge of ethnic agitation and increased the fine to 400 euros.[93]

In October and November 2009, Elisabeth Sabaditsch-Wolff held two seminars titled "Basic Information on Islam" at the Freedom Education Institute, a political academy linked to the Austrian Freedom Party. She discussed, among many topics, the *hadith* narrating that Mohammed's consummated his marriage with Aisha when she was nine, and asked if that would not be called pedophilia. A reporter from a socialist weekly magazine secretly recorded parts of the first two lectures and comments during breaks. The magazine submitted transcripts to the Viennese public prosecutor's office as evidence of hate speech against Islam.[94]

In 2010, Swedish cartoonist Lars Vilks published cartoons showing Mohammed as a round-about dog and received multiple terrorist

---

90 https://www.legal-project.org/issues/european-hate-speech-laws.

91 https://www.reuters.com/article/us-netherlands-wilders/dutch-lawmaker-wilders-appeals-fewer-moroccans-conviction-idUSKCN1TQ0ZF.

92 https://www.spiegel.de/international/europe/campaigns-of-intolerance-austrian-politician-calls-prophet-muhammad-a-child-molester-a-528549.html.

93 https://www.mtvuutiset.fi/artikkeli/islamin-yhdistaminen-pedofiliaan-toi-halla-aholle-sakot-myos-hovilta/2038802#gs.07op65 and https://yle.fi/uutiset/osasto/news/supreme_court_orders_halla-aho_to_pay_for_hate_speech/6171739

94 https://www.gatestoneinstitute.org/2702/sabaditsch-wolff-appeal.

threats.[95]

In April 2010 in the U.S., the cartoon program *South Park* received death threats from a New York-based Muslim organization. As a result, their sponsors at Comedy Central censored an episode, hiding images of Mohammed.[96]

In April 2010, cartoonist Molly Norris published a single online cartoon calling for an "Everybody draw Muhammad Day." By May 1 she had been forced to publish an apology, and in July she went underground due to a *fatwa* against her by al Qaeda. The FBI reportedly offered no assistance other than advising her to disappear.[97]

In 2010 Danish cartoonist Kurt Westergaard's house was attacked by an axe-wielding assailant.[98]

In 2010, the Danish crown prosecutor sought to lift MP Jesper Langballe's parliamentary immunity so that he could face charges under Article 266(b) for publishing an article about the creeping "Islamisation of Europe" and the subjugated status of Muslim women.[99]

In September 2010 in Austria, formal charges against Sabaditsch-Wolff were filed accusing her of hate speech against Islam and incitement, according to Section 283 of the Austrian Criminal Code (*Strafgesetzbuch, StGB*). Her bench trial began November 23, 2010. The weakness of the evidence against her was made apparent and the judge suspended the hearing until January 18, 2011.[100]

In 2011, the French satirical magazine *Charlie Hebdo* was firebombed before publishing an issue featuring Mohammed.[101]

In 2011, Danish journalist Lars Hedegaard was convicted of hate speech for a conversation critical of Islam; in 2012, the Danish Supreme Court cleared him of all charges. In 2013, he survived an assassination attempt by a man who later joined ISIS.[102]

---

95 https://www.csmonitor.com/USA/Society/2010/0512/Cartoonist-Lars-Vilks-attacked-for-showing-Prophet-Mohammed-in-gay-film.

96 https://www.theguardian.com/tv-and-radio/2010/apr/22/south-park-censored-fatwa-muhammad and https://www.cbsnews.com/news/south-park-episode-201-censored-speech-was-no-joke/.

97 https://www.lambiek.net/artists/n/norris_molly.htm.

98 https://www.theguardian.com/world/2010/jan/04/danish-cartoonist-axe-attack.

99 https://www.legal-project.org/issues/european-hate-speech-laws.

100 https://www.gatestoneinstitute.org/2702/sabaditsch-wolff-appeal.

101 https://www.telegraph.co.uk/news/worldnews/europe/france/11330145/Charlie-Hebdo-attack-2011-firebomb-over-Prophet-Mohammed-issue.html.

102 https://www.nytimes.com/2013/02/28/world/europe/lars-hedegaard-anti-islamic-provocateur-receives-support-from-danish-muslims.html.

In January 2011, the Austrian court added a charge against Saba-ditsch-Wolff—"denigrating religious symbols of a recognized religious group." In February 2011 the Vienna Regional Criminal Court dropped the charge of incitement against Sabaditsch-Wolff, but found that her statement implied that Muhammad had had paedophilic tendencies, and convicted her for disparaging religious doctrines. She was ordered to pay a fine of 480 euros and the costs of the proceedings. In December 2011, the Vienna Court of Appeal upheld the decision.[103]

In June 2012, Wolff filed an application with the European Court of Human Rights, relying on Article 10 (freedom of expression). She stated that the domestic courts failed to address the substance of the impugned statements in the light of her right to freedom of expression. If they had done so, they would not have qualified them as mere value judgments but as value judgments based on facts.[104]

In 2013, the UK government banned U.S. authors Robert Spencer and Pamela Geller from entering Britain because of their criticism of Islamic doctrine and their support for Israel. The ban continued in 2019.[105]

In December 2013, the Austrian Supreme Court dismissed a request for the renewal of the proceedings filed by Elisabeth Sabaditsch-Wolff.

In 2014 the U.S., the Southern Poverty Law Center (SPLC), a far-left organization that publishes annual lists of what it calls "hate groups," broadened its 2010 category of "Anti-Muslim hate groups." The SPLC "Anti-Muslim hate groups" included a wide range of U.S. journalists publishing criticism of Islamic doctrines and practices, listing think tanks, individual writers, researchers and Muslim reformers.[106]

In April 2014, election candidate Paul Weston publicly quoted from Winston Churchill's book *The River War*, and was arrested "on suspicion of religious/racial harassment."[107] In June, charges were dropped after public outcry.[108]

In August 2014, retired French schoolteacher Christine Tasin was convicted after the prosecution argued criticism of Islam was the same

---

103 https://www.gatestoneinstitute.org/2702/sabaditsch-wolff-appeal.

104 https://hudoc.echr.coe.int/eng-press#%7B%22itemid%22:[%22003-6234980-8105265%22]%7D.

105 https://www.bbc.com/news/uk-23064355.

106 https://www.splcenter.org/fighting-hate/intelligence-report/2015/year-hate-and-extremism-0.

107 https://www.telegraph.co.uk/news/uknews/crime/10792895/Election-candi-date-arrested-over-Churchill-speech.html.

108 https://www.bbc.com/news/uk-england-27809890.

as inciting violence against Muslims. She was fined €4,500 and given a 3 month prison sentence. She was the target of numerous death threats. In December 2014, Christine Tasin's conviction is overturned on appeal.[109]

In 2015, the satirical magazine *Charlie Hebdo* was attacked for its criticism of Islam, killing 12 people and wounding 11 others.[110]

In May 2015, the American Freedom Defense Initiative and *Jihad-watch.org* co-sponsored a national "Draw Muhammad Contest" in Garland Texas to defend free speech. The event was attacked by two terrorists, with credit later claimed by ISIS. Police shot the terrorists and a security guard was wounded. Subsequent court documents revealed that the FBI not only had foreknowledge of the planned attack in Texas and did nothing to prevent it, but the FBI undercover informant encouraged the terrorists and photographed the attack as it happened.[111]

In 2015, Swedish cartoonist Lars Vilks was the target in an attack on a café that killed a civilian and wounded three policemen.[112]

In 2015 French politician Marine Le Pen went to trial for comments she made about Islam in 2010. She was later acquitted.[113]

In 2016, French-Jewish scholar Georges Bensoussan was prosecuted in France for "incitement to hatred" against Islam, because he expressed concern about rising anti-semitism, later acquitted.[114]

In 2016, a Danish court convicted a man of making Facebook comments that disparaged the radical Islamic organization, *Hizb-ut-Tahrir*.[115]

In 2016, in the U.S., the Southern Poverty Law Center published another blacklist of writers, lawyers and researchers, "A Journalist's Manual: Field Guide to Anti-Muslim Extremists."[116]

---

109 https://www.meforum.org/islamist-watch/44845/court-of-appeal-overturns-conviction-of-woman.

110 https://www.bbc.com/news/world-europe-30708237.

111 https://www.grassley.senate.gov/news/news-releases/what-did-fbi-really-know-terrorist-attack-garland-texas and https://freebeacon.com/issues/security-guard-injured-in-2015-terrorist-attack-appeals-suit-against-fbi/.

112 https://www.theguardian.com/world/2015/feb/14/copenhagen-blasphemy-lars-vilks-prophet-muhammad-krudttonden-cafe.

113 https://www.theguardian.com/world/2015/oct/20/marine-le-pen-trial-charged-anti-muslims-hate-speech.

114 http://www.israelnationalnews.com/News/News.aspx/226359.

115 https://globalfreedomofexpression.columbia.edu/updates/2016/02/some-things-rotten-denmark-criminalizing-blasphemy-hate-speech-law/.

116 https://web.archive.org/web/20161116001905/https://www.splcenter.org/20161025/journalists-manual-field-guide-anti-muslim-extremists.

In 2017 in Germany, Michael Stürzenberger received a 6-month prison sentence for publishing historical facts on Nazi-Muslim collaboration on Facebook. He has been prosecuted multiple times in Germany and Austria.[117]

On January 20, 2018 in France, Pierre Cassen was convicted of "incitement to hatred against Muslims" and a fine of $12,000 was imposed on him. He was also given a three-month suspended prison sentence.[118]

On October 25, 2018, the European Court of Human Rights ruled against Elisabeth Sabaditsch-Wolff's appeal.[119]

From 2016 to the present, at the SPLC's urging, financial corporations (PayPal, credit card companies, banks, crowdfunding sites, online advertising networks) and social media companies (Google, Facebook, Twitter, YouTube) coordinated a national campaign to deny services to individuals and groups on the "Anti-Muslim" SPLC lists.[120]

In January 2019, the judge dismissed a lawsuit filed against the FBI by the security guard who had been wounded in the 2015 Garland shooting at the "Draw Mohammed Contest" co-sponsored by the American Freedom Defense Initiative and *Jihadwatch.org*.[121]

In March 2019, the Grand Chamber Panel of the European Court of Human Rights rejected Sabaditsch-Wolff's request for referral, stating that the judgment in her case was now final.[122]

In August 2019, the terror state of Iran issued a threat against the Washington, DC think tank Foundation for Defense of Democracy, "threatening that any actions taken against it by 'security apparatuses'"will be 'considered legitimate' by Tehran."[123]

—Henrik R. Clausen has two decades of professional media experience, and is author of two books about democracy and international law. A human rights fundamentalist, he holds a deep conviction that classical liberties and inalienable rights are the true sources of freedom and pros-

117 https://www.osce.org/odihr/339161?download=true.

118 https://www.gatestoneinstitute.org/12051/france-islam-free-speech.

119 https://hudoc.echr.coe.int/eng-press#{"itemid":["003-6234980-8105265"]}.

120 https://dailycaller.com/2018/06/06/splc-partner-google-facebook-amazon/.

121 https://www.jihadwatch.org/2019/01/miscarriage-of-justice-judge-dismisses-lawsuit-alleging-fbi-role-in-2015-jihad-attack-on-afdi-free-speech-event.

122 https://hudoc.echr.coe.int/eng-press#{"itemid":["003-6361015-8328848"]}.

123 https://www.washingtonexaminer.com/news/terror-sponsor-iran-threatens-washington-think-tank-with-actions-by-security-apparatuses.

perity. In over 15 years of pro-freedom activism. Henrik has researched many historical and legal topics, and has shared his analysis in many articles, in particular about Islamic history and the workings of *shariah*.

— Christine Brim is a researcher and writer in the U.S.

BY AARON RHODES

The European Court of Human Rights' Assault on Natural Rights

Lisabeth Sabaditsch-Wolff's account deserves close attention by all concerned about the erosion of liberty in liberal societies, and especially by those who are not.

Totalitarian states deny the existence of human rights, and authoritarian states restrict human rights. This is not difficult to understand. But what does it mean when United Nations human rights institutions endorse and legitimate the violation of freedom of speech; when laws in nominally liberal, democratic societies violate fundamental freedoms; when international courts uphold those laws; and, when the civil society human rights community is largely supportive of these restrictions on liberty? What does is mean when the laws of European countries sanction behavior in the manner of the blasphemy laws of Islamic theocracies, which, along with secular authoritarian states, exert strong influence on the interpretation and enforcement of international human rights standards?

These are among the questions raised by this book. They are questions that show the challenges we face in trying to secure freedom now, and for future generations.

As a human rights advocate, I have been disappointed by a number of decisions by the European Court of Human Rights (ECtHR) over the past several years. One can and should question the Court's judicial activism in watering down authentic human rights, and for rulings that have intruded into questions that should be decided democratically, not by judges. But perhaps most egregiously, the Court has also not protected religious freedom.

The freedom to criticize religious beliefs, dogmas and practices is essential to religious freedom itself, and really inseparable from it. A large portion of my human rights activity has been devoted to defending members of Muslim communities—in the Balkans, in Chechnya, in Central Asia, defending the Ahmadi Muslims in Pakistan and elsewhere; and, opposing discrimination against Muslims in European countries. When France imposed a ban on forms of religious clothing, a ban really aimed at Islamic practices, my colleagues and I were confident it would be rejected by the ECtHR. But in 2014, it was upheld in a ruling that revealed the shaky ground beneath human rights in Europe. The Court placed vague social goals over the right to religious freedom. The Court said wearing the burqa could undermine the notion of "living together," thus upholding the French assertion that the veils "breached the right of others to live in a space of socialization which made living together easier." Aside from undermining the freedom of religion, indeed any exercise of freedom that might be interpreted as at odds with "socialization," the ruling alienated many Muslims and has thus arguably contributed to radicalization. The decision received only muted criticism from major human rights groups. The establishment human rights community tends to regard international human rights courts and human rights institutions as sacrosanct.

By the time it ruled on Ms. Sabaditsch-Wolff's case, the Court had thus established a record of failure, and the ruling described in her book should have surprised no one. All the same, it shocks and depresses. The ECtHR undermined a basic human right with the argument that speech is only protected as long as it does not hurt the feelings of others. Elisabeth was convicted by an Austrian court for "disparaging religious doctrines in a manner capable of arousing justified indignation." The ECtHR ruled that this did not violate the European Convention on Human Rights, the charter set up to protect our basic freedoms from laws imposed by governments—a bill of rights for Europeans to defend their natural, inherent rights.

According to the Court, religion may be criticized, but only in the right "manner," in order to ensure "religious peace." The implication is clear: we are legally required to address religious questions only in a certain way, in order to avoid violent reactions on among those who might be justly indignant, and react in an un-peaceful manner. In other words, the responsibility for religious peace lies in restricting speech, not restricting reactions to speech. This is demeaning, and wrong—seeing individuals in a programmatic way, as if they bear no free will with which to rein in their passions, and bear no responsibility for civil behavior. We have no right not to be offended, but we do have a legal and moral obligation, and individual responsibility, to express our indignation in a nonviolent way.

Once again, as in the ruling against Muslim attire, the ECtHR's language included a multitude of ambiguous terms, which as we know, often allow authoritarian regimes to repress freedom through the politically-motivated manipulation of vaguely worded laws. Since the Enlightenment, it has long been a foundation of human rights reasoning and practice that no one has a right not to be offended, but apparently that no longer holds. The decision said Elisabeth had not discussed the question of the Prophet Mohammad's marriage to a nine-year old girl in a "neutral" manner. This may to be true, but how much public debate about controversial moral questions is, in fact, "neutral?" Given its deeply partisan and ideological character, and the distance and anonymity offered by social media, the charge is irrational. Indeed, is "neutrality" desirable, or even possible? Are we now under the control of overlords who monitor the "manner" in which we discuss social and moral questions, and penalize us for violations based on highly subjective and arbitrary criteria?

The ECtHR decision endorsed what is in effect a blasphemy law. Blasphemy laws are laws that restrict and punish speech that is considered offensive to the faithful and leaders of religious communities. Austria's legislation follows principles one finds in archaic Islamic jurisprudence: the Islamic prohibition of slander set down in *The Reliance of the Traveller* (*umdat al-Salik*), an Islamic manual of jurisprudence written in the fourteenth century and considered to contain absolute legal rulings. It defines slander as "to mention anything concerning a person that he would dislike." (r2.2)

The law is one of numerous pieces of anti-"hate speech" legislation that European Union member states have installed, in part directed by the EU itself, which mandates such legislation. Hate speech legislation also has its basis in Article 20 of the International Covenant on Civil and Political Rights (ICCPR), which obliges parties to the treaty to pass legislation against "any advocacy of national racial or religious hatred that constitutes incitement to discrimination, hostility or violence." This language, because of its inexact, and thus dangerous, language ("hatred," "discrimination," "hostility") had been proposed by communist dictatorships and authoritarian states, and strenuously opposed by liberal democracies that knew it could be misused for political purposes.[1] But the anti-liberal UN members won in the process. Many of the liberal democracies that objected then, now boast of, and promote, hate speech legislation. And while the UN Human Rights Committee has insisted that the dangerously vague language in Article 20 must not be interpreted as supporting blasphemy laws, yet in effect, it does.

Such laws are deeply injurious to the right to freedom of religion and conscience; they thwart the exercise of reason, which can bring us together as a main element of our common human nature. They are recognized as incompatible with human rights, although about a quarter of all the nations of the world have them, and in a number of those countries, blasphemy may be punished by the sentence of death. At an international meeting to defend religious freedom convened by the United States in the summer of 2019, 27 countries condemned blasphemy laws. They called on governments that utilize these laws "to free any individuals imprisoned on such grounds, and to repeal blasphemy, apostasy, and other laws that impede the exercise of freedoms of expression and religion or belief, in a manner inconsistent with international law." Few European states joined this appeal.

The ECtHR reasoning for upholding a blasphemy law suggests a form of pseudo social science, or social engineering, whereby courts interfere with individual freedom in the interest of supporting social goals. But human rights are not there to shape our actions, by the use of penalties, in the service of any particular vision of the good society; they are there to protect liberty so that citizens can ensure that society is just and fair, through political processes. The utilitarianism of the ECtHR's approach is incompatible with the principle of individual liberty, but it reveals a backward social science nonetheless, a social science based on discredited determinism. Restrictions on freedom of speech, and freedom of religion and conscience, do not necessarily make societies stronger, more humane, or more tolerant. The evidence of history suggests otherwise.

Upholding the standards of responsibility and civility that allow a pluralistic society to peacefully exist requires the cultivation of reason and moral character. A democratic ethos is not something that can be

---

1   Mchangama, Jacob, "The Sordid Origen of Hate-Speech Laws," *Policy Review*, December, 2011.

imposed by courts, but must instead emerge in the family, in education, in religious institutions and in other parts of civil society, in processes that inform the way individuals think and act towards one another, how they go about supporting the principles they consider paramount for the good of individuals and their communities. According to the Dutch theologian Hans-Martien ten Napel:

> This democratic ethos will need to be developed by citizens through their participation in various institutions and civil society organizations, among other things. In order for these institutions and organizations to flourish, natural rights such as freedom of religion, freedom of expression, and freedom of association and assembly are prerequisites. By limiting such freedoms, without realizing it, liberal democracies are cutting off the very branches on which they rest. At a minimum, restrictions on these natural rights will result in a transformation of the nature of liberal democracy. From a system in which citizens are free to pursue the good life they have chosen for themselves, it runs the risk of changing into a system which imposes one particular conception of the good life on society as a whole.[2]

The idea of inherent, universal human rights comes to us from the idea of Natural Rights, an idea that in turn is rooted in visions of a Natural Law, to which the laws of rulers and legislatures must conform if they are to avoid impinging on our common human nature. The insouciance with which legislative bodies and courts in supposedly "liberal" democracies now violate basic liberties is without doubt due to our contemporary lack of appreciation for the principle of Natural Rights, which is the foundation for freedoms that are not to be conditioned by arbitrary laws.

The inclination to limit our most basic and original human right to freedom is on the ascendant, and it operates within the framework of international human rights, a field that has partially morphed into a political-correctness regime promoting, rather than fighting, speech codes, and siding against those citizens forced to participate in same-sex marriage rituals against their religious beliefs. When the U.S. Secretary of State, Mike Pompeo, announced the formation of a commission to examine what has happened to the idea of "unalienable rights," most of the human rights community strenuously objected. A coalition of 430

---

2 Hans-Martien ten Napel, "The Natural Law and Natural Rights Tradition: A Foundation for Religious Freedom," London School of Economics Religion and Global Society Blog, 15 July 2019.

human rights, civil rights, foreign policy and faith organizations, leaders and scholars sent a letter to Pompeo urging him to dismantle the new Commission on Unalienable Rights. In their letter, the groups wrote that "(W)e view with great misgiving a body established by the U.S. government aimed expressly at circumscribing rights through an artificial sorting of those that are 'unalienable' and those to be now deemed 'ad hoc'.….*These terms simply have no place in human rights discourse.*" (emphasis added)[3]

If, indeed, it is believed that a distinction between inherent human rights, and those rights that have their basis not in nature, but in politics, has "no place in human rights discourse," it is a sure sign that that discourse is not one capable to defending liberty. By the same token, the conviction of Elisabeth Sabaditsch-Wolff and the incapacity of the European Court to rule against a thought-terminating blasphemy law, can, and must, have a silver lining if we are to believe freedom of thought has any future in Western societies. It can show us what is wrong with the way we are treating our most cherished freedoms, and help us revive our commitment to honoring and defending them.

—Aaron Rhodes is president of the Forum for Religious Freedom-Europe, and the author of *The Debasement of Human Rights* (Encounter Books, 2018).

---

3 *National Catholic Register*, 25 July 2019.

Epilogue

THE LAMENTABLE JUDGMENT of the European Court of Human Rights, which upheld the blasphemy law in place in Austria, has seamlessly integrated itself into a series of measures repressing the right to freedom of speech on both sides of the Atlantic. This has always been my greatest concern: we are witnessing a tsunami of suppression of thoughts that are outside the Overton Window, outside the already very narrow corridor of acceptable discourse.

I am deeply troubled by how many people, old, young, intelligent, not so intelligent, are currently subscribing to a phenomenon called "groupthink," which is a concept introduced by the late Professor Irving Janis. Groupthink describes a pattern of behavior with three distinctive features:

- A group of people come to share a particular view or belief without a proper appraisal of the evidence.
- This leads them to insist that their belief is shared by a 'consensus' of all right-minded opinion.
- Because their belief is ultimately only subjective, resting on shaky foundations, they then defend it only by displaying an irrational, dismissive hostility toward anyone daring to question it.[1]

Whether Professor Janis' concept is applied to Islam or "global man-made warming," the result is the same: people stop thinking for themselves, becoming instead "true believers" and thus losing their individuality by hooking onto a movement, any movement, that will ease their pain by giving them a sense of belonging.[2] Propaganda is so pervasive

---

1 https://www.thegwpf.org/content/uploads/2018/02/Groupthink.pdf.

2 For more insight into the concept of the "true believer," read *The True Believer* by Eric Hoffer, Harper, 1951.

that it is becoming a colossal challenge to avoid it. The mainstream media is drumming the same tune day in, day out, making escape nearly impossible. There is very little opposition, for reasons in the third feature of Groupthink and those described throughout this book.

How times have changed! How little one can safely say nowadays. What began in the 1970s with the introduction of the concept of Islamophobia, that is, accusing critics of Islam of an illness, has gradually morphed into the relentless persecution of those heretics, now called "haters," "racists" and "white supremacists," the latter of which don't even need to be of white skin color! We are strangled by the idea of hate speech—anything that the "other" may not like to hear, which is eerily similar to the Islamic concept of slander. We are being conditioned to self-censor, even before thinking a thought. We are told by (EU) law that there are groups that are favored and may not be criticized or "hated," like migrants or Muslims, but we can hate priests or the rich; they are not protected. We must fear a midnight visit by the German police for one of our Facebook comments. We can no longer say that there are only two biological sexes. We cannot argue in favor of a family consisting of a man, a woman and a child or children. We cannot protest the "man," who turns out to be a not-so-underage migrant who illegally entered a country and who brutally rapes and kills a 14-year-old girl. Mourning the senseless death of a child makes one a hater. We must understand the motives of the murderer. Your personal opinion may lead to loss of your job, the job which pays your mortgage and puts food on your table. If you are unlucky, you will be visited by child services for your belief in free speech. And if it's a dark day and the wrong country, you might even be locked up for being a citizen journalist.

All of the above describes what has been happening both in the United States and in Europe. One country is protected by the First Amendment, the other by a framework called the European Human Rights Convention. One guarantees God-given rights, the other grants rights.

Despite the numerous attacks on the First Amendment, Americans can still, for the most part, speak their minds. In Europe, the situation is completely different: once you are caught in the crosshairs of the law, be it for hate speech or blasphemy, you know there is no chance to disentangle yourself successfully. Just ask any of my friends who have experienced what I have, or who are still fighting their charges, at great personal cost. Or ask Dr. Karen Siegemund, a Los Angeles native, who recently lost her teaching job for defending Western civilization. Or perhaps you belong to the 68 percent of Americans who believe they can only speak openly and safely about race or Islam with people who hold similar opinions. More than half of the American populace says there is "pressure to think a certain way" about the topics of race, gender, immigration and Islam.[3] In other words, Americans, like their European brothers and sisters, are staying silent out of fear.

I am often told that what I say and how I say it is too acrimonious and that I stir up hatred with what I say. My reply is an echo of one of my closest allies who shall remain nameless:

> I can accept your charge of acrimony only partly. Either a statement is true or it is not. Describing gruesome actions in an appeasing manner is not the correct path. Are we doing the same thing with National Socialism?
>
> If a person who has no clue about what is happening gets up and disgustedly leaves [a speech I am giving], then that's his prerogative. I will do nothing to ask him to return by using "softer," less confrontational rhetoric. Knowledge is to a certain degree also an obligation. It is not my job to be a shrink for those people who refuse to acknowledge reality and simultaneously feel morally superior.
>
> Education, confrontation and the Christian notion of discernment of spirits is what I consider my job. I do not want to be loved, respected or praised for that; I'm certainly not getting paid for that either. As people's own perceptions increase, they will seek for themselves the truth and hold accountable those who under orders deny reality will have inflicted incomprehensible damage on them.
>
> Only radical analyses enable coherent (political) applications. Weak diagnoses always give rise to radical (and often inhuman) therapeutic measures, and, as a consequence, excessive physical violence always plays a dominant role. You will see that our task in the near future will be to keep people who are today still soft as butter from implementing unacceptable and blanket draconian measures.

So you may wonder what is left to do. I will close with two quotes, one from the UN Rapporteur on freedom of expression and one by a well-known German and Jewish writer.

> The strategic response to hate speech is more speech: more speech that educates about cultural differences; more speech that promotes

---

3 Lane, Charles, "We're staying silent out of fear," *Washington Post,* October 15, 2018. https://www.washingtonpost.com/opinions/we-need-the-exhausted-majority-to-speak-up/2018/10/15/160440fa-d090-11e8-83d6-291fcead2ab1_story.html?utm_term=.b264e46dd581.

diversity; more speech to empower and give voice to minorities, for example through the support of community media and their representation in mainstream media. More speech can be the best strategy to reach out to individuals, changing what they think and not merely what they do.

—UN Special Rapporteur on freedom of opinion and expression[4]

We should all take the following words by the deceased Jewish writer Ralph Giordano not only to heart, but to follow them vigorously:

> So, in the future I will dare to say what I think and what makes me uneasy. I will dare to say that I am deeply repulsed by the sight of shrouded women and that my repulsion is not directed at them, but at the patriarchal, religious system that compels them to be wrapped up. I will still dare to say that I consider *shariah* law to be notoriously awful. I will write and tell it the way it is in the same name of cultural self-assertion, under the title: 'Immigration is not the problem. The mosque is not the problem. Islam is the problem.'

Finally, I urge you, dear reader, to never give up and never give in to the tyranny of hate speech and Groupthink. I implore you to defend and uphold the United States Constitution. I invite you to return to thinking for yourself, to seek and find the truth, and to defend it with all your might.

---

4 https://www2.ohchr.org/english/issues/religion/docs/SRJointstatement22April09.pdf

Appendix A

EUROPEAN COURT OF HUMAN RIGHTS
COUR EUROPÉENNE DES DROITS DE L'HOMME

Press Release
issued by the Registrar of the Court

ECHR 360 (2018)
25.10.2018

Conviction for calling Muhammad a paedophile is not in breach of Article 10

In today's Chamber judgment[1] in the case of E.S. v. Austria (application no. 38450/12) the European Court of Human Rights held, unanimously, that there had been:

no violation of Article 10 (freedom of expression) of the European Convention on Human Rights.

The case concerned the applicant's conviction for disparaging religious doctrines; she had made statements suggesting that Muhammad had had paedophilic tendencies.

The Court found in particular that the domestic courts comprehensively assessed the wider context of the applicant's statements and carefully balanced her right to freedom of expression with the right of others to have their religious feelings protected, and served the legitimate aim of preserving religious peace in Austria. It held that by considering the impugned statements as going beyond the permissible limits of an objective debate, and by classifying them as an abusive attack on the Prophet of Islam which could stir up prejudice and threaten religious peace, the domestic courts put forward relevant and sufficient reasons.

Principal facts

The applicant, E.S., is an Austrian national who was born in 1971 and lives in Vienna (Austria).

In October and November 2009, Mrs S. held two seminars entitled "Basic Information on Islam", in which she discussed the marriage between the Prophet Muhammad and a six-year old girl, Aisha, which allegedly was consummated when she was nine. *Inter alia*, the applicant stated that Muhammad "liked to do it with children" and "... A 56-year-old and a six-year-old? ... What do we call it, if it is not paedophilia?".

On 15 February 2011 the Vienna Regional Criminal Court found that these statements implied that Muhammad had had paedophilic tendencies, and convicted Mrs S. for disparaging religious doctrines. She was ordered to pay a fine of 480 euros and the costs of the proceedings. Mrs S. appealed but the Vienna Court of Appeal upheld the decision in December 2011, confirming in essence the lower court's findings.

A request for the renewal of the proceedings was dismissed by the Supreme Court on 11 December 2013.

Complaints, procedure and composition of the Court

Relying on Article 10 (freedom of expression), Mrs S. complained that the domestic courts failed to address the substance of the impugned statements in the light of her right to freedom of expression. If they had done so, they would not have qualified them as mere value judgments but as value judgments based on facts. Furthermore, her criticism of Islam occurred in the framework of an objective and lively discussion which contributed to a public debate, and had not been aimed at

---

1. Under Articles 43 and 44 of the Convention, this Chamber judgment is not final. During the three-month period following its delivery, any party may request that the case be referred to the Grand Chamber of the Court. If such a request is made, a panel of five judges considers whether the case deserves further examination. In that event, the Grand Chamber will hear the case and deliver a final judgment. If the referral request is refused, the Chamber judgment will become final on that day.
Once a judgment becomes final, it is transmitted to the Committee of Ministers of the Council of Europe for supervision of its execution. Further information about the execution process can be found here: www.coe.int/t/dghl/monitoring/execution.

COUNCIL OF EUROPE

CONSEIL DE L'EUROPE

defaming the Prophet of Islam. Lastly, Mrs S. submitted that religious groups had to tolerate even severe criticism.

The application was lodged with the European Court of Human Rights on 6 June 2012.

Judgment was given by a Chamber of seven judges, composed as follows:
Angelika Nußberger (Germany), President,
André Potocki (France),
Síofra O'Leary (Ireland),
Mārtiņš Mits (Latvia),
Gabriele Kucsko-Stadlmayer (Austria),
Lətif Hüseynov (Azerbaijan),
Lado Chanturia (Georgia),
and also Claudia Westerdiek, Section Registrar.

Decision of the Court
\
Article 10
The Court noted that those who choose to exercise the freedom to manifest their religion under Article 9 of the Convention could not expect to be exempt from criticism. They must tolerate and accept the denial by others of their religious beliefs. Only where expressions under Article 10 wentbeyond the limits of a critical denial, and certainly where they were likely to incite religious intolerance, might a State legitimately consider them to be incompatible with respect for the freedom of thought, conscience and religion and take proportionate restrictive measures.

The Court observed also that the subject matter of the instant case was of a particularly sensitive nature, and that the (potential) effects of the impugned statements, to a certain degree, depended on the situation in the respective country where the statements were made, at the time and in the context they were made. Accordingly, it considered that the domestic authorities had a wide margin of appreciation in the instant case, as they were in a better position to evaluate which statements were likely to disturb the religious peace in their country.

The Court reiterated that it has distinguished in its case-law between statements of fact and value judgments. It emphasised that the truth of value judgments was not susceptible to proof. However, a value judgment without any factual basis to support it might be excessive.

The Court noted that the domestic courts comprehensively explained why they considered that the applicant's statements had been capable of arousing justified indignation; specifically, they had not been made in an objective manner contributing to a debate of public interest (e.g. on child marriage), but could only be understood as having been aimed at demonstrating that Muhammad was not worthy of worship. It agreed with the domestic courts that Mrs S. must have been aware that her statements were partly based on untrue facts and apt to arouse indignation in others. The national courts found that Mrs S. had subjectively labelled Muhammad with paedophilia as his general sexual preference, and that she failed to neutrally inform her audience of the historical background, which consequently did not allow for a serious debate on that issue. Hence, the Court saw no reason to depart from the domestic courts' qualification of the impugned statements as value judgments which they had based on a detailed analysis of the statements made.

The Court found in conclusion that in the instant case the domestic courts carefully balanced the applicant's right to freedom of expression with the rights of others to have their religious feelings protected, and to have religious peace preserved in Austrian society.

The Court held further that even in a lively discussion it was not compatible with Article 10 of the Convention to pack incriminating statements into the wrapping of an otherwise acceptable expression of opinion and claim that this rendered passable those statements exceeding the permissible limits of freedom of expression.

Lastly, since Mrs S. was ordered to pay a moderate fine and that fine was on the lower end of the statutory range of punishment, the criminal sanction could not to be considered as disproportionate.

Under these circumstances, and given the fact that Mrs S. made several incriminating statements, the Court considered that the Austrian courts did not overstep their wide margin of appreciation in the instant case when convicting Mrs S. of disparaging religious doctrines. Overall, there had been no violation of Article 10.

The judgment is available only in English.